SALMONBELLIES VS. THE WORLD

Caitlin Press Inc.
8100 Alderwood Road,
Halfmoon Bay, BC V0N 1Y1
www.caitlin-press.com

Edited by Barbara Adamski.
Text and cover design by Hayes+Company.
Cover image by Phillip Chin.

Printed in Canada

Caitlin Press Inc. acknowledges financial support from the Government of Canada through the Canada Book Fund and the Canada Council for the Arts, and from the Province of British Columbia through the British Columbia Arts Council and the Book Publisher's Tax Credit.

Library and Archives Canada Cataloguing in Publication
MacDonald, Bruce, 1956-, author
    Salmonbellies vs. the World : the story of the most famous team in lacrosse
    & their greatest opponents / W.B. MacDonald.

Includes bibliographical references.
ISBN 978-1-927575-26-0

    1. New Westminster Salmonbellies (Lacrosse team)–History.
2. Lacrosse–British Columbia–New Westminster–History.
I. Title. II. Title: Salmonbellies vs. the World.

GV989.M22 2013   796.34'70971133   C2013-905003-5

SALMONBELLIES VS. THE WORLD

THE STORY OF THE MOST FAMOUS TEAM IN LACROSSE & THEIR GREATEST RIVALS

W. B. MacDONALD

CAITLIN PRESS

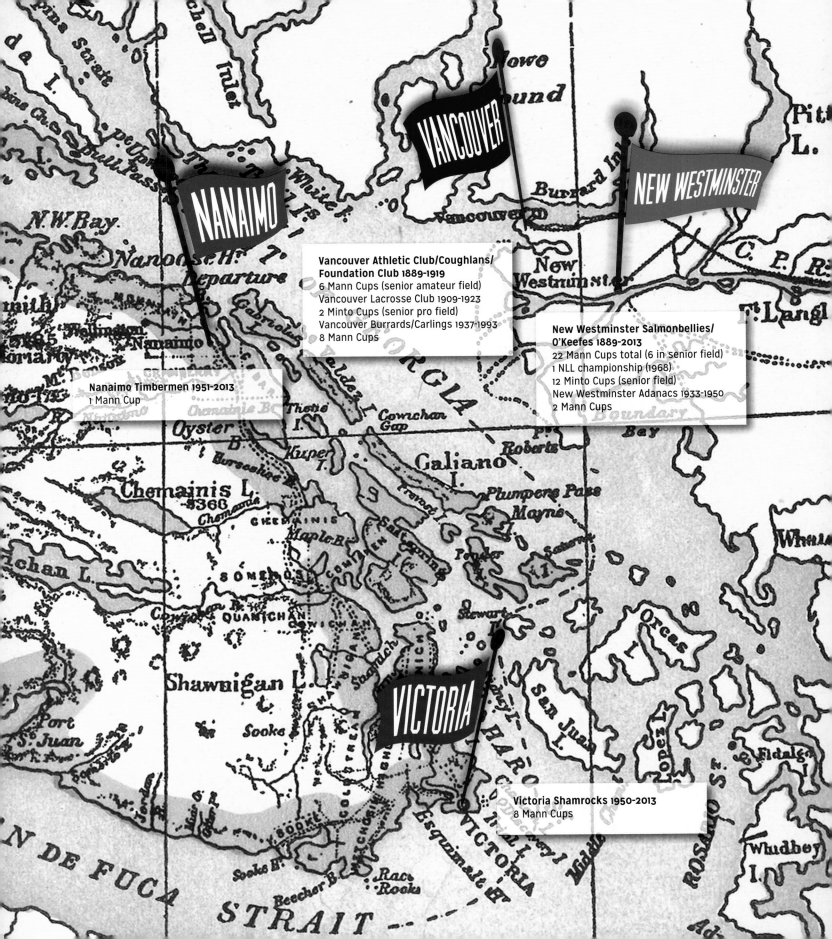

NANAIMO

VANCOUVER

NEW WESTMINSTER

VICTORIA

**Vancouver Athletic Club/Coughlans/
Foundation Club 1889-1919**
6 Mann Cups (senior amateur field)
Vancouver Lacrosse Club 1909-1923
2 Minto Cups (senior pro field)
Vancouver Burrards/Carlings 1937-1993
8 Mann Cups

**New Westminster Salmonbellies/
O'Keefes 1889-2013**
22 Mann Cups total (6 in senior field)
1 NLL championship (1968)
12 Minto Cups (senior field)
New Westminster Adanacs 1933-1950
2 Mann Cups

Nanaimo Timbermen 1951-2013
1 Mann Cup

Victoria Shamrocks 1950-2013
8 Mann Cups

CONTENTS

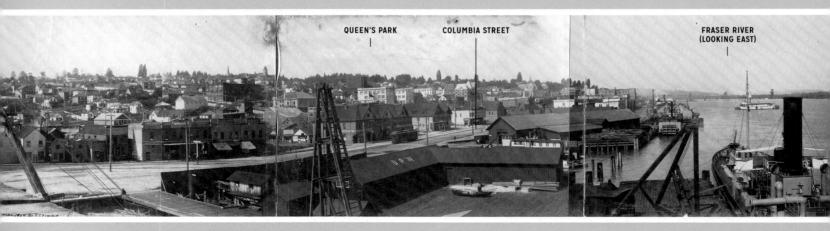

QUEEN'S PARK COLUMBIA STREET FRASER RIVER (LOOKING EAST)

The city of New Westminster, its port and downtown, and the Fraser River as they appeared to an east-pointing camera in 1908. The city's principal commercial thoroughfare, Columbia Street, and the Canadian Pacific Railway line run parallel to the river, known for its sockeye salmon. The derrick in the middle of the photo points to a ridge of trees in the distance. This is Queen's Park, home of the Salmonbellies.

PHOTOGRAPH BY PHILIP TIMMS. CITY OF VANCOUVER ARCHIVES.

3RD AND 1ST STREET PARK MAIN ENTRANCE AGRICULTURE BUILDING WOMEN'S BUILDING INDUSTRIAL BUILDING MIDWAY

The Royal Agricultural and Industrial Society ran the annual fall Provincial Exhibition on the grounds of Queen's Park. (Seen here in 1909.) The park's oval was home field to the Salmonbellies from 1890 to 1931. Vancouver lacrosse fans in the thousands rode the BC Electric Railway Company line to the park's entrance, the white arch at Third Avenue and First Street. Grandstands to the right of the tramway car partially block a view of the lacrosse field. The fence surrounding the field served as a kind of penalty box; offending players were sent "to the fence" to serve their time. Fire destroyed most of the buildings in 1929, including the impressive Agricultural Building, towering over the north end of the field. The site is now a parking lot. Queen's Park Arena was built approximately on the location of the Women's Building. The large white building to the right is the Industrial Building. A midway runs the length of the field's east side. One of the tents advertises "Mowgli." (Possibly an attraction based on Mowgli the feral boy in Rudyard Kipling's 1894 story collection, *The Jungle Book*.) Another promotes "Cannibal Chili." Sour cream with that? Beyond is the reservoir, now disguised by tennis courts.

CITY OF VANCOUVER ARCHIVES. PHOTOGRAPH BY PHILIP TIMMS.

So far as lacrosse is concerned New Westminster is the most independent place in Canada. They grow their own players. About the first word the tiny infant learns is "lacrosse"; they learn to toddle from chair to chair by the aid of a lacrosse stick, and when, as young boys, they begin to play in the parks, they would laugh at anyone suggesting any game but lacrosse. Consequently they have lacrosse teams by the score, of all grades and ages, and the sole ambition of all is to secure a place eventually on the senior team. With one or two intermediate and three or four junior teams, it will readily be seen that when a vacancy occurs in the senior ranks the management are never worried about any possible trouble in filling the vacancy. The new players are all recruited from lower ranks in the city clubs, where they learn thoroughly all the fine points of the game. The Westerners are always in perfect condition, and from youth they are trained to "play to win."

F.C.P., journal unknown, August 8, 1908

It's standing room only at Queen's Park as the Salmonbellies successfully defend the
Minto Cup, defeating Montreal 13-5 on July 23, 1910.

Before there was a Minto Cup and a Mann Cup, the National Lacrosse Association of Canada awarded a pennant (called a "flag") to the senior men's national championship team. In 1867 "national" effectively meant Montreal. Because a Montrealer named Claxton donated them, they are known as the Claxton Flags.

*"A few hard knocks were given and received,
for lacrosse is no parlour amusement."*

The *Daily Columbian,* July 30, 1894

CHAPTER ONE
TAKING TO THE FIELD: 1880-1899

In 1859, Colonel Richard Clement Moody selected a hill on the north bank of British Columbia's Fraser River as the site of what would become New Westminster. Moody's Royal Engineers, "sappers," began to cut down the 200-foot trees that forested the hill in preparation for the city's construction.

Within months of their arrival, they cleared a small, rough playing field on a flat, elevated piece of land on the western side of a ravine. The site (where Woodlands School later stood) was known as the cricket grounds. Moody's British soldiers were especially fond of the sport.

About a year later, in Montreal, Queen Victoria's son, Albert Edward, Prince of Wales, watched a display of lacrosse. In addition to Iroquois and Algonquin players was a team of Caucasians from Montreal, with 17-year-old dental apprentice William George Beers in goal.

Shortly after, Beers wrote a pamphlet of rules for lacrosse. In 1867, the year of Canada's confederation, he expanded on those rules. He set the number of players on a team at twelve, established the authority of umpires, and decreed that matches would be decided by the winning of three games out of five. A "game" was not a game in the sense understood today, but rather a unit within a match. The first team to score a goal won the game. Another game was then played. And so on up to five games. A match could be more than five games, if agreed to by both teams. With no time limit on individual games and with the first goal winning the game, every game was, in today's terminology, "sudden death." Some games lasted seconds while others lasted as long as an hour or more. A five- to ten-minute rest was allowed after each game. Once a match began no substitutions were allowed, except for injured players.

Goals could be placed at any distance from each other, but in actual practice the ideal distance was somewhere between 110 and 125 yards. The goalposts, commonly made of brass, were to stand six feet high and six feet apart. (Later, a crossbar was added.) The goals did not have nets. A small flag sat on top of each post, giving rise to the expression that a goal-scoring player had "dropped the ball through the flags." A crease was to be drawn in front of each goal, six feet from the flagpoles. The crease was used to determine offsides, rather than to mark off an area for the exclusive use of the goalie.

The first national governing body for sport in Canada, the National Lacrosse Association, was formed in 1867, adopting Beers's rules. While lacrosse spread rapidly throughout Quebec,

Ontario, and even into Manitoba, the sport grew exponentially in Montreal, from nine clubs in 1861 to twenty-five in 1881. In 1869, after campaigning unsuccessfully to have lacrosse recognized by Parliament as Canada's national game, Beers published *Lacrosse: The National Game of Canada.*

In 1880, two young lacrosse players from Ontario, Joseph and Frank Reichenbach of Elora, settled in New Westminster with their family, bringing with them two lacrosse sticks, "the old long type with wide gutted web."[1]

In 1886, Victoria and Vancouver organized lacrosse teams, but it took the CPR's completion of a spur line to New Westminster in November of 1886 to solidly establish the sport in New Westminster.

Lewis Allen Lewis, of Dresden, Ontario, arrived in New Westminster on May 24, 1887. The 23-year-old excelled at track, baseball, rugby, cricket, and tennis. When he heard about a 100-yard sprint competition with a $100 first prize, he approached race official Thomas Mowat[2] about entering the contest. In the race, Lewis wore a pair of spiked running shoes and assumed the new crouch-style starting position he'd learned in Ontario. Mowat, unsure about the shoes and the legality of Lewis's unorthodox style, ordered Lewis back ten feet. Lewis won anyway, "allowing his backers to make a big clean-up in the betting," according to the *Daily Columbian.* Impressed, Mowat corralled Lewis after the race, wondering if he played lacrosse. Yes, Lewis did.

The same year, William John Corbett of Kingston, Ontario, arrived in New Westminster, bringing with him a stick made by Kingston's Lally Company, the country's largest maker of lacrosse sticks at the time. A tinsmith by trade, Corbett found work at James Cunningham's hardware store on Columbia Street. He placed an order for Lally sticks, which arrived later in 1887.

At the same time, Henry Valentine Edmonds, a prominent BC real-estate investor and insurance agent, who resided in New Westminster, purchased two lacrosse sticks in Victoria for his teenaged sons, William and Henry.

On Saturday, May 12, 1888, a meeting to form a lacrosse club was held on New Westminster's cricket grounds. Frederick Robertson Glover, city editor of the *Columbian,* was appointed temporary chairman. Lacrosse-playing sprinter Lewis Allen Lewis, an accountant at Royal City Mills, was made secretary and treasurer. Membership in the lacrosse club was set at two dollars. Practices were every Wednesday and Friday evening at Townsend's field, at the northwest corner of Queen's Avenue and St. Patrick Street (now Third Street).

Townsend's field was rough and uneven, but relatively flat and treeless. Playing there was far better than playing on Columbia Street, where players dodged wagons, horses, and pedestrians. The field, along with most of the property on the east side of St. Patrick between Queen's Avenue and Pelham Street (Third Avenue), belonged to William Borridaile Townsend, who'd served in the British Navy, worked for the Hudson's Bay Company, and was a Cariboo gold rush miner before settling down in New Westminster in 1875. He became the city's mayor in 1889. Previously, he'd allowed his field to be used for carnivals and circuses and was happy now to lend it to the cause of lacrosse, a sport, as time would prove, that was often both a carnival and a circus.

Club chairman Glover, via his notices in the newspaper, urged all players to attend practices to not only become familiar with each other and with conditioning, but also to learn the basic skills of the game. Several would-be players had never even held a lacrosse stick before.

In 1888, while New Westminster's lacrosse players organized, Alfred Ernest "Bony"

A lacrosse ball hand carved by August Jack Khatsahlano of Vancouver in the early 1890s from the discarded rubber tire of a steam tractor.

OLD HASTINGS MILL STORE AND MUSEUM. PHOTOGRAPH BY PHILLIP CHIN.

Suckling and J.B. Simpson paid a visit to Winnipeg-born brothers James and David Smith at their carpet store on Vancouver's Water Street.[3] (Suckling and James Smith had been lacrosse teammates in Winnipeg.) They asked the Smith brothers to join them and others in a friendly lacrosse match in Victoria on the Queen's birthday. The brothers happily agreed. Vancouver won the match. The following July 1, Dominion Day, the Victoria team played a rematch in Vancouver and won, forcing a third match in Victoria, which Vancouver won, thereby capturing the first BC championship.

In late April 1889, the New Westminster lacrosse club met at Hyack Hall, the city's wooden firehall on Columbia Street. John Connal Whyte, militia member and construction superintendent of the city's water works, acted as chairman. James Wilton Harvey, who managed his father-in-law's dry goods business on Columbia Street, was elected president. Thomas Mowat became first VP, and his younger brother, Maxwell Mowat, a fisheries inspector, was appointed secretary treasurer. F.G. Strickland, of New Westminster's Strickland & Co., millwrights and engineers, took on the role of second VP.

A team was selected. Whyte was chosen to act as the team's playing field captain. A field captain could be a player in the match or a non-player. If he was a non-player he couldn't carry a stick or wear a uniform. A non-playing field captain ran the length of the sidelines, shouting instructions and encouragement to his team. (The field caption function eventually split into two separate roles: the team captain, a player; and the coach.) As field captain, Whyte was responsible for choosing a referee and umpires (they had to be unanimous choices, a task that was almost a sport in itself: on one occasion New Westminster and Vancouver argued over the choice of referee for over an hour), calling the coin toss for choice of goals, and he represented the team in disputes. For example, in the case of a disputed goal, field captains had the unilateral right to dismiss the referee or the goal umpire and have a new one appointed.

In the first game Whyte would play "between the flags." In a sport where a game was won or lost by the first goal, the goalkeeper was the single most important position and often the best athlete on the team. Whyte, widely considered the best all-around athlete in BC, had earlier distinguished himself in Ontario playing on two provincial rep rugby teams.

BC-born Harry Thompson would play point, the last line of defence before the goalie. His job was to harass the opposition's offensive ("home") players and prevent them from shooting. To be effective, the point needed to be stronger than any home player he faced.

Thomas Carrie, who'd moved from England to Canada as a boy, would play cover point, working in defensive tandem with the point. His range of motion was greater than point, so speed was slightly more important than strength.

"Newt" White would play third man, a defensive position that required the ability to break up plays before they started.

Richard Bailey Lister, a police officer, and John Corbett would play the two defence field positions. Lister, a rugby player, had captained one of the city's teams for several seasons.

James Gow, a tireless runner with a knack of being in the right place at the right time, would play centre. He took faceoffs and patrolled the field from end to end, intercepting opponents' passes and feeding the ball to the primary attackers. When opportunities presented themselves, he became a goal scorer. At 34, Gow was well past his lacrosse prime, but he was an experienced and exceptionally fit player.

James Arthur McMartin, a customs officer from Ontario, would play "outside home" (winger). Opposite him was "inside home" (winger) Frederick George Turner, the son of Royal Engineer George Turner and a clerk at the city's land registry office. Turner was promoted from intermediate (today's junior) to senior ranks for the match. Wingers were

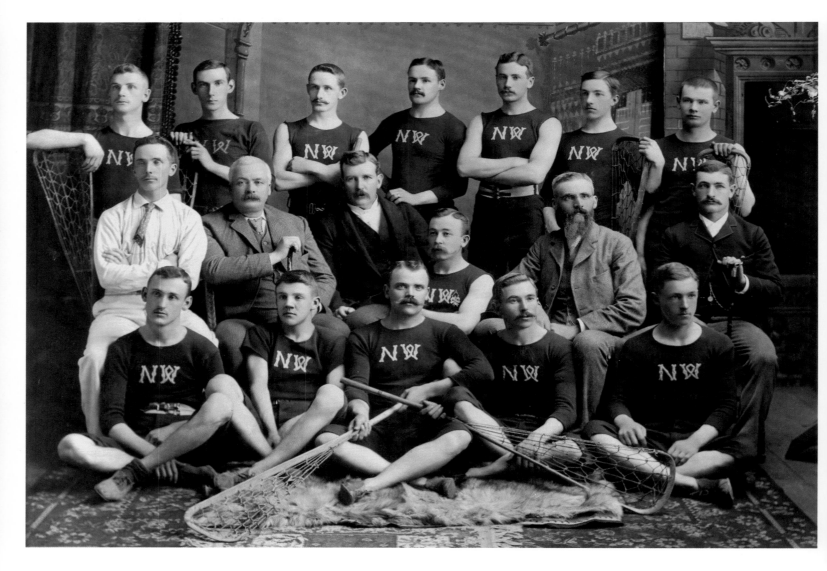

In their second season (1890) the New Westminster Lacrosse Club won all four games to finish first over Vancouver and Victoria.
Back row: Charles C. Stewart, Herb Ryall, C.S. Campbell, Col. John Connal Whyte, A.B. MacKenzie, Percy Peele, Z. Ketchum.
Middle row: James Gow (field captain), James Leamy (president), J.G. Jacques (1st VP), H.M. McGregor, Mayor J.C. Brown (honorary president), Max Mowat (honorary sec. treas.) **Front row:** Harry Thompson, W. Clute, J.J. Cambridge, Lewis Allan Lewis, H. Peele. Whyte, Lewis, Gow and Thompson played in the team's first game in 1889. Lewis was the team's leading scorer in 1890 followed by Stewart.

NEW WESTMINSTER MUSEUM AND ARCHIVES. PHOTOGRAPHY BY HALL AND LOWE, VICTORIA.

supposed to be fast. Their primary job was to draw out defenders and pass to open first or second home players.

At first home would be the winner of the $100 sprint, L.A. Lewis. His job was to "be a past master in the art of turning everything that comes his way into goal."[4] J.R. Polley, a real-estate broker, played second home, a position that also called for scoring.

George O'Mahon Dockrill would play third home, the connecting link between the wingers, centre, and other home players. When first home fought for the ball behind the goal, second and third home became temporary first homes, so they had to be great shooters. But Dockrill, a teacher and member of the BC Brigade Garrison Artillery, was a cricket player, not a lacrosse player. Both Dockrill and Lister had probably never handled a lacrosse stick until their early twenties.

All of these players were small by today's box lacrosse standards. None was over five-foot-eleven, the average height being about five-foot-eight. And no player weighed over 180 pounds, the lightest weighing in at 128 pounds.

New Westminster played its first match on a sweltering Saturday, June 8, 1889, at Townsend's field. Vancouver player James Smith described the grounds as, "a couple of lots near a judge's residence [no] larger than 100′ by 100′ and there were a number of small stumps scattered about it."[5] The New Westminster team was short players, so Vancouver lent them two or three men (as allowed by the rules), along with some equipment.

A "Mr. Clarke" was chosen to referee, with C.S. McDonnel and George Armstrong acting as umpires. A large number of spectators were on hand. The match was scheduled for three o'clock, but the Vancouver club[6] was late. (Until the creation of an inter-city tramway system, travel between New Westminster and Vancouver was by stagecoach or CPR train. The indirect, roundabout train line ran through Westminster Junction, now Port Coquitlam.) The match finally got underway at 4:20 p.m.

One of Vancouver's home players, McDougall, struck first, scoring after seven minutes of play, ending the first game. Turner scored New Westminster's first goal in the second game at about five o'clock. "At the end of 25 minutes of all-over-the-field play," wrote Glover in the *Columbian*, "the ball was faced to the side of Vancouver's goal; Lewis got it, passed to Turner, who dropped it through the flags . . . " After a short break, Dave Smith of Vancouver scored at the three-minute mark to win the third game. Just after six o'clock, following thirty-five minutes of play, Vancouver scored once more, winning the fourth game and the match 3–1. Glover singled out Vancouver's Suckling and Quigley for their exceptional play and lavishly praised New Westminster's efforts. He also pointed out that they had played poorly as a team, frequently leaving four or five opponents unchecked and often throwing the ball blindly and wildly. After the match, the teams met at the Colonial Hotel on Columbia Street for an evening of toasts, speeches, and dinner hosted by the New Westminster club.

As New Westminster and Vancouver played on Townsend's field, Queen's Park was taking shape a few blocks to the east. The park would become home to the Royal Agricultural and Industrial Society (R.A.&I.S.), the operating body of the annual provincial exhibition. Among other features, a large playing field, enclosed by a horseracing track, was laid out. The field was built on a north-to-south downslope that it famously retained for decades. It ran parallel to Park Lane (First Street) between the main entrance to Queen's Park at Pelham Street (Third Avenue) and just short of Queen's Avenue. A small grandstand was erected about halfway down Pelham Street. A magnificent home for the exhibition, the Agricultural Building, was constructed at the north end of the field.

Designed by New Westminster architect George William Grant, the Agricultural Building was a monument to symmetrical geometry, with its rectangles, squares, and pyramidal roofed turrets. During the annual provincial exhibition, its barn-like interior housed various agricultural exhibits, including displays of the Fraser Valley's fruits and vegetables. The massive building accommodated five thousand people and provided dressing rooms for athletes. It overlooked the playing field, and its recessed, second-floor balcony provided photographers with a unique vantage point for panoramic photographs of lacrosse games. For photographers shooting from the opposite direction, the building served as an iconic backdrop. Its matching entranceway turrets resembled gigantic goalposts, right down to the flagpoles seemingly representing lacrosse's goalpost flags. The Agricultural Building made a statement: this was no cow pasture; this was New Westminster, a place of significance. Over the next forty years, the fortunes of New Westminster, Queen's Park, the Agricultural Building, the R.A.&I.S., the provincial exhibition, and the Salmonbellies would be inextricably linked.

Representatives of lacrosse teams from Victoria, Vancouver, Nanaimo, and New Westminster formed the British Columbia Amateur Lacrosse Association (BCALA). In early 1890 a constitution and rules were drawn up. A two-hour limit was placed on matches, with the team winning the most games winning the match.

On Saturday afternoon, July 12, 1890, a train stopped by special arrangement at the foot of New Westminster's "Asylum Hill." Formerly the cricket grounds, the site was, at that time, occupied by a psychiatric hospital. A man disembarked hurriedly and climbed into a waiting carriage. The horse and carriage whisked him the mile or so to the new lacrosse field at Queen's Park, where team officials waited with his jersey. Within ten minutes of arriving in the city, Herb Ryall was playing lacrosse. Born in 1867 in Paris, Ontario, where he learned the game, Ryall had been with Brandon, Manitoba's senior team for four years before being invited to join the New Westminster club. Ryall scored his first goal for New Westminster in the second game.

There was a new man playing for Vancouver as well, Elijah "Lige" Scurry. A defence fielder, Scurry was a 19-year-old black man born in Owen Sound, Ontario. (His father, Hiram, and mother, Martha, moved Elijah, his four brothers, and his sister to Vancouver in 1886, making them one of Vancouver's earliest pioneer families.) As the game progressed, a number of young spectators singled out Scurry and insulted him with "cowardly epithets." The majority of the crowd found their bad conduct and reprehensible language intolerable and forcibly stopped it. "Of the whole audience there was not a dozen who did not heartily condemn the remarks turned against Scurry. And he had their warmest sympathy," according to the *Columbian*.

The 1890 season finished with New Westminster in first place with four wins and no losses; Vancouver with one victory, two losses, and a tie; and Victoria with three losses and a tie. At the season's-end banquet at the Hotel Douglas, Gordon Courbould, recently elected MP for New Westminster, spoke about his hopes for the future of lacrosse. One of the main reasons for cricket's popularity in the United Kingdom, he claimed, was the respect shown for umpires' decisions. He believed that if the same were true of lacrosse where brawling and disputing umpires' calls were common, then lacrosse would "occupy an even higher position than it does now."

In another speech that night, insurance man A.B. McKenzie reminded those gathered of the importance of keeping lacrosse an amateur sport. Lacrosse teams were clubs with members who paid dues and their own expenses. They were proud to be amateurs; professionalism was equated with Americanism and baseball. Lacrosse players, in theory at least, played for the joy of the sport itself. L.A. Lewis won the Brown Cup as the club's first scoring champion. In his acceptance speech, he graciously acknowledged his teammate and *Columbian* newspaper typesetter C.C. Stewart, who had scored only one less goal.

A twelve-mile electric railway line was completed in 1891, linking Vancouver and New Westminster. A one-way trip took less than an hour. Prosperous businessmen and merchants erected houses in the streets and avenues near Queen's Park. Along the riverfront, sawmills, canneries, and dockyards were busy. Fraternal societies such as the Oddfellows and Masons were in vogue, and you could not turn a corner without bumping into a church (there were eighteen in total, and an even greater number of bars).

On April 29, 1891, electric lights lit up the exhibition buildings in Queen's Park for the first time, and a new fence was installed around the perimeter of the lacrosse field. About four feet high, the fence contained errant balls, kept spectators off the field, and served the same function as today's penalty bench. Penalized players were "sent to the fence."

The public was keenly interested in the lacrosse club's practices. People turned out to watch the team go through its paces. The *Columbian* reported not only on league matches but also on the team's performance during practices. The turnout of players, intensity of the scrimmaging, and general level of fitness were all noted.

Vancouver's matches were played at Brockton Point in Stanley Park. Spectators arrived on foot, by carriage or bus, and by ferry steamers running between downtown Vancouver and the Point. A return tramway fare to Brockton Point, including the ferry, cost a New Westminster supporter eighty-five cents.

Unsportsmanlike behaviour continued to mar the games. In condemning unnecessarily rough play, the *Columbian* singled out Scurry. He incurred the scorn of the paper in July 1891, when he was accused of purposefully throwing the ball out of bounds in the sixth and final game in order to preserve a 3–2 Vancouver victory. Commenting on the brutality of the same game, the paper noted that Scurry "seemed to think he was on the field for the sole purpose of disabling his opponents."[7] The disabling spread.

On August 8, the rivals met at Queen's Park. Again, the *Columbian* had plenty to say, writing that the match was "the most unfortunate interpretation of Canada's national game ever seen in the province . . . rough beyond all reason, and positively brutal at times." The paper went as far as saying that lacrosse was no longer a game deserving of public patronage.

The trouble occurred in the third game, after Vancouver had got ahead by two. "The game was by far the most unpleasant to witness ever seen on Queen's Park," the paper wrote. "Even the disabling and nearly killing of Allan had no effect on the play." The paper provides no details on the "nearly killing of Allan," but it does provide a graphic description of a collision near the end of the third game that illustrates the intensity of play: Draper got the ball away from Ketchum, passed MacKenzie and Campbell and rushed in towards the goal. As he turned to shoot on the flags, Coldwell (playing point) ran out and checked sharply, their heads coming together with terrific force. Draper's lip was badly split, and Coldwell's ear suffered a similar injury.

Scurry again came in for censure, the paper accusing him of being "without exception, the roughest man on the field, and should have been ruled off a dozen times." The game, slowed by penalties and the evacuation of the wounded, lasted eighty-two minutes. Many people left well before the end because "the slaughter was more than they could stand." The fourth game was only two minutes long and the fifth was over in seventeen minutes. Vancouver won the match 4–1.

When New Westminster's lacrosse players were not battling Vancouver, they were teasing the players of a more genteel sport. Moody Square, now known as Moody Park, was the site of British Columbia's first golf links, the Westminster Golf Club. Sharing the park with the golfers, the lacrosse players delighted in picking up a player's golf ball and playing a game of catch with it. The worst offenders of all were Wells Gray and L.A. Lewis.[8]

In early October, Scurry was again in trouble. At the close of the match, a 3–1 New Westminster victory at Queen's Park, centre (and field captain) James Gow accused Scurry of directing "a very offensive epithet" his way, and called on Constable Box to arrest him.[9] The officer complied, much to the displeasure of Vancouver's players and supporters, who mobbed the policeman. Scurry was eventually released, but the matter was far from settled. The *Vancouver World*, as partisan a paper as the *Columbian*, used the incident to strike back, alleging that Gow had started the row when he called Scurry a "nigger."[10] It went further, alleging that the

Beginning in 1891, the BCER (or one of its predecessors) carried lacrosse fans between Vancouver and New Westminster. The line ceased operating in 1958.

VANCOUVER PUBLIC LIBRARY.

New Westminster players—"ragged urchins" and "unruly school boys"—all commonly used the same language for which Scurry had been arrested. The *Columbian* was outraged, calling the allegations an "infamous lie." "No true man," wrote the paper, "would use that epithet to a fellow—it is only in use among the lowest blackguards."

The *Columbian* then diverted the blame for all of lacrosse's problems to "a clique of gamblers and betting men who back the Vancouver team for money," implying that gamblers would go to any length to procure a win—including importing eastern players—even, by some contorted logic, a black man if necessary. Vancouver may have decided that the Scurry controversy was not worth the trouble (he was missing from the team's 1892 roster), but the 1891 season ended with Vancouver in top spot with three wins and no losses, New Westminster with two of each, and Victoria winless.

Lacrosse's popularity in New Westminster was immense. Any evening of the week at Queen's Park over 100 players were practising, a remarkable number given the city's total population of about 4,000.

Players represented various age groups and organizations. Following the lead of the senior teams, the intermediate players (the same age as today's juniors) formed clubs, with Victoria leading the way. In 1892, Vancouver had two intermediate teams and New Westminster had two: the West Enders and the Moonlighters. The Moonlighters practised at night in Queen's Park (in what today is the outfield of Queen's Park Stadium) under newly installed electric arc lights. Henry Edmonds, possessor of one of the city's first lacrosse sticks, led the Moonlighters. These two intermediate teams supplied most of the players for New Westminster's senior team.

Violence in the sport continued. On July 14, 1893, in the fourth game of a match against Victoria at Queen's Park, L.A. Lewis was struck twice on the head by Harry Morton's stick. Morton, a professional, had learned his lacrosse in Ontario, having played a total of ten years for St. Catharines and Niagara Falls. He'd been kicked out of the St. Catharines club for playing under an assumed name. Morton's second whack at Lewis knocked Lewis unconscious, "blood spurting from a ghastly looking wound in his head."[11] As angry New Westminster supporters flooded the field, a dazed Lewis got to his feet and ran to Morton. The men grappled and Lewis again fell to the ground insensible. Lewis was carried off the field and the club's physician, Dr. Fagan, dressed an inch-long cut in the side of his head. A small artery had been severed.

Lewis wanted to keep playing, but Fagan would not allow it. Play resumed and the Victoria club, down 3–0, scored their first goal, winning the fourth game. They scored three more to take the match 4–3. Morton's strategy of taking out the opposition's leading scorer worked, but he was charged with assault. At the hearing, one witness testified that he had heard Morton say to Lewis, "I'll settle you" just before striking him.[12] Another witness testified that as Morton was going to the dressing room between the third and fourth games, he said, "Wait till I get onto that fellow [Lewis] and I will fix him."[13]

Morton denied saying anything to anybody. Asked if he had bet any money on the July 14 match, Morton replied that he had not. The magistrate found that assault on a lacrosse field was still assault, and ordered Morton to trial. Morton's attack rendered Lewis deaf, and although Lewis partially recovered, he was hard of hearing for the rest of his life. He returned to the field, however, on September 28, scoring the first of the club's four unanswered goals to beat Victoria 4–0.

There were now two Vancouver intermediate teams as well. The rivalry between Vancouver and New Westminster was intense, and the Moonlighters won eight straight matches with only one goal scored against them. In a match against Nanaimo they scored four goals in two and a half minutes of play.

The senior team struggled, winning only one match out of six during the 1893 season. This was unacceptable to the New Westminster Lacrosse Club. Wholesale change was necessary for the following year, starting with the defence. The club recruited "Bob" Cheyne as a playing "coach." The five-foot-eight, 144-pound glazier of Irish descent hailed from Toronto. He'd played in net for Montreal when they captured the Canadian championship in 1890, and played point for Vancouver in 1892 and 1893.

"One of the master minds of the game," according to trainer Tim Mahony, Cheyne revamped the way New Westminster's defence played.[14] Under Cheyne's guidance, the team abandoned the standard practice of hurling long passes downfield to their forwards. Instead, defencemen worked the ball upfield with short, quick passes, which made players work together and allowed them to share both the glory on a win and the blame in a defeat.

Games between Vancouver, New Westminster, and Victoria were, more often than not, bitter grudge matches. Victoria and New Westminster, formerly the best of friends, especially disliked one another. Victoria was importing more eastern players. Four or five of them, according to the *Columbian*, did little or no work during the season. Because these players did not appear to be independently wealthy, people assumed that they were being paid to play. In other words, they were pros in an amateur sport.

If that rankled New Westminster, so did other Victoria antics. Before a match in Victoria on July 14, Victoria's trainer, Professor Foster, ran with a bulldog up and down in front of the grandstand, firing up Victoria supporters. Although the New Westminster team did not understand what the professor was trying to communicate, they did not appreciate it. Victoria scored first, taking the game, then went after Lewis.

Once again, almost a year to the day, Harry Morton cracked Lewis on the head, sending him reeling to the ground, giving "great delight to the hoodlums that lined the fence."[15] Lewis's kid brother, Jimmy, tussled with Morton, resulting in a two-game suspension for Morton and a one-game suspension for Jimmy.

Victoria took the second game. Not content to be winning, Victoria continued its chippy play, with an extremely accomplished all-around athlete from Montreal, A.E. "Archie" Mac-Naughton, laying out New Westminster's Snell.

Despite MacNaughton's hard check on Snell, New Westminster won the third game and had the better of the play in the fourth, when Victoria's Belfrey slashed J.J. Cambridge in the head, sending him crashing to the ground. Play continued and MacNaughton again went after L.A. Lewis, whacking him over the head with his stick. Lewis had to leave the field, and MacNaughton scored to put Victoria up 3–1. In the fifth game, Morton, having served his two-game penalty, hacked H.J. Peele in the head, sending him to the dressing room in a semi-conscious state. With Morton off and Peele out of the game, Ryall scored. Time was called and the match went to Victoria, 3–2.

New Westminster's next match, against Vancouver in Queen's Park, was played in a downpour. While the game was hard played, it was, according to the *Columbian*, "in the fair, manly style that should characterize every contest of the kind. Of course," the paper continued, "a few hard knocks were given and received—for lacrosse is no parlour amusement—but never once during the match was it necessary to call time to bandage wounds or carry a man off the field." New Westminster won 4–2, and Cheyne was singled out for his brilliant play.

New Westminster lost the return match against Victoria on August 4. Lewis, still recovering, was unable to play, while Morton had agreed not to play for the remainder of the season.

The match to determine the provincial champion was played October 22, between New

Westminster (6–2) and Victoria (6–2) at Vancouver's home park, Brockton Point. Lewis was back in action. So was Morton, despite his gentleman's agreement not to play anymore. He may have believed that his prohibition applied only to the end of the regular season, and not to the championship match. The contest, as usual, started late, this time because the tram in which the New Westminster team was riding broke down, stranding them temporarily between cities.

With the score 3–2 in Victoria's favour, and darkness falling, New Westminster's Cambridge, seeing his last opportunity for revenge, lined up and flattened Morton behind Victoria's goal. The *Columbian*, delighted that Morton had finally received his pay back, dryly noted that

Born in Yorkshire, England in 1872, Thackray Oddy joined New Westminster in 1895. At 126 pounds he was the smallest man on the team.

CANADIAN LACROSSE HALL OF FAME.

Cambridge had the "misfortune" to lay him out. Morton was carried from the field. Cambridge went to the fence.

Moments later, the referee called the game because of darkness, declared it a draw, and ordered the match replayed. Victoria protested to the BCALA, arguing that New Westminster had sealed its own fate by arriving late. They were leading 3–2 when the sixth game was called. The score should stand, they should be declared the winner, and the championship should be theirs.

But the association backed the referee's decision. The match would have to be replayed. A date was set, but Victoria threatened not to show. On the prescribed date, New Westminster took to the field. And waited. When Victoria failed to appear, the match and the provincial championship went to New Westminster.

Piqued, Victoria resigned from the association. The association then ordered Victoria and New Westminster to play a match at Brockton Point to decide the provincial championship. When Victoria failed to appear on the field, they forfeited, handing the championship to New Westminster. Meanwhile, at the intermediate level, the West Enders took provincial honours.

Victoria eventually overcame its pique and, calling themselves the Triangles, rejoined Vancouver and New Westminster in the association for the 1895 season.

Joining New Westminster was Thackray ("Thack") Staten Oddy, who, at 126 pounds, was the smallest player on the team (average weight was around 150 pounds). By mid-August each team had at least two wins, with Vancouver on top of the standings with four wins and two losses, and New Westminster with four wins and three losses.

The Vancouver team continued to work hard in pursuit of the provincial championship, practising every evening at five o'clock. Despite their efforts, they were defeated by New Westminster in the teams' final encounter of the season. With Vancouver and Victoria having one more match to play, Vancouver's record was 4–3, New Westminster's was 5–3, and Victoria's was 2–3.

Had Vancouver won against Victoria, they would have taken on New Westminster for the championship. But Vancouver, short a few key players, was denied a request to postpone the Victoria match by a week. When they failed to appear at the scheduled match, they forfeited to Victoria, giving New Westminster the championship.

The season ended with New Westminster and Vancouver's senior and intermediate teams playing exhibition matches in Tacoma and Seattle, respectively.[16] The Americans had pushed for the matches to be played on a Sunday, but the devout Gow, speaking on behalf of both

Canadian teams, refused to play on the Sabbath. The matches were held on Monday instead. New Westminster finished the 1896 season with a 1–6–1 record. In the final match, Vancouver won 4–3 to capture the provincial championship.

The first reference to the New Westminster team as "salmon bellies" occurred in the *Columbian* on August 9, 1897, but the name was in use well before that time.[17] Years before, in June 1892, the team decided on a standardized uniform. George Leaf (the team's first waterboy, in 1892) described the sweater's colour as "deep salmon red"[18] for it brought to mind the red flesh of spawning salmon, the fish that ran in the millions in the Fraser River.

New Westminster's choice of colour was a gift to Vancouver's fans, who, according to James Smith, were quick to make the salmon connection and, in the best gamesmanship tradition of sports, were soon deriding New Westminster as a bunch of "salmon bellies"—the section of a salmon containing white, fatty meat, considered a delicacy and often cooked fresh or preserved by pickling or salting.

New Westminster had no comeback until Vancouver, originally in blue sweaters, switched to grey, to hide mud splatters and stains. They were immediately branded "greybacks," slang for lice.[19] Worse name-calling was to come. Leaf recalled teenage fans from Vancouver taunting their New Westminster peers before games at Queen's Park, the thrust of it being that the Vancouver team was going to eat the "salmon bellies" alive. New Westminster supporters, in turn, branded Vancouver "crab eaters."[20]

On the same principle, Victoria's players were called "clam diggers."[21] While crab and clam meat today are highly valued delicacies, in BC at the turn of the twentieth century, they were considered by Caucasians to be practically worthless.

In effect, fans were calling each other what they considered to be the lowest of the low: Indians. But if salmon bellies were regarded by Caucasians of the time as delicacies, or at least as food worthy of a white person, why is calling a team "salmon bellies" a pejorative? "We always had Salmon-Bellies for breakfast at the Brunette Mills cookhouse," recalled John Warren Bell. "Old Jim Kee, the Chinese cook, dished up the same kind of food every day. Oatmeal porridge, Salmon-Bellies with boiled potatoes and flap jacks. I asked him once why did he not have a change. 'Allee time same—salmon-belly—Siwashie chicken.'" (Indian chicken. "Siwash" is a pejorative term for Aboriginal people, derived from the word "savage" in the west coast's Chinook jargon.) Jimmy Gifford, who was with the Salmonbellies from 1904 to 1912, took a different view of the matter. He understood the name salmon bellies as a racial slur against Caucasians. As far as he was concerned their opponents' fans were calling his team "soft and white," like the texture and colour of salmon bellies.[22]

An alternative or possibly corroborating story about the origins of the team's name concerns an excited shoeshine man. "It was on the Cambie Street grounds that the famous New Westminster lacrosse players first got the sobriquet 'Salmonbellies,'" according to Vancouver pioneer Albert Beck, a lawyer, court registrar, and government agent. "It was given them by an Italian bootblack, a well-known character about town, formerly of New Westminster, latterly of Vancouver, and who, following the usual custom of those days, carried his polishing outfit over his shoulder wherever he went. One day in the early 1890s, the Westminster lacrosse boys came over to Vancouver for a game with the sticks. Vancouver gathered together a scratch team, and both teams, followed by a straggling crowd of pioneer 'fans' assembled on the Grounds to play it off. The bootblack was 'rooting' for New Westminster. The New Westminster men got the ball down towards the Vancouver goal, and tried to rush the net. The bootblack was 'rooting' vociferously, and in his excitement yelled, 'Git there, salmonbel-

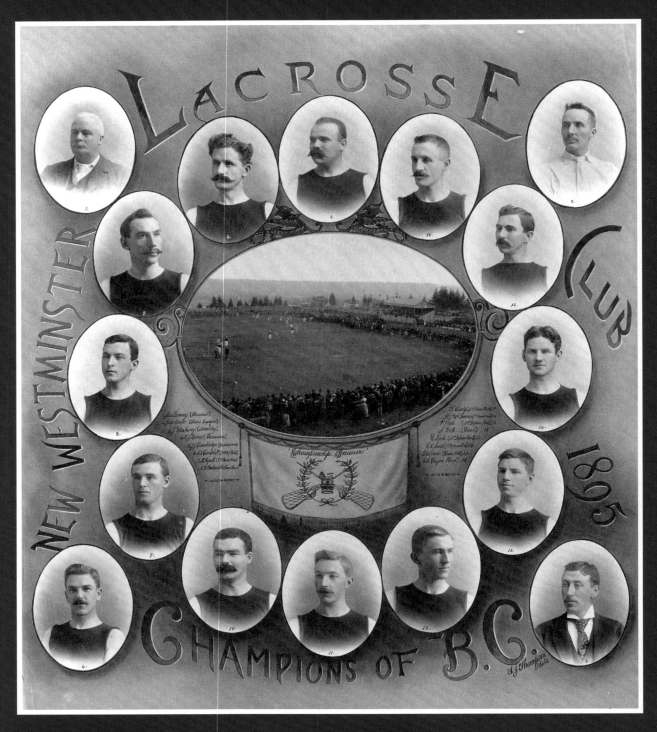

The 1895 New Westminster team orbits a photo of Queen's Park. They defeated Vancouver in the final game of the season to retain the BC championship. **Upper left:** James Leamy. **Upper right:** James Gow. **Lower left:** Thomas James Lewis. **Lower right:** Joseph Mahony. **Starting at middle top and moving counterclockwise:** John James Cambridge, Charles Stewart Campbell, Herb Ryall, William "Barlow" Galbraith, Thackray Oddy, Daniel J. McQuarrie, Percy Peele, Stanley Peele, Clarence Dale "Biscuits" Peele, Charles Knightley Snell, Lewis Allen Lewis, Robert Hodgson Cheyne.

lies!' The epithet tickled the jocular fancy of the onlookers—everyone heard it—much hilarity followed, especially among the Vancouver supporters, and the descriptive nickname fitted so well that it has survived ever since, and in a measure has attached itself to all who hail from the old salmon town."[23]

George Leaf agreed with Beck, writing, "Following a few years of such doings a gathering of rabid NWLC boosters entertained the idea of adopting that word Salmonbellies as the name for their highly prized team."[24] While men may have liked the name, not every woman did. "What a vulgar name for a team—simply horrible—could they not get a more suitable name—most ridiculous—indecent," complained a female spectator, her Victorian sensibilities clearly offended by the anatomical slang, "belly."[25] Another spectator pointed out to her that the salmon belly was the choicest part of the fish. "Of course Salmon-Abdomen might be more refined but we are not cultured folk for we were brought up on Salmon-Bellies and love 'em." The lady replied, "What rot—perfectly ridiculous."

With the transit system between New Westminster and Vancouver consolidated as the BC Electric Railway Company, ridership increased steadily, as did attendance at lacrosse matches. To accommodate the greater numbers, more seats were added to Queen's Park.

On Saturdays, businesses often closed for the afternoon in order to take in the matches, always scheduled for three o'clock sharp (although the visiting teams' late arrival often meant that games didn't get underway until four o'clock). For major matches, even the sawmills closed down.

A "master mind of the game," Alexander Thomas Turnbull, of Paris, Ontario, joined the team in early August 1897.[26] A former centre with the Toronto Tecumsehs lacrosse club, Turnbull arrived in New Westminster after a short stay with the Nelson, BC, lacrosse team. He was an instant sensation with the fans. Turnbull was on the short side at five foot six, and weighed 145 pounds, but he was a fitness fanatic, far ahead of his time, and spent an hour every morning swinging clubs, lifting dumbbells, skipping rope, and shadow boxing, which was a novelty for the 1890s. But his workout regime could not hide his baldness, which made him look considerably older than the 25 years of age he actually was. His teammates called him "Dad," and it stuck. Over the years Dad was content to let others believe he was much older than he was, gaining, perhaps, a psychological edge on the field. At the very least, his supposed advanced age earned him widespread admiration. Dad was that rare athlete with a sixth sense for where he should be at any point in a game relative to where the play was about to be. He was also quick. One commentator remarked that the only hope the man checking Dad had was to get himself a polo pony and ride it. Dad spearheaded the team's attack while Cheyne anchored the defence.

To their roster, the Salmonbellies also added 20-year-old first home player William "Will" Gifford, the first of five sons born to Thomas and Anne Gifford. Thomas, a Scottish watchmaker-jeweller, moved his family to New Westminster in 1887 and set up the Lower Mainland's first jewellery store on Columbia Street. The family house was on Third Street, directly across from Townsend's field and a couple of short blocks from Queen's Park.

In July, the Salmonbellies defeated Victoria in Victoria for the first time in five years to lead the league with three wins, a draw, and a loss. They then split the matches with Vancouver, setting up a final match for the provincial championship. On October 2, 1,200 fans showed up at Queen's Park. As dusk fell, the score was tied at one in the third game. Dad, in what would become his signature style of play, sprinted past Vancouver players, received a pass from Stan Peele, and whipped the ball past goalkeeper John Quann to seal the victory. Thousands of delirious fans flooded the field, wanting to shake Dad's hand.

In June, Thack Oddy's brothers George and Richard joined the team, George at first defence and Dick at centre. The Salmonbellies practised hard preparing for a match with Victoria, a team that was starting to make a habit of defeating them. Not this time, if New Westminster could help it. "There is blood on the moon," read the *Columbian*, meaning that danger lay ahead for Victoria. The Salmonbellies defeated Victoria 4–1 in "glorious weather, if a trifle warm."

The weather stayed "a trifle warm"—94° Fahrenheit in the shade—for the next match against Vancouver. That was extremely hot for the usually temperate and rainy west coast. The Salmonbellies defeated Vancouver 3–1. More than twenty years later, Turnbull singled out that season as the most strenuous he'd ever played: "For good, hard work I really believe that the series of 1898 between Vancouver and New Westminster takes the prize . . . They gave us some real battles and you knew you had been through a game after playing against them."[27]

On August 20, Vancouver defeated Victoria, and on September 3, New Westminster defeated Vancouver. The Salmonbellies now led. On Friday evening, September 9, the Salmonbellies scrimmaged with the intermediate team in preparation for their match with Victoria. "The game," reported the *Columbian*, "will be a hot one." The following night, most of downtown New Westminster burned to the ground. The lacrosse season was delayed while the city recovered.

On a cold and wet November 24, Thanksgiving Day, the Salmonbellies arrived at Caledonia Park (now Royal Athletic Park) in Victoria to play the delayed final game of the season. They were informed, contrary to an agreement, that they would not be receiving any gate receipts. They refused to play. After a heated discussion, Victoria relented, agreeing to part with half the receipts. Because it was already late in the day, and night might fall before the natural end of the match, the referee, in keeping with association rules, declared that in the event of darkness, he would call the match and declare the team with the most goals the winner.

The game got underway. For the first time ever, results were relayed to New Westminster by telegraph, an operator being stationed at the Park. Thack Oddy won the first game for New Westminster and, despite Victoria "hoodlums" hurling chunks of sod and mud at the Salmonbellies, also scored to win the fourth and sixth games.

With the score 4–3 for New Westminster, official time almost up, and night falling fast, the president of the association suddenly stepped in and overruled the referee's earlier terms. New rules that were not yet published, he said, meant that there was actually twenty minutes left.

The match continued. After twenty minutes of play in semi-darkness, without any goals, the game was called. Initially the referee awarded the contest and the championship to the Salmonbellies, but upon consultation with the association president, he announced he would reserve his decision pending further consultation. A few days later, the association awarded the championship to New Westminster.

In early June 1899, at Brockton Point, the Salmonbellies faced Vancouver for the second time that season. A female Vancouver supporter thought her team could win if, she said, they could break the "thin red line" of New Westminster's red jersey clad defenders.[28] Her remark caught on with other spectators and somehow made its way back to the Vancouver team. Even though Vancouver lost 3–2, the team was tickled enough by her observation to purchase a copy of British painter Robert Gibb's popular 1881 painting "The Thin Red Line" and present it to the Salmonbellies after the game. Gibb's painting depicted the red-coated, kilted, and outnumbered Sutherland Highlanders repulsing a Russian cavalry charge during the Crimean War's Battle of Balaclava.

The next cavalry charge came from Victoria's James Bay Athletic Club. The former Victoria team, largely composed of imported eastern players, had folded at the end of the 1898 season. James Bay's junior team stepped up to senior for 1899. The young team had upset New Westminster 3–2 on July 24 to close within one win of the Salmonbellies. Five days later, the rivals met again at Queen's Park. The Salmonbellies prevailed 7–0. On August 5, in a match against Vancouver, Thack Oddy had the ball and was getting away from his check, when another Vancouver player cut him down. The crowd jumped over the fence, and a fight ensued, lasting for several minutes. The *Columbian* reported that the injuries Oddy received were "pretty severe." Vancouver's captain, Sykes, was so disgusted with the treatment Thack received and the "disgraceful" way his team played in general that he quit lacrosse for good, saying, "baseball should be given a turn now." With seven wins against one loss, the Salmonbellies retained the provincial title.

After an exhibition match, the Salmonbellies and their opponents from Nelson, BC, sat down in the ballroom of New Westminster's Hotel Guichon. Crossed lacrosse sticks adorned the walls and fresh cut cedar boughs decorated the ceiling. The meal consisted of, in part, oyster soup, deviled kidneys on toast, and boiled ham in Champagne sauce. While they ate, Darcy's orchestra played the 1899 hit parade. Supper done, "fragrant weeds" were smoked, the Queen was toasted, and the unofficial national anthem, "The Maple Leaf Forever," was sung: "In days of yore, from Britain's shore/Wolfe, the dauntless hero, came. . ." The teams toasted each other, the Nelson contingent heartily encouraging the Salmonbellies to start playing eastern teams on eastern soil. Speeches were followed by the singing of "For They Are Jolly Good Fellows." Judge Alex Henderson rose and recited "Jim Bludso of The Prairie Belle," a popular poem about a Missisippi riverboat engineer who died saving his passengers. The subjects of the poem are duty, courage, and self-sacrifice, qualities prized no less in lacrosse players than in red-coated Highlanders.

In late September the Toronto Lacrosse Club (the Rosedales) arrived in New Westminster for a two-game exhibition series. The team included 22-year-old "Charlie" Querrie of Markham, Ontario. Of medium height and 135 pounds, Querrie was an elusive runner and a tricky stick handler. An outstanding playmaker and scorer, Querrie was the scoring star of the Markham Seniors Lacrosse Club when they won the Ontario championship in 1899. He went on to play with the Toronto Lacrosse Club from 1900 to 1903, and for the Toronto Tecumseh team from 1904 to 1917, where he was a perennial top-ten point-getter until 1913.

Due to a mix-up, Toronto had to play with borrowed sticks and uniforms. New Westminster's reputation for "scrapping on the slightest provocation"[29] caused Toronto to be timid on the attack. The Salmonbellies won the first match 7–2. The Toronto team had their own uniforms and sticks for the second match, but still lost 7–3. On the afternoon following a night of banqueting at the Hotel Guichon, the team was bid farewell at the CPR station. As the train pulled out, the teams gave each other "3 cheers and a tiger."[30] Toronto's war cry was answered by the crowd singing, "For They Are Jolly Good Fellows." Then, as the end of the train passed the platform, a number of Toronto players serenaded a cluster of teary-eyed female admirers: "Goodbye, ladies! Goodbye, ladies! Goodbye, ladies! We're going to leave you now!"[31]

When these badges featuring the club's war cry debuted in 1900 "they sold like hot cakes and exhausted the supply of ribbon" in New Westminster.

CANADIAN LACROSSE HALL OF FAME. PHOTOGRAPH BY PHILLIP CHIN.

"We are champions of the world now, and if they want it back they will have to come to our little town."

Tom Gifford in a letter to his mother reprinted in the *Daily Columbian*, September 8, 1900

CHAPTER TWO
GOD'S GREAT JUDGMENT SEAT: THE 1900 TOUR

"An enterprising local man got out a badge on which a fine salmon was conspicuous below a lacrosse emblem, and above the words of the club's fish war cry," noted the *Columbian* in 1900. "They sold like hot cakes and exhausted the supply of ribbon in town."[32] The war cry:

> *"Ala Veepore, Ala Veepore, Veepore Viper Vum—*
> *Bum get a sockeye—Bigger than a coho—Bigger than a coho—*
> *Humback, Humpback ziz boom bah—Oolichans Oolichans Rah Rah Rah."*[33]

The war cry equated the Salmonbellies with sockeye (also known as humpbacks), the smallest but reddest fleshed and most valuable species of salmon. Coho, averaging seven to eleven pounds, are bigger than sockeye, while the oolichan is a small, silvery fish that appears in Pacific coastal waters in spring. In short, the cheer was for the fish of the Fraser River, including, most importantly, the fish whose colour the New Westminster team wore, the bright crimson spawning sockeye.

Younger spectators, finding the war cry difficult to perform, came up with one of their own: "Hobble gobble, hobble gobble, hiss boom bah! Westminster, Westminster, rah rah rah!"[34] The morning after a match, early in the 1900 season, Matt Barr, an up-and-coming Vancouver businessman and member of the Crab Eaters, woke up in a New Westminster hotel to discover the front of his coat plastered with Salmonbellies badges. The team had its nickname and now its identity, and did not mind letting everyone, including Matt Barr, know about it. Sis boom bah.

The Salmonbellies won the BC championship for 1900. They had defeated Vancouver's and Victoria's best teams for four years running. But could they overcome the best Ontario and Quebec clubs? Seven teams were lined up: Montreal Amateur Athletic Association, Nationale de Montreal, Montreal Shamrocks, Ottawa Capitals, Quebec City Lacrosse Club, Toronto Lacrosse Club, and Toronto Tecumseh. The Salmonbellies would play seven matches in two weeks in four cities.

The tour was mostly financed by a wealthy backer, but a benefit concert held at Herring's Opera House helped offset his expenses. As steamboats whistled on the busy Fraser River, an audience of about 500 people enjoyed an evening of entertainment featuring cornet and banjo solos, an exhibition of East Indian club swinging, marches performed by the eighteen-member New Westminster City Band, a sword dance, a Highland fling, an Irish jig, and a tongue-in-cheek recitation of Rudyard Kipling's *Ballad of East and West*: "Oh, East is East, and West is West, and never the twain shall meet/Till Earth and Sky stand presently at God's great Judgment Seat."

On an overcast Wednesday morning, August 15, hundreds of people thronged the CPR station on Columbian Street at the foot of Eighth Street, later the home of the Keg restaurant. Boys with Salmonbellies badges pinned to their chests climbed onto the shoulders of friends, hoping to catch a glimpse of the team. Under bowler hats, stiff-collared men beamed with pride, shaking the hand of every player within reach. Young women, in white pouter pigeon blouses, trumpet skirts, and broad-rimmed, beribboned hats, snuffled tears into silk handkerchiefs. On the banks of the river, just a stone's throw from the station, fishermen waited for the last salmon run of the season, rumoured to be coming around Point Roberts, heading for the Fraser. It was a good omen, east-bound salmon and east-bound Salmonbellies. The players wore their Salmonbellies badges proudly. "Tom Gifford," wrote Dad, "nearly had a fit when a lone traveller saw our salmon badges and took us for a fishing club."[35]

The train they boarded, the *Imperial Limited*, was the CPR's finest. Operational for just over a year, it crossed Canada between Vancouver, Montreal, and Quebec City. The Vancouver to Montreal leg was a four-day, 2,881-mile route. The train, pulled by a coal-burning steam locomotive, featured luxurious sleeping and dining cars. Fast and well appointed, the service was exceptional and the emphasis was on comfort. As the train pulled out, the team shouted their war cry. Mothers and girlfriends shed more tears and waved their handkerchiefs.[36]

Settling down in their seats, the players reached for the many food hampers they had received, not that anyone was going to starve, each player receiving two 75¢ dining car vouchers per day.[37] Still, Tom Gifford checked to make sure he had a proper supply of pickles, a necessity as far as he was concerned.

Dad admired his new tin teapot, warning his teammates to keep their hands off it. Biscuits Peele endured the ribbing that came with his discovery of a supply of dog biscuits mixed in with lemon and orange peel.

One hamper held a number of linen dusters, protection for anyone venturing onto an open platform against the heavy black smoke belching from the engine. Stan Peele, intending to stick his head outside from time to time, had the foresight to bring along a pair of goggles.

The morning after their arrival, the Salmonbellies toured the Montreal AAA clubhouse and gymnasium. On August 22, they met Beers's team, the Montreal AAAs, the weakest team in the National Lacrosse Union (NLU), on their grounds in Westmount, where Westmount High School now stands. The lacrosse field bordered the edge of an escarpment that dipped steeply into a valley full of factories, rail yards, and brick row houses, an Irish working-class area known as Griffintown. The south-facing pavilion and grandstand afforded a panoramic view of the St. Lawrence, Lachine Rapids, Nuns' Island (Île des Sœurs), and, to the east, Victoria Bridge.

The match was sportsmanlike, and the Salmonbellies won handily. Montreal won only two games to the Salmonbellies' five. Back in New Westminster, where bulletins of the game were posted outside the CPR Telegraph Office, a large crowd cheered each goal, while many of the team's lady admirers "regretted they were not permitted to throw up their hats."[38]

The team departed by steamer for Quebec City, shooting the Lachine Rapids as they left Montreal. On August 25, in front of a crowd of 1,500, they did more shooting, winning twelve

The 1900 New Westminster Salmonbellies. **Back row:** William "Barlow" Galbraith, Arthur Wellesley "Wells" Gray, Herb Ryall, Tommy Gifford, Jack Mahony, Stan Peele, Bob Cheyne. **Middle row:** George Oddy, Clarence "Biscuits" Peele, Archie MacNaughton, Harry Latham, Fred Lynch. **Front row:** Alex "Dad" Turnbull, Will Gifford, Charlie Snell.

games to Quebec's one. A spectator surmised that the Salmonbellies could easily have won thirteen, but didn't, for fear of bringing bad luck.

After some sightseeing, the Salmonbellies caught an express train back to Montreal for an August 27 date with the Montreal Nationals on their home grounds at Maisonneuve, a suburb on Montreal's eastern edge. It was hot (90° Fahrenheit) and humid. The Nationals struck first, but the Salmonbellies answered in the second game. They won five more games while the Nationals won two more, and then, to underline their point, the Salmonbellies won the next three games in a combined fifty seconds. The score was 9–3 for New Westminster on three goals by Peele, two each by Gifford and George Oddy, and singles from Lynch and Turnbull. Montreal had never seen anything like it. "They are all strong and muscular, but there is more strength than grace in their work. They bat the ball quite frequently instead of picking it up and passing. However, there is an amount of back passing and fancy passes that is astonishing."[39] Cheyne, Gray, and Galbraith were "impenetrable." Galbraith was ruled off in the third game for clobbering a National who was "taking liberties." Snell struggled on an injured leg. MacNaughton was disappointed with the team's share of the gate receipts, a paltry $100. Later, back in New Westminster, he was asked by the *Columbian*'s editor for his thoughts on the game. "They paid a dollar or two to learn better," he said, "and I've got some of it." As for Tom Gifford, he thought the match was easy and the Nationals' goals total flukes.

Two days later, on August 29, the Salmonbellies faced the Shamrocks, a working-class team based in the Irish Catholic slum neighbourhood of Griffintown. The Shamrocks were the defending NLU champions. Their best point-getters were Jack Brennan, Albert Dade, Bert Henry, and Henry Hoobin. Drilled from boyhood by his lacrosse-playing father, Hoobin, at an early age, acquired incredible stick handling skill and a mastery of the game's fine points. He was a tall, powerful athlete with blistering speed, already famous for his broken field rushes in on goal. Running at full speed he could snag a pass one-handed and shoot from any angle.

The CPR Telegraph Company stationed a special operator on the grounds. Goals reached New Westminster in three minutes flat and loud, prolonged cheers went up after each one. The crowds in Vancouver were equally loud in support of the Salmonbellies.

The score was even after four games, but the Salmonbellies scored three with ease before battling hard for their final goal, making it 6–2 for New Westminster.

In Vancouver, the betting was heavy. One real-estate developer was rumoured to have won $6,000 so far on the Salmonbellies. In New Westminster, bets were smaller, but a local hotelkeeper had won $500 from "admirers of the old Griffintown champions."[40] In Ladner, ten miles west of New Westminster on the Fraser River, Captain Baker of the steamer *Transfer*, hearing the news of the Salmonbellies' triumph, hoisted his ship's flags in celebration. The *Montreal Gazette* compared the Salmonbellies' attack on goal to a cavalry charge, while another Montreal paper attributed the Salmonbellies' victory to heavy checking and stamina. As far as they were concerned the Salmonbellies played old-fashioned lacrosse, not "pretty, modern lacrosse."[41]

The most anticipated match of the tour pitted the Salmonbellies against the NLU-leading Ottawa Capitals. Three thousand people filled the grandstand at the University of Ottawa's varsity oval, and the CPR stationed another special telegraph operator on the grounds. Ottawa pressed hard in the first game, peppering Cheyne with shots, but Dad opened the scoring for the Salmonbellies, firing a goal on a ball misplayed by Ottawa's netminder "Bouse" Hutton.[42] The match quickly escalated into vicious crosschecking, stick slugging, and tripping. Trainers on both sides were kept busy. Will Gifford had his lip stitched, while Dad and Latham came in for scalp repairs. Latham's cut required four stitches, but the internal effects of his "close hair cut" were with him for a week, during which time he was "on queer street."[43]

The *Gazette*'s take on the fouling was that Ottawa was trying to slay the visitors. Dad's play was, as usual, brilliant. Positioning himself on the defensive side of centre, he unerringly made tactically correct passes before sprinting straight in on the Capitals' goal. MacNaughton, the old warhorse, could not resist getting in on the action. Early in the match a 15-year-old wise guy in the grandstand shouted, "New Westminster couldn't beat a carpet!"[44] The hot-tempered redhead took exception and went up into the stands, saying dramatically that his team could lick the Capitals and the spectators as well. A crowd of boys razzed MacNaughton for the rest of the match.

Latham and Will Gifford scored to put the Salmonbellies up 3–0. Then Ottawa scored. After the fourth game, boys on the grandstand's roof pelted MacNaughton with gravel. As the teams retired to their dressing rooms for a breather, goalie Hutton had words with MacNaughton. Whatever Hutton said MacNaughton didn't like, and he threw a punch at the Caps' goalie. Three or four Capitals jumped in and pinned MacNaughton to the grandstand wall. Police intervened, separating MacNaughton and the Capitals, and chased threatening spectators back into their seats.

In the dressing room, one of the Salmonbellies balked at returning to the violent match. MacNaughton told the player that either he took his chances on the field with the others or he, MacNaughton, would give him a good licking right there in the dressing room. The player chose the Capitals.

Although hobbled, Stan Peele scored the Salmonbellies' fourth goal to win the game. New Westminster's defence ragged the ball for the final seven and a half minutes of the match, concerned that their offensive teammates might get killed if they even so much as touched the ball. The final score: 4–1 for the Salmonbellies.

After the match, the Capitals were still angry with MacNaughton, one player giving him a swat as they made their way to the dressing room. The animosity continued, police having to form a line to keep back incensed Ottawa supporters as the Salmonbellies made their way to waiting carriages. "The people went nearly crazy," wrote Tom Gifford, "to think that a team from British Columbia should defeat them on their own grounds."[45]

Again, New Westminster's close and stiff checking carried the day. The *Ottawa Citizen* claimed that there were "no gleaming stars on the Western team" but their defence was a "stone wall" and offensively they were "remarkably aggressive around the goal, where they shot sparingly, but with much precision and effect."[46] The *Montreal Gazette* noted that their play seemed effortless.[47]

The Salmonbellies arrived at the Toronto Lacrosse Club's home grounds feeling tired and sluggish after a fitful sleep through a hot and sticky Toronto night. It was to be their sixth match in four cities in thirteen days.

Charles Almeron Welsh, a New Westminster grocer and keen Salmonbellies supporter, was in Toronto the day of the match. He reported that the Salmonbellies were looking worse for wear. Snell and Peele were "more or less crippled," Dad had lost fifteen pounds, Will Gifford was "thin as a rail," and Harry Latham was "like a shadow."[48] Despite that, with Oddy distracting Toronto's goalie, Biscuits opened the scoring on a long shot. Toronto won the next two games. Dad tied it, but then Cheyne, who had been hit in the eye by a ball at the start of the game, could not continue. Ryall replaced him in goal for a short time, then Gray went between the flags, everyone moved back a position, and Ryall went in at home. Toronto took the fifth game, scoring after just one minute. Lynch, off a Will Gifford pass, scored with a quick throw to win the sixth.

The seventh game lasted all of ten seconds, Lynch grabbing the ball from Dad's faceoff and passing to Ryall who, on fresh legs, scored almost before Toronto could move. The *Montreal Gazette*'s reporter, by now familiar with the Salmonbellies, paid close attention to Dad in Toronto, in particular to his faceoff technique: "Turnbull lifts at the draw, and he is a wonder at it. It drops into Latham's or Gifford's stick, and there is immediately half a field of territory gained."[49]

The Salmonbellies were ahead 4–3 and trying to hold on, but second home, Charlie Querrie, evened the match. A ninth game got underway, but with Toronto pressing hard, the referee called time. The Rosedales argued for an overtime game to determine a winner, but the exhausted Salmonbellies, under no compulsion to continue, declined. The Rosedales protested to no avail. The draw stood. A day later, MacNaughton challenged Toronto to a rematch, but now it was Toronto that declined.

The Salmonbellies had four days to rest and recover before meeting the Toronto Tecumseh Lacrosse Club of the NLU, a rival league to the Canadian Lacrosse Association. The Tecumseh team took their name from the Shawnee military commander who became a Canadian hero when he played a major role in Canada's repulsion of an American invasion in the War of 1812. Could the Tecumsehs repulse the Salmonbellies?

The battle took place on Saturday, September 8, at the Tecumseh's home field, Hanlan's Point, on Toronto Island, a short ferry ride from the city's downtown. Hanlan's Point, billed as Canada's Coney Island, featured a large hotel built and at one time owned and operated by Ned Hanlan, Canada's celebrated world champion rower. The island also featured a variety of rides, slides, concessions, amusements, picnicking spots, and a stadium fronting on Lake Ontario. Shawnee warriors or not, the match was predicted to be a walkover. And it was: 7–1 for New Westminster.

On August 31, the day before the Ottawa scrap, a young New Westminster soldier, Private William H. Brooking, arrived in Quebec City, not long from the veldts of South Africa. He'd been engaged in a different sort of scrap, the Boer War. Brooking was a member of A Company, Special Service Battalion, Royal Canadian Regiment of Infantry and part of the First Canadian Contingent to South Africa. He'd been injured at the Battle of Paardeberg, stricken with typhoid fever, and discharged. Arrangements were made for him to return to New Westminster with the team.

Snell, Dad, and Lynch hung back in Toronto. The rest of the team and Brooking boarded the westbound *Imperial Limited*. Four nights later, they pulled into New Westminster. The engineer turned on the train's bright signal lights and fuses. Exploding fireworks were nearly drowned out by jubilant cheering from thousands of people, including Vancouverites, lining the track and packed around the station. The Salmonbellies made their way to waiting horse-drawn carriages and a procession. As everyone settled into seats, the procession, headed by the bugle band, began to move east on Columbia Street, flanked by 250 torchbearers. Columbia Street's merchants left on their lights, windows glowing brightly, revealing decorations and welcome-home banners. Hundreds of people lined the streets as the procession made its way to the Armories on Sixth Street. The Armories was crammed to "suffocation." As Brooking, the team, and dignitaries took their seats on a raised platform, the band played a popular 1894 tune, "Soldiers of the Queen."

Mayor Scott addressed the crowd, praising Brooking and his "gallant little band of eight" and welcoming him back to the city.[50] He thanked the Salmonbellies for "advertising the city in a manner that cannot fail to bear fruit in the business sense" before equating them with soldiers. "Those very qualities which have made you victors are the same which, displayed on South African battlefields, have sent the name of Canada to the front of the Empire's roll of honor."[51]

Retired Salmonbellie J.J. Cambridge then called for three cheers, and the band launched into "For They Are Jolly Good Fellows." Ryall spoke briefly and joined his team in their "Ala veepore" war cry. A young lady fainted in the overheated atmosphere.

Anticipating the triumphant return of the team, city-hired contractors painted the grandstand and other buildings at Queen's Park Salmonbellies red in their honour. More spoils of victory awaited the team. A stove was installed in their dressing room so that the players' jerseys could actually dry between practices, and their rubdowns could happen in warmth and comfort.

The *Columbian* printed a song written by Walter James Walker, an Englishman who had come to New Westminster in 1885. In his song, "New Westminster," the city is maternal, a mother whose "sons" fight "in distant lands." In the first two stanzas, Walker compares victory on the lacrosse field to victory on the veldt. In the third stanza, he predicts that mother New Westminster, though still showing the "blackened scars" of the 1898 fire and "burdened sore with debt," will, with the love of her sons, be triumphant many more times.

A rare, early First Nations stick used for the game the Mohawk called tewaarathon ("little brother of war") and the Ojibwe called baggataway ("bump hips"). Also known simply as stickball.

CANADIAN LACROSSE HALL OF FAME. PHOTOGRAPH BY PHILLIP CHIN.

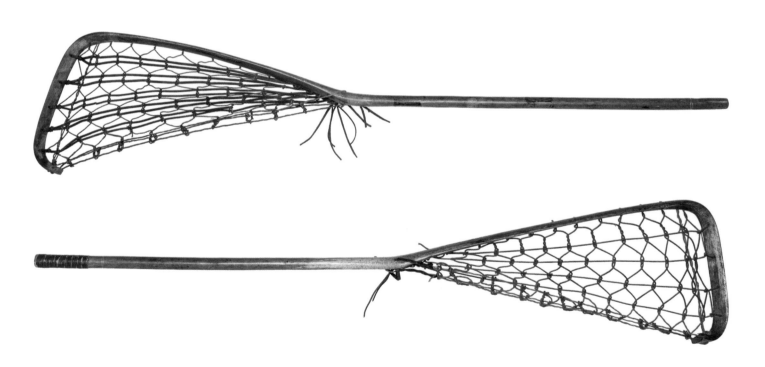

Early field lacrosse sticks could be any length, but could not be more than one foot in width. They had to be woven with "cat-gut" (rawhide, gut or clock string) and could not be "bagged," which meant the netting was stiff enough to prevent a pocket from forming.

CANADIAN LACROSSE HALL OF FAME. PHOTOGRAPH BY PHILLIP CHIN.

THE MINTO CUP
PRESENTED BY
THE EARL OF MINTO,
GOVERNOR GENERAL OF CANADA.
1901.

Any team in Canada could challenge for
the Minto Cup, but between 1908-1924
the Salmonbellies relinquished it only twice.

CANADIAN LACROSSE HALL OF FAME.
PHOTOGRAPH BY PHILLIP CHIN.

"If I am satisfied, you ought to be."

Tom Gifford

CHAPTER THREE
IN PURSUIT OF LORD MINTO'S CUP: 1901-1908

The Salmonbellies went east in 1900 wearing badges, literally trying on their identity, but for the 1901 season they would wear that identifier, the salmon, on the front of their sweaters for the first time. Although they would only wear the salmon-crested sweaters for one season before reverting to the plain deep red style, the die was cast.[52] The YMCAs, a new Vancouver team managed by Archie MacNaughton, was formed to challenge the Salmonbellies. MacNaughton signed Walter Miller. The Salmonbellies objected, claiming correctly that Miller was a professional baseball player and therefore ineligible to play in an amateur league. The YMCAs denied the allegation. The Salmonbellies warned the YMCAs that if they intended on playing Miller at their upcoming match, they would call it off. The YMCAs shrugged their shoulders and made their way to New Westminster. Fans, unaware of the situation, arrived at Queen's Park only to find no gatekeepers, no tickets, and, it appeared, no game. About 2,000 people gathered at the lacrosse field anyway. The YMCAs came out, threw the ball around for a few minutes, claimed a victory, and gave themselves three cheers.

MacNaughton's tactics did not sit well with Leaf, a self-confessed "strong home town rooter as well as a heavy opposition roaster."[53] Leaf was verbally giving it to MacNaughton "hot and heavy" during a game when Leaf felt a "stinging slap" across his face. MacNaughton's wife, standing next to him, had hit him with one of her long kid gloves, sparking a "merry free-for-all." Among the combatants was a New Westminster-born man of Chinese descent, Joe Quoy, who, with a fellow Salmonbellies' supporter named Jack Cheery, simultaneously threw hard rights that "floored their opponents and put their lights out for a few minutes," thereby bringing hostilities to an end.[54]

When the dust finally settled, the Salmonbellies emerged with the 1901 league title. With the exception of one defeat by Victoria in the spring of 1898, the team had gone three seasons without a loss, including the games of the 1900 tour. They had beaten everyone. Who was left? Or better yet, what was left?

The answer came from Gilbert John Elliot-Murray-Kynynmound. Kynynmound, better known as the Fourth Earl of Minto, was the governor general of Canada. He presented a silver trophy, the Minto Cup, to be awarded annually to the best senior men's amateur lacrosse team in the country. In 1901, the Montreal Shamrocks defeated the Cornwall Colts to win the cup.

No sooner had they captured it than the Vancouver YMCAs challenged them. The YMCAs were partially financed and fully managed by the irrepressible MacNaughton, who also played on the team.

There was resentment in New Westminster. The Salmonbellies, reigning provincial champions for five straight years, thought of themselves as the rightful cup challengers. While the Salmonbellies were clearly the greater threat, the Shamrocks took MacNaughton's team seriously. They insisted that they would play only one match against the YMCAs, although the rules stipulated two. A few days prior to their departure for Montreal, the YMCAs beat the Salmonbellies in a fiercely contested exhibition match, lending some moral legitimacy to their cup challenge.

Still sore from the exhibition and tired from the long rail journey, the YMCAs nevertheless battled evenly for thirty-eight minutes before the Shamrocks scored. Another twenty-eight minutes passed before the Shamrocks won the second game. They won three more games to win the match 5–0, retaining the cup.

Dad wired MacNaughton in Montreal, teasing him to "bring back at least a photo of the cup."[55] MacNaughton blamed the defeat on the effect of the tough, physical match against the Salmonbellies and the long, tiring rail journey. What the team had needed, he claimed, was a week's rest once they reached Montreal.

In June of 1902 the Salmonbellies, managed by New Westminster Mayor William Keary, boarded a chartered Pullman railway car for the journey to Montreal and an appointment with the Shamrocks to contest for the Minto Cup. Joining veterans Cheyne, Gray, Galbraith, Latham, Lynch, Tom and Will Gifford, Biscuits and Stan Peele were brothers George and Tom Rennie, Alex Cowan, and Trevor Wilkinson, promoted from the intermediate ranks. Mahony had retired as field captain.

Cheyne was at the far end of his career. Stan Peele's fractured ankle had healed, but he favoured it. Two of their reliable scorers, Ryall and Snell, had retired. The defence was intact, but if it came to that, could they beat the Shamrocks by denying them goals? Also, the Irish team would be ready for them this time; surprise was no longer a factor. The Salmonbellies were, as ever, confident, but cautious. Keary was worried that his team was overtrained and had arranged for massages all the way to Montreal. For good measure, the CPR's *Atlantic Express* made frequent stops, allowing the players to get out and stretch their legs. When they reached Montreal, they would have five days to acclimatize and, under the eye of a top-notch trainer, get themselves ready for the best-of-three series. They were heeding MacNaughton's advice.

On Saturday, June 28, New Westminster's citizens once again crowded around the CPR's bulletin board. The Shamrocks took the lead. Penalties were costing the Salmonbellies. Gray was ruled off for the match early on for "cutting down" Paddy Brennan. The foul was bad enough that he had a police escort from the grounds. With Dad out of action for five minutes for cross-checking, the Shamrocks scored twice. To top it all off, Stan Peele's ankle gave out. He was replaced by Wilkinson. The new offence was not scoring; the old defence was struggling. The Salmonbellies were "badly whipped" 6–1.[56] New Westminster was stunned. Communications were slow in reaching the city; telegrams were short and cryptic. "Hope to do better," read one. "Boys are all fine," read another. Charlie Welsh wired Dad, asking if the cause of the defeat was superior play or bad luck? "A little of both," responded Dad.[57]

On July 1, in the second match, the Shamrocks scored first after twenty-six minutes. The Salmonbellies evened the score on a goal by Gifford. And then disaster struck. Montreal scored four in a row. Lynch got the Salmonbellies' second goal, but it did not matter: 5–2 Montreal. The cup was staying in Quebec. Somewhere, Archie MacNaughton was gloating. The team,

The third and deciding game of the Salmonbellies' 1902 non-Minto Cup series against the Shamrocks at Queen's Park was a hard checking, defensive battle that ended in a 2–0 New Westminster victory.

smarting from the defeat, elected not to play any other games in the east. Three months later, in early October, the Salmonbellies renewed their acquaintance with the Shamrocks. Montreal was in New Westminster for three games over exhibition week. The series, with the Minto Cup not at stake, was won by the Salmonbellies two games to one.

In early July 1903, Vancouver beat the Salmonbellies at Brockton Point. On the afternoon of the return match, later that month at Queen's Park, the grandstand was packed. The Vancouver team, looking sharp in their green jerseys with red shorts, lined up, and after the field was cleared of "dogs and superfluous boys,"[58] the match got underway. It was not long before a young Vancouver fan in the bleachers called Wells Gray a "butcher," although there were one or two words preceding the butcher part for which the *Columbian* thought the spectator should have been arrested. When he repeated the foul terms, Gray jumped the fence and "tapped" his stick over the youth's head. The youngster opened his mouth wider than ever and started crying, causing a young woman beside him to shriek and faint. Incensed Vancouver fans rushed the field, which brought out the Salmonbellies' fans. But order was quickly restored and the game resumed. When time was called, Vancouver finally had the big prize, having defeated the Salmonbellies on their home grounds 7–5 in front of 5,000 fans.

On August 31, the great rivals played at Brockton Point in front of 10,000 spectators. Gate receipts were a tidy $2,700. The bleachers were packed tight. Every elevation was occupied, even the roofs of the adjacent clubhouses. Spaces between clubhouses and the athletic arena were a congested mass of horses and vehicles of every kind. The match ended in a 3–3 draw. It would have to be replayed sometime before the end of the regular season on the Salmonbellies' home grounds.

On September 21, the Salmonbellies faced Vancouver at Queen's Park. Five hundred Vancouver fans arrived on a special-excursion CPR train, joining a large contingent of Pitt Meadows and Coquitlam residents. Many of the spectators wore "the famous salmon-bellie ribbons," purchased at Ryall's drugstore.[59] Not unnoticed in the crowd were two young fence jumpers. One of them, trying to save the price of admission, got caught by a nail and tore a strip off a $6 pair of pants. Later, an excited team of mules bolted from the park. Seemingly as caught up in lacrosse as everyone else, the mules returned in time to see the end of the first quarter. Mules and fence jumpers were nothing new, but down on the field something revolutionary was happening. The game was being filmed. Wanting to lure more people west, the CPR in 1902 hired a British company under Charles Urban to produce short films—advertising, really—depicting Canadian life.[60] The CPR provided the Bioscope Company of Canada with a flatcar pushed by an engine, and the filmmakers set out on a route that took them from Quebec to Victoria. On September 21, 1903, they were in New Westminster to capture the province's most popular sport and pastime. The filmmakers concentrated their efforts on faceoffs, leading the *Columbian*'s reporter to wonder what the uninitiated would make of a game where the only action was two crouching men jostling for a ball.

If the mules and the young man with the torn pants were Salmonbellies fans, they went away from the game happy, the Salmonbellies winning 10–1. They scored a second victory at the box office, netting $1,000.

In late September, the Montreal Shamrocks arrived in New Westminster. They were in town at the invitation of the R.A.&I.S. to play a series of matches during exhibition week. The Salmonbellies, whipped by the Shamrocks in two Minto Cup games the year before in Montreal, wanted nothing more than to right that wrong. The Shamrocks, strengthened by the additions of "Spike" Hennessy and Ed Robinson, met the Salmonbellies on September 29 in front of about 6,000 people.

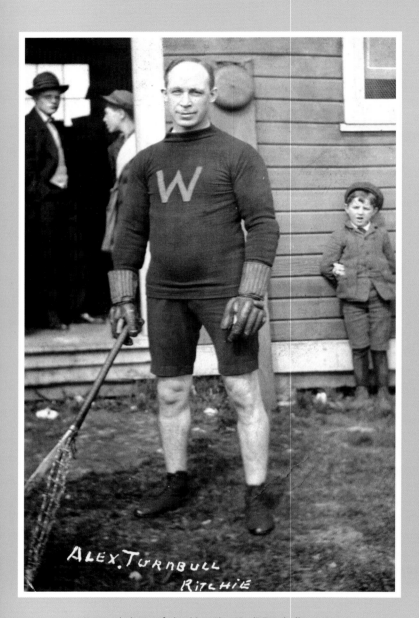

ALEX. TURNBULL
RITCHIE

Your only hope of checking Alex "Dad" Turnbull was to "jump on a polo pony and ride it," quipped one observer.

NEW WESTMINSTER MUSEUM AND ARCHIVES.

G. SPRING
RITCHIE, PHOTO

Gordon "Grumpy" Spring played on nine Minto Cup-winning Salmonbellies teams from 1909 to 1921, retired as the team's leading scorer, and coached or managed the team to five Mann Cups until his death in 1949.

NEW WESTMINSTER MUSEUM AND ARCHIVES.

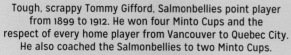

Tough, scrappy Tommy Gifford, Salmonbellies point player from 1899 to 1912. He won four Minto Cups and the respect of every home player from Vancouver to Quebec City. He also coached the Salmonbellies to two Minto Cups.

NEW WESTMINSTER MUSEUM AND ARCHIVES.

Jimmy Gifford was one of five Gifford brothers who played for the Salmonbellies. A blacksmith Monday to Friday, he was a punishing pugilist on Saturday afternoons. His scraps with Newsy Lalonde were epic. He co-founded and coached the Adanacs in 1933. The bell or "gong" on the right was used by lacrosse officials to signal time.

NEW WESTMINSTER MUSEUM AND ARCHIVES.

The Shamrocks were ahead 2–0 at the end of the first quarter on goals by Paddy Brennan and Ed Robinson. Hoobin scored in the second quarter and then Fred Lynch got one for the Salmonbellies. Lynch scored again, then Dad tied it, but with a few minutes remaining in the game the Shamrocks' Finlayson scored to win the match 4–3.

On October 5, they met again, the Honourable Richard McBride, Premier of BC, performing the ceremonial faceoff. The Salmonbellies were up 5–1 at the half on two goals each by Lynch and Dad and one by Gifford and went on to win 7–3. Dad recalled these games as the most grueling he ever played.[61] He was run ragged by Montreal's speedy Tommy Moore. On one occasion Moore headed downfield with the ball. When Dad caught up with him, Moore stopped dead in his tracks, turned, and amused everyone on the field when he said loudly to him, "So, you're de guy de say can run, hey? Well, come on." Moore, according to Dad, left him in his dust.[62]

The Shamrocks then beat Vancouver on October 7, 9–0, proving beyond any doubt that they were the better team, but, with a 1–1 record against New Westminster, were they better than the Salmonbellies? The Shamrocks and the Salmonbellies had played eight matches over the previous three years, with each team winning four. The Salmonbellies had the edge in goals, thirty-seven to the Shamrocks' thirty-one, but the Irishmen retained the Minto Cup.

Following the exhibition week matches, the Vancouver and Montreal teams toured California, playing matches in San Francisco. That did not sit well with the Salmonbellies, who insisted that Vancouver, according to BCALA rules had to play the August 31 drawn match within two weeks of the end of the regular season or forfeit the provincial championship. Time was almost up, and Vancouver was enjoying the attractions in San Francisco. Vancouver telegraphed that they could hardly be in two places at once, and besides, they had taken two regular-season games from New Westminster. The BCALA sided with Vancouver. The men in the green shirts were the champions for 1903. Outraged, the Salmonbellies seethed until June of 1904, when they resigned from the association.

With New Westminster out, the 1904 season opened with just Vancouver and Victoria in the association. By the middle of August, Vancouver had won all five matches. With the exhibition approaching, the R.A.&I.S. proposed a two-game series between Vancouver and the Salmonbellies. In the end, it was agreed that Vancouver would play Winnipeg and the Salmonbellies would face Nelson. The Salmonbellies bolstered their defence with the addition of Will and Tom Gifford's 18-year-old brother Jimmy. Jimmy was a blacksmith by trade and was incredibly strong from the hard physical labour of turning out log-boom chains and fabricating heavy equipment. The Nelson team was no match for the Salmonbellies, who won the first encounter 8–3.

After the game, the Salmonbellies, desperate for serious competition and trying to find a way of rejoining the association without losing face, issued a challenge. They would play the twelve best players from the Vancouver, Winnipeg, and Nelson teams. If they lost, they would re-enter the association. If the all-stars lost, Vancouver would have to go along with their proposals. Vancouver did not bite. The Salmonbellies, somewhat deflated, played a lacklustre second match and tied Nelson 6–6. In the third and final match, a 10–1 New Westminster win, "Barlow" Galbraith, bored with the proceedings, rushed from his defensive end of the field to the Nelson end and scored, the second goal he had ever scored as a senior player. Wrote the *Columbian*, "His heart jumped as he pictured himself a star home player."

The Salmonbellies swallowed their pride and rejoined the association, which now included a Seattle team, in time for the 1905 season. Beginning with this season, the old scoring system of goals deciding individual games within the timed quarters of a match was replaced by a system of aggregate goals. (The quarters were retained.) A game was now a game in the sense that it is understood today.

A different Salmonbellies team was emerging. Just seven veterans remained. Biscuits was back along with Dad, Barlow, outside home DeBeck, home Harry Latham, George Oddy, Tom Gifford, and all-purpose attacker, Fred Lynch. Gone was their great goaltender, Cheyne, who had decided to retire at 37. Sandy Gray took his place. Stan Peele, his ankle never fully recovered, handed over first home to his old teammate Harry Latham. Rookie James Francis "Pat" Feeney filled Latham's shoes, he and Tom Rennie taking over at second and third home, respectively. Jim Bryson slotted in at inside home, and Barlow's point-playing brother Charlie joined the team. George Rennie and Jimmy Gifford played defence. Waiting his chance at spare was a promising 17-year-old, Clifford Isaac Spring. Spring was born in Bracebridge, Ontario, in 1888, but was raised from an early age in New Westminster. When he was younger, he worked in a bakery, earning the nickname "Doughy."

The Salmonbellies travelled south to play a Seattle team on August 29, winning 10–2. The *Seattle Post-Intelligencer* raved about Dad, saying his performance "was little short of marvelous" and noting his years of experience: "Turnbull was playing lacrosse when most of his teammates were in swaddling clothes, yet he is now the peer of them all."

A month later, the Ottawa Capitals arrived in New Westminster, their first visit west. The Capitals would play three games, one with Vancouver, one with the Salmonbellies, and the third with the winner of the Vancouver-New Westminster contest. But before the series started, the Salmonbellies and Vancouver played for the league championship. New Westminster prevailed 4–1.

On Saturday, October 3, in the opening game of the series, the Salmonbellies faced Ottawa, with L.A. Lewis refereeing. Because Ottawa also played in red jerseys, the Salmonbellies donned white, prompting the *Columbian* to observe wittily that the white spring salmon run was just as strong as the red. The Salmonbellies team on the field that day featured two sets of brothers: Tom and Will Gifford, and George and Tom Rennie. But it was Fred Lynch who scored first. The Caps tied it. DeBeck got the Salmonbellies' second. The Caps tied it. And then the Salmonbellies' Pat Feeney, ten seconds after the start of the fourth quarter, "spoiled the pudding" for Ottawa by scoring the third and wining goal on Alvan "Bun" Clark, who was taking Hutton's place in nets.[63]

A couple of days later, it was Vancouver's turn with the Caps. Starting the second half tied at five apiece, the game slowed to a crawl when both teams and the crowd watched, mesmerized, as an aeronaut in another part of Queen's Park ascended and descended in a gas-filled balloon. The game ended in a draw, 7–7.

The Salmonbellies took on the Capitals in the third game of the series. New Westminster was up 4–1 at the beginning of the fourth quarter when the Caps suddenly found some holes in the Salmonbellies' defence and scored four goals to win 5–4. "It was," said the *Columbian*, "incredible to believe that any team on this terrestrial ball can score four goals in twenty minutes on the New Westminster defence."[64]

In 1906, Victoria withdrew from the league and Vancouver fielded a second team, the Mount Pleasant Maple Leafs. The Salmonbellies lost Oddy to retirement and Dad sat out the season. The team added two young players to their roster, New Westminster-born and bred players Bert Henry and Irving "Punk" Wintemute, son of pioneering New Westminster furniture maker Robert Wintemute. Punk would develop into one of the better stick handlers in the game and would score a lot of goals in an unusual move that involved jumping and turning as he shot.

Developments in the NLU were affecting the game in the west. Every senior player in eastern Canada had turned pro and was drawing a salary. The money was substantial; total gate

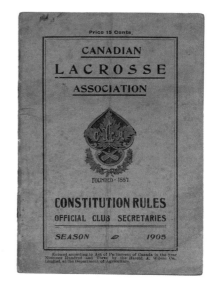

In 1905 the CLA adopted aggregate goals to determine winners, rather than the team winning the most games within a match.

CANADIAN LACROSSE HALL OF FAME. PHOTOGRAPH BY PHILLIP CHIN.

Nº 42 — TOMMY BURNS, Vancouver Team.

Nº 43 — J. BRENNAN, Montreal Team.

Nº 44 — A. DADE, Montreal Team.

Nº 45 — H. SCOTT, Montreal Team.

Nº 52 — F. SCOTT, Montreal Team.

Nº 53 — R. FINLAYSON, Montreal Team.

Nº 54 — N. NEVILLE, Montreal Team.

Nº 55 — J. WINTEMUTE, New Westminster Team.

Nº 62 — W. TURNBULL, New Westminster Team.

Nº 63 — L. TURNBULL, New Westminster Team.

Nº 64 — T. RENNIE, New Westminster Team.

Nº 65 — JAS. FEENEY, New Westminster Team.

Nº 72 — A. LANGLOIS, National de Quebec.

Nº 73 — J. METIVIER, National de Quebec.

Nº 74 — A. De BEAUMONT, National de Quebec.

Lacrosse was so popular in Canada that in 1910 and 1911 Imperial Tobacco created and issued a "Lacrosse Series" of cards featuring the players of the country's professional teams, including the Salmonbellies. These "premiums," inserted in cigarette packages, were meant to increase sales. Today they are highly collectible.

CANADIAN LACROSSE HALL OF FAME. PHOTOGRAPHS BY PHILLIP CHIN.

receipts for the eastern season were $115,000.[65] Charlie Welsh, now president of the BCALA, said that when the game went professional, he would get out. He believed that the Salmonbellies would do better as an amateur team. Said Salmonbellies secretary, Ryall, "We have enough players who will play for the game's sake."[66] A pro team would not, he believed, be a paying proposition in BC, with the possible exception of Vancouver, whose population might be able to support one.

Vancouver lacrosse enthusiasts were indeed keen to introduce professional lacrosse for 1908, arguing that it was justified as a means to better teams and larger gate revenue.

The Salmonbellies went 8–1 in 1906, their only loss coming at Brockton Oval at the hands of the Maple Leafs. New Westminster scored eighty goals and allowed thirty-five as they won the provincial championship for the eleventh time since 1889.

In the spring of 1907, the Salmonbellies defeated the Victoria Maple Leafs to capture the new Kilmarnock Cup, emblematic of the provincial championship. Salmonbellies' trainer Tim Mahony brought the trophy home ahead of the team, placing it with great pride in Ryall's drugstore window.

On June 17, at Queen's Park, the Salmonbellies crushed an all-Canada team 17–0. In a June 29 game against the Maple Leafs at Brockton Point, Dad, then 35 years old, re-injured his leg early in the game. The referee refused to let him leave the field because his check would also have to go off to even up the sides, so he spent the game in one spot, limping around, seldom touching the ball. The Salmonbellies lost 8–4.

The Toronto Tecumsehs, eastern frontrunners, were signed to play during exhibition week. Welsh had previously signed the Vancouvers (as they were then called) and the Maple Leafs. The winning team would get $800, second place $600, third place $400, and fourth place $200. Concerned about an amateur team playing a pro team, a representative of the Canadian Amateur Athletic Union met with Salmonbellies' president Reverend Henderson and Charlie Welsh and warned them the team would lose their amateur status if they played the Tecumsehs for money.

The Tecumsehs arrived at Westminster Junction on Saturday, September 28. They led the seven-team National Lacrosse Union (NLU) for most of the season, but finished second to the Shamrocks. The Tecumsehs were known for their polished stick handling and "good dodging."[67] Querrie was now their manager and playing captain, the "wonder" of the NLU. He won the league scoring title with thirty-four points in sixteen games in 1906 and finished second in 1907.

"We want that $800 prize," he said, "and will do our best to pull out with our gloves on the big roll."[68] They appeared to have the manpower to back their confidence. Their leading goal-getter, with twenty-nine, was Harry "Sport" Murton. Murton, born and raised in Fergus, Ontario, was a serious Scot who put his heart and soul into everything he did. He could go past a defender on either a straight run or on a turn, without slacking his speed, and often leaping five or six feet in the air. He "took such desperate chances that few, if any, defencemen could stop him."[69]

But every home player on the Tecumseh team had scored more than ten goals during the regular season. Even the powerful Shamrocks had only four players scoring more than ten goals. The Tecumsehs led the league in goals with a hundred and one, against fifty-seven scored against them. They were not short on defenders either, with Stewart, cover point, and Griffiths, point, both weighing in at over 190 pounds and both with exceptional speed.

Between 1899 and 1906 there was no brighter lacrosse star than Montreal Shamrocks' attacker Henry Francis Hoobin. A knee injury effectively ended his career at 27 years old, although he attempted a comeback against the 1908 Salmonbellies.

NEW WESTMINSTER MUSEUM AND ARCHIVES.

After wresting the Minto Cup from the Montreal Shamrocks, the 1908 Salmonbellies played an exhibition against the Tecumsehs at Hanlan's Point Stadium in the Toronto Islands. The stadium was adjacent to an amusement park, hence the roller coaster behind the team. **Left to Right:** J.A. McGowan (trainer), George Rennie, Jimmy Gifford, Irving "Punk" Wintemute, Len Turnbull, Clifford "Doughy" Spring, Clarence "Biscuits" Peele (team manager), James "Pat" Feeney, Tom Rennie, Alexander "Sandy" Gray, Tommy Gifford (captain), Charlie Galbraith, Bill Turnbull. (Missing: Pete Latham, Alex "Dad" Turnbull, Jack Bryson.)

On October 1, the Tecumsehs, with Wells Gray and Bob Cheyne refereeing, easily defeated Vancouver 17–7. Despite that, the oddsmakers still favoured New Westminster. Before the match, the Tecumsehs announced, as a measure of their sincerity, that they had pooled their money, about $200, and were betting on themselves to win. The Salmonbellies won 12–6. Tom Gifford held Tecumsehs' Murton scoreless. Tom Rennie did the same to Querrie. Having overcome his injuries and playing like a 20-year-old, Dad was carried from the field by his admirers, while the team was hauled by a joyous crowd from the park to the city after the game.

The Tecumsehs showed themselves to be good sports when manager Keary revealed that they would not accept the $600 second prize, allowing the Salmonbellies to retain their amateur standing. The Salmonbellies had scored sixty-nine goals on the season against forty scored on them. They also led in the penalty department, players being ruled off fifty-three times. Len Turnbull, the youngest senior player in BC, led the league in scoring with seventeen goals in eight games, followed by two Maple Leafs players, then Jim Bryson with eleven, Bill Turnbull[70] with ten, Pat Feeney with eight, and Bert Henry with seven. Sixty thousand people had attended the exhibition, and Saturday's paid attendance at the big game was 18,000, counting only people in the bleachers, grandstands, and around the fence. Charlie Welsh credited the game with keeping the crowd until Saturday, swelling gate attendance, and making the fair's management happy with the receipts.

On Saturday, October 12, a complimentary banquet for the team was held in New West-minster at Mrs. Cook's restaurant. Addison's orchestra supplied the music. Wells Gray, who had refereed the Tecumseh match along with Vancouver's Matt Barr as judge of play, spoke, saying, "All the Tecumsehs asked for was fair refereeing, and when they got it they didn't like it."[71] At the end of a humorous speech, Herb Ryall made a serious pitch to keep the game amateur. He strongly disapproved of bringing professionalism into amateur sports. It was no sport when players had to be paid whether they won or not. Mayor Keary spoke, saying that he looked forward to the day when New Westminster and Vancouver would be one. This was met with "cheering and cries of 'Greater Westminster!'"[72] Keary then announced that two men were prepared to finance the team if they wished to travel back east next year in pursuit of the Minto Cup. He was also heartened by the absence of liquor at the banquet. The Mayor then launched into "The Veteran's Song," a popular tune by the man who wrote "Danny Boy," English lyricist F.E. Weatherly.

Robert Eickhoff followed with Eugene Field's nursery rhyme "Little Boy Blue."[73] The poem, which Eickhoff sang, is about a boy who dies in his sleep, leaving his toy dog and tin soldier to wonder "what has become of our Little Boy Blue/Since he kissed them and put them there." His encore was American Charles Adams' 1878 comic doggerel "Leedle Yawcob Strauss," a father's ode to his mischievous son.

Beneath the syrupy lyrics and the silly stereotyping, the songs are about duty, about doing what must be done despite difficulty or suffering. A former British soldier, now old and infirm, calls out for his faithful Martini-Henry rifle to steady him as he waits for the king to pass by in a parade; a toy soldier rusts, maintaining his post as ordered by his command-ing officer, the little boy; a father can only shake his head at the antics of his young son. But the old infantryman must rise to honour the king, the toy soldier dare not abandon his post, and Mr. Strauss cannot but love his son. The message to the Salmonbellies was clear: you were good soldiers. The team responded with their war cry.

Winning the Minto Cup was the only thing that mattered to the New Westminster Salm-onbellies as the 1908 lacrosse season got underway. They trained by playing against their intermediate team, putting themselves at a two-man disadvantage just to keep things inter-esting. They also played a game against Vancouver, a 4–0 New Westminster victory.

The lacrosse situation in Vancouver was dire. The athletic club was broke. One of the team's executives, Lionel Yorke, approached transplanted Australian and successful Vancou-ver businessman Con Jones about taking over the management of the team on a professional basis. The son of Irish immigrants, 39-year-old Jones had arrived in Vancouver in 1903, his wife and children accompanying him. Where other entrepreneurs saw opportunities in fish, forestry, and mining, Jones saw it in billiards, tobacco, and poker.

A born promoter, the competitive Irish-Australian was just what the Vancouver sports scene needed. Wasting no time, in the summer of 1904, Jones opened Con's Billiard Room. It was not much, just nine tables, but it was a start. In 1908, he took over another pool hall operation and renamed it the Limit Pool Room. A year later he added the Brunswick. In back rooms you could play a friendly game of five-card stud poker. Operating a gaming house was illegal, but Jones got around that technicality by forsaking any part of the stakes, charging only for the use of cards and tables. A soccer fan, Jones organized and was president of the Pacific Coast Association Football League. His familiarity with lacrosse was confined to what he knew from attending games as a spectator. Nevertheless, he accepted Yorke's invitation, and a new era began for BC lacrosse—a pro era.

Early Saturday morning, July 11, the Salmonbellies and their entourage boarded their railway car at the CPR station. As the train pulled away, advertising banners strung along both sides of the railway car boasted: "New Westminster Lacrosse Team. From the land of Fruit, Flowers, Sunshine and Prosperity."[74] No mention of salmon. But, as it was in 1900, the omen for victory was not far beneath the surface of the Fraser River. The sockeye already caught were small, a sure sign, according to fishermen, of a good run on its way.

Four days later, the Salmonbellies stepped off the train at Caledonia Springs, Ontario, a whistle stop on the CPR line, about halfway between Ottawa and Montreal. Its natural spring waters were the only reason it was even on a map. The house elixir, "white sulphur water," won first prize at the 1893 Chicago World's Fair. A sanitarium, the Grand Hotel, had sprung up to capitalize on the reputed health benefits of the water. Since 1835, the sanitarium-hotel had played host to thousands of people suffering from conditions with nineteenth-century names such as catarrh, dropsy and lumbago. They came to take "the cure," a regimen of spring waters, fresh air, rest, and abstinence from alcohol—especially abstinence from alcohol—which was not served or allowed.

The Grand Hotel was a place for wealthy health-tourists, the elderly, alcoholics, and hypochondriacs to park themselves for a couple of weeks and try to get well. The hotel, in the hands of the CPR since 1905, was a bizarre-looking cross between a penitentiary and an aviary. It stood over a village of pavilions, rooming houses, a spring-fed heated swimming pool, and a bottling plant. The CPR had improved the property with the installation of a tennis court, gymnasium, and one of the earliest golf courses in Canada.

As far as the Salmonbellies' handlers and backers were concerned, however, the location could not possibly have been better. There the players could acclimatize, train, swim, receive massages, rest, and not be tempted by big city distractions. "Czar 'Biscuits' refused to allow the boys the indulgence of smokes and in the liquid line nothing stronger than fruit salts was permitted," reported the *Columbian*. The players, stranded about forty rail miles from Montreal, might as well have been confined to barracks. No beer, no women, no bright lights. Instead, they had to content themselves with light practice on the hotel's lawn and glasses of "carburetted hydrogen gas water," whose diuretic and soporific qualities were said to induce "happy dreams."

On the Saturday following their arrival, the team travelled to Montreal to watch a game between the Montreals and the Tecumsehs. "We could have beaten both clubs," wrote Biscuits in a telegram. "Tecumsehs played like dubs."

On July 21, watered and rested to a fault, the Salmonbellies took to the field at the Shamrocks' home park in Montreal's northern suburbs, the Mile End grounds (now Jean Talon market). The Shamrocks wore their traditional green jerseys, the Salmonbellies their red. Outremont, the other side of Mont Royal, was just visible a couple of miles to the south, low, grey clouds and a fine, drizzling rain obscuring the mountaintop. Only 1,800 fans attended the poorly advertised match.

The Shamrocks were the reigning eastern champions, but many of the players had been with the team for a decade. The Brennan brothers, Jimmie Hogan, and team captain Jim Kavanagh were on board. But their big offensive gun, Henry Hoobin, had retired at the end of the 1907 season, a chronic knee injury forcing him out. "Nothing," the 29-year-old superstar said, "could ever induce me to get into the game again."[75] Compared to the Shamrocks, the Salmonbellies were younger, lighter, and faster.

The Salmonbellies' new centre, Pat Feeney, Dad's replacement, squared with his counterpart at mid-field. The referee, Doctor Irvine of Toronto, placed the ball between the centres' sticks and blew his whistle. The Salmonbellies went straight to the attack, with Dad, playing home, directing the offence. The team bore in on the Shamrocks' goal at every opportunity, but their shooting was off. The Shamrocks' Spike Hennessy scored first. The Salmonbellies soon tied it. Tom Rennie opened the scoring in the second quarter, but his goal was answered by goals from Jack Brennan and Hogan. Bill Turnbull tied the score 3–3, but the other Brennan, Paddy, then scored.

And then Dad did what he had done so many times before, scoring twice to end the half: 5–4 Salmonbellies. That was it for Kavanagh. Steve Rochford took his place in the second half and shut down Dad, allowing him and his teammates just one goal in the second half. It was all they needed. Hogan notched one in the fourth, but the Salmonbellies took game one, 6–5.

A disconsolate Hoobin watched from the grandstand. Also watching was the Tecumsehs' "Sport" Murton. "Galbraith, Tom and Jim Gifford and the two Rennies are a pretty well placed defence, the weight shading off from the goal as the speed increases toward the center. They relieve with great cleverness, and field the ball down well,"[76] wrote Murton. He was describing a Salmonbellies' innovation—a "stonewall" defence that today is known as a zone.

Murton thought Jim Gifford was the headiest man on defence: "He scans the whole field and takes his rush down when he sees it will be useful. His cutting off of passes was a feature."[77] On the other hand, Murton did not think Pat Feeney was very good, writing that he "lacked ginger" and "gave no show of the wonderful speed claimed for him."[78] And while Wintemute was not strong enough and Bryson did not come up to expectations, Len Turnbull and Dad combined for many "pretty plays."[79] As much as he admired Dad's play, Murton could not resist getting in a shot. "His bald spot must look inviting to a lacrosse stick," he said.[80]

Back at the sanitarium, the Salmonbellies drank more seltzer water. Trainer J.A. McGowan treated Len Turnbull's knee, injured earlier in the season, and his brother Bill's bad ankle. Doughy Spring took Bill's place, while the ever-dependable Pete Latham took over for Len.

On July 28, the teams lined up again at the Mile End grounds. There was one notable inclusion to the Shamrocks' roster: Henry "nothing-could-ever-induce-me" Hoobin. Biscuits, for one, just shrugged. Hoobin had been out of the game too long, as far as he was concerned, and would not be a factor. His inclusion was only a measure of the Shamrocks' desperation to find some offence. Lally and Irvine, mirroring the adjustments of the teams, switched places, Lally going in as referee.

Dad opened the scoring. Bryson added two more, showing that he was, contrary to Murton's assessment, up to expectations. 3–0 Salmonbellies. The Shamrocks' Hennessy next found the net, but Feeney answered. Brennan scored, Bryson got his third of the game, then Feeney scored his second. Biscuits had been right about Hoobin: the all-time great was valiant, but couldn't score. In the end, the Salmonbellies won 6–2 for a combined 12–7 series victory. At long last, they had taken the coveted cup from the Shamrocks. They also had their share of the gate receipts, $817.50. Lally thought Dad had played so spectacularly "he was entitled to anything from a seat in Parliament to a good looking wife."[81]

But Dad had paid a price. His head and face were a mass of scars, the ligaments in one arm torn, and his legs badly bruised. His injuries were severe enough that he was unable to sleep for several nights after the series.

As soon as the final score was posted at the CPR telegraph office, New Westminster erupted in celebration. The Salmonbellies' president, Reverend Henderson, was hoisted high onto shoulders, and two men raised salmon triumphantly over their heads, leading a boisterous procession east on Columbia Street. The mob stopped at Welsh's store for impromptu speeches. Cheers, whistles, and applause startled the horses. Henderson and Ryall led businessmen, clergymen, lawyers, ranchers, teamsters, steamboatmen, clerks, and just about every other class of society to Albert Crescent, the city's promontory over the Fraser River, near the present-day Patullo Bridge.

By eight o'clock that night thousands of people lined Columbia Street and formed a procession near the CPR depot, from where they marched again to the Albert Crescent grounds led by the city band and torchbearers. Hundreds of boys carried brooms, emblematic of the Salmonbellies' great sweep. Others rattled cowbells, tin cans, sleigh bells, and every conceivable kind of noisemaker while hundreds of young men set off firecrackers. The Crescent Club timed their spectacular fireworks display to the arrival of the procession. Two long strings of Chinese crackers went off, drowning out the city band. They reached the crescent to discover a large bonfire of oil barrels illuminating the grounds. Jack Bryson spoke through a huge megaphone, twice his length, to a crowd of 6,000 people. MLA Thomas Gifford announced that it was the proudest day of his life. The Salmonbellies, he said, "had done more to advertise New Westminster than anything else."[82] New Westminster, he claimed, was now on "the tongues of people from the Atlantic to the Pacific." At about ten o'clock the crowd, their appetites still wet for more celebration, paraded back downtown. Hundreds of people whooped it up on Columbia until one o'clock in the morning "as fancy and mineral water suggested."

In Montreal, the Shamrocks hosted the Salmonbellies at the Windsor Hotel. Shamrocks' president, Slattery, congratulated the victors and wished them well. Welsh accepted the cup and, after thanking the Shamrocks for their hospitality and sportsmanship, said that the country was paying too much attention to the American summer pastime, baseball. He hoped that newspapers would do their part to foster lacrosse and said he was confident that bringing the cup to BC would further the game in the west. In closing, he said he hoped that one day soon a strong lacrosse league in Manitoba would bridge the gap between west and east. The Salmonbellies then boarded their train, the Shamrocks cheering them as the train pulled out of the station.

The team travelled to Toronto where, without injured players Dad and Wintemute, they lost an exhibition game 10–4 at Hanlan's Point against the NLU-leading Tecumsehs. Then it was on to St. Paul, Minnesota, where they defeated the Mohawks. Their next stop was in Winnipeg, Manitoba, where they defeated that city's Shamrocks. Their train was late arriving in Calgary where they were scheduled to play the Alberta champions. It was seven o'clock in the evening before they stepped onto the field.

The Salmonbellies went straight to work on the muddy pitch, paralyzing Calgary with their vaunted attack. Bill Turnbull scored the first goal after four minutes of play. In order to get in a full game before complete darkness, there were no breaks between quarters. At the start of the second quarter, Bill Turnbull again opened the scoring. Having built up a good lead, and starting to tire, the Salmonbellies were content to defend in the final quarter. The play was all around their net, but Calgary could not find an opening: 6–2 Salmonbellies.

On August 13, a Thursday night, the train carrying the Salmonbellies and the Minto Cup pulled into New Westminster. This time, the banners on either side of the car read "New Westminster Lacrosse Team of British Columbia. CHAMPIONS OF THE WORLD." The team had been gone thirty-two days, had travelled over 6,000 miles, and were defeated only once in six matches against five teams. Thousands of people cheered their arrival. A block north, looking down over the city from Carnarvon Street, the brand new Russell Hotel blazed with electric lights, a beacon to the returning team. Its proprietors, Brine and McLean, had turned on everything just for the team's homecoming. In the kitchen, cooks had prepared a special Minto Cup lacrosse menu for the public. Just steps south of the Russell, at T.J. Trapp's hardware store, brothers Thomas and Samuel Trapp had prepared a reception and dinner. A long table, visible from the street, had been set for the players. A huge cooked salmon occupied the table's centre.[83]

A week or so earlier the *Columbian* had summed up the team's victory in verse.

The band is playing somewhere,
But not in Montreal,
For the Shamrocks met Westminster
And they got an awful fall.
Now the cup is coming Westward
To stay for many years,
And the Shams and all their backers
Are shedding bitter tears.
But in this old town there's laughter,
There's happiness, there's fun,
For our boys have got the tinware,
And their backers have the mon.[84]

The Salmonbellies were not shy about proclaiming their status after winning the Minto Cup in 1908.

CANADIAN LACROSSE HALL OF FAME. PHOTOGRAPH BY PHILLIP CHIN.

On September 26, the Salmonbellies faced Con Jones' Vancouver Lacrosse Club at Queen's Park. They were minus veterans Dad and George Rennie, who were on their way to England with Hoobin and Paddy Brennan as members of the 1908 Canadian Olympic lacrosse team. Doughy Spring's younger brother, 19-year-old Gordon "Grumpy" Spring, was added to the Salmonbellies' lineup. (The origin of his nickname is lost to history. He does not seem to have been particularly grumpy.)

An outside home player, Grumpy fit in perfectly with the Salmonbellies' boring-in style of play. He was short, stocky and, while not fast, he could start instantly into a full stride. Positioning himself fifteen or twenty feet behind and to one side of the opposition's goal, he would, at the opportune time, make a sudden dash toward the goalmouth, his quick start and weight usually carrying him at least one step ahead of his check. Just as he angled across the goalmouth, carrying his sawed-off stick close to his chest, a teammate would aim a pass directly at his body, so that he would not have to expose his stick. In what seemed like one motion, he would catch the ball and flip it, at an impossible angle, over the goalkeeper's shoulder and into the net. He was so fast that goalies seldom saw it coming. Once the ball was in the net, he would leap joyously in the air, his stick thrust high over his head. Grumpy's sudden cut to the net, quick ball release, goal, and leap in the air would become a familiar sight to tens of thousands of spectators.

But at the start of the September 26 contest, Vancouver's Green slashed Grumpy's skull, creating a deep gash. Salmonbellies' supporters were incensed and screamed for Green's blood. Green went to the fence for ten minutes, and was later sentenced to serve another five for more slashing. He cursed referee Joe Reynolds, loudly proclaiming that Reynolds was afraid of the Salmonbellies, a laughable claim in light of Reynolds' Vancouver-playing days.

Just before the half, with the Salmonbellies leading 8–0, Green sandwiched himself between his teammate Crosby and the Salmonbellies' Tommy Gifford. Gifford gave Green the butt end of his stick. Green tried to remove Gifford's nose. The two went at each other with their sticks, inspiring everyone else to do likewise. After a few minutes all but Green and Gifford had calmed down. As players from both sides tried to separate the two, hundreds of spectators decided to help Gifford. Swarmed, Green circled the angry mob in a desperate attempt to escape to the dressing room. As the mob chased Green, Vancouver's black trainer, George Paris, drew his revolver. Paris, a native of Truro, Nova Scotia, was a boxer who had trained athletes from Seattle to Dawson City. Without a doubt Paris's intention was to fire a shot into the air as a signal for the mob to stop. But he thought better of it, and shoved the revolver back in his pocket. Green was already safely in the dressing room when Paris reached the door. As he was about to go in, an egg hit him in the side of the head. Out came the revolver. The mob suddenly changed direction, scattering in wild disorder. Detective Bradshaw coolly ordered Paris to lower his weapon, but a spectator, Dave Burnett, unwisely grabbed Paris's gun arm. The trainer threatened to shoot if he was not released. The gun went off. The bullet grazed Burnett's hand on its way through his coat, the powder burning the front of his clothing.

In the grandstand, Bill and Len Turnbull's mother Jessie fainted and was carried to the street. Other women were equally overcome and passed out. Paris, too, was unnerved, and surrendered his revolver. Two officers marched him off to the station. Meanwhile, most of the Vancouver players were in their dressing room, New Westminster's cooler heads barring the door. But the mob, as angry as ever, was still demanding Green. Eggs were flying. Archie MacNaughton, naturally, caught one in the head. Salmonbellies officials pleaded for the crowd to disperse, to no avail. Reverend Henderson tried to lower the temperature, but the mob would not be placated until they had their hands on Green. In the Salmonbellies' dressing room, Tommy Gifford, with a fresh white bandage over his nose, knotted his tie, adjusted his straw boater, and strode out to confront the crowd. His presence silenced them. When he had everyone's undivided attention, he spoke. "If I am satisfied," he said, "you ought to be."[85] And with those eight words, he turned and entered Vancouver's dressing room. There he shook hands with Green. Green, a nasty cut visible on the top of his head, accompanied by Gifford and other officials, exited the dressing room. The mob parted, allowing Gifford and Green free passage.

Paris was charged with carrying a concealed weapon and pointing a loaded weapon with intent to do grievous bodily harm. A conviction carried $150 in fines and two months behind bars. He was held for two days until a "reputable source," probably Con Jones, bailed him out. Vancouver refused to play any more games against the Salmonbellies.

On the day Paris was bailed out, the Ottawa Capitals, runners-up in the NLU, arrived by train to play two games against the Salmonbellies during the exhibition. Archie Allen and Tom Gorman led the Capitals in scoring. Bouse Hutton, who had not been with the team on their 1905 trip west, was in goal. Hutton had two Minto Cups under his belt, 1901 and 1904. In 1902, he was the fullback of the Ottawa Rough Riders, Canadian football champions, and in 1903 and 1904, he won Stanley Cups as the goalie of the Ottawa Silver Seven.

The Salmonbellies led 5–2 heading into the fourth quarter of the first game, when the Caps scored two goals within seconds of each other. Grumpy scored, but the Caps came back with two more to tie. The Salmonbellies scored once more to win 7–6.

The second game was held before 12,000 spectators, a few thousand more than the population of New Westminster. Eight tram cars "loaded to the roof" arrived from Vancouver alone. Fans were treated to a spectacular game. Hutton took a Len Turnbull ball to the solar plexus and was knocked out cold for fifteen seconds. He came to and continued in goal. Despite a valiant effort from the Caps, the Salmonbellies prevailed 9–6 in the second game and 8–4 in the third.

In league matches against two Vancouver teams and Victoria, the Salmonbellies had

Age has blackened it, but this is the game ball from the Salmonbellies' historic 1908 Minto Cup victory over the Montreal Shamrocks.

CANADIAN LACROSSE HALL OF FAME.
PHOTOGRAPH BY PHILLIP CHIN.

En route to New Westminster, the triumphant Salmonbellies posed with the wives who had accompanied them on their journey, the Minto Cup, and the CPR coach that carried them homeward. The banner reads: New Westminster Lacrosse Team of British Columbia. CHAMPIONS OF THE WORLD. **Left to Right:** "Biscuits" Peele (team manager), Jimmy Gifford, Len Turnbull, Jack Bryson, "Punk" Wintemute, Charlie Galbraith, Bill Turnbull (behind trophy), Pete Latham, "Doughy" Spring, George Rennie (wearing fedora), "Sandy" Gray, Tom Rennie, Tommy Gifford, "Pat" Feeney, Charlie Welsh (GM). Ladies on train, l-r: Mrs. Mary Welsh, Mrs. Katherine Peele, Mrs. Lucy Gifford (Tom's wife).

NEW WESTMINSTER MUSEUM AND ARCHIVES.

won all seven games they played, scoring eighty-eight goals, with just fourteen against them. They had dethroned the legendary Montreal Shamrocks in two games and defeated the Tecumsehs, the Mohawks, and the Winnipeg Shamrocks. In their first defence of the cup, they beat Ottawa in three straight. They were the undefeated, undisputed champions of the lacrosse-playing world.

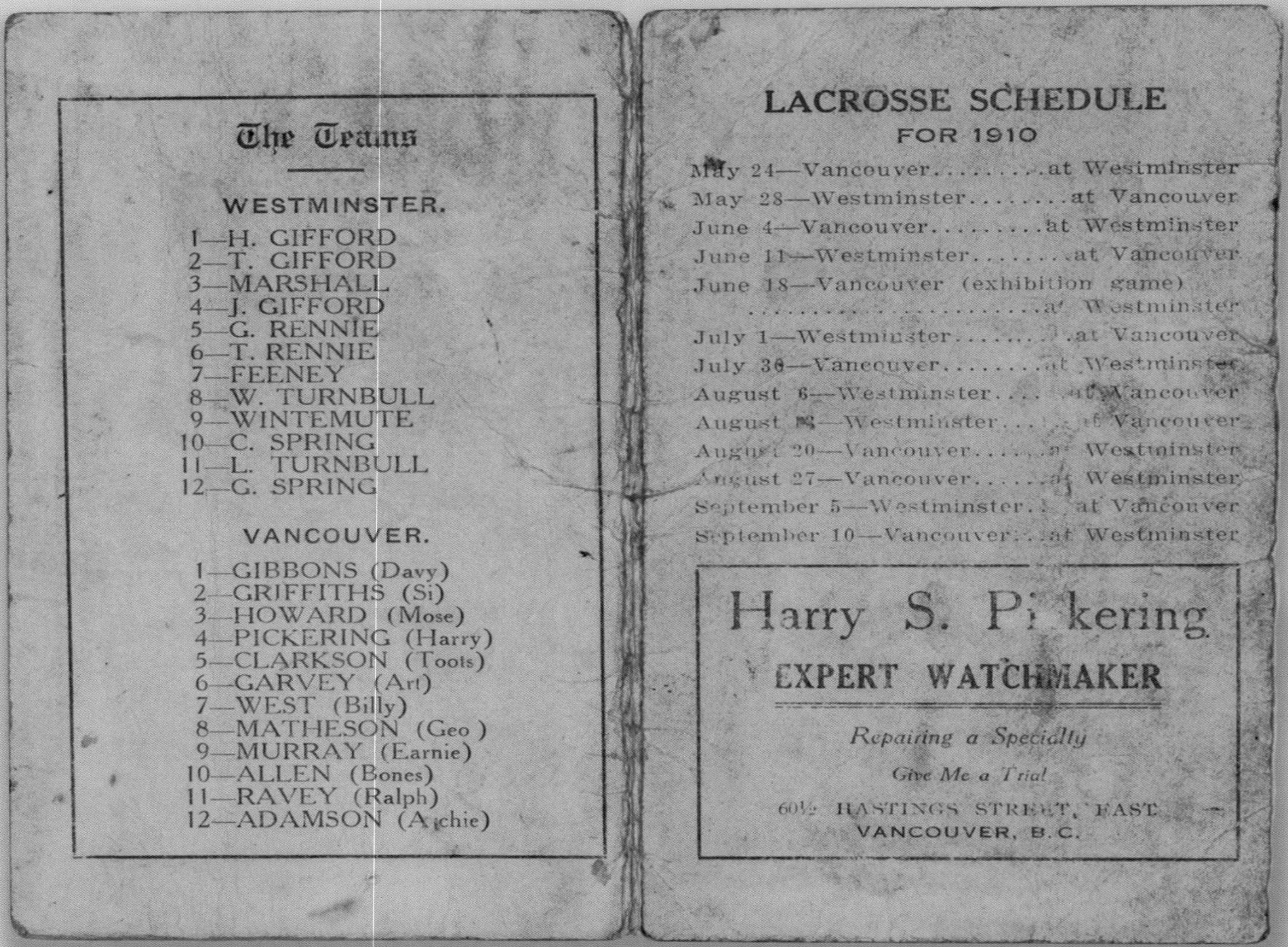

The Teams

WESTMINSTER.

1—H. GIFFORD
2—T. GIFFORD
3—MARSHALL
4—J. GIFFORD
5—G. RENNIE
6—T. RENNIE
7—FEENEY
8—W. TURNBULL
9—WINTEMUTE
10—C. SPRING
11—L. TURNBULL
12—G. SPRING

VANCOUVER.

1—GIBBONS (Davy)
2—GRIFFITHS (Si)
3—HOWARD (Mose)
4—PICKERING (Harry)
5—CLARKSON (Toots)
6—GARVEY (Art)
7—WEST (Billy)
8—MATHESON (Geo)
9—MURRAY (Earnie)
10—ALLEN (Bones)
11—RAVEY (Ralph)
12—ADAMSON (Archie)

LACROSSE SCHEDULE
FOR 1910

May 24—Vancouver.........at Westminster
May 28—Westminster........at Vancouver
June 4—Vancouver.........at Westminster
June 11—Westminster.......at Vancouver
June 18—Vancouver (exhibition game)
.........................at Westminster
July 1—Westminster.......at Vancouver
July 30—Vancouver.........at Westminster
August 6—Westminster.....at Vancouver
August 13—Westminster.....at Vancouver
August 20—Vancouver.......at Westminster
August 27—Vancouver.......at Westminster
September 5—Westminster....at Vancouver
September 10—Vancouver....at Westminster

The Salmonbellies won eight of eleven league games against the Vancouver Lacrosse Club
in 1910 and successfully defended the Minto Cup against two Montreal clubs.

DON OXENBURY. PHOTOGRAPH BY PHILLIP CHIN.

> *"Rule with a firm hand. Thumb off the smart alecs.*
> *Let the coaches rave and the customers howl.*
> *Call 'em as you see 'em and to hell with everybody."*

Fred "Mickey" Ion, *Vancouver Sun*,
November 22, 1927

CHAPTER FOUR
GOING PRO: 1909-1924

In 1909, the Salmonbellies ceased to be amateurs in the eyes of the Canadian Amateur Athletic Union because, while not salaried, they were accepting money for playing, and they were playing professional teams. The BCALA dropped 'Amateur' from its name. But although the Salmonbellies received a split of gate receipts, they had regular jobs like everyone else. Amateur or professional, the Capitals wanted another shot at the Salmonbellies. But the team was not the Capitals of a year earlier. It was a team put together by Regina Member of Parliament William Melville Martin, who had distinguished himself as a scholar and an athlete at the University of Toronto before obtaining his teacher's certificate and later a law degree from Osgoode Hall. Six years after taking up his law practice in Regina, he put together what he hoped would be a formidable lacrosse team, with the help of Sport Murton. As a member of the 1907 Tecumsehs, Murton had failed to defeat the Salmonbellies in two games at Queen's Park. He wanted another shot at them, and if there was a Minto Cup on the line, so much the better. The Regina Capitals was composed of the best professional talent available: inside home Angus "Bones" Allen, defence fielder Tom Gorman, and outside home Jack Shea from the Ottawa Capitals; cover point Dr. Ollie Davidson, goalkeeper Bun Clark, and Murton himself, at second home, from the Toronto Tecumsehs; first home Art Warwick from the Torontos; McLean of Souris, Manitoba; and first defence Johnny Howard from the Montreal Shamrocks.

Gorman and Shea had the richest deal, receiving $250 each for the two cup games plus all travel and living expenses. The rest received between $100 and $200. The final member of the team was Édouard Charles "Newsy" Lalonde. He acquired the nickname "Newsy" as a teenager working at the *Cornwall Freeholder* newspaper. Newsy's professional career began in 1906 with the Canadian Soo Algonquins hockey team in Sault Ste. Marie, Ontario, earning $50 a week as a member of the International Hockey League, the first openly professional hockey league.

In the weeks leading up to the series, BC Electric Railway cars in New Westminster and Vancouver flew streamers advertising the game. Extra cars were added to the line to accommodate the thousands of expected spectators. Despite the Capitals' star power, the oddsmakers had the Salmonbellies doubling Regina's score in the series. New Westminster was a two-to-one favourite. On May 20, Canadian flags flew from every flagstaff in New Westminster, and store windows were decorated with the red and blue of the lacrosse club. Spectators poured

into Queen's Park from not only Vancouver and the Fraser Valley, but also from American towns and cities. The Capitals appeared on the field in red jerseys and grey shorts. The Salmonbellies came out in their new red jerseys, with the recently added big, white W crests, and dark blue shorts, having adamantly refused to give up their red jerseys to accommodate the wishes of the challengers.

Referee Archie MacNaughton faced off the ball, and the game was on in front of 8,000 boisterous spectators. The Salmonbellies played cautiously in the first quarter, while the Capitals played aggressively. But the second and third quarters belonged to New Westminster and, although Regina rallied in the fourth, the game ended at 6–4 in favour of the Salmonbellies.

Ten thousand people filled the stands in anticipation of the second game. Regina did not get on the scoreboard until the second quarter, after the Salmonbellies had already notched seven. Grumpy scored four, while Len Turnbull and Jack Bryson got three each in a 12–2 New Westminster victory.

Murton, as always, had given it everything he had, breaking a couple of ribs in the process. But for the second time in two years, he had nothing to show for his exertions. New Westminster had shown that not even an amalgamation of the best players from across the country was going to take away *their* cup, an assertion they would reinforce throughout the remainder of the season and the coming decade.

Con Jones watched the Regina series with intense interest, and hired defenceman Johnny "Mose" Howard, Newsy, and Bones Allen from the Regina team. Allen was born and raised in Cornwall, Ontario, where he played lacrosse and pro hockey for his hometown before joining the Ottawa Silver Seven, winners of the 1905 Stanley Cup. Scouting in Toronto, Jones hired Tecumsehs' star, Archie Adamson, the third-ranked point-getter in the NLU, with twenty-two goals and four assists. In Montreal, he hired Spike Hennessey, a goal scorer for the Shamrocks since 1903.

The Salmonbellies faced Jones's new team on June 12. Doughy scored four, Grumpy two, and Latham and Tom Rennie one apiece in an 8–5 Salmonbellies' victory. Newsy, playing inside home for Jones, scored his first goal against New Westminster two minutes into the third quarter. The Salmonbellies discovered that Newsy had a way of crowding in on his check and muscling by. He was equally adept at getting his man off balance, at accepting passes at close quarters, and at scoring. He was also a sharp field general in directing an attack. The Salmonbellies discovered one other thing: he liked to argue. His first disagreement occurred in the fourth quarter, when he, Galbraith, and Tommy Gifford went to the fence for ten minutes for delay of game. In the Regina series, Newsy and Gifford, being at opposite ends of the field, had not tangled. Now that they were acquainted, they hated each other.

The Salmonbellies' next encounter with Vancouver ended in a 9–8 New Westminster victory. The game was an especially wild one, ousted players at one point practically "decorating" the fence. The *Columbian* claimed that the Salmonbellies had not won a more decisive victory because they were saving themselves for their upcoming Minto challenge series against the Tecumsehs. But the real issue was that Dad, in hospital with ribs fractured in the June 12 game, was not in the lineup, and Tom Gifford had been called away during the second quarter to deal with a train wreck on the Westminster swing bridge, where he was superintendent.

The Salmonbellies faced the Toronto Tecumsehs at the end of June, their second defence of the Minto Cup in a month. The Tecumsehs, led by Querrie, put up a much tougher fight than the Reginas. Initially, Toronto played "eastern style," moving around the perimeter of the goal looking for an opening. Finding this tactic ineffective, they switched to the western style of "boring in" and began to score goals. The switch, however, came too late, and the Salmonbellies won the first game 6–4.

In 1909 transportation was still split between horse carriages and autos, men wore straw boaters, women shaded themselves under parasols, and the Beaver cigar (reads the banner along the fence) was the best in BC. They were made at a factory in New Westminster owned by retired Salmonbellie Fred Lynch, a player in the 1890s.

NEW WESTMINSTER MUSEUM AND ARCHIVES.

The inscription on the 1910 Salmonbellies' team photo reads: "Champions of the world, defenders of the Minto Cup. They played for joy, not for money. They were respected, beloved, and to small boys they were heroic." **l-r:** Dan McIlroy (trainer), J.A. McGowan (trainer), Jimmy Gifford, Doughy Spring, George Rennie, Charlie Galbraith, unidentified, Bill Turnbull, Thomas Gifford, Tommy Gifford, Buck Marshall, Pete Latham, Bert Kellington (bowler hat), Sandy Gray, unidentified (white hat), Fred Lynch (president, behind gent in white hat), Punk Wintemute, Hugh Gifford, Tom Rennie, Edward Longfellow, Pat Feeney, Tim Mahony (trainer), Charlie Welsh (manager). **On the grass l-r:** Grumpy Spring, boy unidentified (possibly Earle Gray), Len Turnbull. **Missing:** Jack Bryson.
NEW WESTMINSTER MUSEUM AND ARCHIVES. PHOTOGRAPH BY W.T. COOKSLEY.

In the second game, the Salmonbellies were evenly matched on nearly every level. Play was fast and hard on both sides. The Turnbull brothers, Len and Bill, along with George Rennie, outdid themselves, while Harry Pickering and goalie Kinsman were outstanding for the Tecumsehs. But in the end, the Salmonbellies prevailed 6–5 to win the series 12–9, retaining the Minto Cup.

In the grandstand Con Jones watched the play of Tecumsehs' defenceman Fred "Mickey" Ion and liked what he saw. A defenceman from Paris, Ontario, by way of Brantford, Ion had joined the Tecumsehs in 1909. Following the cup series, Jones signed him. He also liked the way Bun Clark played goal and signed him, too.

With the Minto Cup challenges met, regular league play resumed. In a game on August 7, Vancouver's Waldo Matheson, upset over a call by Victoria referee Percy Peele, went after him. When Peele blew his whistle to end the quarter, a mob of Vancouver supporters rushed onto the field and attempted to beat him up. The Salmonbellies surrounded Peele and escorted the badly shaken official to their locker room. He later filed assault charges against Matheson.

The Salmonbellies won the next game as well, 5–4. While New Westminster was giving Vancouver three cheers, Newsy shoved his stick hard into George Rennie's face, raising a nasty welt. Rennie remembered that in the season finale on September 18, when he and Newsy punched it out in the third quarter. The game and the 1909 season ended in a 7–4 Salmonbellies' victory. Newsy won the league scoring honours, netting twenty-three goals in ten games. The Spring brothers tied for second with fourteen goals apiece. In total, New Westminster scored sixty-nine goals against Vancouver's sixty-five.

"This is no picnic," Jones told reporters on May 10, 1910, having put down his foot on mandatory player attendance at Monday, Wednesday, and Thursday night practices. "They have to be in perfect trim to beat New Westminster."[86] Absentees were slapped with a $5 fine. Newsy was absent in a different sense. After playing hockey with the Toronto professionals in the winter of 1909, he elected not to rejoin Jones's team for the 1910 season, signing on with the Montreal Nationals instead.

The Montreal AAA team, reigning NLU champions, arrived on July 12 to challenge the Salmonbellies for the cup. They stayed at the Badminton Hotel in Vancouver and practised at Brockton Point. They took to the field at Queen's Park on July 16, in front of 11,000 spectators. They left the field 10–4 losers. For the Salmonbellies, Grumpy scored four and Len Turnbull three. After their loss, Montreal got drunk. Nursing hangovers on Sunday, they passed up the Salmonbellies' invitation to an excursion up the Fraser River to Pitt Lake, a popular destination for sightseers.

The AAAs went into the second game determined to bottle up Grumpy, but Len Turnbull scored less than a minute into the game followed by Wintemute ten seconds after the faceoff and then again a couple of minutes later. Turnbull ended the match with five goals to Wintemute's three, and the Salmonbellies won 13–5. If it was any consolation to Montreal, they did hold Grumpy scoreless.

Winning was becoming old hat for the Salmonbellies and their fans. Noted the *Columbian*, the Salmonbellies' "boring-in tactics, the pass to the centre while the home comes in toward their opponents' goal, the interference, the running in circles in front of the visitors' goal, the rush of one man across the goal, pretending that he has the ball, all these tactics have been watched by the inhabitants of this city for some time past."[87]

As a publicity stunt, Con Jones hired former world heavyweight boxing champion Tommy Burns to play one game for his team on Labour Day, September 6. Burns, who reigned as champion from 1906 to 1908, grew up playing lacrosse in Ontario. He was mediocre at outside home (he managed one assist), but his presence gave the team renewed confidence. With Vancouver well ahead in the fourth quarter, George Rennie swatted Burns on the leg with his stick. Burns ignored him, so Rennie took a run at the ex-world champ. Burns shook him off and Rennie was banished for the remainder of the game. Vancouver won 7–1, but the Salmonbellies had defeated Jones's greenshirts all season long (in eight out of eleven games) and they retained the BC championship. Jones was disgusted. The team had cost him lots of money and he had nothing to show for it. He swore he was out of the sport "once and for all."[88]

The next challenger for the Minto Cup was the Montreal Nationals. They crossed the country in style on their way to the west coast. The team had one private railway car for accommodation and another that had been converted into a rolling gymnasium. Their topnotch trainer, William Noseworthy, came with them. They played a number of games in cities as they crossed the country. When they finally arrived on the coast they had a good three days to acclimatize. Practising at Queen's Park they complained about the downslope and called it a hay field. Newsy, the captain of the Nationals, had broken the team's goal-scoring record with thirty-one goals. He was confident of victory. "We have a cracking good team," he told reporters a few days before the first game.

Game 1 got underway on September 17. New Westminster scored five goals and held the Nationals scoreless until the middle of the third quarter. The game was widely followed in Ontario and Quebec. In Ottawa, 1,000 people gathered outside the Sparks Street office of the *Citizen* newspaper to read bulletins of the game as they were posted. Len Turnbull scored three goals and Grumpy contributed two on the way to a 7–3 victory. Salmonbellies' defender David "Buck" Marshall checked Newsy scoreless. One of the Salmonbellies slashed Newsy in the face. When his wound became infected, he was hospitalized in Vancouver, ending his season.

One week later in front of about 9,000 spectactors the Salmonbellies ran away with the second game 11–1 on the strength of three goals by each of the Spring brothers and two by Len Turnbull. The Nationals' trainer, Noseworthy, blamed the defeat on the Salmonbellies' ball control or "ragging" style of play. Eastern referees wouldn't have allowed it, he claimed.

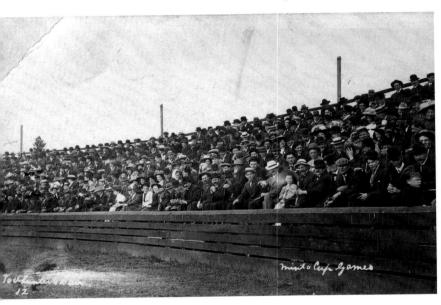

Industries and merchants in New Westminster often closed at noon on Saturdays to allow people to catch important lacrosse games at Queen's Park. Thousands of fans from Vancouver travelled by BC Electric Railway. Men wore suits; women wore long dresses buttoned to the neck. Hat makers got rich.

STAN STEWARDSON.

On May 1, 1911, Newsy, a nineteen-goal, sixteen-game season with the Montreal Canadiens behind him, stepped down from the train at the CPR station at the foot of Granville Street. His contract with Jones was a reported $3,500 for the ten-game season. The Montreal press and Nationals fans were upset by his "defection," but Newsy didn't care. He hadn't forgotten the slash to his face and the nasty infection it caused. He was spoiling for another shot at the Salmonbellies. By his side was fellow Cornwall native and NLU pro, Dalton "Dot" Phelan, a 150-pound, third home player, a newcomer to Jones's stable.

Newsy went straight to Recreation Park at Smythe and Homer Streets, where the Vancouver Beavers pro baseball team were playing. Sports fans recognized him immediately. Frank Patrick approached Lalonde at the game. Patrick, his father Joe, and brother Lester were in the middle of building ice hockey rinks in Vancouver and Victoria to house two of the teams in their new three-team Pacific Coast Hockey Association. (The New Westminster Royals were the third team.) Patrick proposed that Newsy sign on with the Vancouver team, the Millionaires, for their inaugural season. Newsy, however, wasn't interested in committing at that point.

Nick Carter, a second home player originally from St. Catharines, arrived in Vancouver on Tuesday. Carter had spent the 1909 season with the Toronto Lacrosse Club, tallying twenty-one goals and eight assists in ten games, fourth in the NLU. Carter was fast and a skillful stick handler. And his 170 pounds made him the biggest home player on the coast.

Another St. Catharines native, 23-year-old William "Billy" Fitzgerald, arrived in Vancouver on Wednesday. By the age of nineteen, Fitzgerald was playing for the St. Catharines senior club, easily the best in eastern Canada and winners of the Globe Shield, the top prize in the senior amateur league, every year from 1905 to 1912. Fitzgerald had signed on with them in 1907, and for the next two years, they won every game. He turned pro in 1909 with the Toronto Lacrosse Club. Ted Reeve of the Toronto Telegram described him as "a lean, racing, crowd lifting goal scorer who would come in from centre field like the wind, pick a pass out of the air for a flashing shot, or set up a play for one of his inside home men with his sudden take-away burst of speed."[89] The *Toronto Mail and Empire* said that he "had the lacrosse brains of Querrie and Lalonde, and he had the speed that was denied them."[90] Fitzgerald's contract with Jones was even richer than Newsy's: a reported $5,000 for the season, more than that of the highest paid hockey player or the average American baseball player.

Jones called the first full team practice for Wednesday. In addition to Newsy, Allen, Phelan, Ion, Fitzgerald, and Carter, the team consisted of George Matheson, an Ottawa-born Vancouver veteran who started with the Capitals in 1897; Harry Pickering, a strong, versatile defender from Mount Forest, Ontario, who had started his career with the Tecumsehs; Manitoba native Weldy Clark; Vancouver-born Dude Sumner; Billy West; and Pete Muldoon, a boxer and trainer who, in a pinch, could double as a lacrosse player. The team captain was defenceman Harry Godfrey, from Winnipeg, who arrived in Vancouver in 1900. At six feet and 189 pounds, he was the biggest man on the team. All told, thirteen of Jones's seventeen players were former NLU players. Jones was fielding what amounted to an eastern all-star team.

The Salmonbellies were also getting into condition for the home opener. Barring pre-season injuries, the 1911 Salmonbellies would be almost the same team as 1910. All the brothers were back: the Giffords, Rennies, Springs, and Turnbulls, along with Sandy Gray, Punk Wintemute, Pat Feeney, and Buck Marshall. Other than Marshall, defenceman Johnny Howard was the only non-native of New Westminster on the team. Plucked by Con Jones out of the 1910 Regina all-star team, Howard played for Vancouver the same year, but fell out with Jones and signed a one-season contract with the Salmonbellies for $1,500, making him the only salaried player on the team.[91] He would earn his money. His primary task for the coming season was to keep Newsy from scoring.

In sharp contrast to the Vancouver team, the Salmonbellies were almost exclusively a team of New Westminster-born and bred lacrosse players. On the basis of population statistics, New Westminster shouldn't have been able to compete with Vancouver, let alone metropolises such as Toronto and Montreal. New Westminster's population grew from 6,500 people in 1901 to 10,000 in 1911, but was dwarfed by Vancouver's population of over 100,000. On the basis of money, again, New Westminster should have been uncompetitive, lacking a Con Jones. Each Salmonbellies player, other than Howard, received a split of the gate receipts, about $300 a season. Jones's players were all paid large salaries. And yet, the small-town Salmonbellies, heading into the 1911 season, were the three-year defending Minto Cup champions. The day before the opener, Salmonbellies' manager Charlie Welsh was confident of victory, but conceded that they were expecting a close game. Jones was all smiles, saying only that people should expect a few surprises. The betting odds favoured New Westminster—slightly. Not a little money had been wagered on the result, reported the *Daily Province*.[92]

The eastern pros of the Vancouver Lacrosse Club and the Salmonbellies met for the first game on May 24, Victoria Day. About 10,000 people streamed toward Queen's Park for the three o'clock faceoff. City streets were unpaved and the traffic raised a thick cloud of dust. "On game

The goal umpire, in his derby hat, watches closely as the Salmonbellies apply pressure around Vancouver's goal, about 1912. The goals were 6' x 6'.
STAN STEWARDSON. POSTCARD.

days you could scarcely see the houses across the street," recalled lacrosse fan Laura Sinclair.[93]

The teams emerged from their respective dressing rooms in the Agricultural Building, Vancouver in their green sweaters, the Salmonbellies in their red. With referee Matt Barr presiding, Grumpy scored three and a half minutes into the game, and although the Salmonbellies were down two men at one stage, Vancouver could not find the back of the net for an equalizer.

Injuries to Vancouver's home players disrupted their attack. Tom Gifford's slash to Allen's leg opened the flesh to Bones's bone, earning Gifford a ten-minute penalty onto which another ten minutes was added once the severity of Allen's injury was known. Gifford's penalty and other Salmonbellies' infractions kept New Westminster a man short for most of three-quarters of the game. In the second quarter, Newsy, entangled in front of the Salmonbellies' net, suffered a concussion and left the game bound for Vancouver's St. Paul's Hospital.

THE WESTMINSTERS STAND INVINCIBLE AGAINST THE WORLD.

Salmonbellies' captain Tommy Gifford straddles the globe. Having easily dispensed the Regina Capitals, he's ready to take on Minto Cup challenges from Vancouver, Toronto, and Calgary. "The Westminsters stand invincible against the world," reads the caption. It wasn't hype. The Salmonbellies were unbeatable in 1909.

BRITISH COLUMBIAN.

While Vancouver's defence was strong, New Westminster's—with Gifford at point and Howard at coverpoint—was "about as pleasant and inviting . . . as a bunch of grizzly bears after a lean winter."[94] The game ended 1–0 New Westminster.

Jones was not unhappy. His team had been together only three weeks but held the three-time defending Minto Cup champions to just one goal. His big defencemen—Griffith, Pickering, Godfrey, Matheson, and Ion—anchored by Bun Clark in net, had shown how stingy they were going to be in allowing goals. As for the offence, they had yet to gel, but when they did, he was certain they were going to score—frequently. Just to be safe, and possibly to keep them out of the hands of the Salmonbellies, Jones signed Vancouver's own Davy Gibbons, goalkeeper, and defenceman "Toots" Clarkson. At the same time, Toronto wanted back Fitzgerald, Carter, and West, and asked them to name their price. In New Westminster, players had named a price also, but it was not one that Charlie Welsh was willing to pay. Welsh, an advocate of amateurism, threatened to resign.

Jones's greenshirts raised a pool of money to bet on themselves to win the second game. The Salmonbellies did the same, putting up $400. The teams met for the second time on May 27 at Recreation Park in front of about 11,000 fans. Vancouver's Fitzgerald opened the scoring, but Grumpy scored twice in a row in the second quarter to give the Salmonbellies a 2–1 lead. Carter, West, and Adamson, however, scored three goals, one after another, in the fourth quarter to win the game for Vancouver, 4–2. It was one of the better displays of lacrosse in years—despite plenty of penalties, brawling, and irate fans throwing seat cushions. Bill Turnbull took a vicious swipe with his stick at Lalonde's head, meaning to knock him out cold or worse, but scored only a glancing blow. Wintemute picked up Ion's stick and broke it over his knee. Referee Wells Gray, no stranger to rough play and crazy behaviour, was so upset with the lack of respect he was shown by the fans that he resigned from any further refereeing. The league practically begged him to reconsider, but he was adamant, he was out. For good.

Lacrosse fans snapped up the reserved seats for game three at Recreation Park. The Beavers baseball game, originally scheduled for one o'clock Saturday, was moved to six o'clock to accommodate the lacrosse match, slated, as usual, for three o'clock. Newsy scored soon after the faceoff. Then Fitzgerald scored, and Newsy followed up with two more. The first quarter ended 4–0 Vancouver.

The Salmonbellies had a hard time finding a way through Vancouver's defence and were forced to shoot from long range, but Len Turnbull found the net in the second quarter and

Doughy scored in the third. By the fourth quarter, New Westminster, down 4–2, was exasperated. Tom Gifford fouled, but instead of serving his penalty where he was supposed to, on the bench, he sat, like a petulant child, in the grass at the upper end of the park. After a few minutes, he decided that he'd served enough time and invited himself back into the game. Jones brought Gifford's act to referee Galbraith's attention. Galbraith blew his whistle to signal a temporary halt while he conferred with the penalty timekeepers. But the crowd, strangely forgetting that a gong, not a whistle, signaled the end of a game, decided they would pour onto the field anyway. Maybe they were mocking Gifford by imitating him. Megaphone-wielding park officials managed to get people back into their seats. Gifford sulked. The game ended a few minutes later, a 6–3 Vancouver victory.

Nine thousand fans gathered at Queen's Park for game four, among them Jimmy Gifford's wife, Maisie, who was wheeling one-year-old son Stu in a pram. At the entrance to the park a handsome, well-dressed gentleman stopped to have a peek at the infant. "Oh," said the man, "Is this Jimmy Gifford's son?" "Why yes, it is," said Maisie, pleased. "I thought so, he has the face of a real horse's ass," said Newsy, tipping his hat and walking away.[95]

On the field, Newsy and Jimmy Gifford battled, scuffled, and fought at every opportunity. At one point they exchanged blows until, exhausted, they wrestled each other to the ground. And still they threw punches. More time passed, but neither man would relent. A couple of Newsy's teammates grabbed hold of his ankles and attempted to pull him to safety. But Gifford was not about to let go of Newsy's ears and was dragged along with him. Somehow they were separated.

The first quarter ended with the Salmonbellies up 3–1. George Rennie shut down Newsy, repeatedly stealing the ball from him, much to the delight of the hometown partisans. But Vancouver rebounded in the second quarter, edging the Salmonbellies by one. It was a rough match, with New Westminster drawing most of the penalties. At one point only eight Salmonbellies were on the field against Vancouver's eleven. Grumpy tied the game in the third quarter and then brother Cliff got the winner. 5–4 Salmonbellies. The defensive realignment had worked, Newsy and Fitzgerald being held to just one goal each.

Manager Charlie Welsh resigned following the match, joining Wells Gray on the retired list. He cited "business" as the reason, but clearly he did not like the direction in which the game was going. He said in 1907 that if the game ever went professional, he would be out of it. He'd stuck with it for three years, but he was now fed up. However, unlike Gray, he recanted. The team needed him. He would stay, for now.

The teams next met in the first of a two-game, total-goals exhibition series proposed by Vancouver Mayor Louis Taylor, the winning team to receive medals specially struck in honour of the June 22 coronation of George V. On June 22, about 8,000 people at Recreation Park saw Vancouver take the first coronation match 6–2.

For the second match, the Salmonbellies were without Len and Bill Turnbull, Doughy, and Sandy Gray. Hugh Gifford suited up with brothers Tom and Jim. In the second quarter, Jimmy and Newsy went at it. The mortal enemies exchanged rights and lefts, but Newsy drew the five-minute penalty. Newsy's fellow Cornwallian, Dot Phelan, scored the first of his two goals, and the half ended with Vancouver up 3–0. In the third quarter, Hugh Gifford took a run at Newsy and got five minutes for his trouble. Godfrey, in retaliation, hammered a sprinting George Rennie, knocking him to the grass, blood flowing from his broken nose. Rennie went off and Adamson joined him to even up the sides. The Salmonbellies did not take kindly to Godfrey's handling of Rennie. The Giffords in particular were displeased. The moment play resumed, Tom and Jimmy mixed it up with Newsy and Fitzgerald, giving "a lively exhibition

New Westminster's identity as the home of the Salmonbellies reached into every corner of civic life. This Citizen's Picnic ribbon from 1910 gave the Salmonbellies and the Minto Cup top billing.
CANADIAN LACROSSE HALL OF FAME. PHOTOGRAPH BY PHILLIP CHIN.

of club-swinging."[96] The sight of the four men trying to decapitate each other brought others into the fray, including some spectators. The police broke it up. Newsy and the Giffords got ten minutes each, while Fitzgerald drew five. Vancouver took advantage of the Salmonbellies' lack of discipline and scored three more goals.

In the fourth quarter, Newsy and Tom Gifford resumed hostilities and were benched for the rest of the game. When the gong sounded, Vancouver realized a long cherished dream—skunking the Salmonbellies for the first time ever, 6–0.

A few days later, Grumpy admitted to the press that he'd turned down Fred Thompson's $5,000 offer to play for the Toronto Lacrosse Club for the nine games remaining in their season, saying, that $50,000 could not take him away from the team at that time.[97] Thompson denied having offered Grumpy any such sum.

Despite steady rainfall on Dominion Day, July 1, more than 12,000 fans turned out for the fifth game at Recreation Park. The bleachers and the edges of the field were black with umbrellas.

The association was hoping to restore order on the field. For the first time, instead of the usual single referee, they would try two. The first half ended 0–0. Ion opened the scoring fifteen seconds into the third. Grumpy answered a few minutes later. Then Newsy got the go-ahead goal, followed by Matheson with one for good measure. Vancouver's defence was nearly impenetrable. A frustrated Tommy Gifford took it out on Ion, applying some hickory stick to Ion's leg. Referee Ditchburn tried to issue a penalty chit, but Gifford ran all over the field to avoid him. As play continued, referee Cusack joined Ditchburn in chasing the chit-disturbing Salmonbellies captain around the field. Cusack finally snagged Gifford's jersey, stuffing the chit down the jersey's neck and ordering Gifford out of the game. Gifford started for the clubhouse, but changed his mind, running instead to Vancouver's net, where he stood while the ball was in play at the other end of the field.

When the play came toward Vancouver's goal, Gifford cross-checked Harry Griffith from behind. Griffith turned and slashed his stick at Gifford's head, cutting a large gash in Tommy's cheek. Gifford swung back with his stick and dodged to one side, swinging, in turn, at Allen, Adamson, Fitzgerald, and Newsy and receiving the same back from each one of them. Feeney then went after Nick Carter, the two of them swinging sticks at each other with deadly intent. When that failed to settle the matter, they dropped the sticks and fought with fists, Feeney getting

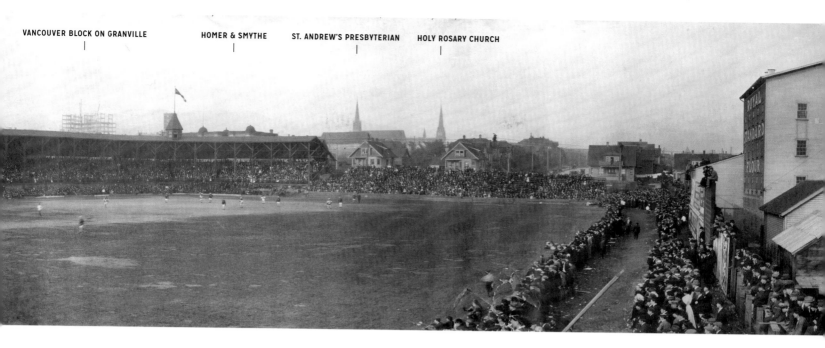

A sellout crowd at Recreation Park watches the Toronto Tecumsehs challenge Vancouver for the Minto Cup in 1911.

VANCOUVER ARCHIVES.

the worst of it. In the midst of it all Hugh Gifford came barreling out of the dressing room and onto the field to throw a punch at Griffith. Griffith dropped Hugh with a hard right cross.

By that point, a number of spectators had dropped their black umbrellas, swarmed the field, and squared off in dozens of fights. Park officials and the police eventually separated all the combatants and the game resumed, minus a subdued if unrepentant Gifford, who was escorted from the grounds. With two minutes remaining, Bill Turnbull's shot missed wide. As the gong sounded Vancouver's delirious supporters spilled onto the field, this time in celebration. Final score: 3–1 Vancouver.

Ditchburn's report to the association called for the league to make an example of Gifford. "There was no excuse for him and he should not be allowed to play again," the *Daily Province* quoted him as saying. And he meant *never* again.

The debate about what to do about Gifford lasted over two hours. New Westminster's representatives admitted they could not vote in favour of any resolution to bar Gifford. Vancouver's delegates declared that they had no interest in depriving the Salmonbellies of a valuable player. They did not want the Minto Cup unless they won it with Gifford on the field. Even a motion to fine Gifford $50 was defeated.

The Salmonbellies, having managed a paltry three goals in as many games, adjusted their offensive lineup in preparation for the sixth match at Queen's Park. Doughy and Feeney switched positions, Doughy going to first home and Feeney going to centre. Ernie Murray replaced the slumping Wintemute at second home.

On a sweltering July afternoon Grumpy, happy to be united with Doughy, went on a spree, scoring five goals, two in the first quarter and one in each of the other three. Despite taking heavy punishment from the much bigger Griffiths, Grumpy's spirited play lifted the entire team. Len Turnbull scored twice while Tom Rennie and Doughy scored one each. Even defenceman Buck Marshall netted one.

But Newsy saw to it that the Salmonbellies' success came with a cost, knocking George Rennie out of the game by knocking out four of his teeth. After serving his ten minutes, Newsy went after Ernie Murray, clobbering him with a stick to the head. He served another ten minutes, but by then it was all over, the Salmonbellies winning 9–2. The season was now even at three games apiece.

After repeated incidents of breaking training, Jones fired Nick Carter. Dot Phelan was slated to replace him—at second home, not first—but within two days, Carter was back with the team. Centre Billy West, out with an injured ankle, was replaced by Toots Clarkson, who went to cover point while George Matheson moved from third defence to centre.

The seventh game took place on Saturday, July 29, at Recreation Park. The Salmonbellies had just scored two goals in a row early in the fourth quarter to tie the game at six apiece, when Newsy scored twice in quick succession, breaking things wide open. Fitzgerald added two more and Carter one. The five unanswered goals gave Vancouver an 11–6 win and a 4–3 edge on the season.

Before the eighth game on Saturday, August 5, the Salmonbellies held a meeting behind closed doors to decide who should play. Team management was not invited. Clearly, the players believed that the only way to avoid losing the Minto Cup was to take matters into their own hands.

Vancouver's Newsy was of the same mind about the Minto Cup and scored three goals, one in the second quarter and two in the third. One of his shots, from ninety feet out, was so hard it broke goaltender Gray's stick on its way into the net. Fitzgerald scored two, and Vancouver, decisively outplaying New Westminster, defeated the Salmonbellies 7–4, the Salmonbellies' first defeat at Queen's Park in two years. No one took the loss harder than longtime trainer Tim Mahoney. He was heartbroken.

The *British Columbian*, at a loss to explain the team's poor play and poor sportsmanship, issued an apologia: "When they see defeat staring them in the face they sometimes do things that they would not think of doing were it not for the sting of defeat that stirs the primeval passion in their breasts."[98] Primal passion or not, no amount of rhetoric was going to erase a 5–3 season deficit. The Salmonbellies had to win the next game just to stay alive.

Dad took over coaching the team following the loss.

Newsy Lalonde, Con Jones and "Léo" Dandurand at the CPR station at the foot of Granville Street in Vancouver, 1912. Dandurand, another eastern lacrosse star, ended up not playing for Vancouver and went on to co-own, coach, and manage the Montreal Canadiens from 1921 to 1935, winning three Stanley Cups.

Over the next two weeks, he ran the Salmonbellies' practices, hoping to help them find the edge they needed. In Vancouver, the greenshirts were no less earnest. During a scrimmage just three days before the ninth game, Vancouver's defence was merciless on its offence, laying out Phelan, Fitzgerald, and Allen. "They'll get it in the game," said one of Vancouver's defencemen, "so let them learn to like it now."[99] Jones asked the defenders to ease up, but they would not. He called off the practice when it looked as if the two sides would stage a battle.

On August 19, before a crowd of 11,000 at Recreation Park, Vancouver, two-to-one favourites, and the Salmonbellies went at it with everything they had. Tom Gifford gave it a little more than he should have, breaking one rib and fracturing another attempting to finish off Newsy once and for all. Newsy emerged unscathed; Gifford was carried from the field in agony.

Halfway through the match, some Vancouver fans put into circulation hundreds of black-bordered cards, in imitation of funeral service programs, containing verses that cast "unpleasant insinuations" on the citizens of New Westminster and their lacrosse team. But the

Salmonbellies were far from dead. With six minutes left in the game, Doughy scored to put them in the lead 5–4.

Salmonbellies' supporters were still cheering wildly when, seconds later, Fitzgerald ran half the length of the field and scored unassisted to tie it. Newsy scored moments later, so he thought. The greenshirts were starting to celebrate victory when the umpire ruled that the ball had actually hit the post. And then, with just four seconds remaining on the clock, Doughy broke through Vancouver's defence and scored the winner: 6–5 New Westminster.

In advance of the tenth and deciding game, the brash Jones, anticipating planting kisses on the Minto Cup, wired the NLU-leading Tecumsehs an offer of $4,000 to play two games against his team if they defeated New Westminster. Jones would have the Minto Cup if Vancouver triumphed over the Salmonbellies, but only by defeating the best team in the east could he really lay claim to being the national champion. Querrie wired back in the affirmative. Now all Vancouver had to do was win.

The match was set for September 4, Labour Day. One man would definitely not be playing: Tom Gifford was wearing a plaster cast. Howard would try to fill his shoes at point, while George Rennie assumed the captaincy. Unable to agree on a local referee, the teams chose Joe Lally, if he was available. Lally was respected—bordering on revered—across Canada as the best referee in the game. He had not refereed in some time, but he took the assignment in the interests of the success of the national game.[100] Forty-three years old and out of shape, Lally skipped rope in a baggage car as the train rolled westward. By the time he reached the coast he had, he claimed, lost fifteen pounds and had begun to acquire the wind he would need to keep pace with the players.[101]

Betting odds were five-to-three in favour of the Salmonbellies. Jones promised the team $1,000 if they won. Fourteen thousand fans crammed into Queen's Park on Monday, September 4. Feeney, out of action since July 17, let everyone know he was healthy again, beating goalie Clark at the first minute mark of the first quarter.

Newsy tested Lally early in the game by taking a well-practised dive in the hope of drawing a Salmonbellies' penalty. Lally ignored him. Play continued. Newsy, realizing his ruse had failed, got up and chased after the play.

Adamson tied the game ten minutes later and then, in the second quarter, Fitzgerald scored, followed by Adamson again, then Dot Phelan.

Vancouver led 4–1 at the half and looked invincible. The Salmonbellies came out for the third quarter looking "downcast and anything but hopeful."[102] A few minutes into the quarter Len Turnbull tried a long, low pass from midfield in the general direction of Vancouver's goal and perhaps one of the Spring brothers' sticks, but the ball somehow rolled into Vancouver's net. The fluke goal lifted the Salmonbellies' spirits.

Twenty seconds later, Bill Turnbull scored. Then it was Wintemute's turn. He was followed by Len Turnbull, George Rennie, and Grumpy. With each goal, the fan-generated decibels rose higher. Vancouver's defence was in complete disarray. The quarter ended with the Salmonbellies up 7–4.

Fitzgerald scored once in the fourth, but Grumpy got his second goal to end the game: 8–5 New Westminster. The season was tied at five wins each. Jones was not amused; the cup was once again slipping away.

No one scored more goals or knocked out more teeth than Vancouver's "Newsy" Lalonde.

VANCOUVER ARCHIVES.
PHOTOGRAPH BY W.J. CAIRNS.

The season was to be decided by two games, the total number of goals to determine the winner of the cup. Seven thousand fans turned out at Queen's Park on Saturday, September 9, for the first of the tiebreakers. Fifteen British newspapermen covered the game from the press box. Lally refereed. The score was 3–2 Vancouver at the close of the third. With rain pelting down at the start of the fourth quarter, Bill Turnbull tied the game. Vancouver ragged the ball rather than risk another New Westminster goal, but ragging was illegal and Lally called them for it. Fitzgerald won the ball at the ensuing centre-field faceoff, raced in, and beat Sandy Gray with a shot: 4–3 Vancouver.

In anticipation of a sellout crowd, a dirt bank was built along the south side of Recreation Park, adding extra standing room. Jones again offered the team $1,000, to be paid in cash immediately following a victory. Ticket scalpers did a brisk if careful business, the police being on the alert for the illegal sales. An estimated 15,000 people—all but 1,000 of them paying customers—squeezed into Recreation Park on Saturday, September 16. Many more watched from neighbouring rooftops and balconies.

From the faceoff, most of the play was in New Westminster's end. Battered and bruised Salmonbellies defenders mustered the vestiges of their energy. Howard checked Newsy closely, poking him hard in the ribs every chance he got. While Newsy was held scoreless, Howard was often on the bench, opening up Vancouver chances. The first quarter ended tied at 0.

Adamson scored first in the second quarter, followed by Phelan and Allen. Fitzgerald, who had been keeping Gray hopping for two quarters, finally scored three minutes into the third. Bill Turnbull answered, but Adamson notched his second right after. George Rennie found the net in the fourth, but again Vancouver came back, with Phelan scoring his second. When the gong sounded it was 6–2 Vancouver for a two-game total of ten goals to the Salmonbellies' five. At long last, after three years and two months, Jones and his team had the Minto Cup.

Thousands swarmed onto the field, delirious with joy after so many seasons of defeat. Before Jones and his players could offer the customary three cheers for the losing side, they were hoisted onto shoulders and carried to their dressing room. A large green and red flag bearing the letters VLC was unfurled to a rousing ovation. Fitzgerald, with fifteen goals in twelve games, and Newsy, with twelve, led Vancouver in scoring. For the Salmonbellies, Grumpy equalled Fitzgerald's tally, and Len Turnbull equalled Newsy's total.

With the victory, Bones Allen and Newsy joined Bouse Hutton as the only men to play on Minto Cup and Stanley Cup winning teams. Amidst all the hoopla, the Salmonbellies hung their heads and disappeared into their dressing room. One clever newspaper editor equated Jones's capture of the cup to MacBeth's capture of the Scottish throne.[103] "Thou hast it now: King, Cawdor, Glamis, all . . . Though thou play'dst most foully for't."[104]

The newly crowned greenshirts made a triumphant tour of Vancouver in horsedrawn carriages before disembarking at the Rainier Café, at the corner of Carrall and West Cordova Streets in Gastown. There, team captain Harry Godfrey presented Jones with a solid gold stopwatch, a token of the team's appreciation.

The Salmonbellies turned over the cup at a formal banquet at the Westminster Club. In accepting, Jones said that it was the happiest day of his life, or rather, that the previous Saturday had been. He added that Vancouver took off its hat to New Westminster for bringing the cup to the west in the first place.

Charlie Welsh was bitter, saying in his speech that he did not think the Vancouver team superior, just luckier. He added that he would not return to manage the Salmonbellies in 1912, citing business reasons. The one thing everyone agreed on was Lally's faultless refereeing. The teams united in presenting him with a diamond ring. As for the cup itself, it took up residence in the window of Godfrey's sporting goods store on East Hastings.

Charlie Querrie's Tecumsehs, having agreed to Jones's $4,000 offer, arrived in Vancouver as scheduled in late September to challenge for the Minto Cup. Jones offered his team another $1,000 for a win, and they prevailed in the two-game, total-goals series 7–3 with a 5–0 win and a 2–3 loss. Vancouver was now the true national champion.

Billy Fitzgerald, "the lean, racing, crowd lifting goal scorer," was paid even more money than Newsy to play for Jones' 1911 Minto Cup winners.

CANADIAN LACROSSE HALL OF FAME.

James "Pat" Feeney, the centre man that ably filled Dad Turnbull's shoes in 1908.

NEW WESTMINSTER MUSEUM AND ARCHIVES.

Other than goalkeeper Gray, who retired and was replaced by Vancouver's Bun Clark, the Salmonbellies' lineup for 1912 was identical to that of 1911.

In Vancouver, Jones replaced Clark with Cory Hesse, but lost Fitzgerald to the higher-paying Toronto Lacrosse Club. As for Newsy, he initially signed as Toronto's player-manager, but a bidding war broke out for his services. Con Jones offered him $2,500. The Toronto Rosedales offered $3,500. The eventual highest bidder was Jones at $5,500 for the season. By contrast, Newsy's salary with the Canadiens was only $1,300. The average Canadian worker was earning about $700 a year, meaning Newsy was earning almost as much per game as the average Canadian worker was earning in a year.

Although Jones's businesses were doing well—he held licences in Vancouver for sixty pool tables—Newsy's salary was a lot of money. But Jones knew he had no chance of retaining the Minto Cup without him, so he paid. Newsy broke his contract with Toronto and travelled to Vancouver via the United States for "fear of being attacked and taken off the train."[105]

Jimmy Gifford and Newsy, the "$5,500 beauty,"[106] fought in the season's first game and would have gladly paid a multiple of the league's $35 fine (each) for the privilege of knocking the other out—or worse. On Dominion Day at Recreation Park, before 11,000 fans, Newsy celebrated Canada's forty-fifth birthday by permanently dislodging four of Tom Gifford's teeth.

Jimmy Gifford and Nick Carter mixed it up. Vancouver mayor, James Findlay, apparently unfamiliar with lacrosse, was outraged by Jimmy's actions and ordered him arrested, over Carter's strenuous objections. Jimmy was halfway to the paddywagon when Matt Barr intervened and had Findlay call off the law.

After the match, won 4–3 by the Salmonbellies, Jones confronted referee Dad Turnbull, criticizing not only his work on the field but also his character, threatening to tell the public "what kind of a man he was." Dad listened to the tirade and coolly replied, "Is that so?"[107]

A delay in the rough, penalty-filled fourth game (June 17) of the 1911 season. Combatants sit on the grass and the referee watches as a trainer administers to a downed player. New Westminster won 5-4.

NEW WESTMINSTER MUSEUM AND ARCHIVES.

Jimmy Gifford may have avoided jail, but he was not so lucky when it came to hospitals. Taken suddenly ill on July 12, he was rushed to Royal Columbian. The surgeon, expecting to find a bad appendix, found an abscess. Jimmy's season was over, and Sandy Gray came out of retirement to replace him. Three days later, the Salmonbellies and Vancouver were again on the battlefield. That game went from bad to worse—at one point, the Salmonbellies had five penalized players sitting on the bench. The game ended in a free-for-all fight. Violence such as that seen in the match would eventually kill lacrosse if it were not immediately eliminated, wrote the *Columbian*.

With Jimmy Gifford recovering in hospital, George Rennie and Tom Gifford suspended, Tom Rennie injured, and Doughy ill, Salmonbellies' manager Wells Gray informed Jones early Saturday morning that they were unable to field a team. A frantic Jones offered to let Gifford and Rennie play, and also to bench two of his best players. Gray turned him down. Jones was understandably upset, as were 3,000 mostly Vancouver fans who, expecting a game, showed up at Recreation Park. Jones lashed out, claiming that not only had the Salmonbellies forfeited the game and incurred a $500 fine, but that they had also forfeited their professional franchise. Furthermore, he swore he would never again send his team to play the Salmonbellies.

True to his threat, the greenshirts did not show up for the next match at Queen's Park. Meanwhile, Jones, knowing that the future of western professional lacrosse was at stake, caught a train east and met with lacrosse team owners, hoping to secure matches that would keep fans interested.

In a connected bid to keep pro lacrosse alive, Jones met with parties in Victoria who were interested in fielding a team. The plan called for seeding the team with a mix of Vancouver and eastern players, whose salaries would be covered by a combination of a guaranteed lacrosse salary, gate splits, and regular jobs. But there was one last thing to look after. With Vancouver's Recreation Park due to close by the end of 1912, Jones's professional teams, soccer and lacrosse, and their fans needed a purpose-built stadium to call home.

Taking his cue from the Patrick brothers' Denman Arena, Jones put down money on a property west of the Pacific National Exhibition grounds. A wooden stadium went up, enclosing the playing field, with an overhanging roof all around. He called it Con Jones Park.

In Vancouver and New Westminster, heads cooled, and the adversaries agreed that the forfeitures cancelled one another. The teams got back to playing. With Jimmy Gifford out for the duration, Newsy set his sights on Hugh Gifford, smashing his stick into Hugh's face at the first opportunity. But other than that, the match was clean, fast, and entertaining, with few penalties. Jones, feeling confident once more, watched from the sidelines, all smiles in his trademark straw boater hat.

With two games remaining in the season, Hugh got even with Newsy, laying him out with a stick to the face. But Newsy had the last word. In the final game, he used the butt end of his stick to send Tom Rennie reeling to the grass. The Salmonbellies, however, won the game and finished the season 9–3, the Minto Cup back in their arms.

The Cornwall Colts challenged for the cup during exhibition week, but went down in the two-game, total-goals series 31–13. Newsy, his pockets full of cash from Jones, was traded by Montreal to the Patrick brothers' Vancouver Millionaires hockey team, joining Fred "Cyclone" Taylor and Si Griffis. The Millionaires, playing out of the arena the Patricks' built on Georgia at the foot of Denman, were mediocre in 1912, but Newsy led the Pacific Coast Hockey Association that winter in scoring—twenty-seven goals in fifteen games.

In 1913, Tom Gifford retired, after playing fourteen seasons of senior, winning four Minto Cups, and serving as captain for many years. Whenever one Gifford dropped out of the rotation, there was another waiting to take his place. Now it was young Jack's turn. Like all Gifford boys, Jack joined the senior team at eighteen. In early May 1913, Jones re-signed Newsy, Adamson, Matheson, Phelan, Allen, and Griffith, his new playing manager and captain. But he could not land Fitzgerald. A skilled carpenter, Fitzgerald took time off from lacrosse to concentrate on

Before the start of the second coronation medals game on June 23, 1911, 1,000 lacrosse sticks were handed out to boys under the age of twelve, courtesy of Con Jones.

VANCOUVER ARCHIVES.
PHOTOGRAPH BY STUART THOMSON.

Lacrosse fans board BC Electric flatbed cars eastbound on Hastings at Carrall, about 1910. Con Jones' Brunswick Pool Room at 58 East Hastings is nearby. The trip to New Westminster took about an hour.

BC SPORTS HALL OF FAME.

his housebuilding business.

The Salmonbellies were up five games to two when Ion and Griffith refused to obey a league-ordered suspension and suited up for a July 5 match at Hastings Park. Led by Tom Gifford, the Salmonbellies walked off the field before the start of the game. Five thousand spectators rose as one, jeering and hooting as the Salmonbellies headed to the dressing room. Vancouver claimed a $500 forfeit. With neither side giving an inch, on July 13, when Vancouver did not show up for the match, the Salmonbellies scored on an empty net to claim the game and the forfeit money. "We have the advice of two lawyers," said Gifford, "and we positively refuse to play unless Ion and Griffith remain off the field."[108] That was too much for Vancouver, who withdrew from the league on July 17. The two rivals went to court over the forfeiture money,

Angus "Bones" Allen (white shorts) joined the VLC in 1909. Allen, Newsy Lalonde and Bouse Hutton are the only men to play on Minto Cup and Stanley Cup winning teams. Hutton actually won both cups twice.

but the judge told them to settle it themselves. Jones proposed that if the Salmonbellies completed the schedule, including three games with Victoria, he would forgive them their $500 fine and pay them $500, but Ion and Griffith had to play. No deal. Jones then quit, turning over the club to Newsy and a committee of Harrys—Pickering, Godfrey, and Griffith. It had cost Jones $40,000 in salaries to field the 1913 team. He honoured his contracts, telling Newsy that despite the losing record, he had "earned every cent of it."[109] Newsy and the three Harrys reformulated the team as the Vancouver Athletic Club and challenged the Salmonbellies for the Minto Cup. The Salmonbellies defeated them, too, 9–1 and 5–3, for an overall total of 14–4.

As the 1914 season approached, the lure of professional money was too strong for Doughy and Len Turnbull. The two goal-getters joined Querrie's Tecumsehs. To make up for the loss, Tom Rennie moved from first defence to centre, and Jack Gifford switched from third defence to Len Turnbull's spot at outside home. Defenceman Johnny Howard also jumped ship, joining the Quebecs. The Salmonbellies compensated for Howard's loss by recruiting Vancouver defenceman Ion and bringing in homegrown Wilson Douglas "Willis" Patchell, who was raised in New Westminster's Sapperton district, near the BC Penitentiary, where his father was warden. Willis had been playing, along with his older brother Bill, for New Westminster's senior amateur team, the Royals.

The Salmonbellies lost that season's opener to the Vancouver Athletics. On the same day, a few thousand miles away, Doughy scored at will for Toronto in a 17–8 victory over Quebec. The Salmonbellies won their next two matches, but spectators were few and far between, and gate receipts barely covered expenses. And, unlike anything the Salmonbellies had ever known, there was no cheering. People's moods had darkened and their pocketbooks had taken a beating. In 1913, the US stock market had collapsed, ushering in a worldwide depression. Vancouver and New Westminster's real estate bubble burst, commercial rents declined, and loans went unpaid. In New Westminster, the Dominion Trust Company building on Columbia Street sat unfinished, the workers being laid off after the company's financial failure.

In Europe, Austria-Hungary's Archduke Franz Ferdinand was assassinated in Sarajevo, Bosnia and Herzegovina, on June 28, 1914. The world was on the brink of war, but lacrosse continued. In early June, Doughy scored a goal in the game against the Nationals. The Nationals' Newsy more than countered, banging in five. In Victoria, the Salmonbellies lost the fourth match of the season to the Athletics in front of just 1,500 fans, but won the next contest. The Athletics took the next match to even the season at three wins apiece. Rumours started to circulate in New Westminster that the Salmonbellies would be hanging up their sticks for the remainder of the season. Not a chance, announced captain George Rennie. "The boys will finish the season even if they do lose money," the *British Columbian* quotes him as saying. They needed to stay in shape for the coming Minto Cup challenge.

Newsy was enjoying a 66-goal season for the Nationals. "The players are not anxious to see any of those eastern players on a world championship team," said Rennie, "especially Newsy Lalonde of the Nationals."[110] Although war was almost certain to break out in Europe at any time, the Salmonbellies' main concern was preventing Newsy from winning another Minto Cup.

People, however, were not turning out to games. The Athletics were losing money and could not continue to pay players. Vancouver's team disbanded on July 8, and the Salmonbellies retained the Minto Cup, by default.

Con Jones made a proposal to get pro lacrosse restarted. He would pay Vancouver's and the Salmonbellies' expenses and salaries for the rest of the season—three games in Vancouver, three in Victoria. In return, the Salmonbellies would surrender to him their team's ownership, management, name, identity, and colours—and the Minto Cup. "It will be a pretty warm day when we let Jones boss us," was the Salmonbellies' published reply.[111]

On August 5, Great Britain declared war on Germany, committing Canada automatically. The 104th Westminster Fusiliers of Canada became a training unit for battalions of the Canadian Expeditionary Force. The exhibition buildings at Queen's Park were converted to barracks. New Westminster was at war.

On September 19, the Salmonbellies and a Vancouver all-star team played a game to raise money for the war relief fund—they could agree on at least that. Appeals for men to join the 131st Westminster Battalion appeared in New Westminster. "Lacrosse made New Westminster famous," read one poster. "Boys, make her famous for her soldiers!"

Despite the war, a lacrosse season was organized for 1915. The Salmonbellies and a Vancouver all-star team—without Newsy—planned a twelve-game schedule.

The Salmonbellies had won seven of eleven games when the final game was cancelled, the outcome being meaningless to the standings. New Westminster retained the Minto Cup. In Montreal, Newsy won the NHL scoring title with thirty-one goals and led the Canadiens to their first Stanley Cup victory. But with the war in its second year, organized senior lacrosse in Canada was finally suspended in 1916.

Roughly 2,000 Canadian lacrosse players served in WWI, including many from New Westminster. Twelve of fourteen Salmonbellies signed on. Willis Patchell, in England awaiting transfer to the front, took third place out of over a hundred entrants in the 100-yard sprint at the Military Games and anchored the winning relay team. In Flanders he rescued a wounded comrade, W.D. Milne, trapped under heavy fire. Patchell was badly wounded in the leg. Milne wrote a poem in Patchell's praise, which reads in part, "Back from the E-2 Wilson rushed/Through showers of pointed lead."[112]

Following the Canadian Corps' capture of Vimy Ridge in April 1917, the YMCA, in cooperation with the Corps, organized an extensive sports program. Athletic goods were shipped to France, including 720 lacrosse sticks and sets of gloves, and 600 balls. Army units competed at the brigade and divisional levels. The brigade games were played one or two evenings a week, the winners receiving badges. Two New Westminster men with the 6th Battalion Canadian Railway Troops, Thomas Leonard Purvis and Leo Andre Lusier, played in a lacrosse match on July 2, 1917, in a delayed Dominion Day celebration. "The [Dominion Day] sports were splendid," reported New Westminster resident Private Robert Percival Dauphinee, "but it was

Harry Godfrey hoists the VLC flag at Recreation Park in 1911 after defeating the Salmonbellies to capture the Minto Cup.

BC SPORTS HALL OF FAME.

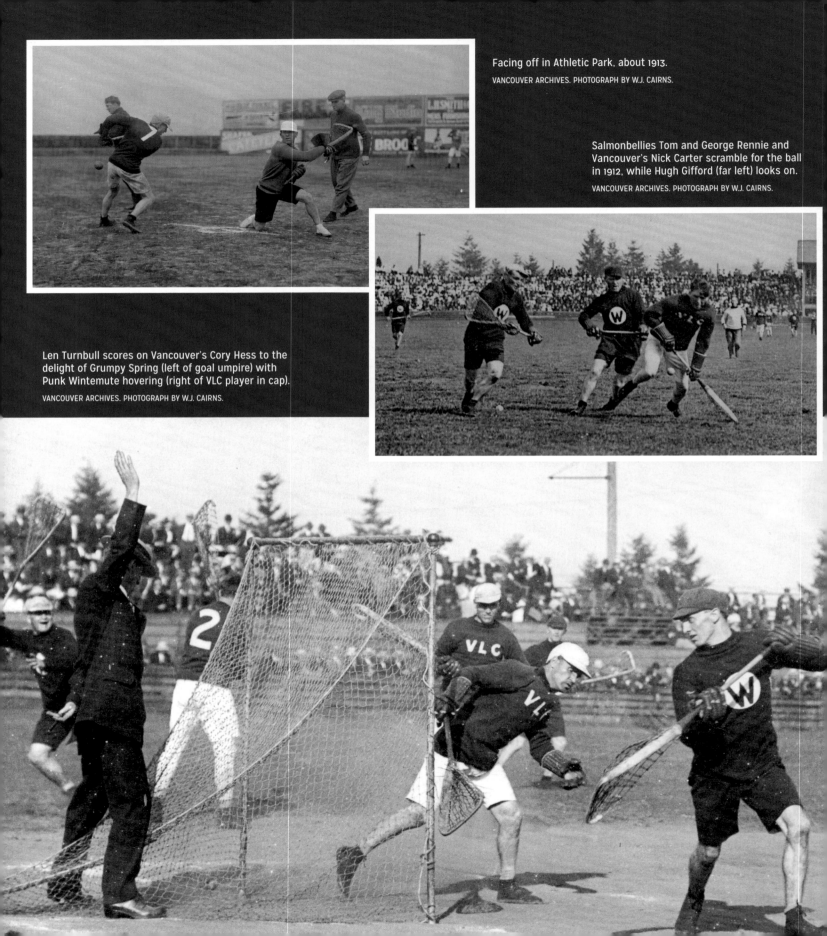

Facing off in Athletic Park, about 1913.
VANCOUVER ARCHIVES. PHOTOGRAPH BY W.J. CAIRNS.

Salmonbellies Tom and George Rennie and Vancouver's Nick Carter scramble for the ball in 1912, while Hugh Gifford (far left) looks on.
VANCOUVER ARCHIVES. PHOTOGRAPH BY W.J. CAIRNS.

Len Turnbull scores on Vancouver's Cory Hess to the delight of Grumpy Spring (left of goal umpire) with Punk Wintemute hovering (right of VLC player in cap).
VANCOUVER ARCHIVES. PHOTOGRAPH BY W.J. CAIRNS.

Goalie Bun Clark thwarts #9 Bones Allen at Brockton Point. Hugh Gifford hovers (behind Clark and Allen) and Johnny Howard defends against a pass as goal umpire Harry Godfrey leans for a better view.

VANCOUVER ARCHIVES.

Bun Clark has stopped Newsy Lalonde's shot, but Newsy and Mag McGregor (between #6 Johnny Howard and Tom Rennie in white cap) are hoping to steal back the ball, 1912.

VANCOUVER ARCHIVES. PHOTOGRAPH BY W.J. CAIRNS.

Defenders Tom Gifford, Johnny Howard and Tom Rennie are too late to stop Newsy Lalonde from putting one in the net behind Bun Clark, 1912.

VANCOUVER ARCHIVES. PHOTOGRAPH BY W.J. CAIRNS.

the weirdest lacrosse match I ever saw . . . German shells were dropping close around us, while the players carried on their struggles for the ball as seriously as though they were playing an old-time game in Queen's Park."[113]

 In 1918, with a trickle of war veterans returning home, the Salmonbellies and the Vancouver "greenshirts" played under the banner of the improvised Mainland Lacrosse Association (MLA). After Patchell wounded his leg, doctors thought he would never play lacrosse again, but the then 28-year-old confounded them and everyone else, joining both the New Westminster fire department and the Salmonbellies. The team's best checker, he was assigned to Newsy. After Flanders, Newsy must have seemed easy, but the ever-slippery goal scorer went on to lead the MLA in scoring with twenty-three goals in seven games as Vancouver compiled a 6–2 record and won the Minto Cup—or so they thought.

The team that finally defeated the Salmonbellies for the Minto Cup, the 1911 Vancouver Lacrosse Club. **Standing:** Harry Cowan (team exec.), Harry Wardman (asst. trainer), Billy West, George Matheson, Mickey Ions, Harry Godfrey, Con Jones (owner), Harry Pickering, Harry Griffiths, Bun Clark, Pete Muldoon (trainer), Lionel Yorke (team exec.) **Sitting:** Matt Barr (team exec.), Nick Carter, Archie Adamson, Billy Fitzgerald, Newsy Lalonde, Dot Phelan, Sebby Nicholls, Dude Sumner, Bones Allen.

In May 1919, the Minto Cup's trustees and the BCLA jointly refused to recognize the MLA and the 1918 season. Vancouver argued that the MLA was legitimate and that they had every right to the cup. The Salmonbellies sided with the trustees and the BCLA. The Minto Cup stayed in New Westminster.

Newsy sat out the 1919 lacrosse season. The Salmonbellies won the twelve-game Minto Cup series seven to five over the Vancouver Terminals, now partially owned and managed by Harry Pickering.

Harold "Haddie" Stoddart joined the Salmonbellies in 1920. Goal scorer Thure Storme was slated to join Stoddart on offence.

Storme's name, of Scandinavian origin, translated to "thunderstorm," an apt description of his scoring ability. "Storme weighs about 130 pounds," said one observer, "But dynamically he weighs a ton. He can shoot from the most difficult angles, and can take a pass with his check draped all over him. So long as he is on his feet near the goal, he is the most dangerous home player in the business."[114]

Many of his goals were the result of an unusual, highly effective underhand shot. The five-foot-ten, blond athlete had played his first organized lacrosse in 1911 in New Westminster and helped the city win the senior amateur lacrosse title, the Mann Cup, in 1915. In 1916, he enlisted, going overseas with the 131st Battalion. Storme starred on many military athletic teams until he was wounded in the arm in May 1917. Returning home in March 1918, he played senior amateur lacrosse for New Westminster against the Vancouver Coghlans. Turning down professional offers, he led the league in scoring in 1919.

Salmonbellies Manager Tom Gifford had had big hopes for Storme in 1920, but lost him for the season to a broken leg suffered in a soccer game. With Storme out, Tom turned for goals to his brother Jack. The youngest Gifford responded and the Salmonbellies defeated Vancouver in their first four encounters.

And then Newsy returned, instilling confidence in the Vancouver team.[115] On Dominion Day, Newsy led Vancouver to a 6–5 victory. In a late July match, he and Jack Gifford were sent off for the remainder of the game after triggering a donnybrook involving players, managers, trainers, spectators, and police.

But Gifford captured the scoring title with twenty-five goals, against Newsy's fourteen. The Salmonbellies narrowly won the regular season, and the Montreal Shamrocks were signed to play for the Minto Cup, although they had to mortgage their clubhouse and grounds to afford the trip.

But the Shamrocks cancelled at the last minute. It was the height of the post-war economic depression, and money was scarce. Organizers scrambled together a three-game, total-goals Minto Cup series between the Salmonbellies and Vancouver.

In the first game, Newsy attacked Jack Gifford, knocking out two molars. The referee, former Vancouver player Harry Godfrey, summoned all his nerve to separate the blood-spattered, wild-eyed, stick-swinging combatants. The game ended in a tie. In the second game, Newsy scored twice, despite Patchell's close checking, and Vancouver won.

About 8,000 people turned out for the third game. The Salmonbellies won 4–1, but Vancouver won the cup on total goals, thirteen versus eleven. Newsy and the Terminals held the Minto Cup for the first time since 1911. Grumpy led the Salmonbellies in cheering the new champions.

Throughout the 1921 lacrosse season, Grumpy could not win a coin toss to save his life. Whether or not it was on Vancouver's field or at Queen's Park, if he called tails, it was sure to be heads. It got to be a running joke. At Queen's Park, losing the toss actually did mean a small disadvantage: the loser had to start the game playing up the field's slight but noticeable slope. It also meant that the downslope team's goalkeeper would be facing into the afternoon sun.

In Vancouver, team co-owner and manager Harry Pickering was tired of running the show. He sold his interest to 1890s vintage player Bony Suckling, then in his early sixties. Con Jones

Vancouver Lacrosse Club owner Con Jones trademarked his "Don't Argue" brand of tobacco products in 1914, but he continued to argue with the Salmonbellies well into the 1920s.

CANADIAN MUSEUM OF CIVILIZATION. 2001.185.37. S2002-6940

Don't Argue tobacco stores were scattered throughout Vancouver. In 1929 this one was at the corner of Granville and Dunsmuir.

VANCOUVER PUBLIC LIBRARY. PHOTOGRAPH BY STUART THOMSON.

After Canadian troops took Vimy Ridge in April 1917, the Canadian Corps and the
YMCA co-sponsored athletic competitions, including lacrosse games, behind the lines
as part of a program of rest, recreation and recuperation.

proposed a rival league to the BCLA and organized Vancouver and Victoria teams—he had a stadium to fill. Jones's league lasted only to the end of June.

In New Westminster, Grumpy's bad luck with coins didn't matter. The Salmonbellies defeated Vancouver on the season and won back the Minto Cup. With the cup again in New Westminster's hands, Grumpy retired as the team's all-time leading scorer. His 187 goals in 134 regular season games makes him the greatest goal scorer in western Canada during the professional era. In the seven seasons that he played against Newsy, Grumpy scored 126 goals, the same as Newsy. But Grumpy's most impressive statistic is that he was on nine Minto Cup winning teams, from 1908 through 1921.

Before the start of the 1922 season, Tom Gifford resigned as Salmonbellies' manager. His senior playing career had begun in 1898 and stretched into fifteen seasons, during which the team won four Minto Cups (1908–10 and 1912). From 1913 to 1915, he managed the team to three more cups, and from 1919 to 1921, he was at the helm for two cups. Nine Minto Cups in total. Gifford passed the manager torch to Pat Feeney.

Goalkeeper Bun Clarke also retired. His career had begun in 1898 as well, with the Toronto Tecumsehs, and after spending the 1911 season with Vancouver, he joined the Salmonbellies in 1912. His play in nets helped the team to six cups. Doughy was the early favourite to replace Clarke, but his teammates needed him more on offence, so Bernie Feedham got the net job.

Just before the season opener Con Jones proposed yet another Vancouver professional team to compete with the Salmonbellies. The choice of which team to play against, Jones's or the existing club, rested entirely with New Westminster. They assessed the two "offers" and made a decision on merit. The existing Vancouver team, under new management, had already signed seven proven players. What was Jones holding in his hand? Was he in? No, he folded, and staged senior amateur games at his park instead, paying the Vancouver Elks, New Westminster Royals, and a Victoria team $75 a game.

Lacrosse-playing BC soldiers of the 4th Divisional Ammunition Column in Petworth, England, 1917. Duncan McPhaden (centre) played for the senior amateur Salmonbellies.

DON OXENBURY.

But he vowed to be back in professional lacrosse the following year, saying he hoped to pick up enough youngsters around the city and from Ontario to field a third team in the BCLA. "Then things will get real interesting," he said.[116] But Jones made things "real interesting" only a month later when he reversed himself completely and announced that he would back the Vancouver Lacrosse Club and a new New Westminster team, the Young Royals, in a new professional league. Not only that, but Grumpy and Willis, among others, were on board with him, Grumpy as the team's player-manager.

Willis Patchell was not nearly ready to call it quits, but both men were looking for an opportunity to extend their careers, add to their income, and own a piece of the professional lacrosse action going forward. The league, however, never got off the ground. Grumpy coached the amateur Royals team instead, while Willis went back to the Salmonbellies, joining older brother Bill on defence.

On June 17, Newsy scored an unassisted goal right after the opening faceoff. Two minutes later, he knocked Haddie Stoddart "cuckoo" with a body check. Stoddart left the game. With Stoddart and Patchell out and Buck Marshall not in the lineup, Vancouver had a free hand offensively, and ran up a 6–0 lead.

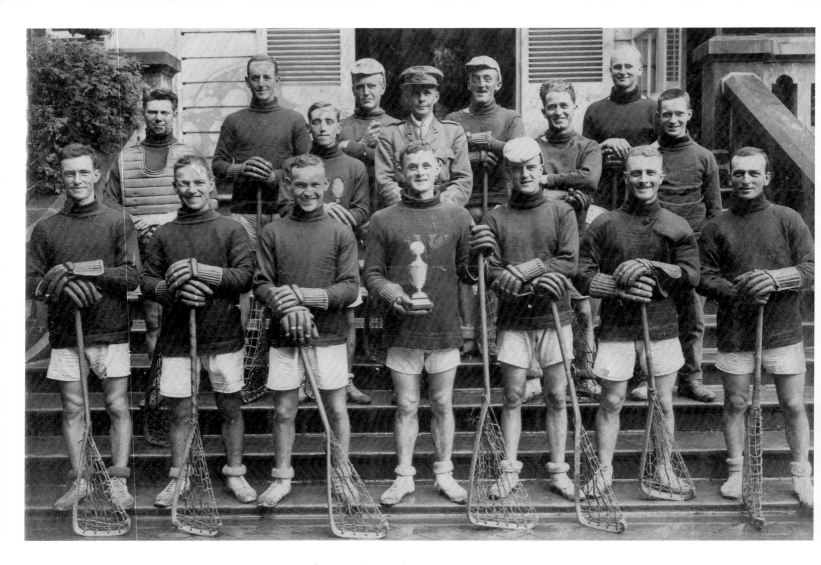

New Westminster's Duncan McPhaden (standing, far right) and his 5th Canadian Divisional Ammunition Column teammates won the 1917 Canadian Corps fall lacrosse championships in Villers-aux-Bois, France.

DON OXENBURY.

The game got progressively scrappier. Pat Feeney and Bay Carter, fighting against the fence, kicked up "mountains of dust."[117] In the third quarter, Vancouver's "Fat" Painter and Lawrey Nelson went at it. And then late in the fourth, inevitably, Lalonde and Jack Gifford tangled. Gifford, no doubt, had not forgotten the two molars Newsy had cost him. Hugh Gifford raced across the field and entered the fray, which brought in players, managers, and officials, and brought spectators to their feet, the fans in the boxes leaning over to get a closer look. "It was a beautiful picture, while it lasted," reported the *British Columbian*.

Vancouver won 7–3, Newsy adding three goals, but subtracting no molars. The loss did not sit well with the Salmonbellies. A week later, the Salmonbellies built up a 3–0 lead. But at the start of the second half, Vancouver's Stan Carter, a redhead like Archie MacNaughton and just as feisty, tussled with Haddie Stoddart. Stan's brother Bay rushed in, bringing in the rest of the players. After about five minutes, tempers appeared to have cooled when Jack Gifford, clouted over the ear without warning, retaliated with his stick, trying to decapitate the offending McLaren. The battle was on again. This time the spectators got into it, hundreds of them—men,

SALMONBELLIES VS. THE WORLD

women, and children—pouring onto the field, New Westminster's citizens versus Vancouver's.

Jimmy Gifford, "like an old war horse that sniffs the battle from afar," headed straight for his old adversary Newsy.[118] Fists flew. Umbrellas and canes swung. Hats, collars, ties, billfolds, loose change, gloves, sticks, and other personal effects soon littered the ground. Youngsters, eager to get in on the fighting but thrown out of the scrimmages, foraged among the fallen objects, spiriting away anything of value that they could lay their hands on. The police blew their whistles and tried to restore order, but it was a full-scale riot. They did the only thing they could: they called in the fire department. The hose and ladder brigade arrived and, using their biggest megaphone, threatened to drench everyone with water if they did not cease and desist. The rioters got the message and the field began to clear—a full thirty minutes after the fighting had begun. It wasn't Passchendaele, but when the dust settled there were eight serious casualties on the sidelines, players being treated by doctors. There was almost one more casualty when Pat Feeney, heading to the dressing room, managed to block Archie MacNaughton's swinging cane with his stick.

Most of Vancouver's sticks and gloves were missing—the battlefield scavengers having picked the grass clean—so the Salmonbellies scrounged up equipment for the Terminals and the game resumed, with eight men a side. It was, observed the *Columbian* matter-of-factly, "the most strenuous fight since 1913." The game ended in an 8–2 Salmonbellies' victory.

The teams continued to battle through the remainder of the season. Storme was unlucky again, suffering a broken shoulder halfway through July. Newsy took a poke at an umpire when he was denied a goal, but scored lots anyway, eventually winning the individual honours with nineteen, compared to Doughy's and Storme's fifteen apiece. Grumpy refereed his first senior game and managed the Royals to the senior amateur title, the Mann Cup, the team's third in a row. The season concluded in the worst rainstorm in years, with players slipping and sliding while the spectators jammed together under the grandstand roof at Queen's Park. Len Turnbull scored the winner in a 3–2 Salmonbellies' victory, clinching the Minto Cup 9–7.

Meanwhile, in Montreal, Paddy Brennan of the Shamrocks, frustrated by the frequent stoppages in play in field lacrosse, moved lacrosse indoors for the first time at Montreal's new Mount Royal Arena.[119] The arena, a natural ice rink, was home to the NHL's Montreal Canadiens from 1920 to 1926. On January 10, 1920, in the first hockey game played at the arena, Newsy scored six goals in a 14–7 Canadiens victory over Charlie Querrie's Toronto St. Patricks. Following Brennan's indoor lacrosse experiment in the summer of 1922, two Ontario Amateur Lacrosse Association (OALA) teams played eight-men-aside box lacrosse in Toronto's Mutual Street Arena. While the experiments in Montreal and Toronto were promising, conditions were not yet ripe for box lacrosse to supplant field.

The Salmonbellies and the Terminals—minus Newsy—traded wins though the summer of 1923. Thure Storme, his broken shoulder mended, started where he'd left off in 1922, scoring goals in bunches. In a match on August 13, he scored four with Grumpy-like flips over his shoulder and signature underhand scoops. He was neck and neck with Vancouver's Dot Crookall for the scoring title.

By middle of September, Vancouver was within one game of tying the Salmonbellies on the season. With the annual exhibition approaching, the Salmonbellies applied to the city to stage free games at Queen's Park. Alderman Goulet shook his head in disbelief and invoked Shakespeare's *Hamlet*. "There is something wrong in Denmark," he said, "when they mean to play without a charge being made."[120] He was right, there was something very wrong—the professional Salmonbellies were on their last legs, again. The city referred them to the R.A.&I.S., who had jurisdiction for September. But no professional lacrosse was played during the

Salmonbellies defenceman Willis Patchell anchored the winning relay team at the Military Games in England and rescued a wounded comrade under heavy fire in Flanders.
STAN STEWARDSON.

exhibition. Instead, the season was abandoned with two games remaining. Baseball, however, drew huge crowds.

With the professional Salmonbellies struggling to survive, the talented senior amateur Royals picked up the slack, defeating the Victoria Capitals for the Mann Cup in a two-game, total-goals series, 1–2 and 7–2.

Con Jones wanted one more crack at the Salmonbellies and the Minto Cup. In 1924, he took charge of the Terminals. Jones knew better than anyone the importance of star power. Without big name players to draw paying customers, a professional league in any sport did not stand a chance. He recruited the best players he could find, including the two instrumental in capturing the 1911 cup, Newsy and Fitzgerald.

Fitzgerald was then almost thirty-six. He'd played for the Toronto Lacrosse Club in 1912 and sat out the 1913 season. After the 1914 season with Vancouver, Fitzgerald accepted a coaching position at Hobart College in Geneva, New York. He returned to St. Catharines after the war and, in an attempt to revive interest in the sport, organized a semi-pro Ontario lacrosse league. Jones was betting that Fitzgerald and Newsy would lead the team to victory, but if they could not, he was prepared to spare no expense in hiring others to get the job done. Fitzgerald arrived in Vancouver in time for just one practice prior to the season opener. Newsy wasn't far behind.

The Salmonbellies and the Terminals took to the field at Queen's Park for the May 21 opener. A good-sized crowd showed up and paid half the admission price of a year earlier. With cigar maker Fred Lynch as referee, the teams played to a 3–3 draw. The light, fast offence of the Salmonbellies was offset by the weight and flypaper checking of the Terminals. Feeney, Storme, and Gib Adams scored for New Westminster. Fitzgerald, while clearly out of condition, played well, but did not score.

Jones was ecstatic with what he saw. As the game ended and the players caught their breath before overtime, he pranced onto the field to offer his congratulations. Whatever else you do, he urged them, do not let them score in overtime. His meaning was clear: preserve the tie. The Terminals did as instructed. Jones "was as proud as a kid with his first watch."[121] It was only one game, and a tie at that, but Jones could not restrain himself. "If that's the best New Westminster can do," he said, "we are going to win the cup without much trouble. We are going to be stronger as the season advances. Lalonde will be with us for the next game."[122] To Jones, it looked like 1911 all over again.

Saturday's game got underway at 2:30 p.m. before 3,000 fans at Con Jones Park. Newsy, as foxy as ever but out of shape, gave the Terminals confidence. Fitzgerald struck first, a back-hander eleven minutes into the first quarter. He scored again, less than a minute into the second. Then the teams scored five goals in just over five minutes. Storme got one off a pass from Feeney and Jimmy Gunn got a second on a pass from Stoddart. The Terminals charged back for two more, then Bill Patchell scored. No one could find the back of the net in the third and fourth quarters. The game was Vancouver's, 4–3. Jones gloated. At last, he believed, he had another

The sign at Hastings Park reads 'Penalties' and that's where things are going as Doughy Spring has taken a swipe at a VLC player, knocking the cap off his head.

VANCOUVER ARCHIVES.
PHOTOGRAPH BY STUART THOMSON.

Vancouver's Everett McLaren faces off against Salmonbellies' George Feeney at Brockton Point in 1920, while referee Fred Lynch prepares to get out of the way.

VANCOUVER ARCHIVES.
PHOTOGRAPH BY STUART THOMSON.

team capable of defeating the Salmonbellies.

But Jones had forgotten about Doughy, who was in far better condition than Fitzgerald and Newsy. In fact, although he had practised only once with the team, Doughy was likely in better shape than anyone on the field. In game 3 at Queen's Park, he scored three goals with two assists to spark the Salmonbellies to a 10–1 victory. Newsy got the only Vancouver tally.

Jones was disconsolate. The Salmonbellies and the Terminals went into the fourth game at Con Jones Park with 1–1–1 records. Fitzgerald opened the scoring off a rebound. At the end of the second quarter, it was 2–2. And then, with a minute to go in the third quarter, "Fitzgerald put Vancouver one to the good near the end of the third on a pass from Lalonde."[123] It was the last goal that either of them would score. The Salmonbellies went on to win 6–4.

Following the contest, Jones called off the season. If not even Newsy and Fitzgerald, two of the greatest players the game had ever seen, could lead his handpicked team to victory over the Salmonbellies, what hope was there? His physician, he said, had ordered him to sever all connection with the game. He wasn't faking; he'd been suffering from hypertension for years.

Newsy stuck around Vancouver, and Fitzgerald departed on the next train east. Jones was asked if he would allow the players to use his park for free for the good of the game. "No," he said. New Westminster had crushed his spirit. Con Jones was done. And so was professional field lacrosse in BC. The Minto Cup went into storage.

The Salmonbellies pose before the start of a game in 1922. In June at Queen's Park a scrap between Vancouver's McLaren and Jack Gifford resulted in hundreds of rioting fans. It took thirty minutes and threats of a hosing by the fire department to quell the fighting. **Standing l-r:** Buck Marshall, Bill Patchell, Gib Adams, Pat Feeney (player/manager), Haddie Stoddart, Bernie Feedham, Thure Storme, Hugh Gifford, Lawrey Nelson, Jack Gifford. **Squatting:** Len Turnbull, Doughy Spring.

NEW WESTMINSTER MUSEUM AND ARCHIVES.

The sockeye salmon emblem debuted briefly in 1901 and reappeared on sweaters on May 24, 1927. With a few exceptions, the salmon has been prominent on New Westminster lacrosse team sweaters ever since. This one belonged to Dad Turnbull's son Bob, who wore it between 1934 and 1936.

THE OLD HASTINGS MILL STORE AND MUSEUM. PHOTOGRAPH BY PHILLIP CHIN.

CHAPTER FIVE
THE DEATH OF FIELD: 1925-1931

The Salmonbellies petitioned the BC Amateur Athletic Union at the end of the 1924 season to have players reinstated as amateurs. Many of their veterans had retired. The team pulled together the best amateurs they could find, most of them from the Royals. With the collapse of the professional league, Vancouver tried to put together a team to be called the All-Canadians. But the All-Canadians withdrew before the 1925 season even got underway.

Without their traditional Vancouver opposition, the now amateur Salmonbellies turned to the one other possibility: the Vancouver Indians. The Indians had their origin in the vision of a dynamic Squamish leader, Andy Paull. Born in 1892, Paull had begun organizing and coaching a group of Indian youngsters in 1921. Although a qualified lawyer, Paull, by the rules then in place, could not practise without losing his Indian status. Working as a longshoreman, he organized Indian orchestras, employment services, beauty contests, and the lacrosse team. His goal—his dream—was to create an all-Indian team capable of winning the Mann Cup.

In 1918 a Squamish Indian team competed as juniors against three Vancouver teams: Seaforths United, Adanacs, and West Ends/Towers. The following season, they competed in the Vancouver Amateur Lacrosse Association against the Vancouver National Athletic Club and the Vancouver Native Sons. In 1922, under manager and coach Paull, the Squamish team went 12–1 on the season against four other teams in the Vancouver association league. In 1923 they faced the senior amateur Salmonbellies and the Vancouver Native Sons, compiling a respectable 2–5–3 record. In 1924, they played as the North Shore Athletics.

When 1925 rolled around, the Indians were a seasoned team of predominantly First Nations players with their own version of the Giffords—the Bakers: Bob, Ray, Dominic and Henry. They also had Moses Joseph, Gus Band and sharpshooter Elmo Ems. White players included seasoned vet Cory Hess in goal, Riley McLaren, Les Dickinson, and Joe Shillingford.

The Salmonbellies were down to just one Gifford, Bill (Will's son), who was making his first appearance for the seniors. The Royals' Ken Calbick played defence along with Leo Gregory, "Buck" Ettinger, Andy Hunter, and Bob Mackie. Howard Crandall was in nets. Up front the Salmonbellies had Jack Rennie, a centre man with the Royals, and veteran home players Nels Atkinson, Jack Wood, and "hot tempered" Johnny Vernon.

Vernon, from New Westminster, played the game Gifford-style: hard, fast, and take-no-prisoners. Spectators knew he was about to blow his stack when he turned down the earflaps on his padded cap. On Saturday afternoons, he was a ball of fire, but during the week he delivered milk for a local dairy.

The BC Coast Lacrosse Association formed around the Salmonbellies and the Indians. Con Jones reversed his decision and allowed the Indians to use his park as their home field. To shore up fan support, the association brought in new rules to make the game more appealing and less prone to hooliganism. Spectators were now required to use the stands. Only players, managers, and officials were allowed on the field. An "anti-defence" area was designated around the goals to prevent defenders from bunching up. This precursor to the box lacrosse crease was meant to encourage more goals. Night games were four twenty-minute quarters. In case of a tie, two five-minute periods would be played, the first goal winning. Fewer and fewer fans showed up as the season wore on. Ticket prices were cut back to 25¢.

In August, the Salmonbellies and the Indians tied again at three. The teams decided to replay the game at a later date. Thinking they had the championship in the bag, in August, the Salmonbellies lost two games. The Indians could still capture the title. But on September 2, the Indians lost 5–3. The Salmonbellies were willing to replay the 3–3 game, but because Queen's Park was already booked for soccer during the exhibition, they had to play at Sapperton Park. With fan interest at nearly zero, and with no chance of earning any gate money at the wide-open park, the Indians declined and the Salmonbellies retained the Mann Cup.

Jack Wood won the individual scoring honours for the second time in two years with eighteen goals. Elmo Ems led the Indians and took second place overall with fifteen. In September, the Salmonbellies received news that Stoddart, Feeney, and the Patchell brothers had been granted reinstatement in the Amateur Athletic Union of Canada. The players would have to sit out a season, however, before resuming play. Following the 1925 season the Salmonbellies turned over the Mann Cup to the CLA.

From 1910 to 1925 the cup had been, like the Minto Cup, a challenge cup. The Vancouver Athletic Club won it four years running, 1911 through 1914. New Westminster won it in 1915 and repeated as champions in 1916 and 1917. Two different Vancouver clubs won the trophy in 1918 and 1919. In 1920, New Westminster won it back and retained it every year through 1925. But the challenge format no longer benefited the sport. Instead, as a way of fostering the sport nationally, the Canadian Lacrosse Association (CLA) instituted a national playoff system.

The BC Coast Lacrosse Association folded in May 1926, leaving the game again in the hands of the BC Amateur Lacrosse Association. The BCALA comprised the Salmonbellies, the Vancouver Lacrosse Club, and the Richmond Farmers. The Farmers had fielded a senior team in the Vancouver Amateur Lacrosse Association in 1920, winning the league with an 8–2–1 record. There was no league play in 1921, but in 1922, the Farmers finished third among five teams, with the Indians on top.

The next generation of Salmonbellies featured returning centre Bill "Red" Fraser, Johnny Vernon, Bob Mackie, Nels Atkinson, and Cyril "Flickie" Doyle. Haddie Stoddart's brothers Len and Johnny joined the roster. But the team lacked the defensive power of the Patchells and the scoring instincts of Haddie, Thure Storme, and George Feeney. Richmond won the BCALA's truncated regular season (over by the middle of August) with six victories against two losses, then beat the Salmonbellies in the two-game, total-goals league playoff series 7–6.

In the Kilmarnock Cup, the Farmers again faced the Salmonbellies in the form of a team from Ocean Falls, a rain-soaked coastal town about 300 miles north of Vancouver. In the early 1920s, Ocean Falls was home to about 2,000 people, including a number of ex-New Westminster residents, many of them quality lacrosse players who'd found work at the town's pulp and paper mill. The Ocean Falls "Salmonbellies" narrowly defeated the Farmers in a hard-fought, two-game, total-goals series 9–8 (6–6, 3–2) to advance to the western finals against the Winnipeg Tammany Tigers. Ocean Falls was as narrowly defeated by Winnipeg 13–12 (5–6, 8–6) as they had defeated the Farmers. The Toronto Westons subsequently swept Winnipeg in the Mann Cup 11–3 and 11–3.

Grumpy had every reason to be excited as his team worked out at Queen's Park on a rainy Monday night in May 1927. For one thing, he had back in his lineup a number of key former professionals—the Patchell brothers, George Feeney, and Haddie Stoddart and the best of the former Royals. The only one not back that he would have liked on the roster was injury-plagued Thure Storme. For Grumpy, it was the classic dilemma. He had the best veterans and the best of the next generation, but would they gel?

On Empire Day, May 24, at Queen's Park, the renewed Salmonbellies came out of the dressing room in new uniforms. For the first time since 1901, the team visually acknowledged their nickname. A big white salmon was set against the traditional red jersey, with a white band running along the bottom. The team fired on all cylinders, hot-tempered Johnny Vernon scoring five goals as they trounced the Vancouver Province Bluebirds 12–3.

A week later, they faced the Richmond Farmers at their Bridgeport field. The grass was uncut and the field wasn't limed, allowing the spectators to crowd in. The Salmonbellies complained, but had no real excuse in a 3–2 loss. The defeat strengthened their resolve, and they went on to win their next nine games.

In July, with Haddie Stoddart's brother Johnny in goal, they held their opponents scoreless in three of four games. On the season, they allowed just twenty-three goals in twelve games, just a fraction less than two per game, while scoring seventy-nine, an average of over six per game. The statistics were, and remain, unprecedented in Canadian lacrosse. In the playoffs for the Kilmarnock Cup, the Salmonbellies shut out the Farmers in the two-game series, defeating them 9–0 and 6–0 to advance to the Mann Cup with the defending Toronto Westons.

The R.A.&I.S. guaranteed the Westons a large sum of money to come to New Westminster during exhibition week. They arrived in late August. The Westons had won the Canadian Amateur Lacrosse Association regular season title from 1923 to 1925. In 1926, after defeating Montreal, they defeated the Winnipeg Tigers to capture the Mann Cup. Coached by former Toronto professional lacrosse player Eddie Powers, the Westons had been together, with only two exceptions, for four years. Furthermore, they were coming off an undefeated 1927 season. They were a formidable team; the Salmonbellies would have their hands full.

Rules had changed since the Salmonbellies last competed in a national series against an eastern team. The referee, from Ontario, insisted on a thirty-foot circular "bull ring" in lime to mark off centre field. Only the two centre men could enter the ring for faceoffs. Moreover, no player was allowed to move, let alone enter the circle, until the ball had gone out of the ring. There was more. For the first time in the west, a crease circled the nets, and goals within the crease were disallowed. A free throw was awarded to a player who had been fouled. And one more new rule: any time the referee blew his whistle to stop play, substitutes were allowed onto the field.

The new rules did not bother the Salmonbellies, who took the first game 6–3. Three days later, on Saturday, September 12, in front of 6,000 fans, the Salmonbellies were down by two goals three times. From the front row of the grandstand, former defensive great Tom Gifford

The referee's whistle used by former VLC player George Matheson in the 1920s.

CANADIAN LACROSSE HALL OF FAME. PHOTOGRAPH BY PHILLIP CHIN.

acted as Grumpy's assistant coach, calmly but loudly giving strategic direction to the players while Grumpy handled the bench.

At the Westons' bench, Eddie Powers was beside himself, confusion, bordering on panic, reigning. Vernon got the third tie. And then, playing three men short in the fourth quarter, Flickie Doyle hit Red Fraser with a pass. From long distance Red unleashed a shot. As he let it go, three Westons jumped on him, burying his face in the grass. But the shot went in. Westons could not equalize. The Mann Cup was back in New Westminster. Six thousand fans and the team exploded as one, but the happiest of all was Grumpy, who congratulated and thanked every single player as he made his way to the dressing room.

The victory was accredited to the Salmonbellies penetrative style of play. Crease rules or not, New Westminster could still find the back of the net. Comparisons were made to the Salmonbellies of the 1890s and 1910s. At the banquet for the teams following the match, the Kilmarnock Cup, sent down by the Ocean Falls team, graced the centre of the head table. Many of the old Salmonbellies were there, players and supporters, including Joe Lally and former field captain Jack Mahony. Defenceman Leo Gregory accepted the Mann Cup on behalf of the team. Meanwhile, back at Queen's Park, Red was still strolling around when the exhibition shut down at 10:00 p.m., a big smile on his face and three attractive young women by his side.

With their 1927 Mann Cup victory, the Salmonbellies earned the right to represent Canada at the 1928 Olympic games in Amsterdam. In New Westminster, merchant and team business manager Dan MacKenzie was doing everything in his power to scrape together the necessary $13,000 funding. In Vancouver, BCALA president Jim McConaghy was busy twisting arms on the team's behalf. The Canadian Olympic Committee, ashamed that the team might be relegated to third tourist class on its transatlantic voyage, kicked in an extra $1,000 on top of the miserly $1,000 already promised to ensure that the team travelled cabin class like all the other Canadian athletes. The team's supporters were anxious that the fund be enough to enable the Patchell brothers, George Feeney, and Haddie Stoddart to make the trip, despite their not being able to play in the Olympics due to their former professional status. The International Olympic Committee, however, saw no issue with taking money from a first time sponsor, the Coca-Cola Company.

Canadian Olympic team crest worn by Salmonbellies in 1928.

CANADIAN LACROSSE HALL OF FAME.
PHOTOGRAPH BY PHILLIP CHIN.

The team sported natty new white jackets and slacks, but had to rely on Vancouver's Universal Knitting for fresh jerseys—white with a red maple leaf, emblazoned CANADA. The Dominion Rubber Company provided new playing shoes, and Joe Lally donated sixteen new lacrosse sticks.

But with three weeks to go, the "On To Amsterdam" fund was still short $5,000. MacKenzie was frantic, putting the touch on everybody in New Westminster, particularly the business class, pitching them on the idea that the team represented a great publicity opportunity for the city and its fresh-water port facilities. What's more, every man, woman, and child was urged to do his or her bit to send the team to Amsterdam. On July 10, the fund stood at $11,640.53—close enough.

The next morning, the Salmonbellies gathered at the Great Northern Station and boarded a chartered Pullman coach stocked with enough pure British Columbia water to satisfy everyone's thirst as far as Quebec City. Twenty years earlier to the day, another Salmonbellies team had boarded a train bound for Montreal and the Minto Cup. Biscuits Peele, Jack Bryson, and others from that team were on hand to bid the Olympians farewell.

Grumpy had been a question mark all along due to ill health and business concerns. But he boarded the train with the team too, although promised to go only as far as Montreal.

The Salmonbellies played exhibition matches as they travelled across the country, hoping to stay in shape and to raise additional cash. They defeated Edmonton 8–1 and Winnipeg 5–2.

In Winnipeg, Hop Wilkie was hospitalized with an abscessed throat. In Toronto, Salmonbellies' goaltending great Bun Clark, now operating a grocery store, greeted the team on their arrival and acted as a goal umpire in the game against the Westons-loaded Toronto All-Stars. The All-Stars won 7–4. In their last tune-up before the Olympics the Salmonbellies defeated Montreal 10–0. The exhibition series raised an additional $700. Wilkie, his throat on the mend, rejoined the team.

Two publicity stills from 1928. **Gillnetter boat:** Leo Gregory (in stern), Nels Atkinson and Johnny Vernon (toward bow) hope to net some funding for the team's trip to the Olympic games in Amsterdam, where they represented Canada. **Fish dock:** Atkinson, Vernon and Gregory at the Canadian Fishing Company cannery on New Westminster's waterfront.
MYDSKE FAMILY.

After the Montreal game, the 1908 Olympic lacrosse team hosted a dinner in honour of the 1928 team at the Windsor Hotel. Later that night, they boarded a train for Quebec City. Grumpy was forced, as he had feared, to leave the team in Montreal, and Bill Patchell took over as coach. On July 18, the Salmonbellies left Quebec City aboard the *Empress of Scotland*. It was the first Atlantic crossing for all but George Feeney and Willis Patchell. The last time, they had been on their way to the Western Front.

While McKenzie and McConaghy had scrambled to secure funds, the president of the US Olympic Committee, Major General Douglas MacArthur, arranged an elimination tournament among the nation's six best teams: Johns Hopkins, Army, Navy, Maryland, Rutgers, and the heavily favoured Mount Washington Lacrosse Club, the equivalent of a pro team today.

Ray Van Orman coached Johns Hopkins. Van Orman was a former football coach who had never even seen a lacrosse game when he took the lacrosse coaching reins at the university in 1926. He built an organization whose teams would compile a 71–11 record and win six national championships over the next eight years. On June 9, at Baltimore Stadium, sixth-seeded Johns Hopkins stunned everyone by downing Mount Washington. Hopkins then beat Army and Maryland to claim the trip to Amsterdam. The beneficiary of $19,000 worth of gate receipts from the elimination series, Johns Hopkins boarded the chartered United States Lines' S.S. *President Roosevelt*. On board was most of the US Olympic team, including General MacArthur and swimmer Johnny Weissmuller, not yet famous as Tarzan. The lacrosse team, under the steady gaze of Van Orman, stayed in shape with calisthenics and laps around an on-deck track.

The Salmonbellies arrived in Holland on July 27. They toured the Olympic site with its beautifully proportioned and strikingly modern stadium, designed by Dutch architect and artist Jan Wils. At the entrance to the stadium, they craned their necks to take in the graceful Marathon Tower, also designed by Wils, with four balconies for horn-blowing heralds, an upper gallery for loud speakers (a novelty at the time), and, at the pinnacle, a bowl to house the Olympic flame, to be lit for the first time ever.

On Saturday night, July 28, the Salmonbellies received a visit from US player Louis Nixdorff. "It looks," Nixdorff later wrote in his diary, "as though we will be in for a busy afternoon next Sunday."[124]

On Monday, three Salmonbellies paid a return visit, not to the team's lodgings on board the *President Roosevelt*, but to their practice field. "We shammed for a very dub team," noted Nixdorff (1920s sports slang: "We pretended to be a bad team"). Patchell and Van Orman met to agree on the rules. Patchell preferred to forgo goal creases, but Van Orman wanted them. They compromised: creases in front of the goal would be four feet instead of the usual six. They also agreed to play two thirty-minute halves rather than the usual four twenty-minute quarters, with each team having three substitutions a half. Nixdorff thought his team had come away with the best of the deal. With the game looming, he admitted that Johns Hopkins was "a little bit scared."[125] The American team's intelligence on the Salmonbellies was that they were "very cocky" and certain their superior experience and stick work would win for them.[126] Master strategist Van Orman took note.

The Americans were calm the day of the game, August 5. They ate at three o'clock, dressed, and left for the stadium, sure of winning but not overconfident.[127] The game got underway in front of 30,000 spectators, almost all of them there to witness the end of the marathon. Johns Hopkins used tight man-on-man riding tactics, featuring a lot of stick checking, as ordered by Van Orman, to frustrate the Salmonbellies' usual style of play. Jack Wood scored one, but the half ended with Johns Hopkins up 4–1.

Before the mid-game break ended, the marathoners entered the stadium, delaying the start of the second half. France's Algerian-born Boughera El Quafi took the gold. Lacrosse resumed. "If the first half was rough," wrote Nixdorff, "the second was a nightmare."[128] Struck by a stick and cut over the eye, Vernon, forgetting the world stage he was on, pulled down his ear flaps and retaliated as he would have back in Queen's Park, getting into a full-on brawl with Hopkins's John Lang. Jack Wood scored two more goals for the Salmonbellies, but the Americans also scored two more and took the game 6–3.

A hard working defenceman like his brother Willis, Bill Patchell was barred from playing in the 1928 Olympic games because of his former pro status. Instead, he coached the team in the absence of Grumpy.

CANADIAN LACROSSE HALL OF FAME.

Afterwards MacArthur raised hell with Lang and the other Hopkins players involved in the Vernon skirmish. But the crowd was amused with the rough tactics, as well they might have been, this being the Olympic games where the brotherhood of nations was supposed to prevail. "To more than a few of the spectators lacrosse was viewed as a kind of genteel murder," wrote the *New York Times*. "The opinion which most prevailed was that the players were just there to beat each other up with the sticks."[129]

Beat up with sticks or just plain beat up, the Americans faced the British squad the next day. The champions of the North of England league, centred in Manchester, had won the right to represent Great Britain. The Americans knew instantly it was not going to be a walkover, the British, in Nixdorff's opinion, being "as good if not better than the Canadians."[130] The score was 4–3 Hopkins at the half. The teams traded goals and leads until the English were on top 7–6. The Americans fired shot after shot, the ball bouncing everywhere but in, until George Helfrich scored—or thought he had. The umpire ruled that the American had been in the crease and disallowed the goal, giving Van Orman and his players reason to regret his insistence on a crease. England won; an upset, yes, but they had been helped by the Salmonbellies. The American team was beat up, bruised, and worn out from back-to-back matches. "Such post-mortems," wrote Nixdorff, "and sad, gloomy faces."[131] Their moods worsened when MacArthur, peeved by the fighting, cancelled the team's planned match in Manchester. "Such great spirit in a general I have seldom seen," wrote Nixdorff, sarcastically.[132]

On August 7, with Jack Wood scoring another three, Canada defeated England 9–5. Other scorers were Vernon with two and Gregory, Fraser, Burnett, and Mackie with one apiece. The result was a three-way tie, with one win and twelve goals each. The US suggested a playoff, to which Canada agreed but England didn't. And so it ended. Lacrosse was a demonstration sport, and no medals would have been awarded no matter the outcome.

But that wasn't the case in track and field, where the biggest winner of all was Canada's Percy Williams, taking gold in the 100m and 200m sprints. Many of the Salmonbellies, including Jack Wood, witnessed his victories. Williams's performance was matched by Weissmuller's gold medals in the 100m and the 4 x 200m freestyle swimming events.

The Salmonbellies played exhibition games in England, Montreal, and Ottawa before arriving back in New Westminster on September 4. Wearing their crisp, white Olympic uniforms, they were lionized, a motor cavalcade taking them from the train station to Queen's Park, where in front of a large, cheering crowd, Mayor Wells Gray praised their performance. The team had been gone two months, with eleven wins and two losses to show for their efforts. But it was the loss to Johns Hopkins that mattered—and stung.

With the Salmonbellies in Amsterdam, there had been no league play in BC. The Mann Cup finals, however, were played, the Ottawa Emmetts defeating the Winnipeg Wellingtons for the trophy.

A couple of weeks after the Salmonbellies' return, at a party at the home of team president Llewellyn Douglas, the players set aside a number of bottles of rum in honour of their Olympic adventure. In a sort of tontine agreement, the players agreed to meet each year and drink to the team. This would happen until only two players were left. Ab Brown built a wooden case, and the bottles went into storage.

In 1924, Con Jones built a large Dutch colonial revival-style house in Vancouver's upscale Shaughnessy district, where he liked to entertain lavishly. But the party ended for Jones when, long afflicted with hypertension, he fell ill at a league final soccer game at his stadium, Con Jones Park, on May 29, 1929. He died of a brain hemorrhage six days later at his house, just short of sixty years of age. Jones was gone and lacrosse appeared to be headed for the same fate.

In Quebec lacrosse had suffered a steep decline from its heyday, but with a concerted push from Paddy Brennan and Newsy Lalonde, a five-team Quebec-Ontario Senior Lacrosse League was formed in 1929, helping revive player and fan interest in and around Montreal. In Toronto, former Tecumsehs star Charlie Querrie led the attempt at reviving field lacrosse.

In Vancouver, a charabanc drawn by six horses carried old Salmonbellies stars Cheyne, Turnbull, Tom Gifford, and others through the streets of Vancouver on the way to Brockton Oval for an old-timers' match. A trumpeter announced their progress while the players chanted their old "ala veepore" war cry. It was a measure of the club's desperation that they would resort to such blatant nostalgia in a bid to revive some interest in lacrosse. Another old-timers' game, this one in New Westminster, was held in June, partially to promote lacrosse, but with the gate receipts—about $1,400—going to Punk Wintemute, paralyzed from the waist down and blinded after a failed surgical procedure to relieve arthritis.

On Sunday, July 14, at about 6:00 a.m. a fire began in the 39-year-old Agricultural Building. As the dry wooden structure went up in flames, the fire spread rapidly to other exhibition buildings. Before long everything of significance was consumed. The heat from the blaze was so intense that it cracked the east-facing windows in exhibition manager Duncan MacKenzie's house at the corner of First Street and Third Avenue. New Westminster and its citizens had lost their prized exhibition buildings, but the Salmonbellies had lost even more. For four decades the Agricultural Building had been the stage overlooking their battleground and the iconic backdrop against which their fortunes played out. The entranceway turrets, reminiscent of goalposts, were now ashes. Gone too were the steps on which Tom Gifford in 1908 said to an angry mob, "If I am satisfied, you ought to be." Gone was the second floor deck from which photographers shot panoramas. Only the game itself remained, and even that was in jeopardy.

The box built by Ab Brown in 1928 to house bottles of rum. The rum was to be used by the surviving members of the 1928 Canadian Olympic lacrosse team to toast their teammates.

CANADIAN LACROSSE HALL OF FAME. PHOTOGRAPH BY PHILLIP CHIN.

Despite the loss of the Agricultural Building, the Salmonbellies continued to frustrate their BCALA rivals, the Vancouver Waterfront Workers. In one game, with Vancouver playing with just eleven men, players brawled all over the field. Three Salmonbellies and four Vancouvers received one-game suspensions. Arriving at Queen's Park for the next match, Salmonbellies players found the door to the clubhouse locked. A key was finally located, and the door was opened by—a sign of the times—the manager of a baseball team.

Down five players, Vancouver did not show up for the next match. Paying fans were offered refunds, but most declined in the hope that the 50¢ would benefit the Salmonbellies. It had come to charity.

The Salmonbellies won six of eight regular-season games to retain the Kilmarnock Cup. The R.A.&I.S. decided to stage the exhibition despite the fire, with large tents replacing buildings. Seven thousand fans showed up at Queen's Park on September 2 for the first match of the

1929 Mann Cup. A large part of the draw was Winston Churchill, who, on an extended tour of Canada and the US, was in New Westminster to give a speech opening the exhibition. He congratulated the city for carrying on despite the fire, but his presence did nothing for the home team. They lost 9–5 to the Oshawa General Motors. Oshawa also won the second game 2–1 to capture the cup.

A few weeks later, in late October, the US stock market crashed, setting off the Great Depression. The decline in stock prices caused bankruptcies and severe economic problems, including business closures, contraction of credit, firing of workers, bank failures, and the decline of the money supply in the US, Canada, and around the world. At first, the effects of the Depression were not felt in New Westminster. But soon they would be.

On February 1, 1930, the Salmonbellies' long-time trainer, 50-year-old Tim Mahony, died.[133] The Irish-born Mahony had arrived in New Westminster in 1889. In addition to training the team, Mahony wrote that he repaired sticks "for more years than he cares to own up to," adding that he always swore he would "never fix another stick, but no one believes him, not even himself."[134]

Over years of service, Mahony became a beloved figure, not only with the Salmonbellies, of which he was made a life member, but also with all the teams they faced. The Reverend Canon d'Easum conducted his funeral service at Holy Trinity Cathedral. One hundred athletes from New Westminster and Vancouver marched to his gravesite overlooking the Fraser River. As d'Easum closed his Bible, Norman Rattray, Salmonbellies' manager, stepped forward. In his hand was the stick that Mahony had selected and strung for Buck Marshall. Rattray placed it on Mahony's coffin as it was lowered into the earth.

As the 1930 season got underway, the Salmonbellies watched from their grass field as a building was constructed to the north, more or less on the site of the Women's Building, burned to the ground less than a year earlier. The new building was so close that any one of the players could have winged a ball and hit it. It was intended to be a civic auditorium and an indoor ice rink, a place for hockey, among other uses. But, as far as lacrosse players were concerned, it had nothing to do with their game. As the team warmed up, casually passing and catching, no one thought for a second that their new home was being built, that the future would play out on wood, not on grass.

The Depression was tightening its grip. The Salmonbellies' most devoted fans came to the games, but hardly anyone else did. Their only league opponent, once again, was the Vancouver Lacrosse Club. In the second-to-last regular season match, turnout was feeble, no more than thirty. The season ender was cancelled, partly because of homecoming celebrations for the Westminster Royals, newly crowned Canadian senior men's soccer champions. The situation was no better in Ontario, where only the Brampton Excelsiors, the Oshawa General Motors, and the Toronto St. Simon's were active. In the end, the Salmonbellies won eight of ten against Vancouver, retaining the Kilmarnock Cup. In the Dominion playoff, they defeated the Edmonton Native Sons 17–0, and in the western Canada final they beat the Winnipeg Argos in two games by a combined score of 17–8, earning a Mann Cup berth against the Brampton Excelsiors.

Brampton in the 1930s was a town of 5,500 people, best known for Dale's Nursery, a cut-flower business that at its height was the largest in North America. The Excelsiors formed in 1883, played in their first Mann Cup in 1913, folded for the duration of WWI, and played continuously through the 1920s. By 1930, they had a very strong team. They met the Salmonbellies at Toronto's Varsity Stadium on a hot and humid Saturday, August 30.

Eddie Power, a former star defenceman with Toronto in the NLU and a "fine disciplinarian,"[135] coached the Excelsiors. But the team's leader on the field was a genial, grey-haired, 40-year-old insurance agent and devout Baptist named George Sproule. Sproule, an inside home, played in his first Mann Cup sixteen years earlier, in 1914, against the Vancouver Athletics. In the 1930 eastern finals against the Montreal Amateur Athletic Association team, Sproule scored three goals in the second half of a 4–1 Brampton victory. His play reminded the old Montreal reporters in the press box of Henry Hoobin. It was twenty-two years since Hoobin last played—in game 2 of the 1908 Minto Cup series against the Salmonbellies. But, triggered by Sproule, Hoobin was still playing in their memories.

In front of 7,500 boisterous spectators, the Salmonbellies lost the first game 8–1, Brampton's Norm Zimmer scoring or assisting on half the goals and Stoddart scoring New Westminster's only goal. The Salmonbellies' Richard "Sonny" Douglas scored twice in the early going of game 2, but Brampton tied it just before the half. Their supporters "went crazy and many a good hat was lost."[136] The Excelsiors scored twice on George Mackie in the third quarter, but Sproule, in scoring one of the goals, broke his ankle. Still, Brampton seemed in control of the sluggish Salmonbellies. But Stoddart fired two shots past goalie Bert Large to tie it, then whipped in an underhand shot in the fourth to win the game and tie the series.

In Wednesday's deciding game, with 8,000 fans looking on, Johnny Vernon gave the Salmonbellies the lead. After a scoreless second quarter, Jack Wood notched the Salmonbellies' second goal, but referee Charlie Querrie ruled him in the crease and disallowed the goal. Zimmer then tied the game, Jerry Kendall added a second, and Hank Gowdy made it 3–1. As Brampton's band, anticipating a victory, played "Hail, hail, the gang's all here," the Excelsiors successfully ragged the ball until six-foot-four Ted Reeve and Zimmer set up Jerry Kendall for Brampton's fourth goal and first Mann Cup. After dining with the Excelsiors, the disappointed Salmonbellies boarded a 10:00 p.m. train. As they headed home, the building they had watched going up in Queen's Park, the civic auditorium that would become the Arena, was only two weeks away from its official opening.

In 1931 a new enterprise, the International Professional Lacrosse League (IPLL), backed by eastern hockey interests and paying players as much as $75 a week, was set to take the game inside. Envisioned by Montreal's Joe Cattarinich as a complementary summer league to the National Hockey League, the IPLL started play in June 1931 with two Montreal teams, the Canadiens and the Maroons; a Toronto team, the Maple Leafs; and the Cornwall Colts. Cattarinich and Leo Dandurand, owners of the Canadiens hockey team, owned the Canadiens lacrosse team. Pete Campbell operated the Toronto team, backed by the Leafs' Conn Smythe and Frank J. Selke. The Colts were owned by Joseph Lally, lacrosse-stick manufacturer and respected referee. But would people pay to sit indoors on hot summer nights?

Newspaper columnists saw the league as a bastardization of the field game, invented by hockey businessmen solely to keep their arenas full of paying customers in the summer. But that overlooked the lacrosse credentials of businessmen like Dandurand and Lally and the résumés of the former lacrosse greats they picked to coach their clubs. Lalonde, for example, was behind the bench for the Canadiens, while Paddy Brennan, former Montreal Shamrocks great, guided the Maroons.

Other experienced lacrosse people filled managerial positions with the clubs. Some of the stars of the new league were famous hockey players—Charlie and Lionel Conacher, Ace Bailey, and Nels Stewart—who were just as good with a lacrosse stick, but who had, due to their professional status, been unable to compete in amateur lacrosse. But the IPLL's rank and file players were recruited largely from Ontario's senior teams.

With established pros and the best former amateurs set to begin playing indoor box lacrosse, younger Ontario and Quebec players jumped into the new game. In fact, they beat the pros to it. A Montreal intermediate league was the first to organize around box lacrosse. Lalonde gave the league instant credibility when he offered to donate a cup bearing his name. On June 21, two days before the IPLL's first match, the Montreal intermediates began play. Newspaper pundits took note. With young amateurs embracing the new version, they could no longer claim the game was a cynical money grab by hockey interests. "It looks perhaps like the game of the future and perhaps the salvation of the grand old pastime," wrote the *Montreal Star*'s Basil O'Meara.[137] In the end, however, not enough people paid to see the games and the pro league folded after just one season, costing Selke and Smythe an estimated $20,000.[138]

Quebec and Ontario senior players continued with field lacrosse for 1931. Defending Mann Cup champion Brampton lost six players to the IPLL, opening up the distinct possibility of one of the Quebec teams winning the league and competing for the Mann Cup. And a cup win would mean representing Canada at the 1932 Olympics.

After Cornwall's senior amateur field team dropped out of league play, their better players having joined the IPLL's Colts, the remaining players took up the box game, playing an exhibition match with the St. Regis Indians in Brockville before a large crowd in July. The Indians formed a box team and played Cornwall in Prescott in September. On the success of those matches, Brockville, Prescott, Cardinal, and Smiths Falls formed an autumn indoor league. Small communities, unable to field competitive twelve-man sides, had no problem coming up with seven players, and took immediately to the box game. Cornwall created its own box entity in October: a three-team intra-city league.

On July 7, 1931, senior field players under the jurisdiction of the OALA forged ahead with an unsanctioned entity: the Sunnyside Box Lacrosse League. Games were played at Sunnyside Stadium, on Lake Ontario, west of downtown Toronto. The new league was a huge hit with fans, and Charlie Querrie blessed it with a championship trophy in his name.

Throughout the summer of 1931, Sunnyside teams played exhibition games in southern Ontario, in small towns like Brantford, Woodstock, and Orangeville. Wherever they played box lacrosse, teams sprung up in their wake. The six-team field league did not fold, but soldiered on, awaiting its fate. As it happened, fate was a shrinking base of support while box prospered. Death came when the OALA was ineffectual in dealing with a riot incited by a playoff game between the Brampton Excelsiors and Toronto St. Simon's.

In New Westminster and Vancouver, lacrosse officials paid close attention to eastern developments. But the younger generation of Salmonbellies refused to have anything to do with box lacrosse. Instead, they nominated a number of New Westminster and Vancouver's former professionals or "old boys" to try it out. The old boys started working out in preparation for BC's first box game, an exhibition trial run, scheduled against the amateur Vancouver Home Oils at Vancouver's Athletic Park. The park, located between Granville and Hemlock Streets and West Fifth and West Fourth Avenues, was built by Bob Brown in 1913 to replace the demolished Recreation Park. It was levelled in 1951 to make way for the new Granville Street Bridge.

On the evening of Tuesday, July 14, old boys Jimmy Gunn, Thure Storme, Bernie Feedham, Dot Crookall, Bay Carter, and others took to the boxed-in field. Among the others was Doughy, now into his fourth decade of senior lacrosse. The playing field was cut in half, and the width narrowed. Without much midfield, the game, in theory, would be faster, quicker, and higher scoring, making the game more interesting to play and watch. Balls flying out of play were still an issue—it caused too many boring stoppages of play—but boards and netting could eventually be erected to contain the action.

Under new floodlights, the teams played eight men a side: three defence fielders, a centre, three home players, and a goalie. Within the first hour, a total of twenty-one goals had been scored, ten by the Salmonbellies' old boys.

Unlimited substituting was allowed, which kept up the pace of the game and allowed different combinations of players. But Crookall, Storme, and Spring, old-school to the bitter end, refused to be substituted and played the entire game.

Spectators had a great time, much preferring it to field lacrosse. Reported the *British Columbian*, "Box lacrosse made a great hit last night. The fans left Athletic Park convinced that the 8-man game is far ahead of the 12-man variety from the standpoint of the spectator."

Nine days later, the Salmonbellies' old boys took on the Squamish Indians. That game too was a success from every standpoint. Somewhat encouraged, on July 28, the younger generation of Salmonbellies tried the new game against the Vancouver Home Oils, with ten men a side. The team found that play was snappier, with more passing on the attack and less bunching in front of the goal by attackers, leading to more goals.

Conceived as a civic auditorium, what came to be called Queen's Park Arena was built on the ashes of the exhibition's Women's Building at a cost of $61,440.

On the same night, a double header, the Salmonbellies' old boys once more played the Squamish Indians. Two days later the old boys again took on the Home Oils, this time defeating them 15–10. The younger generation of Salmonbellies were still unconvinced about the new version of the game and continued to play field.

On August 4 the Salmonbellies met the Home Oils in the season's final regulation field game, winning 24–4 and advancing to the BC championship against the North Shore Squamish Indians. After defeating the Indians 22–9 (7–6, 15–3) they again faced the Brampton Excelsiors for the Mann Cup and the privilege of representing Canada at the 1932 Olympic games in Los Angeles.

The New Westminster Parks Board renovated Queen's Park, building bleachers and a grandstand closer to the field. A loudspeaker system was installed and used for the first time. Forty-six hundred spectators showed up for the first game of the series. The *Columbian* wondered if the Salmonbellies might suffer from stage fright, so unaccustomed were they to performing in front of such a crowd.

Burnaby resident Forbes Adams and his eight-year-old son, Cliff, were among the spectators. Forbes was a die-hard lacrosse fan, almost addicted, in his son's words.[139] Father and son took their seats near the top row in the grandstand. Nine or ten rows in front of them, a 29-year-old vendor was peddling 5¢ bags of peanuts from a tray strapped around his neck. Forbes signaled for a bag. The vendor tossed it up, straight into Forbe's hand. Cliff had seen him do it many times before. He never missed with his tosses. The vendor was Nat Bailey, founder of White Spot restaurants.

Brampton, having lost six outstanding players from the 1930 championship team to the International Professional (box) Lacrosse League, was an underrated team at the start of the season. They were also fast, fit, and young. Once rolling, they did not stop, defeating the Toronto St. Simon's, Montreal AAA, Winnipeg Wellingtons, and Calgary Rangers on their way to New Westminster.

In the opener, the Excelsiors substituted freely; the Salmonbellies lacked the bench depth to match. But the real issue was penalties. New Westminster took forty-five minutes' worth compared to Brampton's five. The Salmonbellies' Johnny Vernon was the worst offender, with twenty minutes. Brampton's Core scored three goals and "Bucko" McDonald three in an 8–4 victory.

The Salmonbellies came back to win the second encounter 7–3 in front of 1,500 fans. Patchell checked Core scoreless, Brown turned good shots aside, and the team got goals from six players, including George Feeney with two.

On Thursday, September 10, 1931, the Canadian Amateur Lacrosse Association adopted box as its official game. The third match of the Mann Cup finals would, therefore, be the last league-sanctioned senior amateur field game. Automobiles and roads had given people somewhere to go on Saturday afternoons besides lacrosse games. Picnicking sites or golf courses were now within easy distance. The rising popularity of baseball, both for players and spectators, had drawn athletes and fans away from lacrosse, which had developed into a slow, boring, defensive struggle featuring too many penalties, too much stick swinging, and not enough goal scoring. The Depression didn't help. Without income from ticket sales, the game struggled to meet expenses. On Saturday, September 12, many lacrosse greats gathered in front of the grandstand to witness field lacrosse's funeral. Joining them were 4,500 fans, paying their last respects.

Haddie Stoddart's goal in the second quarter of the third game of the 1931 Mann Cup was the last of the Salmonbellies' field era, a bookend to Fred Turner's first in 1889, forty-two years earlier.

CANADIAN LACROSSE HALL OF FAME.

Grumpy's team took to the field. With New Westminster up 2–1 in the second quarter, Stoddart was tripped with only Brampton's goal-keeper, Wally Large, to beat. He took a penalty shot from thirty feet out, but Brampton centre, Ollie Carey, illegally blocked it. He received a five-minute penalty, and Stoddart was given another shot. That time the veteran scored, putting the Salmonbellies in front 3–1. Brampton's George "Mush" Thompson scored less than two minutes into the second half, and captain Stewart Beatty added one—a long bouncer—about thirty seconds later to tie.

With the Salmonbellies' Wally Mercer serving his third penalty, the Excelsiors pressed even harder. Bucko fired one from long range and found the net behind Brown. The quarter ended with Brampton up 4–3.

The Excelsiors played defensive lacrosse in the fourth, ragging the ball whenever they could for as long as they could. The Salmonbellies had their chances but could not score. The fourth ended as it had begun. The Excelsiors had successfully defended the Mann Cup. Stoddart's goal in the second quarter was the last of the Salmonbellies' field era, a bookend to Fred Turner's first in 1889, forty-two years earlier. It was fitting that a stalwart like Stoddart score the final goal, complementing the first by the rookie Turner. It was also unusual, coming as it did on a penalty shot. As Stoddart fired it past Wally Large, no one at the park that day could have known that it was the Salmonbellies' final field lacrosse goal. The third and fourth quarters had yet to be played. But there were no more Salmonbellies' goals. As the teams headed for the showers and the fans filed out of the park, the old game had been put to rest.

September 12, 1931. The faceoff at the start of the third and deciding game of the 1931 Mann Cup championship at Queen's Park. It was also the last Canadian field lacrosse championship before the switch to box lacrosse. Brampton Excelsiors' centre Ollie Carey (facing camera) appears to have won it from Salmonbellies' centre Bill "Red" Fraser. #9 is Brampton's Claude Jennings. The referee is Hugh Gifford.

VANCOUVER ARCHIVES. PHOTOGRAPH BY STUART THOMSON.

During half-time of the third and deciding game of the 1931 Mann Cup championship, William James Moore, a Vancouver commercial photographer, set up his Kodak Cirkut camera at centre field to capture what everyone present knew was the last Canadian field lacrosse championship game. The large format camera, set on a tripod, would rotate slowly 360 degrees, driven by a spring-wound, clockwork motor. What the lens saw would be captured on a negative eight inches high and six feet, nine inches long. Moore was an old hand at Cirkut photography, having taken his first in Vancouver in 1911. By 1931 he had captured hundreds of panoramic and 360 degree views, including one of a May Day celebration in 1923 in the very spot on which he now stood. He ran the motor, listening to how smoothly it was running. It sounded a little off. He ran it once more. Satisfied, he spoke with one of the referees who signaled the teams out onto the field. As they ambled into position *Columbian* newspaper sports editor and announcer Vic Andrews spoke over the new public address system. A circular photograph was going to be taken, he told the 4,500 spectators, would everyone please stay still until the camera had completed its rotation. He need hardly have said it; everyone present knew the drill. The teams' defenders took up their positions in front of their respective goals, the Samonbellies at the south end, the Excelsiors at the north. Brampton's home players gathered on the west side of the field, about twenty yards away from the camera, their folded arms resting on the butt ends of their sticks. One black-capped Salmonbellies player stood next to an Excelsior, their postures indicating that, despite the stakes, the two were on friendly terms. Facing his camera south toward the field house, Moore started its clockwise rotation, a full circle lasting seven or eight minutes.

The camera turned while time stood still.

Or rather 4,500 people plus two referees and two teams stood still. Most of them anyway. As it turned to the west, three Salmonbellies—the first players photographed—decided either to have a little fun or to improve on their images. Knowing full well that the camera in completing its 360 degrees would return to photograph them a second time, they stepped forward a few paces and separated, the player in the middle going ten feet to his left. His teammates, thinking that possibly they would look better wearing their caps, put them on. The other distinct possibility is that they were bored, restless, and wanted to get on with the game. The photograph completed, the players waited a little longer while Moore packed up his equipment and left the field. Former Vancouver players Stan Carter and Ernie Murray replaced Hugh Gifford and Mike Rodden as referees.

THE D. D. MANN TROPHY

EMBLEMATIC OF THE

AMATEUR LACROSSE CHAMPIONSHIP

OF CANADA

1910

Sir Donald Mann, a Canadian railway tycoon, donated in 1910 a trophy in his name to be awarded annually to the senior men's amateur lacrosse champions of Canada. New Westminster won it for the first time in 1915 and retained it for most of the next 15 years.

CANADIAN LACROSSE HALL OF FAME. PHOTOGRAPH BY PHILLIP CHIN.

"The little city on the banks of the Fraser probably never assembled a club with a fighting spirit, in the face of overpowering odds, to compare with the present Salmonbellies."

Don Tyerman, *Vancouver Sun*,
October 12, 1937

CHAPTER SIX
CHASING THE MANN: 1932-1938

In 1932, the Salmonbellies left the grass of Queen's Park for the dirt floor of Queen's Park Arena. The Salmonbellies formed the Senior Box Lacrosse League (under the BCALA umbrella) along with the North Shore Squamish Indians and the Vancouver Athletic Club. New rules and regulations were in force. Dan McKenzie, vice-president of the CLA, explained the new game on radio station CJOR. The sport was now played seven men a side, with five substitutes and an extra goalie. Substitutions were allowed at any time, but the retiring player had to reach his bench before a new player came on. A minor penalty was two minutes; a major penalty was five. And all players had prominently displayed numbers on their jerseys.

The first Salmonbellies box team was composed of Jack Coulter, Wes McLeod, Sonny Douglas, S. Mahoney, Johnny Fraser, Johnny Vernon, Red Fraser, Stu Gifford, Willis Patchell, and goalkeeper Jimmy Mosdell. Grumpy was manager and coach.

On July 1, the Salmonbellies met their first opponent, the Squamish Indians. With the Indians up 2–0, Coulter, a big defenceman from Weston, Ontario, scored the Salmonbellies' first official box goal. Wes McLeod got the second, and Sonny Douglas got the third. Sonny scored two more goals to lead the team to a 12–9 victory.

Within days of the game Sonny became ill with quinsy (peritonsillar abscess), a complication of tonsillitis. Hospitalized, he missed the July 8 game against Vancouver. The infection spread to his lungs. On July 15, at the age of twenty-five, Sonny died of pneumonia in Royal Columbian Hospital.

Doughy's son, Bryce, took Sonny's place on the team. With Brampton unable to represent Canada at the 1932 Olympic games in Los Angeles, an all-star team, with Grumpy and Dan McKenzie as co-coaches, was chosen. Six Salmonbellies and one Squamish Indian made the side: Roland Mercer, Stu Gifford, Johnny Fraser, Bryce Spring, John McQuarrie, and Red Fraser, the only player also on the 1928 Amsterdam squad. The Indian player was goalkeeper Henry Baker. As in 1928, they faced coach Van Orman's Johns Hopkins University team, which represented the United States.

Lacrosse was played on the afternoons of August 7, 9, and 12. The first match took place in front of about 75,000 spectators. Most were there to see track and field events. Olympic officials interrupted the second half of the game to allow for the finish of the marathon, just as they did in Amsterdam. With the sun setting, shadows gathering, and cool breezes blowing in off the ocean, trumpets sounded to announce the entrance of Argentina's Juan Carlos Zabala. A few minutes later, he crossed the finish line and lacrosse resumed, the US winning 5–3. Any advantage the Canadian team might have had as individual players was offset by the cohesiveness of the Johns Hopkins team.

But Canada played aggressively in the second game, the most fiercely contested of the series. The score was tied at four just before the end of the game, when, with an all-out effort, Canada scored.

The deciding game of the series was played before a large crowd, but the second half was shortened to just fifteen minutes to allow the Canadians to catch their ship home. The Americans won the truncated game 7–4, taking the series and the Lally Cup two games to one.[140]

Queen's Park Arena in 1938, the year the famous wooden floor was installed.

Back home in New Westminster, the Salmonbellies struggled, not so much with the new box game as with an aging team, and finished the season in last place with three wins, eight losses, and a tie. The Andy Paull-led Indians took top spot and beat Calgary in the western Canada semifinal, but lost to the Winnipeg Argonauts in the western Canada final. The Mimico Mountaineers beat the Argonauts for the Mann Cup.

In the spring of 1933, many Salmonbellies still opposed giving up the field game. By late April, the team would normally have been out and practising for the coming season, but that year the team hadn't even held its annual meeting. In New Westminster, people were thinking the unthinkable: would there be a Salmonbellies team? The *Columbian*, as in the dark as anyone else, speculated that the Salmonbellies had been hit hard by the Depression.[141]

Grumpy was back as coach. The real issue was players. With a number of veterans dropping out and others at the ends of their careers, how were they going to field not just a team, but a winning team? The answer was to have Salmonbellies' veterans join forces with Andy Paull's up-and-coming Squamish Indians players.

While the Salmonbellies scrambled to put together a team, 1932 Olympic team players Stu Gifford and John McQuarrie, along with Max "Scragg" MacDonald, inspired by the example of the Canadian champion Adanacs basketball team, decided the youth of New Westminster needed an alternative to the Salmonbellies. There was plenty of young lacrosse talent around, but with the Salmonbellies relying on aging veterans and out-of-town Squamish Indians players, the graduating juniors had no place to play in New Westminster. Officers of the Adanacs basketball team were made officers of the new lacrosse club, with Jimmy Gifford agreeing to serve as coach.

Gifford's team, arrayed like the hoopsters in purple and gold, was far from a group of eager young juniors. In fact, it featured aging field players, most of them ex-Salmonbellies. Adanacs' president, Bill Martin, put up the $100 bond the league required, trainer Sam McNee barely scraped together the money to buy sticks, and Cam McKenzie scoured the city in search of bargain-priced running shoes. Jimmy put the team through its paces four evenings a week.

The Salmonbellies, having won their first two games, met the twice-defeated Adanacs for the first time on June 14, 1933. The crowd, noted the *Columbian*, was noticeable by its absence.[142] The new rivals played a clean, fast, entertaining game, won 6–5 by the Salmonbellies.

About six weeks later, the teams met again. Referee Hugh Gifford called a foul on his nephew, Stu Gifford, for roughing Alfie Davy. Stu objected. Hugh told him to keep quiet or he would be banished for the remainder of the game. Later, Hugh called another penalty on Stu, but, as far as the Adanacs were concerned, missed an obvious Salmonbellies' foul. The period over, coach Jimmy Gifford let his brother Hugh know what he thought of his refereeing. Hugh gave it right back to him and then, after turning to go to his dressing room, turned back and swore at Jimmy. That did it; the brothers staged a battle.

In the end, the Salmonbellies won the game, 15–4. Following their losses, the dispirited Adanacs headed straight for Jimmy and Maisie's house. "They came for post mortems and I presided as coroner," said Maisie.[143]

On August 16, the Salmonbellies pitted their old-timers against the upstart Adanacs. The proceeds from the game were to help out with Punk Wintemute's medical and living expenses. Some of Punk's teammates played, including the Rennies, the Giffords, and Buck Marshall. Recently elected New Westminster mayor Fred Hume, an old senior amateur player, also took a few turns on the floor.

Born in 1892 in New Westminster's Sapperton area, Hume left school to support his mother and siblings after the death of his father. He sold newspapers; worked as a store clerk, fisherman, teamster, millworker, fireman and telephone lineman; and found time to play field lacrosse. With a tool kit and $50, he and his brother set up an electrical repair business that grew into Hume and Rumble, the largest electrical contracting firm in western Canada. As a means to selling radio sets, he started BC's second radio station, CFXC, serving as co-owner, manager, and disc jockey. Hume became a New Westminster alderman in 1924 and Mayor in 1933. As affable and popular as he was, "friendly Fred" liked to succeed.

The Salmonbellies won the league 18–6, over Vancouver St. Helen's Hotel, Vancouver Abbotsford Hotel, and the Adanacs. Alfie Davy's brother Les was the Adanacs' top shooter, scoring forty goals to finish third in the league, behind Alfie (sixty-one) and St. Helen's Hotel's Bill Morphett (fifty-seven). The Adanacs won seven of twenty-four games, tying for last place with the Abbotsford Hotel. The Hotels edged them 18–17 in a two-game series to grab the last playoff spot. Of the seventeen Adanacs players only six would return for another season.

The Salmonbellies defeated the Province Bluebirds to advance to the Mann Cup finals against the Hamilton Tigers. The youthful Tigers surprised the Salmonbellies and the spectators with a new tactic, substituting all their players except the goalie every time the ball went out of play. The Salmonbellies adjusted, but after losing the first two games, Dad Turnbull faced off the ball in the third.

Grumpy was animated behind the bench, exhorting his troops, alternating between a megaphone and a cigar. Jack Bryson called the play-by-play into a telephone connected directly to Punk Wintemute.

The Salmonbellies were down a goal in the fourth quarter of the third game when Doughy arrived to watch. Suddenly the team was up by one, hanging on for an 8–7 victory. At the buzzer Grumpy erupted with joy, doing his war dance with his arms around Willis Patchell's neck. And why not? Had the team not rebounded from a poor 1932 season to at least one win in the Canadian finals?

Between October 9, 1933 and May 7, 1935 Alf Davy scored at least one goal in forty-one consecutive games—a record that stood for over forty years until broken by Victoria's Kevin Alexander. Davy sat out the 1937 Mann Cup with a broken arm.

CANADIAN LACROSSE HALL OF FAME.

Invigorated, the Salmonbellies won game 4, 12–10, on the leadership and hard defensive work of Patchell and the inspired offence of the "sly and elusive" Stoddart, who played nearly the entire sixty minutes, scored the winning goal, and added the twelfth.[144] But the team paid a price. In the dressing room, three Salmonbellies collapsed from exhaustion and had to be revived by a doctor.

The fifth game went Monday night. Scalpers were asking and getting $10 for a pair of tickets. Queen's Park was crammed. But the Tigers pulled out a win, 12–7, and took home the Mann Cup.

The Great Depression hit its lowest point in 1934. The Senior Box Lacrosse League was renamed the Inter-City Lacrosse League (ICLL). At Queen's Park Arena, lacrosse fans were kept informed of developments on the floor by way of a newly installed public address system. Vancouver radio station CJOR broadcast the first regular-season lacrosse game. Behind the microphone was Lionel Edward "Leo" Nicholson.

Forty-three years old, Nicholson looked like a fading screen idol with his slicked-back hair and pencil moustache. He wore a natty suit and tie, a silk handkerchief spilling out of his breast pocket. At Queen's Park he called the games from front row seats, not from the press box. His loud, machine-gun-like cadence captured the speed and excitement of the games. "He's burning up those far boards fast," was typical of Nicholson's patter.[145] Every Monday and Friday night during the lacrosse season, thousands of listeners tuned in to hear the man that made the phrase "the fastest game on two feet" famous. Nicholson's broadcasts did more to popularize box lacrosse and bring people out to the games than any other factor. "You could walk half a mile along any street in White Rock during the summer and never miss a play, everyone would be outside with the radio tuned in to Nicholson's broadcast of the lacrosse game," recalled Salmonbellie Ralph Burton.

The 1934 season ended with the Salmonbellies in second place with fourteen wins and ten losses. Alfie Davy scored eighty-one goals with nineteen assists to win the league scoring honours, becoming the first Salmonbellie to reach 100 points in a season.

New Westminster defeated the third-place Vancouver Province Bluebirds in the league semi-finals, then met the league's first-place team, the Vancouver St. Helen's Hotels. Davy was outstanding in the opener, a 20–9 Salmonbellies' victory. "Little Alf Davy was the man who stole most of the glory during the battle," reported the *British Columbian*. "Although slashed at, cut down, tripped and generally mauled around, and for the greater part of the evening covered by two or three men, the Fishmen's scoring ace banged in 8 goals to lead his team to an overwhelming triumph."[146]

The Salmonbellies lost two games to Vancouver, but won two more to advance to the western finals against the Winnipeg Wellingtons, coached by Art Somers, a Stanley Cup winner with the 1933 New York Rangers. The Salmonbellies took game one 12–8. In the second game, on September 27, Davy set marks that still stand, scoring twelve goals—a record—with four assists, for a total of sixteen points—another record. The final score was a merciless 33–5 Salmonbellies victory.

The Salmonbellies boarded a train for Ontario, where they faced the Orillia Terriers in the Mann Cup. North of Toronto, Orillia is located on the shores of two connected lakes, Simcoe and Chouchiching, home to the Huron and Iroquois, who played baggataway, lacrosse's fore-runner. The Mann Cup, however, was to be played in Barrie, about twenty-two miles south of Orillia. Its citizens were excited to host the first national championship of any kind played in their town.

Playing on a clay floor, the Salmonbellies lost the opener 21–8. Bill Wilson's "weaving hips

In the 1933 Mann Cup the Hamilton Tigers surprised the Salmonbellies when they used a new tactic, substituting all their players except the goalie every time the ball went out of play.

CANADIAN LACROSSE HALL OF FAME. PHOTOGRAPH BY PHILLIP CHIN.

and brilliant runs carried him through the sieve-like Salmonbellie defense"[147] in the second game, in which he recorded nine goals and five assists in a 19–6 Terriers' victory. Wilson had nearly out-Davy'ed Davy. Orillia then won the third game 13–6 to capture the national title. It was little consolation to Davy, but in the five games that constituted the Mann Cup playoffs (two Winnipeg games plus three Orillia games), he scored a total of twenty-two goals—another record that still stands seventy-eight years later.

Back home in New Westminster Grumpy explained the Salmonbellies' poor showing: "There are only three reasons why we lost. The Terriers are one darned good lacrosse team, the lighting was poor, and the floor was made of clay, and …" he continued, citing the fourth of his "three" reasons, "those eastern referees certainly were terrible."[148]

Hume had accompanied the team to Barrie and watched with dismay as the Terriers swept the series. It did not sit well with him; the Salmonbellies were due for an overhaul. He began by asking the Adanacs if they were interested in combining forces. They weren't.

Before the start of the 1935 season, Hume released several Squamish players and let others go to Richmond. He lost Alfie Davy to the Vancouver Bluebirds and was left with a lot of aging field stars, including Doughy, goalie Bernie Feedham, Bob Turnbull, Red Fraser, Johnny Vernon, and Jack Wood. Wood's old Olympic teammate, Flickie Doyle, played four games in 1935 and netted one goal. Hume filled in the rest of the roster with players from senior B.

Andy Paull picked up the six Indians released by Hume, added ten other Squamish players, and recruited five standouts from Brantford, Ontario's Six Nations team, including Stu Bomberry, Jack Squires, and Russell Smith. The North Shore Indians were back in business and stronger than ever.

Early in the season, the Salmonbellies took on their former teammates at the Arena. Old teammates or not, the two sides went at it with a vengeance. When a fight broke out between Doughy and Stan Joseph, Salmonbellies' trainer Fraser Rowan made the mistake of walking behind the Indians' bench. Coach Andy Paull promptly crowned him with a megaphone, attracting the attention of the Salmonbellies' Wilf Hill. The "megaphone battle" was on, both benches emptying. Before the game was over, rookie Salmonbellie Bill Tyler needed five stitches to close a gash in his head—no penalty called.

Paull's action with the megaphone was not an isolated event. "Andy

Leo Nicholson, the unmistakable voice of box lacrosse in BC from 1933 to 1945. He put people in seats for lacrosse games like no one else. A trophy in his name has been awarded annually since 1948 to the outstanding senior goalkeeper in the west.

CANADIAN LACROSSE HALL OF FAME.

The microphone of the PA system used in the early days at Queen's Park Arena. It was donated to the Canadian Lacrosse Hall Of Fame by the Salmonbellies' first water boy, George Leaf.

CANADIAN LACROSSE HALL OF FAME.
PHOTOGRAPH BY PHILLIP CHIN.

The 1937 Salmonbellies, Mann Cup champs and "the downright fightingest club" ever. **Back row:** Max Turner, Ralph Burton, Sonny Smith, Pete Meehan, Raymond "Punch" Thompson, Harold Henry, Jack Coulter, Bill Wilkes. **Centre row:** Fred Foreman (trainer), Ken Featherstone, Harry Campbell, Lorne Munro, Louie McKinnon, Tommy Gordon, Willis Patchell. **Bottom row:** Jack Hughes, Pete Anthony, Bill Wilson, Mayor Fred Hume, Grumpy Spring, Bill Tyler, Ed Downey, Red Fraser. One of Grumpy's sons sits in front of Hume. **Missing from picture:** Alfie Davy, Hop Ayles, Lloyd Cameron. The photo was taken before practice against Queen's Park Arena's rear doors. Burton and Thompson, junior players, travelled from White Rock to practice with the team, and arrived late. Grumpy told them not to bother getting into their practice gear and to get in the picture.

CANADIAN LACROSSE HALL OF FAME.

Paull loved the game of lacrosse to the point where he would become violent or argumentative if he didn't agree with the outcome or decision,"[149] lacrosse statistician Stan Shillington is quoted as saying. Upset after a game, he once tried to jam a referee's tobacco pipe down the official's throat. On another occasion he blew a whistle, halting the opposing team's breakaway and allowing his team to catch up. Lacrosse fans loved his antics and came out in the thousands—up to 10,000 a game—to see the talented Indians play at their home arena, the Denman Street Forum in downtown Vancouver.

The Salmonbellies met the Indians in a game meaningless to the playoff picture, but of personal interest to Johnny Vernon and Indians' star Ray Baker, who were vying for league scoring honours. Baker scored four goals and one assist to Vernon's three and one, and with one game in hand, eventually overtook Vernon to win the scoring race by just one point.

Jack Wood, who, along with Vernon, had rallied the team all season long, fittingly scored the team's regular season-ending goal, suffering a broken rib and torn side muscles in the effort: 15–10 Salmonbellies. Wood got a measure of consolation when he won the Maitland MVP trophy. "I think we dropped something like 14 games by 1 goal," he recalled in 1954, "but we had a lot of fun that summer."[150]

Richmond won the league with eighteen wins in twenty-four games, and the Salmonbellies ended up in last place with just four wins. Worse, they finished behind their upstart city rivals, the Adanacs, who won five more games. Paull's Indians were 14–10. The Richmond Farmers defeated the Indians three games to one in the league finals, earning the right to meet the Orillia Terriers for the Mann Cup.

As far as Hume was concerned, "the great Salmonbellies machine was wrecked."[151] He had financed the Westminster Royals soccer team to three Canadian championships. He promised to do the same for the Salmonbellies. "I'm not talking through this hat of mine. I'm in the market for a championship team. You know what we did with the Westminster Royals. Well, we're going to do the same thing in lacrosse next season."[152]

Hume devised a plan. And he had the money, reputation and influence to make it happen. During the Mann Cup series, Hume arranged to meet the Terriers' four best players (Bill Wilson, Bill Wilkes, Ed Downey, and Lorne "Toar" Munro) at their lodgings at the Hotel Vancouver. Jobs were scarce, and money was in short supply. In the hungry '30s, a position on a team meant a job and security. Hume offered them permanent jobs or, if work was unavailable, he would guarantee them each $20 a week. They signed. Later, Hume also secured the services of Bill Mullis and of Canada's best goalkeeper, Pete Anthony.

Despite the addition of the Ontario stars and the Adanacs' Pete Meehan, the Salmonbellies' 1936 season got off to a bad start, even before their season opener. Wilson, a bus driver by day, was in an auto wreck; Anthony got struck in the eye by a ball during practice; Wilkes twisted his ankle; and Mullis, who worked with Wilkes at a New Westminster service station, suffered a leg injury when the brakes of the car they were positioning for the hoist failed, pinning Mullis against a concrete wall. But by May 7, all the easterners except Wilkes joined the Salmonbellies veterans at Queen's Park for the season opener against the Adanacs.

When the team hit the floor, the fans barely recognized them, with all the new faces in brand new jerseys—dark red with a light stripe across the shoulders and on top of the arms, a sharp departure from the old red and blue uniforms. It was a new team with a new look, but could they win?

Not that night against the Adanacs, an 18–11 defeat. And not in their second and third games, either, with losses to Richmond and the Indians. The team still struggled, unable to gel.

Hume stepped in. The Salmonbellies' president, mayor of the city and one of BC's most powerful businessmen, told them they had to sort out their differences and start playing as a team. It wasn't intended to be inspirational; it was a threat. They got the message and turned themselves around, winning nine straight league games to finish with fourteen wins and ten losses.

Known among his teammates for the constant comic ribbing he dished out, team captain Wilson was all business when it came to scoring, more than doubling his 1935 stats with seventy-seven goals and twenty-seven assists—best in the league by sixteen points. Jack Wood

The Orillia Terriers won the Mann Cup three years in a row (1934-1936) before Salmonbellies president Fred Hume enticed four Terriers–Bill Wilkes, Bill Wilson, Ed Downey, and Lorne Munro-and Hamilton's goaltender Pete Anthony to New Westminster in 1937. l-r: Ernie Curran, coach Frank Carroll (wearing hat), Bill Wilson, Bill Wilkes, Len Wilkes, Bruno Cavello. Ken Pethick behind Carroll and Tommy Scott immediately behind Pethick. Two players in upper left unidentified.

DOWNEY FAMILY.

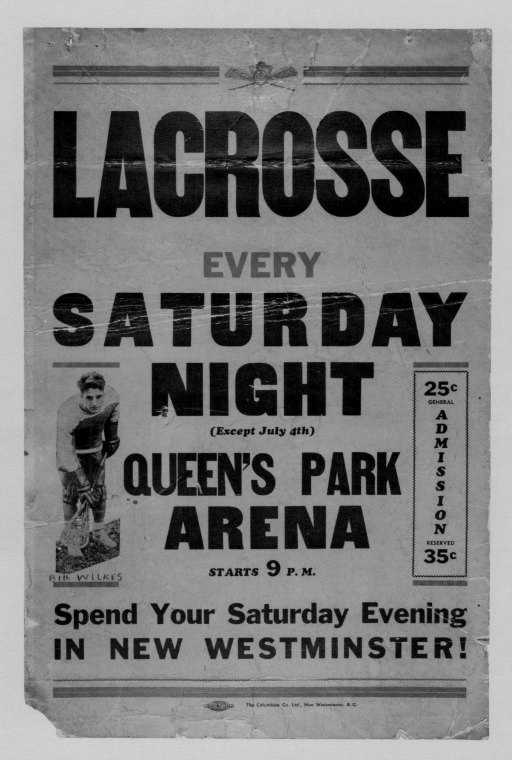

A fierce intra-city rivalry between the Salmonbellies and the Adanacs combined with big name attractions such as Wilkes, Downey and Wilson, and with Leo Nicholson broadcasting the games over the radio, Queen's Park Arena was packed to capacity on Saturday nights in 1937.

CANADIAN LACROSSE HALL OF FAME. PHOTOGRAPH BY PHILLIP CHIN.

finished fourth with seventy-four points. But Paull's North Shore Indians swept the Salmonbellies 3–0 for the BC championship.

The Indians went to the Mann Cup at Toronto's Maple Leaf Gardens, but lost the first game to Orillia 10–8. The Indians tied the series, winning game two 8–6. Paull, ever the promoter, had the team out to various evening functions. Their weariness showed in the third game, an 11–9 loss. But the Indians were front-page news and more than 10,000 fans attended game 4. Unfortunately for Paull and his team, they suffered a 20–9 loss. It was the Terrier's third straight Mann Cup. Paull took it hard. It was his team's first Mann Cup appearance and it would be their last.

The 1937 Salmonbellies practised hard. "The practices were tougher than the games," recalled Ralph Burton. "We suffered more injuries in practice."[153] It paid off— they won their first eight games. The Arena sold out for just about every contest. At the end of the regular season, the Salmonbellies topped the standings at 22–6. The Adanacs finished second at 15–13.

A new team, the Burrard Olympics, founded by Les Dickinson, Bill Calder, and Ed Bayley, finished last in the standings, but young players like Les Dickinson's son Bill, Chuck Morphett, and John and Roy Cavallin showed great promise. The Olympics played out of the Vancouver Forum. Built in 1931, it seated about 5,000 people, half of what the Denman Arena, which had burned down the previous August, once held.

Bill Wilson led the Salmonbellies in scoring, averaging five points a game. His smooth style of play—the press called him "the blonde ghost"—made it look easy. Line mate Bill Wilkes was productive too, averaging more than four points per game and earning league MVP. Wilkes was also a pesky defender, irritating opponents with his stick checks, delivered rapid fire to wrists and forearms. "Little twelve inch chops" is how Vancouver Burrards' Johnny Cavillin described them. "But you'd swear he was winding up with an axe the way he jolted you."[154] Opponents' arms would be black and blue by the end of games.

Mann Cups seemed to follow Ed Downey. He won one with the Hamilton Tigers in 1933, two with the Orillia Terriers in 1934 and 1935, and two with the Salmonbellies in 1937 and 1943.

DOWNEY FAMILY.

Seventeen games into the regular season, Alfie Davy broke his left arm, knocking him out of further competition. Davy had been on a record-breaking tear, scoring sixty-four goals with twenty-two assists—over five points a game on average—prior to his injury. When the regular season wound up eleven games later, his eighty-six points were still good enough for fourth best in the league behind the three Bills—the Olympics' Dickinson and the Salmonbellies' Wilkes and Wilson.

Spring's men faced the Richmond-Homes Combines in the league finals. Hume promised the players new hats if they won the first game. They did. Hume promised bands on their new hats if they won the second game. Getting in on the act, another supporter, "Toots" Phillips, promised the team new ties and Grumpy a new shirt, if they won the second game. But the Salmonbellies lost the second game. They did, however, win the next two to capture the league title, and ended up getting those new hats and ties for the team and shirt for Grumpy. They then defeated the Trail Smoker Eaters 2–0 for the BC championship and waited for the eastern representatives—presumably the Orillia Terriers—to arrive for the Mann Cup.

The Terriers faced a more grueling route to the championship than the Salmonbellies did. The defending Mann Cup champions tied Mimico Mountaineers for first place in the seven-team Ontario league, and defeated Brampton Excelsiors in the quarterfinals, St. Catharines Athletics in the semifinals, and the Mimico Mountaineers in the finals. They then defeated Cornwall at home in Orillia in the eastern semifinals and the Montréal Canadiens in the finals. In the Dominion quarterfinals, they defeated Winnipeg's Elmwood Pats and, in the final, Alberta's Calgary Rangers. Having battled through sixteen playoff games—practically a season in itself—and already racking up thousands of railway miles, the team boarded a train bound for the west coast.

The Terriers had not won the Mann Cup three years running without being an exceptional team with great coaching. They had 59-year-old Frank Carroll behind the bench, a man who excelled at not only coaching but at boxing (he was the 1906 Canadian welterweight champ) and hockey. Between 1913 and 1923, he was involved as a trainer or a coach with a number of amateur and professional championship hockey teams in Toronto, including coach of the St. Patricks, the precursor to the Maple Leafs, in 1920–21. But Carroll was best known in his day as the coach of the Springfield Indians, a minor league hockey team owned by the New York Rangers. He took the Indians to three league championships in the late 1920s and early 1930s. In 1928 he coached the Canadian boxing team at the Amsterdam Olympic games. In May of 1932, he was appointed coach of the Montreal Maroons in the short-lived IPLL. He gave up coaching hockey in 1933 and turned again to lacrosse, taking the helm of the Terriers prior to the start of their Mann Cup run in 1934.

In his ten seasons (1936-46) with the Salmonbellies, Bill Wilkes scored a combined 845 points over 284 games, an average of three points a game. His outstanding performance despite a painful, badly sprained, tape-encased ankle in the 1937 Mann Cup finals at Queen's Park ranks as one of the all-time great efforts in Salmonbellies history.

CANADIAN LACROSSE HALL OF FAME.

Spring's bench was not nearly as deep as Carroll's. If the Salmonbellies were going to win the 1937 Mann Cup, they would have to do it on the strength of just seven men: Wilkes, Wilson, Downey, Meehan, Campbell, Munro, and Anthony. Actually, everything depended on six healthy men and one with a badly sprained ankle. Wilkes, the league's second highest scorer and MVP, had injured his ankle during the Trail series and wrenched it again stepping off the train on the team's return to New Westminster. On paper, the Salmonbellies were doomed. Despite having the home advantage and despite the Terriers' long road to the coast, the Salmonbellies would be lucky to win a single game. And yet they were confident of victory. Or more to the point, they were determined to win.

The Terriers arrived in Vancouver, where they would be staying, on the morning of the first game, Friday, October 8. The opener had been sold out since Thursday. Sellout or not, hundreds of fans gathered at Queen's Park anyway, hoping to find a scalper with a seat to flog or to score a spot among the standing-room-only crowd. When most of them could not find a way in, they stuck around outside, just to be near the action. CJOR's Leo Nicholson was ready to call the game. Oscar Swanson, now manning the controls of the newly installed Imperial Tobacco timing clock, took his place at the end of the press box.

A blue cloud of cigarette smoke already hung in the rafters as the Terriers took to the floor, resplendent in their royal purple and white uniforms, the word TERRIERS across their chests running in uppercase through the "O" for Orillia. They received polite applause from the partisan crowd, punctuated by boos and hisses.

The Salmonbellies followed, receiving a thunderous ovation as they appeared in their red jerseys with light blue shoulder stripe, a big salmon set against an even bigger "W" emblazoned across their chests. The centres came together, and referee Hugh Gifford faced off the ball.

The Terriers' Ernie Curran scored first, but the Salmonbellies' little gum-chewing goalie just chewed harder. The Salmonbellies led 3–2 at the quarter and 7–6 at the half. Coach Carroll replaced McArthur—known as "old spindleshanks" because of his age and thin legs—at halftime with young Mortimer. At the end of the third quarter, the Salmonbellies still led by one goal, 9–8. With ten minutes remaining and the Salmonbellies up 11–8, Wilkes sprained his bad ankle and was helped off the floor, his game over. Red Fraser subbed in. Moments later, Downey was sent off for five minutes. Campbell followed him for two.

Short two men, the Salmonbellies fought off Orillia's power play. The Terriers' "Yorky" Jordan scored with three minutes remaining. With more than 5,000 fans on their feet and the Terriers pressing, Downey returned to the floor, followed by Campbell, and the Salmonbellies hung on for Swanson's game ending bell: 11–9 Salmonbellies.

Announcer Nicholson's voice was hoarse; he could barely talk. The fans erupted in jubilation. In the dressing room, Wilkes, his ankle throbbing, lay writhing on a stretcher while trainer Fred Foreman cut off a thick wad of adhesive tape. Munro's three goals—long-range sub-shot torpedoes—and three assists had led the way, but it was the little guy, gum-chewing Pete Anthony, who'd won the game for them, with thirty-two acrobatic stops—eleven in the fourth quarter alone.

The Terriers had gone into game 1 knowing what they were up against. Five of the Salmonbellies' starters were old teammates of theirs. They also knew the Salmonbellies lacked bench strength. The Terriers had expected to win the first encounter on their way to a fourth Mann Cup. What they did not expect was New Westminster's resolve.

Game 2 took place at Vancouver's Forum on Canadian Thanksgiving, the second Monday in October. Wilkes, under team doctor's orders, had stayed in bed and off his ankle at the Royal Columbian Hospital over the weekend. He was now ready to play, his ankle encased in tape.

The game was 2–2 at the end of the first quarter. In the second quarter, referee Gifford crossed his legs when reversing and went head over heels, losing three front teeth on the landing. He must have looked up and half-expected to see Newsy Lalonde.

The Terriers led 6–4 at the half. During the break, Carroll urged his players to slow things down. The Salmonbellies wanted fast play, but Carroll believed a more deliberate pace would allow the Terriers to better control the game. They were up by two goals. Grind it out for another half and they would win. In the hallway outside the dressing room, Ernie Curran shook his head. He didn't want to listen to Carroll. The Terriers had come this far on speed. All of a sudden they were supposed to hit the brakes? Why? Wilkes was hobbled and the Salmonbellies had no second string. They had not substituted a single player so far in the game. At some point, exhaustion was going to catch up to them and they would make mistakes. Why not run them into the ground?

With the third period underway, Spring was unimpressed with his team's hustle. "Well, let's check a couple of guys anyway!" he yelled. "You fellows play lacrosse like I do drop the handkerchief! Come on, let's go!"[155] The Salmonbellies responded, scoring three goals in two-and-a-half minutes. At the end of the three-quarter mark, the Salmonbellies led 9–7. But the Terriers rallied to score three in the fourth to lead 10–9. After the Terriers' third goal the crowd groaned collectively, sensing a shift in momentum and a looming Salmonbellies' loss. But a limping Wilkes passed to Wilson, who tied the score. Sixty-four hundred electrified spectators jumped to their feet. Two minutes later, Wilkes, seemingly oblivious to the pain

A five-foot-eleven, 205-pound defenceman, Downey could also score. He averaged two goals a game in the 1937 regular season and in the nine playoff games leading to a Mann Cup victory, he notched thirty-six points.

DOWNEY FAMILY.

in his ankle, scored to put the team in front. Another four goals followed. The Salmonbellies had pulled out a second win with an incredible six-goal rally. "The blond ghost" led them in scoring with five goals and two assists. "This is the downright fightin'est club I've ever played on," said a grinning Wilson.[156] Wilkes, who had hit the dressing room for fresh ankle tape at the end of each quarter, had somehow managed to score two goals, with three assists. Meehan, Munro, and Wilson had each played the entire sixty minutes. The Salmonbellies had used just three substitutes—Fraser, Hughes, and Tyler. But Tyler, with a knee injury, barely touched the floor. The Terriers had fresh legs out all game long, using thirteen players in total.

After the game, a frustrated Carroll spoke to reporters. "We look dead out there—no pep, no fire—ah, nuts, what's the use? Every one of these Salmonbellies is in perfect shape. It's little wonder such boys as Downey, Wilson, Wilkes, and Munro," he continued, naming each of the players he evidently still thought of as his own, "can go at top speed for 60 minutes. This big guy, Connell, ought to be ashamed of himself—one run up the floor and he's all in."[157]

Hugh "Shipwreck" Kelly won one Mann Cup with Hamilton in 1933 and two with Orillia in 1935 and 1936. In the Terriers' 1937 Mann Cup run he scored 45 points over 18 games.

DOWNEY FAMILY.

The "big guy" was defenceman Jerry "Carnera" Connell, so called because he resembled the 1933/34 World Heavyweight boxing champion, Italian Primo Carnera. Connell and two of his teammates, Bill Curran and Yorky Jordan, would further test their coach's patience. On Monday night, they broke training and spent a night on the town. Carroll was incensed. Connell, Curran, and Jordan were benched for game 3.

The Salmonbellies' chance of winning the third game and the cup, despite two wins under their belts, was thrown in doubt by Campbell's stomach flu, Meehan's recovery from a crippling check in game two, Tyler's stay in the hospital with an infected knee, and Wilkes's bad ankle. But all four were in uniform for Wednesday night's battle in front of 5,506 fans, including, of course, Nicholson, Hume, Swanson, Haddie Stoddart, and more former Salmonbellies and Adanacs than anyone could count.

The Salmonbellies jumped out to a 6–2 lead at the end of the first quarter and led 10–3 at the half. A few minutes into the second half "Shipwreck" Kelly clipped Munro in the head. Foreman wrapped a bandage around it, and Munro stayed in the game, the bandage growing bloodier by the minute. At the end of the third quarter, it was 14–4. With the fourth ticking down and the game won, Spring sent out sentimental favourite Red Fraser. Fraser missed on his first shot, but he found the net on his second. It was his first goal of the series and his last goal as a Salmonbellie. The crowd gave him a standing ovation. When Oscar Swanson rang the bell, it was Salmonbellies 19, Terriers 12. New Westminster had another Mann Cup, its fourteenth ever and its first in ten years.

The Arena exploded. Seat cushions, peanuts, hats, and programs filled the air and littered the floor. Hume hugged Anthony. Spring hugged Wilson. And for good reason. Wilson had scored forty-five points (thirty-one goals and fourteen assists) with just six minutes in penalties during the nine playoff games—five points a game, on average. Campbell was nearly as good with thirty-six points in nine games.

The Terriers showed their sportsmanship, shaking hands with the victors.

Sweat soaked and blood stained, the Salmonbellies made their way to the dressing room. Players sang impromptu victory songs. Grumpy passed around a bottle from his private stock, "too happy to say anything," he claimed.[158] Mayor Hume, repeating, "We've done it at last" over and over, had finally realized his ambition.[159]

A lone figure, his arm in a sling, watched the celebrations from the periphery, happy but envious. He had watched as Wilson with six goals and two assists, Wilkes with three goals and two assists, Munro with five goals and two assists, and Downey with two goals and four assists accounted for sixteen of the Salmonbellies' nineteen goals in the final game. How Alfie Davy, the hometown boy, wished he had been in on it.

For the rest of the night and into the morning, Salmonbellies and their fans gathered to celebrate a lacrosse triumph where so many had gathered to celebrate before—Columbia Street. In front of Oscar Swanson's sporting goods shop they built a bonfire. Swanson threw in his hat to cheers from the mob. Motorists were stopped and not allowed to proceed until they had honked their horns. A fire truck arrived, its siren screaming. Radio announcer Leo Nicholson was aboard, fire hat on head, a monkey wrench serving as his microphone as he "broadcast" the celebratory insanity. When someone tore down a locksmith shop's giant key sign to present the "key" to the city to Munro, the police thought things had gone too far, but Swanson intervened. "Let 'em have it," he said. "They can have my store, too, if they want it."[160] When daylight came, the only damage the city works department found, other than the missing key sign, was a large area of melted, mushy asphalt.

As for the Terriers, they caught a train. The road-weary and defeated team pulled into Orillia on a rainy Monday. In 1934, 1935, and 1936, half the city's population and a marching band had turned out to welcome them back. On that day, there was an empty platform and no music. The Terriers would never again win a Mann Cup. A year later, Frank Carroll, one of the outstanding coaches of his generation, died.

Most of the players from the 1937 Salmonbellies were back the following year, with the notable exception of Bill Wilson, who'd departed for St. Catharines. Defenceman Downey had a ninety-two-point regular season, with sixty-two goals and thirty assists, to lead all scorers in the league. Only the Adanacs' Jim Douglas scored more goals with seventy. The season ended with the Adanacs on top with seventeen wins and seven losses, the Salmonbellies second at fifteen and nine, and the Burrards third at fourteen and ten. The Salmonbellies defeated the Burrards in two games in the first round of the playoffs and faced the Adanacs for the league title for the first time.

The Adanacs had been on a slow and steady upward climb since their founding in 1933. From 1934 through 1936 they had lost more games than they won, but in 1937 they won fifteen of twenty-eight to finish second to the Burrards.

The Adanacs were even stronger in 1938. Douglas, Bradbury, Lee, and Matthison were the Adanacs' big guns (in that order) during the regular season, but it was Lee with nine goals and four assists, Phelan with six and six, and Matthison with five and six who led the Adanacs to three straight wins over the Salmonbellies in the playoffs. The Adanacs then defeated the Nelson Maple Leafs for the BC championship and Medicine Hat for the western championship.

The Adanacs next faced the powerhouse Athletics in the Mann Cup in St. Catharines. The Athletics featured Roy "Pung" Morton, Joe Cheever, Jack "Wandy" McMahon, Carl "Gus" Madsen, "Shipwreck" Kelly, and Bill Wilson. Wilson was only slightly less outstanding for the Athletics than he had been for the Salmonbellies, scoring fifty-five goals in twenty-four regular-season games and ten playoff goals. The Athletics swept the Adanacs 3–0 to capture the Mann Cup. It was Wilson's fifth Mann Cup in seven years, the first coming with Hamilton in 1933, the next two with Orillia in 1934 and 1935, and the fourth with the Salmonbellies.

In 1934 the Orillia Terriers defeated the Salmonbellies in Barrie, Ontario, winning the first of three Mann Cup championships in a row. One of the game balls is preserved in the Canadian Lacrosse Hall of Fame.

CANADIAN LACROSSE HALL OF FAME.
PHOTOGRAPH BY PHILLIP CHIN.

Many Salmonbellies and Adanacs joined the RCAF "team" in the fight
to liberate Europe from Hitler's Third Reich.

Bill Wilkes, *Vancouver Sun*, May 9, 1939

CHAPTER SEVEN
THE WAR YEARS: 1939-1946

For playing in a short-lived California professional league in 1938, Pete Anthony and other Salmonbellies and Adanacs players were suspended by the league. With Anthony unavailable pending a decision on reinstatement, Spring turned to 16-year-old junior prospect William Scuby for the season opener against the Adanacs. Scuby, son of Greek immigrant parents, was born in 1923 in Battle Creek, Michigan, and raised in New Westminster. Scuby and his lacrosse-playing cohort—among them future Salmonbellie Gordon Arrell and future Adanac Sam Kabatow—cleared a vacant lot on Colborne street, near Queen's Park, and "salvaged" Sweet Caps and Coca-Cola sign boards to make a single backstop. The boys could be found playing all day long in the summer.

The young netminder, in his first senior game, was as nervous as the Salmonbellies' defence was porous. The Forum was full. "I was distracted by the crowd; I'd never seen so many people in one place before,"[161] said Scuby. The Adanacs scored thirty-six goals, not all of them on Scuby, who was pulled in favour of Harry Sharpe late in the second period, with the score at fifteen to two. The final score was 36–10.

With the second game of the season looming against the Richmond Farmers, a desperate Spring tried out eight goalies before settling on Dick Walsh, a former Mimico, Ontario, player and Cliff Quayle, a local intermediate. Spring alternated between Quayle and Walsh over the next few weeks. Both players performed well, but the more experienced Walsh won the starting position. Goalies, however, were just starting to experiment with face masks and Walsh wasn't wearing one at practice when he took a ball to the face on a hard shot by rookie Harry Carter, smashing his nose in four places.

With Anthony still out and his interim starter Walsh permanently out, Spring turned once again to Scuby, who had returned to his Knights of Pythias-sponsored juvenile team. Scuby, well on his way to reaching six-foot-two had just finished a game at the Edmonds box in Burnaby. Still sweating, he watched as a large black touring sedan with running boards pulled up. Out of the automobile came the familiar figure of Grumpy, overcoat flapping, Fedora on his head, cigar clamped in his mouth. "Hey, kid," he asked Scuby, "You wanna play a game tonight?" Sure he did. "Okay, hop in, we're late."[162] The pair set off down Kingsway, heading for Vancouver's Hastings Forum. As Spring drove, Scuby asked who they were playing. "North

Shore Indians, kid." "Oh, God!" thought Scuby. The Indians had a well-deserved reputation for scoring goals.

Outside the Forum, Spring tossed Scuby a Salmonbellies' jersey. Looking down the tunnel into the building, Scuby could see the team already warming up. With just minutes to faceoff, he didn't even have enough time to change out of his Knights of Pythias sweater. He took a large breath, pulled the Salmonbellies jersey over his head, and hustled in. This time Scuby went the distance, stopping twenty-two shots in a 35–14 Salmonbellies' rout.

Salmonbellie Bill "Whoopie" Tyler tries to decapitate Adanac "Punch" Thompson in 1939.

Showering after the game, Scuby felt something other than water running down his ankle. Turning, he caught one of his new teammates laughingly urinating on his leg. He was officially a Salmonbellie. He scrubbed hard "for about half an hour" after the baptism.[163]

Anthony and the other suspended players were reinstated in time for the next game, a match against each other's teams. Despite Scuby's performance against the Indians, Spring opted for his veteran keeper in the next game. Thinking of Walsh's bashed-in nose, Anthony started the game wearing a mask, but it was uncomfortable, so he discarded it for the second and third periods.

Anthony's play in that game and the next few was as uneven as the rest of the team's performance. By the middle of July, the Salmonbellies were nine and seven. Spring constantly shuffled his line up, bringing in new players just about every game. He needed a couple of big defencemen, but there were none to be had. He also needed to stop the revolving door at goalkeeper. This kid Scuby, he thought, might be the one, but he needed more seasoning. In the meantime the Salmonbellies kept battling—and mostly lost.

The Burrards led the league, trailed by the Adanacs. The Salmonbellies held third, while Richmond was fourth, and the Indians fifth, with only one win in sixteen games. Anthony, his concentration wavering, was letting in easy shots. He told Spring he wanted opportunities to play out of net. Spring obliged. With the veteran often more out than in, Spring put between the posts whoever he could find, including occasional goalie George "Hop" Ayles, a 21-year-old attacker with three Salmonbellies' seasons already behind him. Ayles was in net when Anthony scored his only goal, the team edging the Adanacs seventeen to fifteen at the Arena.

The Salmonbellies concluded the regular season with thirteen wins, eleven losses, third place behind the Adanacs (18–6) and the Burrards (19–5).

The Salmonbellies and the Adanacs met in the semifinals. The Adanacs, backstopped by Ed Johnson, took the first two games 17–12 and 17–11. But in a practice before the third game, they lost Bob Lee to an eye injury. He was out for the rest of the playoffs.

The Salmonbellies, with Anthony turning in his "best display of the year,"[164] won game three 13–8. Anthony received rave reviews. He made "miraculous saves," "9 great stops," and was "spectacular," wrote the British Columbian.

After the game, Anthony claimed that the first team to score thirteen goals in a game always won, no matter how many more goals were scored—an odd thing for a goalie to say with his team heading into a must-win game in a best-of-five series. Anthony let in eight of nine shots in the first quarter of game 4, one of two shots in the second, and eight of ten in the third. The Salmonbellies couldn't have done much worse with an empty net. By Anthony's reckoning the Salmonbellies had already lost the game halfway through the third quarter. The "spectacular" and "miraculous" goaltender was suddenly awful.

The play was almost incidental to the fighting. Three bouts broke out in the first quarter, one featuring Adanac "Dutch" Hadden who, after Ken Fetherston's stick raised a large bump over this eye, "went berserk."[165] But those scraps were merely the undercard.

With five minutes remaining in the game, Bill Wilkes, usually the most sportsmanlike of players, dropped his gloves and started pummelling rookie Adanac Brud Matheson, who'd been slashing him all game long. The referee stayed well back as the men had at it, the teams barely managing to restrain themselves. But when blood oozed from Brud's face after a punching marathon, Adanacs and Salmonbellies sprang from their benches, squaring off. The Adanacs' coach, Jimmy Gifford, grabbed Wilkes from behind and hurled him to the floor. Salmonbellies' small but feisty Jack Hughes retaliated, bravely tackling Gifford. As they wrestled, things got even more cockeyed when the Adanacs' team doctor, W.A. Robertson, found himself tussling with little guy Harold "Mousy" Davy, Alfie's brother. Hadden, of the swollen eyelid, wasted no time, vaulting out of the penalty box and going toe-to-toe with Bert Bryant at centre floor.

It took five minutes for the referees to separate the multiple combatants and Constable Gordon Prowse to separate Hadden and Bryant. The game resumed, but the bloodletting was not over. With three minutes remaining, the Adanacs' Ken Matheson, Brud's older brother, and the Salmonbellies' Ken Fetherston mixed it up. The crowd, chanting "Let 'em fight!" got what they wanted, the refs leaving it to field player Constable Red Fraser to break up the fight, hauling Fetherston by the seat of his shorts off Matheson.

The Adanacs scored six goals on six shots in the fourth quarter to win 23–13, knocking the Salmonbellies out of contention. "Someone bribed Anthony," claimed Ralph Burton.[166] A week later the little goalie was sporting a brand-new suit, not bad for a guy with no job other than the little he made playing goal.

The Adanacs now faced the Burrards in the finals. One game into the series, on September 10, Canada officially declared war on Nazi Germany. All the players realized—had realized for weeks or months—that they'd soon be trading their sweaters for uniforms and their sticks for guns.

With war hanging over their heads, the Adanacs went on to defeat Vancouver 20–4 in the seventh game, a game marked by high-sticking and charging as much as by goals, and marred by tomato-hurling Burrards' fans who, upset at every call not favouring their team, barraged referees Harry Gilmore and Hugh Gifford. Gifford, his white ref's shirt stained blood red by one especially juicy beefeater, was later rewarded for his work by being doused with a bucket of water by an angry Burrards' fan. Brother Jimmy exhorted his team to victory, with a constant flow of "Get back!" and "Come on up!" His commands were like a sergeant's, reverberating around the Arena.[167]

In the eleven games of league playoffs, Phelan topped the Adanacs' scorers with forty-one points on twenty-six goals and fifteen assists. Led by Brud Matheson's nine goals and three assists, the Adanacs then disposed of the Nelson Maple Leafs in two games to capture the BC championship and the right to face the team that had demolished them 3–0 in the 1938 Mann

An eye injury kept Adanac Bob Lee off the floor in the 1939 Mann Cup, but he won one in 1947, along with the MVP trophy.

RALPH BURTON.

Cup: the St. Catharines Athletics. The Athletics were a bigger, heavier team than the Adanacs, with power and brute force on their side. Centre Joe Cheevers weighed 180 pounds. Roy "Punk" Morton was "an artist at taking passes and delivering deadly shots on the run."[168] Roy "Bun" Barnard was a hard-hitting defenceman. Even the Athletics' goalie Whittaker was big at six feet and 190 pounds.

The Adanacs were "smooth as kittens" and "fleet as deer" in playing a fast, passing style game.[169] Before the start of the first game, at Vancouver's Hastings Forum, Justice W.A. MacDonald, donor of the ICLL trophy, awarded the Maitland trophy to Adanac Jim Douglas as the league's MVP on the basis of his league-leading seventy-two goals and thirty-two assists. MacDonald wished both teams good luck and asked them to avoid rough play. His request drew a burst of laughter from the 5,000 fans on hand. Everyone knew there was as much chance of avoiding rough play as there was of avoiding war in Europe.

Boyhood friends from White Rock, BC, Adanac Punch Thompson and Salmonbellie Ralph Burton chase a loose ball in 1939.

RALPH BURTON.

The game featured exceptionally close, hard checking. As far as actual fighting went, the two main combatants were the Adanacs' Ken Matheson and the Athletics' Bill Fitzgerald, son of the legendary field lacrosse star. Matheson, also known as "the mosquito," was a fast, feisty, shifty, and highly combative player who buzzed around, dove in for the kill, stung opponents for the ball or a shot on goal, and then was gone before anyone knew what had happened. He'd been assigned to check Fitzgerald, and the two verged on blows several times and went to the penalty box four times each.

After three quarters of "bitter and bruising struggle,"[170] the Adanacs outran the Athletics, who were finally feeling the effects of their long train trip, to win 12–10. Matheson and Fitzgerald traded punches just before the final whistle. League MVP Douglas scored three goals, and teammates Kennedy, Carter, and Saunders scored two each. Sharpshooter Roy Morton scored two for the Athletics, and playmaker Gus Madsen assisted on three and scored one. For their efforts, the Adanacs should have, at the very least, enjoyed hot showers, but for some reason cold water was all that came out of the Forum's showerheads.

Six thousand fans crammed into the Arena for game 2. Smoke from Player's Navy Cut and Export 'A' cigarettes—to say nothing of cigars—formed an oily grey cloud in the rafters.

It was obvious from the opening faceoff that game 2 would be a continuation of game 1—a grim, tight-checking, bruising battle. Goaltenders Bill Whittaker of the Athletics and Johnson of the Adanacs were up to the task. The teams were never more than a goal apart through three quarters and were tied at seven going into the fourth when Joe Cheevers scored to put the Athletics ahead. But Matheson tied it on a spectacular one-handed shot and moments later, Saunders fired a long-distance bullet from the side of the net: 9–8. The Adanacs somehow held off the charging Athletics for the next six minutes for a second win. Matheson, Phelan, and Carter each had two goals for the Adanacs. Gus Madsen had three goals for the Athletics, with

George Coles and Cheever contributing two apiece.

Players on both sides knew they had been in a war. After the bench emptied, Cheevers was found alone, writhing in pain with an injured rib. Adanacs defenceman "Punch" Thompson, a slash having nearly paralyzed his leg, was taken to hospital for treatment.

Even more fans poured into the Arena for game 3. Neither team wanted to grind it out the way they had in the first two contests. Game 3 was going to be won or lost on speed and scoring.

The teams traded goals, with the Adanacs "passing like lightning" and outshooting the Athletics almost two to one.[171] As the game progressed, a man sat alone in his New Westminster Parks Board office, waiting for updates on the game. He was seventy-two years old, his health failing. He had seen parts of the first two games, but was not well enough to attend game 3. At the start of the fourth quarter, the score was even at eight. Then the Adanacs, sparked by Saunders, went on a scoring tear, netting seven goals—"machine gun bullets"—in seven minutes to win the game 15–11 and with it the Mann Cup.

When news of the outcome came to the old man, he said simply, "The Adanacs have won; I can die happy."[172] Although he'd played lacrosse for the Salmonbellies in the 1890s and served the club in a variety of roles over many decades, it did not matter to him that it was not a Salmonbellies team winning the Cup; it only mattered that it was a New Westminster team.

After his playing days ended he had served the Salmonbellies as treasurer and, later, secretary. In 1921, he sold his business and in 1929, he was elected to the New Westminster Parks Board, where, after the 1929 exhibition buildings fire, he was instrumental in rebuilding Queen's Park as a recreational centre. He supported facilities and athletes, often reaching into his own pocket when funds were not available. A familiar figure at sporting events in the city, he was rarely seated, usually too busy fraternizing with his many friends, two of whom, Charlie Welsh and Thomas Gifford, were Columbia Street merchants and life-long Salmonbellies supporters like him. The man in the Parks Board office was pharmacist Herb Ryall.

Thousands of New Westminster citizens and their Adanacs gathered near the firehall at the southwest corner of Royal Avenue and Eighth Street to celebrate the victory. Hundreds of pieces of scrap wood—planer ends supplied by Adanacs' president and lumberman J.R. Murray—were piled high and set on fire in a vacant lot adjacent to the firehall. The happy mob then spilled down the hill toward the CPR station on Columbia Street. After parading on foot and in automobiles east and west along Columbia, the celebration settled at the Canadian Legion auditorium and carried on into the early hours.

When the city finally awoke, it was to newspaper headlines proclaiming that Great Britain and France had rejected Hitler's peace terms as "impossible." On a large square of city-owned property between Eighth and Tenth Avenues and Sixth and Eighth Streets, the sappers busily erected army huts and barracks.

A few weeks after the Adanacs' victory, Herb Ryall died. Teammates Tommy Gifford and Alex Turnbull were among the six men who carried his coffin from Holy Trinity Cathedral to

The New Westminster Adanacs defeated the Ike Hildebrand-led Mimico Mountaineers for their first Mann Cup in 1939.

NEW WESTMINSTER MUSEUM AND ARCHIVES.

the waiting hearse. The cortege made its way up Sixth Street's steep hill and passed his house on Queen's Avenue on its way to Queen's Park. There it slowly circled the fountain square in front of the Arena, one last trip in the park that had meant so much to him.

The irrepressible Grumpy was back in 1940 as both Salmonbellies manager and coach. Other than Anthony, who had decamped to Ontario, the core of the team was identical to 1939's. In the pre-season, Grumpy tinkered with his lines. He was still short one or two sturdy defencemen cut from the Downey cloth, but he had every confidence in his new starting goalie, Scuby. The big Greek kid, like all goalies in that day, played with no pads to speak of, just a ribbed, leather baseball catcher's chest protector and thin, floppy shin guards. A ludicrous little flap, part of the chest protector, hung down over his groin. On his feet was a pair of old sneakers, like the kind people wear when cleaning their boats. Sometimes he wore a baseball catcher's mask.

On May 6, the Salmonbellies played the league's season opener against the Adanacs. Jimmy Gifford had turned over coaching duties to brother Jack, but he was never far from the bench. The Salmonbellies were defeated, and they continued to lose games. Spring tried out new recruits every game, searching for goal scorers.

The night that British Prime Minister Winston Churchill delivered his famous "We shall never surrender" speech, the Salmonbellies surrendered to the Richmond Farmers 19–15. But ten days later, with young newcomer René Leatherbarrow of Richmond in the lineup, the Salmonbellies surprised the league-leading Burrards 20–14.

In early July, the Salmonbellies defeated the Adanacs 27–10. "The goalie, young Bill Scuby, was well nigh invincible," wrote the British Columbian, "robbing Adanacs players of goals on frequent occasions when he was the only man to beat." The Salmonbellies then lost 32–11 to the Burrards.

No matter what Grumpy did or didn't do, no matter what combination of veterans and rookies were in the lineup, the Salmonbellies could not find any consistency. The team closed out another losing season, 7–17, with a loss to the Burrards, who defeated the Adanacs for the league title, but lost the Mann Cup to the St. Catharines Athletics. Bill Wilson had ten goals and seven assists for the Athletics in his sixth Mann Cup.

In the 1940s, the lacrosse ball was the first thing up the floor, with defencemen following in hot pursuit. The emphasis was on the individual, on beating checks any way possible. Games were won on fast breaks, one-on-ones, and two-on-twos. There were six runners, including a rover. Players played both ways, without changing over from offence to defence, and there was no thirty-second clock. A player could rag the ball as long as he liked or until someone took it away from him. Chopping, slashing, and just about anything else was allowed. A defender could hit a player winding up to shoot hard across his gloves without penalty. Players still did not wear helmets. (During his lacrosse career, "Blackie" Black's head received 152 stitches.)

Goal nets were much higher and wider than today, and net minders, with barely more padding than any other player, were expected to stop shots any way they could, throwing in front of a ball whatever part of their body seemed most likely to stop it.

More than 30 goals in total in a game were common. There was no goal crease, so players could be right on top of a goalie and shoot. It was dangerous, so in 1941, the crease rule came into effect. The crease rule was initially not popular with the goalies it was designed to protect. They preferred to outguess attackers who were rushing in.

By July of 1941, the Salmonbellies' and the Adanacs' rosters had been decimated by retirements and war service. In one game, it was overwhelmingly rookies versus rookies, the Salmonbellies fielding veterans Meehan and Tyler, while only one player from the previous year's Adanacs, Gordon Saunders, hit the floor, potting two goals and seven assists in a one-goal Adanacs' victory.

As close and exciting as the game promised to be and was, few spectators showed up, something unheard of just the year before. The war, of course, was uppermost in everyone's minds, lacrosse fading into the background with the loss of many of the marquee players. With the great players went winning ways, and with the Salmonbellies fourth in the standings and the Adanacs third, New Westminster's fans stayed home.

The temperature was another reason to avoid the Arena. On July 14, it soared to 95° Fahrenheit. It was even hotter and more humid inside the Arena, despite the fact that the roof received several soakings in an effort to cool things down. The heat wave continued. On July 16, goalie Crick collapsed from heat prostration in the fourth period and had to be carried off the floor. The following day the temperature hit 99°.

Harry Carter, in his third season with the Salmonbellies, won the league scoring title with 101 points on 75 goals and 26 assists. Carter was a disciplined, thinking player with the ability to change pace and direction extremely quickly. "He didn't make too many moves that didn't count," recalled teammate Jake Trotzuk.[173] Carter played twenty-four games in 1941, giving him an average of slightly more than four points per game. Even more impressive, he scored his goals on just 148 shots, scoring a little better than 50 percent of the time. In a game on July 19, he scored nine goals with five assists, tying Adanac Jim Douglas's 1939 record. But a few weeks later "Whoopie" Tyler chalked up eleven goals and two assists in an implausible 49–20 victory over the Indians at Queen's Park.

Regardless, the Salmonbellies were still mired in fourth place. The season ended with a riot, the Salmonbellies venting their frustrations on the Richmond Farmers, eight players in the final quarter alone going to the penalty box for fighting. But in the end, the Farmers, led by high-scoring Wilf Hamson, Blackie Black, and Art Noble, and backstopped by the outstanding goaltending of one-eyed Herb Delmonico, ran away with the league, having won their first eleven games and beating the Burrards in four straight games for the league championship.

It took the St. Catharines Athletics to stop the Farmers, three games to two in the Mann Cup. Former Salmonbellie Bill Wilson had seven goals and three assists in the series to earn his seventh, and last, Mann Cup. He played two more seasons for St. Catharines in 1942 and 1943, both as player-coach, before retiring. As of the 2012 season, Wilson was number sixteen on the all-time total goals list, with 748 over twelve seasons.

As the 1942 season came around, the Salmonbellies did everything in their power to avoid the fate of the Adanacs and the Farmers, who, with so many players lost to the war, had been forced to fold. The ICLL now comprised the Salmonbellies and three Vancouver-based teams: the Burrards, North Vancouver Ship Repair Yard Norvans, and Burrard Drydock Wallaces United. Burrard Drydock was Canada's busiest shipyard, building freighters, corvettes, minesweepers, and tank landing ships. Of its thousands of workers, many were lacrosse players.

The Army was using Vancouver's Forum, so games were played at Con Jones's old outdoor stadium, now known as Callister Park, and at Queen's Park Arena. Enlisted players for all the teams came and went as dictated by the Army, Navy, and Air Force or, in the case of the Norvans and Wallaces, as dictated by shifts.

As players were absorbed into the war effort, Grumpy and Wood were forced to juggle their ever-changing lineup. They welcomed Adanac Johnny Douglas and Richmond Farmer Blackie Black to the team. Douglas was a natural fit, being a New Westminster native. Black, a blonde, six-foot, 180-pound centre, lived and worked in New Westminster as the manager of

Tip Top Tailors. A sizable dent in his forehead above his right eye and a scar to match—the legacy of a childhood encounter with a kicking horse's hoof—added a raffish, pirate-like quality to his square-jawed, handsomely chiseled features.

Black starred on the Vancouver Bluebirds junior team when they lost three games to two to the Orillia Baby Terriers in the 1937 Minto Cup, the first year the Minto was awarded to the Canadian junior champions. He wanted to play for the Salmonbellies in 1938, but the league would not allow it, fearing it would make New Westminster too strong a team. Instead, he spent four seasons at centre with the Richmond Farmers, thrilling fans with his slick play-making, scoring, and pugilism. Wherever he played, Blackie got "more boos on the floor, and more applause."[174]

Black had won the league scoring title in 1940, with sixty goals and thirty-four assists. In 1941 he led the Farmers against the St. Catharines Athletics in the Mann Cup, with six goals and seven assists in five games, earning the Mike Kelly Memorial trophy for series' MVP the first year it was awarded, even though the Farmers did not win the cup and Black was second in scoring to teammates Art Noble and Doug Ross.

With Johnny Douglas and Black in the mix, the 1942 Salmonbellies were a greatly improved team. As the season got underway Grumpy was constantly chewing gum, smoking cigars, laughing, and cutting up oranges for the players. Before home games he could be found in his big black touring auto outside the Arena, a wad of tickets in his hand, ready to peel off as many as a player wanted for friends and family. In contrast, Wood was known for his quiet, confidential approach with players. He would lean in close and talk, punctuating his points by pounding his right fist into his left palm.

At Callister Park, the Salmonbellies' Gordie Arrell scored five goals with three assists in a July victory over the Wallaces but was lost to the Army before the next game. In that game "Kip" Routley had three goals—and then reported to a military training camp. Bill Tyler played his last game in August before trading in his playing shorts for the bell-bottomed pants of the Royal Canadian Navy. Harry Carter played for most of the season, but entered military service in late August. Scuby was outstanding all season long and in late August, with the team needing a win to secure a playoff bye, he made sensational saves on the Wallaces' sharpshooters Bill Brunskill and Art Pruden, stopping fifteen of their nineteen shots in a 14–8 victory.

On August 17, the Salmonbellies regained first place with a win over the Norvans. After hearing about a fight-filled encounter between the Norvans and the Burrards, Fred Hume said to Grumpy and Wood, "They can't do that to us. We have to get Bill Tyler to stop all this, he can do it."[175] Tyler, also known as "the human tank," was one of the more vicious checkers on the team, and maybe the best fighter. The only trouble was, he was in the Navy. Hume made some calls to Navy brass, but to no avail. The Salmonbellies would have to beat the Norvans without Tyler.

Playing with just twelve men, the Salmonbellies faced coach Bill Dickinson's team in the first game at Queen's Park. The Norvans were loaded with great players, including Johnny Douglas and Bert Bryant, the latter a Salmonbellie for all but two years of his ten-year career. The Salmonbellies lost the first game 13–11, but won the second game 11–7 and the third game 17–9. In the fourth game on the hard-packed dirt of Callister Park, "'Scoop-'em-up' Scuby filled his net, rarely leaving a corner," wrote the *Vancouver Sun*'s Jack Patterson. "Long shots or short he shoved a glove, a knee, a foot or an expansive chest in front of everything."[176] Scuby stopped all but two of twenty-two shots in the 8–2 win.

When the Fraser River's fishermen resumed work on the Monday following the Salmon-bellies' victory, they caught far more sockeye than the canneries could process. The run was

The 1942 Salmonbellies at Callister Park, formerly Con Jones Park. **Front:** Gordon Arrell, Johnny Raitt, Bill Wilkes, Bert Houston, Reg Fallowfield. **Back:** Bill Tyler, Gordon Saunders, Blackie Black, Jack Wood (coach), Alan Askew, Ed Johnstone (goalie), and Ed Downey. **Missing:** Jim Douglas, Harry Carter, Kip Routley, Pete Meehan, Bill Scuby and Alf Davy. Before the war, Saunders and Johnstone played for the Adanacs.

BILL SCUBY.

the heaviest since 1913. Between Monday and Wednesday one million fish ended up in nets—always a good omen for the Salmonbellies. On Wednesday night, they won the fifth game and the league title. Pete Meehan, now a New Westminster police officer, scored twice in the 10–5 victory, and earned a three-star selection. Continuing his excellent play, Meehan scored four goals in a 15–5 Salmonbellies' win in the first game of a two-game, total-points series against the Victoria United Services. They defeated the Victoria squad in the second game 12–8. Bill Wilkes was awarded the Maitland MVP trophy for the second time.

On Sunday night, September 27, the Salmonbellies boarded the train in New Westminster for the trip east to face the Lachine-Ville St. Pierre Combines. Several hundred fans sent them off.

Quebec cultural life seemed to invigorate the Salmonbellies, who banged in eighteen goals to Lachine's four in the first game, although they lost Art Matthewson to a dislocated shoulder. Lachine's René Couture lost only his dignity when his shorts split neatly in two and fell to the floor. Blackie squared off at centre with "Red" Storey, who, in 1938, scored three touchdowns for the Toronto Argonauts, helping the team win the Grey Cup. The Salmonbellies took the second game 19–8, but lost the services of Wallaces' loanee Doug Ross, who suffered a split kidney. They also lost several sticks.

In "Toronto the Good" conditions were puritanical. Newspaper deliveries were prohibited after midnight Saturdays and theatres and ballparks were closed on Sundays. Even tobacco products were banned from sale on the "Lord's Day."

The Etobicoke Indians lent the Salmonbellies ten sticks before the start of the finals, which got underway at Maple Leaf Gardens. Five thousand spectators paid to see the Salmonbellies—minus Ross and flu-stricken Art Pruden—take on the Mimico-Brampton Combines.

New Westminster's lineup for the 1944 Mann Cup was a mix of Salmonbellies, Burrards, Adanacs and Farmers, but they fell to the Athletics in St. Catharines, three games to two.

BILL SCUBY.

To an already strong team, the Combines had added Arnold "Onions" Smith, Six Nations star and perennial league scoring champion Bill Isaacs, and Gus Madsen. Madsen had starred for the St. Catharines Athletics when they won the Mann Cup in 1938, 1940, and 1941. With Arabian facial features, a moustache, and a flamboyant style of play, he was nicknamed "Ali Baba" after the hero of *Ali Baba and the Forty Thieves.*

Like Downey, Madsen was a high-scoring defenceman. But unlike Downey, he was a showman who liked to hop, step, and jump before shooting. When he drew a penalty—which was rare—he would draw attention to himself by waving his arm in mock-shameful acknowledgement. When checked, he wasn't above diving or grimacing in fake pain when he knew the ref was watching.

The opener featured great goaltending at both ends from Scuby and Bert Large. The contest went to the fourth quarter, tied at 7, but Downey took a controversial slashing penalty and Masters scored on the power play. The Combines added another power play goal and one more goal to register a 10–7 win.

The Salmonbellies' bad luck with injuries, lost sticks, and illness continued, with "Kip" Routley suffering a broken bone in his ankle and joining Matthewson, Ross, and Pruden on the sidelines. Grumpy wired west for reinforcement: send Tyler ASAP.

In the second game, Scuby was once again superb, holding the Combines to a pair of first-quarter goals. But the Combines' Masters, McLean, and Ontario scoring leader Ken Dixon brought the crowd to their feet with end-to-end rushes, and the easterners dominated the second and third quarters, not letting up until the last fifteen minutes. Final score: Combines 15, Salmonbellies 9.

The Salmonbellies needed to win three straight to become the first western team to win the Mann Cup in Ontario. The Combines gave them a chance when coach Chuck Davidson inexplicably sat Large in favour of ex-Salmonbellie Pete Anthony in the next game. With announcer

Foster Hewitt in the gondola broadcasting the game over the CBC Radio Network, the Salmonbellies took advantage of the rusty Anthony, immediately scoring three goals on three shots.

Bill Tyler, still in Navy uniform, had arrived by plane over the weekend. He scored early in his first shift. Routley, his ankle heavily tapped, was also back in action. By the fifteen-minute mark it was 6–3 Salmonbellies. They went on to post a 14–8 victory. Jimmy and Johnny Douglas accounted for two and three goals, respectively, while Wallaces' loaner Art Pruden, recovered from the flu, counted a hat trick. Wood credited the win to a packed zone defence and Scuby's stopping of twenty-five of the thirty-three shots he faced. Had he been less charitable, he might also have credited Davidson and Anthony.

Hewitt was again in the gondola to call game 4 for the CBC. The game was also broadcast by direct wire over Vancouver station CKWX. Bert Large was back in goal, but the Salmonbellies led 9–6 at the start of the fourth quarter. With less than ten minutes remaining, the Combines' Arthurs sprinted the length of the floor and scored. "Ali Baba" Madsen then set up Gimblett to close the gap, 9–8. With minutes to go, Madsen shot from in close. Scuby made the save. Madsen's momentum carried him to the side of the net where he ran into Downey and another Salmonbellie. Seizing the opportunity, he acted as if he'd been flattened. The mesmerized referee blew his whistle. Downey went off for two minutes. Madsen was not finished with his theatrics. "Gus took his time walking up to the penalty shot line," wrote reporter Jack Gatecliff, "waggled his stick twice before shooting, then bounced the ball past the western goaltender."[177] The Salmonbellies pressed, but Large blocked everything. With time running out, Madsen found Isaacs with a long pass. Isaacs passed to Masters. Masters' underhand drive beat Scuby. 10–9 Combines. "You don't mind losing," said Downey after the game, "but you hate to see it decided on a cheap penalty. You've got to hand it to Madsen though, he really staged a good act."[178] Coming from anyone but Downey, it would have been sour grapes. "Ed got unfairly blamed for that penalty at the end of the fourth game," said Scuby. "It wasn't his fault."[179] "Ali Baba" and his "thieves" had stolen a victory and with it, the Mann Cup.

While Scuby was playing for the Mann Cup, the Army had contacted his mother. Back in New Westminster, Mayor Hume took the big goalie aside and offered him a deal. If Scuby continued to play for the Salmonbellies, Hume would get him a job working on a large hangar Hume and Rumble was wiring in Richmond. Scuby accepted. But it was not long before Chief of Police Bruce showed up on the job site. Not wanting to distract Scuby from his Mann Cup duties, he had kept his enlistment papers from him until after the series. But now he had to serve them.

Hume had tried, but as powerful as he was, he was no match for the Army; defence of Canada took precedence over defence of the net.

In May 1943, the Salmonbellies had the Arena in which to play, but, with eleven of the previous year's team in military uniforms, could they find enough players? In Vancouver, the Burrards had enough players, but, with the Hastings Forum now a military training base, they had no indoor arena. The Army was ready to field a team, but only if the Salmonbellies were in. They would not outfit a team without the gate receipts to pay for it. No Salmonbellies, no ticket sales, no lacrosse.

Hume, Grumpy, and Wood canvassed their veterans. Could they, would they play? Vancouver arranged to play at Centre Park, at Fir and West Broadway, just west of Granville, where all the city tramlines converged. With gas rationed and travel restricted, public transit was the order of the day.

The city was even willing to exempt the field on game nights from the wartime blackout policy. They could have the lights until 11:00 p.m. Work began on a lacrosse box and dressing rooms. Hume, Grumpy, and Wood cobbled together a team. Only Blackie and the Dickinson brothers, Bill and Eric, had been a part of the 1942 Salmonbellies, the Dickinsons just for the post-season. The Adanacs' Ed Johnson took Scuby's place in net. The youngest addition to the team was 16-year-old Isaac Bruce "Ike" Hildebrand. Winnipeg-born and New Westminster-raised, Hildebrand was a lacrosse prodigy. Only five-foot-seven and 140 pounds, "Ike the tyke" was extremely fast, very shifty, and an excellent shot.

He was on the floor at the Arena for a season-opening exhibition contest with the Vancouver Island-stationed Royal Canadian Air Force squad, the Patricia Bay Flyers. The Flyers' Johnny Smith, formerly a Richmond star, scored six goals in the contest, while ex-Adanac Bob Lee tossed in three in a 17–7 Flyers' victory.

Not to be outdone by the Air Force, the Army team took the early lead in the schedule. But on July 10, the Salmonbellies were out in full force. Team captain Wilkes, Douglas, Bryant, Routley, and Fetherston combining for twenty-one Salmonbellies' goals in a 27–6 "heavy barrage"[180] over Army. Harry Carter, a member of the 1942 Salmonbellies, scored six of Army's goals.

At the beginning of August, Ed Downey and Pete Meehan, two pre-war stalwarts, "enlisted" with the Salmonbellies. The 1942 Mann Cup finalists were back together, minus Ralph Burton, Gordie Folka, Bert Houston, and Black, who had played five games before being claimed by the Army.

A team crest from the 1940s.

CANADIAN LACROSSE HALL OF FAME.
PHOTOGRAPH BY PHILLIP CHIN.

Black had played his last game. Between 1935 and 1943, he played 215 senior games, scoring 365 goals and 247 assists for 612 points, nearly three points a game. Burton and Folka were in the Air Force. Houston was at a Commonwealth Air Training Plan station learning gunnery and would soon find himself in the Royal Air Force, 103 Squadron, in a Lancaster bomber. He would fly forty missions, eleven daylight trips, and twenty-nine as a pathfinder, marking bombing targets with flares to increase the accuracy of the main force. As a rear gunner, Houston faced backwards. "You didn't know where you were going," he later remarked, "but you knew where you'd been."[181]

Also absent from the lineup was Scoop-'em-up Scuby. After basic training in Peterborough, he underwent specialized engineering training at Petawawa. Corporal Scuby, now versed in all things electrical, from keeping generators running to blowing up bridges, was assigned to a secret base on Grosse Île, an island in the Saint Lawrence River, about thirty miles from Quebec City.

The Salmonbellies were a juggernaut through July and August. And with every passing week, if they lost a player to the war effort, they picked up another one to strengthen an already strong team. They lost Jack Ferguson to the Army (the Army itself, not the lacrosse team), but picked up Johnny Douglas, a sailor assigned to the HMCS *Wetaskawhan*, which often kept him from what he loved best, playing lacrosse. Now that he was temporarily stationed in Victoria, nothing was going to stop him from getting in a game. He got his first chance on August 16 in Queen's Park Arena against Army, scoring four goals with one assist.

Joining Douglas in making first-time appearances for the season were infantryman Johnny Raitt and Bill Tyler (with the Fishermen's Reserve of the Royal Canadian Navy, the so-called "Gumboot Navy"). Raitt scored three with an assist. Tyler did not score, but he did manage a two-minute penalty in what would be his only game of the season and the last of his nine-year career. The top ace on the night was Bill Dickinson, with six goals and two assists in a 20–12 Salmonbellies' victory.

For the final match of the regular season, a must-win game in Grumpy's opinion, the Salmonbellies pulled all the stops, or, rather, pulled all the strings they could, to ensure that every able-bodied player was on hand. Johnny Douglas and Ken Fetherston would be at Queen's Park from their bases in Victoria, and Bert Bryant and "Kip" Routley journeyed from their posts in Chilliwack. The Salmonbellies won 24–17. Meehan, Dickinson, Wilkes, Downey, Jim Douglas, and Fetherston each scored three goals, while Johnny Douglas went one better than his hat-tricking teammates.

The Salmonbellies took the playoff opener against the Bombers 16–14. Wilkes again led the way with five goals, an assist, and endless numbers of "little twelve-inch chops" to his

Grumpy Spring saw an outstanding goalkeeper in a big, tall kid of Greek descent named Bill Scuby. Scuby became the Salmonbellies' starter in 1940.

BILL SCUBY

In eight stalwart seasons with the Salmonbellies, hard-nosed defenceman Bert Bryant racked up 567 points, 329 penalty minutes, and one Mann Cup (1943) in three attempts.

BILL SCUBY

ball-carrying opponents' arms. Pilot Officer Ralph Burton played his first game of the season, scoring three times. The Bombers won the second contest, the Salmonbellies took the third, and then the Bombers tied the series with a win at Centre Park. The Salmonbellies won the fifth match at Queen's Park, after future Canadian Prime Minister John Diefenbaker faced off the ball.

The sixth game was at Centre Park, where the Bombers had a habit of winning on the hardpan surface. Around seven o'clock people began to converge in the Granville and West Broadway area, where the hill crests before descending north to False Creek and, beyond, Vancouver's downtown. The electric tramcars, the old "rattlers," disgorged spectators in front of the Aristocratic restaurant, where you could expect "courteous service" and "quality food." The biggest crowd of the season showed up, jamming into the stands elbow to elbow. Hundreds were turned away at the gate. Residential roofs were dotted with spectators. It was a close-fought, cleanly played game, but the Salmonbellies—despite heroics from Burrards' goalie Walt Lee—prevailed 11–8 on hat tricks by Dickinson and Douglas to win the league and advance to the BC championship against the RCAF team, the Patricia Bay Flyers.

The Flyers, stacked with all-star-calibre players formerly with Richmond, Vancouver, and the Adanacs, proved that their season-opening exhibition win against the Salmonbellies in May was no fluke, winning 23–13. New Westminster took the second game—barely—winning 12–10 after leading 10–5 heading into the fourth quarter. On the same night, October 5, in Toronto, the Mimico-Brampton Combines earned the right to represent the east in the Mann Cup when they defeated the Lachine, Quebec, RCAF team. They caught a train west right after their win. The Combines had beaten the RCAF. Could the Salmonbellies?

In the dressing room before the start of the third and final game, Grumpy read to his players a telegram he had received from the Honourable Wells Gray. Gray, the formidable point player, had just turned sixty-seven. "This is my birthday," wrote Gray, "and the best present you and the Salmonbellies can give me is a victory tonight. My regard to the boys and the best of luck."[182]

Bill Wilkes amassed ten points on three goals and seven assists in a 23–13 Salmonbellies' victory. In the three-game series, Wilkes led all scorers with fifteen. But even more impressive, he took no penalty minutes. Wells Gray had his birthday present, all tied up in a bow. The team dined after the game at the Fraser Café on Columbia Street, purposefully avoiding the bar of the Russell Hotel. There would be a celebration, provided they could overcome the Combines, who were slated to arrive in the morning.

The Combines hit the floor at the Arena just hours after arriving in New Westminster. Only three of them had been to the coast before: Bill Mullis, Downey and Wilkes' old Terriers teammate; sixty-seven-goal man Bill Brunskill, with the Wallace Shipyards team last year; and aging veteran George "Mush" Thompson, who in 1931 helped the Excelsiors defeat the Salmonbellies in the last Mann Cup field championship. Bill Isaacs, outstanding in the 1942 series, was again with the Combines, along with sixty-seven-goal scorer Ken Dixon, a pickup from the Army Bullets. Aside from Dixon, only George Masters and Brunskill were in uniform, Brunskill with the RCAF and Masters with the Navy. Bert Large was once more in net.

As the Combines worked out, Jack Wood and Grumpy, cigar clamped firmly in mouth, looked on. They'd reinforced the Salmonbellies with Army's Harry Carter and the Flyers' Ferguson and Phelan. And, if necessary, the Burrards' Roy Cavalin, Walt Lee, and Don Matheson were ready to play. But as Wood and Grumpy watched, they knew that, despite their home-floor advantage, it was going to be close.

Their fears were confirmed when the Combines, despite being outshot fifty to thirty-three, took game one 10–9 after exploding for six goals in the third period. Just as he had in 1942, Large loomed large in goal. Wood and Grumpy changed tactics. If they could not, with Large in net, count on their goal scorers to win games, they would turn to their defence. Isaacs' two goals, Brunskill's three, and Dixon's one marked them out for special attention. Bill Dickinson—defensive heir to Gifford and Patchell—was assigned to Bill Isaacs, while Bob Phelan was let loose on Bill Brunskill.

In game 2, in front of 4,500 roaring fans, the Combines were allowed just five goals. Isaacs, Brunskill, and Dixon managed just one goal each. For the Salmonbellies, Bert Bryant scored three, Dickinson two, and Phelan one in a total team tally of ten.

Mann Cup-bound Salmonbellies, 1946. **Left:** Ralph Burton. **Back row:** Bill Dickinson, Eric Dickinson, Bill Scuby (in fedora), Red Fraser, Alex Shaw. **Front row:** Pete Meehan, George Friend (trainer), Hank Harrison and Bill Wilkes.

BILL SCUBY.

Game 3 went to the Salmonbellies, 17–9. "They are a good team and never give up," said the *Columbian* of the Combines, "but once their three star goal getters are bottled up the rest of the players seem to lack the initiative."[183]

On the day of game 4, Salmonbellies' goalie Ed Johnston was out with his shotgun for the opening of the duck-hunting season. Having tired himself out shooting, he let in a couple of easy shots at the start of the game. To his credit, he benched himself in favour of Burrards pickup Walt Lee. Lee turned in a brilliant performance, even though it was his first time playing in the series and he came in stone cold, without even warming up. The Salmonbellies' scorers, however, were as warmed up as possible, and went on a spree that did not end until they had racked up twenty-two goals to the Combines' six. The Salmonbellies won the Mann Cup for the first time since 1937. Bill Wilkes won the MVP trophy. There were no hard feelings from the Combines. They joined the Salmonbellies for a celebratory dinner at the Hotel Russell on Sunday evening, before catching their train home.

Scuby stops a shot from Jack "Wandy" McMahon of the St. Catharines Athletics in the 1946 Mann Cup. Bill Dickinson (centre) and Ed Downey (right) look on.

BILL SCUBY.

On May 7, 1944, Salmonbellies' great, Wells Gray, died suddenly of a heart attack at sixty-eight. The team that had given him the Mann Cup birthday present was back in force in 1944, leading league play from the start and holding on, despite late season challenges by the Burrards and the Adanacs.

After disposing of the Burrards in four straight playoff games, the Salmonbellies advanced to Toronto's Maple Leaf Gardens to take on the St. Catharines Athletics. The Salmonbellies and the Athletics split the first two games. In the third match, the Athletics scored with twenty-one seconds remaining to win 11–10. The fourth game was scheduled for St. Catharines, but the Salmonbellies, citing a CLA rule that mandated playing Mann Cup games in enclosed arenas, refused to compete in St. Catharines' open-air, dirt-floor stadium, the Haig Bowl. The Mimico Mountaineers sarcastically offered the Salmonbellies blankets to "keep their jewels warm" should it be a cold night, and Woods accused Athletics' fans of throwing stones at opposition goalies.[184] The game was rescheduled for Maple Leaf Gardens, just after a circus packed up and just before the hockey ice went in. The Salmonbellies won 11–8, Bill Dickinson scoring the winning ninth goal in overtime from a Johnny Cavallin pass, with Cavallin and Meehan getting goals ten and eleven.

The fifth and deciding game was held in Hamilton's Barton Street Arena. Along with five other fresh players, St. Catharines brought in Bill Isaacs, the Six Nations star, widely considered the best eastern player of the era, and paid him $100 for the game.

Grumpy was understandably grumpy about it. The rules stated that only those players on a list submitted prior to the start of the Mann Cup series were eligible to compete. The CLA allowed Isaacs to play because of the anticipated increase in gate receipts that he, a locally born favourite son, would bring. "Six fresh men, eh?" groused Grumpy. "That's just swell. I guess Wood and I will have to strip for our side."[185]

The Salmonbellies battled gamely, without captain Bill Wilkes, who'd suffered an eye injury in game 4. Grumpy and Wood, of course, did not strip and Issacs, predictably, led the Athletics with two goals and an assist to an 11–9 victory. The MVP, however, was Salmonbellie Ike Hildebrand.

Salmonbellies veterans Wilkes, Downey, Bryant, Routley, and Meehan were busy with the war and other important matters in 1945. Goaltending was an issue. Bill Sampson played nineteen games, but the team tried out three other goalkeepers, including Ike Hildebrand, who, at the time, stood fifth in league scoring. After donning pads in the second period of a game, Hildebrand promptly let in five of the first six shots he faced, and Sampson went back in.

The Salmonbellies were second-last in the standings, with seven wins in twenty starts, when Bill Scuby, discharged from the Army, arrived back in town in time for a weekend practice. On Monday, he played in goal in a 21–18 victory over the Burrards. But the next game, a 16–15 loss to the Richmond Farmers, eliminated the Salmonbellies from the playoffs. Defenceman Bill Dickinson wound up second in league scoring with forty-three goals and thirty-eight assists, while failed goalie Ike Hildebrand was fifth with forty-seven goals and twenty-two assists.

The Burrards, led by goaltender Walt Lee, Jake Pugsley, and brothers Roy and John Cavallin, went twenty and four on the regular season, got past the Adanacs in a thrilling seven-game playoff series, and faced the Athletics in the Mann Cup. Vancouver swept the series in three straight games, outshooting the Athletics 136–86 and outscoring them 44–18. It was the Burrards' first national title.

With everyone home from the war that was coming home, the 1946 ICLL—Adanacs, Burrards, Farmers, Indians, and Salmonbellies—was at full strength for the first time since 1939. The Salmonbellies reeled off six straight victories to start the season, despite the absence of semi-retired Ed Downey, who was spending his leisure time golfing. But when Burton and Meehan were injured, Grumpy coaxed Downey off the golf course and onto the hardwood.

His first game was on August 5 against the Indians. He was his usual self and inspired his old comrade Wilkes to score four goals and two assists. The offensive star was Hildebrand, then in his third season, while the defensive star was Scuby, whose performance in net was a source of joy to Grumpy, according to the *British Columbian*.

The Adanacs mounted a charge through July and August, defeating the Salmonbellies 13–5 on August 12 for their eighth win in a row. The Salmonbellies, however, hung on for first place with sixteen wins and a draw in twenty-four games. Hildebrand, with fifty-five goals and twenty-seven assists, won the scoring race, with teammates Burton, Bryant, and Bill Dickinson rounding out the top ten.

The Salmonbellies defeated the Burrard Bombers, defending Mann Cup champions, four games to one to win the league title. They then defeated the Trail Golden Bears in two straight contests to claim the Kilmarnock Cup. After defeating the Winnipeg All-Stars in an exhibition game, the Salmonbellies and their entourage arrived in Toronto.

On September 30 the Salmonbellies faced the St. Catharines Athletics at Maple Leaf Gardens in the first game of the best-of-five games Mann Cup. Doug Favell was in goal for the Athletics, having replaced regular starter Bill Whittaker, who was suspended for attacking referee and former Salmonbellies player Jimmy Gunn the previous season. Favell had spent the war in the Navy as a "look out" or "enemy spotter," highly appropriate training for a goal-tender. Like Scuby, he never took his eyes off the ball, no matter where it was on the floor. In front of Favell, the Athletics were loaded with scorers, and while the Salmonbellies tried to match them goal for goal, the Athletics took the first game 11–10.

Almost 8,000 spectators spun the turnstiles at Maple Leaf Gardens for the second game. It was tied at five at the end of the half, but then the Athletics exploded for thirteen goals, while the Salmonbellies could only manage four. The difference was not a reflection on Scuby, but rather an affirmation of St. Catharines' incredible offensive power. It had only been a question of time. Morton led the way with four goals, while Smith, Cheevers, Madsen, and Urquhart contributed two apiece.

With constant forechecking, the Salmonbellies controlled most of the play for most of game 3, but entering the final fifteen minutes down 8–7, they panicked and shot impatiently at the impregnable Favell. The Athletics' Jack McMahon tried to run out the clock. Three Salmonbellies went after him, leaving Doug Cove wide open for a pass. He scored goal nine and the Salmonbellies, knowing it was over, allowed two more for an 11–7 loss. Favell was awarded the MVP trophy. It was another disappointing loss for the Salmonbellies in a series of Mann Cup losses for western teams playing in the east dating back to 1913.

The team netted about $12,000 on the season. Back home, players received their splits of $250, $100 more than they'd received in 1942. Scuby looked at his cheque and shook his

On their way to the Mann Cup in Toronto, the 1946 Salmonbellies played a game in Winnipeg. **Back row:** Jack Wood (coach), Bill Wilkes, Harry Carter, Bert Bryant, Bill Sampson, Ralph Burton, Bill Dickinson, Johnny Raitt, Gord Folka, Bert Houston, Wilf Hill (team president), Grumpy Spring (manager). **Front row:** Bill Scuby, Kip Routley, George Friend (trainer), Ed Downey, Hank Harrison, Eric Dickinson, Alex Shaw, Reo Jerome, Pete Meehan.

BILL SCUBY.

head. It was a great game, but clearly there was no money in it. After 101 games with the Salmonbellies, including twenty-three playoff contests, he knew he would not be back in net in 1947. But what no Salmonbellie had any way of knowing was that the 1946 Mann Cup series would be their last one for many long, dry years. It would be just as long and dry for St. Catharines. The 1946 Athletics looked like a dynasty in the making, but it was actually a dynasty ending. St. Catharines would not compete again for the Mann Cup until 1958 when, as the Welland-Crowland Switsons, they would be pitted once again against the Salmonbellies.

Well-worn leather lacrosse gloves.

CANADIAN LACROSSE HALL OF FAME. PHOTOGRAPH BY PHILLIP CHIN.

In 1951 the Salmonbellies and the Adanacs merged and became the Commandos,
a name inspired by Canadian troops fighting in the Korean War.

CANADIAN LACROSSE HALL OF FAME. PHOTOGRAPH BY PHILLIP CHIN.

"Why do you whisper, green grass/Why tell the trees what ain't so/Whispering grass/The trees don't have to know, no-no."

Whispering Grass (Don't Tell The Trees),
Fred & Doris Fisher, 1940

CHAPTER EIGHT
SALMONBELLIES + ADANACS = SALMONACS: 1947-1954

In 1947, Bill Wilkes took over from Wood as coach. Downey, Routley, Meehan, Burton, and Shaw retired. Raitt too would bow out before the end of the 1947 season. Ike Hildebrand, the 1946 league scoring champion, elected not to play for the Salmonbellies. At the end of May, Bill Dickinson tendered his resignation, leaving Wilkes with a huge gap he could not fill. Bill's brother Eric, however, stayed put. On the plus side, Ken Fetherston—who had scored lots of pre-war goals while tangling with Adanacs' Ken Matheson—rejoined the team. Lloyd "Puss" Cameron, who had played for the Navy in 1944 and Richmond in 1945 and 1946, took over for Scuby in net.

But the bigger problem was not a lack of players. It was a lack of fans. *Columbian* sportswriter Vic E. Andrew sounded the alarm in June. "Lacrosse officials, civic heads, parks board and business and professional men . . . had better get together without delay or something is going to happen—the break up of a club known from coast to coast." Games, noted Andrew, were not being advertised. Special nights for out-of-town fans were no longer organized. The downtown ticket office was closed, with the exception of one game. Even Fred Hume was worried. Standing behind the Salmonbellies' bench, the former mayor "used up a pouch of tobacco while racking his brain" for a way to get more people into the Arena.[186]

Things did not improve by mid-July. The Salmonbellies finished the season third among five teams, with an 11–12 record. Harry Carter, with fifty-nine goals and forty assists, won the league scoring title, with teammate Reo Jerome second with ninety-five points. The Salmonbellies lost 3–1 to the Burrards in the league semifinals. The Burrards, in turn, lost to the Adanacs in the league finals. The Adanacs went on to defeat the Rossland Redmen in the provincials, earning a berth in the Mann Cup championship against the Mimico Mountaineers.

The Adanacs, coached by former player Max McDonald, started the 1947 season with five players from the 1939 team: Bob Lee, Bob Phelan, Garnie Carter, Ted Bradbury, and Gordon Saunders. Bradbury and Saunders played the regular season, the league finals, and one game in the provincials, but were unavailable for the Mann Cup.

But of all the holdovers from the 1939 team no one wanted the Mann Cup as much as Bob Lee. Lee had suffered an eye injury prior to the 1939 series against St. Catharines and had not played in the games. He was thirty-one, and knew that it was probably his last shot at playing in the Mann Cup.

Rookie Gordie Pogue had been sensational in net for the Adanacs all season long, but an injury to his throat suffered in a practice days before the first game took him out of the Mann Cup. Adanac Garnie Carter, a forward until an accidental gunshot shattered his right foot, took Pogue's place. Carter had played one and a half games in goal in his life. His last turn in nets had been four and a half months earlier.

The Mountaineers, coached by Chuck Davidson, featured, among others, former Salmonbellie Ike Hildebrand, who was a top regular-season point getter, with seventy-four points (tied with teammate Don McPhail). The Mountaineers had finished the regular season in third position, well behind the Hamilton Tigers and the St. Catharines Athletics, who tied for first with twenty-one wins and nine losses each. But in the finals, Mimico swept the Athletics in four games, with Ray Mortimer tending goal.

Former Salmonbellie centre Blackie Black wanted to bring more "ballyhoo" to lacrosse. He agreed to coach the North Shore Indians in 1948. Black, Chief Mathias Joe, Stan Joseph (sitting) and Willard Joseph.

The Arena was packed for game 1. The Adanacs' Whitey Severson, Archie Browning and Jackie Northup took turns smothering Hildebrand—considered the key to stopping the Mountaineers—but Mimico led by two points until the Adanacs tied it 14–14 in the fourth quarter. Northup scored what proved to be the winner and New Westminster scored two more to take game one 17–14. Northup and Jake Proctor, in his second full season with the Adanacs, scored three goals apiece, and Ralph Douglas scored two.

In front of 6,800 fans at the Forum, Bob Lee broke up Mimico's attack time after time and scored four goals to lead the team to a 13–9 victory. Norm Baker, full of Novocain to kill the pain of an injured rib, added two goals to Browning's three and Severson's one.

With Bill Wilkes and Bill Dickinson refereeing, the Adanacs and the Mountaineers faced off in game 3 in front of 5,000 fans at Queen's Park. The Adanacs jumped into the lead and never looked back. So obvious was the outcome that in the break after the third quarter, the Arena's engineers sent icemaking brine through the pipes beneath the wood flooring. Proctor and Lee scored three each and the game ended in an 18–9 Adanacs victory. Lee finally had his Mann Cup and with it the MVP trophy, and Garnie Carter had a Mann Cup as well—one he'd never expected.

In 17-year-old Harry Preston the Salmonbellies found a talented and reliable goaltender for the 1948 campaign. Raised in Newton, in those days a farming community, seven miles south of New Westminster, Preston and his buddy, "Jake" Trotzuk, often rode their bicycles over the Patullo Bridge to play in New Westminster's Moody Park. Preston was the Salmonbellies' primary backstop for the next seven seasons, while Trotzuk played five games for New Westminster as a junior pickup in 1949 before playing five full seasons with the team through the 1950s.

The 1948 Salmonbellies, however, fared even worse than the 1947 team, despite big efforts by the team's smallest players, Bertie Houston and Ike Hildebrand. In a game in early August, Houston scored seven times on nine shots, while Hildebrand picked up eight goals and three assists later in August to finish the season with 104 points. But the only statistic that mattered was the team's performance: they lost fifteen of twenty-four games and finished fourth.

The defending champion, the Adanacs, advanced to the Mann Cup to face the Hamilton Tigers at Maple Leaf Gardens. They split the first four games. After getting off to a 4–0 lead in the fifth and deciding game, the Adanacs succumbed to the checking of the heavier Tigers. Joe Cheevers put Hamilton ahead to stay, and the Tigers won 12–8. Favell became the first to win the MVP trophy twice.

Although an Ontario team had won the cup, all was not well in the east. "Sometime around 1948 lacrosse started to peter out," according to Ken Croft of the St. Catharines Athletics. "There

was a decade there where lacrosse was really down in the doldrums."[187] Things were no better in the west. Veterans had other things on their minds—young families and careers. Lacrosse took a back seat.

Wilkes stepped down as coach before the start of the 1949 season, although he stayed in the game as a referee. Jack Wood as coach was reunited with Grumpy. The two had worked wonders through the war years. Five veterans departed, including high-scoring forwards Jerome and Carter and long-time defenceman Bert Bryant. Wood replaced them with five juniors. The press dubbed the youthful team the "kid corps." One of the juniors was fast-running forward Hugh Cruickshank—all of five-foot-five and 135 pounds.

Hume found a job for Ike Hildebrand, so the scoring star stayed with the team rather than going to St. Catharines as he had planned. Second-year man Harry Preston was back in net.

Salmonbellie Bert Bryant checks an unidentified North Shore Indians player in 1948.

VANCOUVER PUBLIC LIBRARY. PHOTO BY ART JONES.

The league, looking for ways to bring in fans, eased the rules to encourage rough play. Grumpy and Wood put a credible team on the floor, but they ended the season out of the playoffs with a 6–10 record.

The Adanacs, a brilliant 15–1 in the regular season, earned a bye in the first round of the playoffs. The veteran-laden Burrards, coached by John Cavallin and led on the floor by league leading scorers Jim Anderson and MVP Harry Buchanan with 44 points each, defeated the North Shore Indians 3–1 to advance to the finals against the Adanacs. Despite eleven points each from Norm Baker, Jack Northup, and Whitey Severson, the Adanacs fell 4–2 to the Burrards, who were led by Earl McDonald's seventeen goals, Don Matheson's fifteen assists, and playmaking defenceman Jack Byford's nineteen points. The Burrards, in their distinctive knight's cross-emblazoned sweaters, took on the Hamilton Tigers for the Mann Cup.

Coach Jack Wood has the attention of six young Salmonbellies in May, 1950.
Kneeling l-r: Jake Trotzuk, Ian McDonald, Jack Wood.
Standing l-r: Cliff Harrington, Hugh Cruikshank, Jerry Garner, Bud Harradine

The Tigers had wound up their regular season in fifth spot in the seven-team Ontario Lacrosse Association (OLA) league. Their big gun, Jack Dorney, had finished second in scoring with seventy-seven goals and fifty-five assists to Mimico's Ken Dixon's 135 points. Blain McDonald, George Masters, and the legendary Bill Isaacs were Hamilton's other big scoring threats. Doug Favell guarded their goal, but the Burrards' new goaltender, Jack Green, in his first season with the Burrards after a season with the Richmond Farmers, was superb in net behind the firepower of Ernie Smith, Jim Anderson, and Mann Cup MVP Don Matheson. The Burrards disposed of the Tigers three games to one.

Grumpy was sick with cancer as the 1949 season drew to a close. His regime of fifteen cigars a day every day had finally caught up with him. He was down to 125 pounds. In hospital, he needed a transfusion. The call went out and his team responded. But even with Salmonbellies' blood flowing in his veins, he passed away at New Westminster's Royal Columbian Hospital on September 21. "Grumpy was our manager right up until his death and one of the finest men I've ever known," said Jack Wood. "He kept our club together despite everything, yet never used an ill word."[188]

One way or another Grumpy had been with the Salmonbellies for forty-one continuous years. He was the team's leading scorer during the professional era, helping them win nine Minto Cup championships in thirteen years. He coached or managed five Mann Cup championship teams. His death marked the beginning of a long decline in the fortunes of the Salmonbellies.

On June 25, 1950, thousands of North Korean infantrymen, supported by tanks and aircraft, crossed the 38th Parallel and invaded South Korea. Against the backdrop of war, the ICLL reverted to seven-man lacrosse, hoping that the added rover would lead to more goals and more fans—especially more fans. Attendance had been on a steep downward slope since World War II and showed no sign of improving.

Blackie Black, having added coach of the North Shore Indians to his lacrosse résumé, weighed in on what lacrosse needed to regain the spotlight. A salesman and a showman, he called for more "ballyhoo" in "selling an unessential to the public."[189]

The Salmonbellies were defeated 14–13 by the Adanacs when they met for the first time in 1950. The Salmonbellies had not beaten their purple and yellow rivals in four years. But in a different sense, the Adanacs and the Salmonbellies were defeating each other. New Westminster simply could not support two senior teams. There was only one arena, one junior system to mine for players, and one base of fan support—and a shrinking one at that. Frustrated Adanacs' coach Bob Lee announced he would quit at the end of the season. He had no solution for the vicious circle in which the sport was caught, with meagre numbers of fans turning out for games and meagre numbers of players turning out for practices. As a result, the team did not improve, which in turn kept more fans from attending games.

His idea that the league comprise four teams had been kicking around since 1949. The plan was that the Burrards and Richmond form one Vancouver team, and the Adanacs and Salmonbellies form one New Westminster team.

The Adanacs finished the season atop the league standings with a record of 19–10–1. The Wood-coached Salmonbellies finished a dismal fifth in the six-team league at 17–12–1. Garnie Carter and Preston had split the goaltending duties down the middle, each playing fifteen games. Alf Wood led the 1950 Salmonbellies in points with ninety-one, only five points off the Adanacs' Jackie Northup's league leading total of ninety-six.

But it was not Jack Wood's team that advanced to the Mann Cup. It was the Adanacs, for the third time in four years.

That year, the CLA changed the Mann Cup format. Instead of five games, the championship would consist of seven. Their opponents were the Owen Sound Crescents, featuring Lloyd "Moon" Wotton in goal. Their best goal scorers were Doug Gillespie, Don Campbell, Russ Slater, and Arnold "Onions" Smith.

New Westminster-born Jackie Northup led the Adanacs, backed by goalie Gordie Pogue. Northup was a one-man ball-ragging machine with a powerful shot, but Wotton would hold him to just six goals in the first six games. The Adanacs borrowed high-scoring Alf Wood from the Salmonbellies, but it was Reo Jerome, in his first and only season with the Adanacs after four years with the Salmonbellies, who shone in the Mann Cup, notching seven goals and seven assists to lead the Adanacs in scoring. Right behind him with eleven points each were Northup, Bob Bremner, Jake Proctor, and Wood.

In the sixth game, Moon tore knee ligaments, so Doug Favell took his place. Favell, who'd repelled Adanacs' shots in the Mann Cup two years earlier, did it again in the seventh game, giving up just one goal in the final thirty minutes. The Crescents won the game 15–7 and with it the Mann Cup. Moon Wotton was awarded the MVP trophy, the first of three for him. As for the New Westminster Adanacs, it was their last Mann Cup appearance.

The Salmonbellies-Adanacs merger became a reality in 1951, when the joined teams became the Commandos, a respectful nod to the sacrifices made by Canadian troops in Korea. After sixty-two years, the Salmonbellies had ceased to exist. What the First and Second World Wars, the Great Depression, and the switch to box had been unable to do, the war in Korea and dwindling fan support had finally done.

The Salmonbellies and the Adanacs were not the only teams to lose their identities. Vancouver and Richmond also merged, becoming the Vancouver Combines.

Salmonbellies fans, especially the old-time players, including Jack Wood, were not happy with the new name. Oscar Swanson, Billy Gifford, and others pushed for a return to the team's original name, the New Westminster Lacrosse Club. One disgusted fan suggested they call the team Salad, a blend of Salmonbellies and Adanacs.[190] The Adanacs were equally unhappy; it was the end of eighteen years of tradition that had produced two Mann Cups. Perhaps the only player ready for the combination was Lew Landess, who had been an Adanac in 1945 and 1946 and a Salmonbellie in 1948.

Jack Wood stepped aside and Ralph Douglas took the reins as the Commandos' playing coach. Douglas, brother of Johnny and nephew to Jimmy, had played his first season in an Adanacs' uniform in 1941 and had been with the Adanacs continuously since 1945. He had the unenviable, near-impossible task of trying to unite the two factions.

The new team boasted the scoring punch of Adanac Jack Northup and Salmonbellie Alf Wood. The two men had finished first and second in league scoring in 1950. The Adanacs' Pogue and the Salmonbellies' Preston would split goaltending duties.

The Commandos took to the floor for the first time on May 4 at Queen's Park Arena. About 1,000 fans saw a team dressed in yellow and red jerseys with a large, gold, maple leaf crest and navy blue trunks with white stripes. The teams played six-on-six, the league having again eliminated the rover position.

Lew Landess scored the Commandos' first goal in a 15–12 New Westminster victory. The Commandos went on to win nineteen of thirty-two games, finishing second in league

Salmonbellie stalwart and Lancaster bomber rear gunner Bert Houston, Max Skinner and "whirlwind goal reaper" Hugh Cruikshank.

HUGH CRUIKSHANK. PHOTO BY BOB YOUNG.

In 1950 the Salmonbellies would finish fifth out of six teams. Jake Trotzuk, Bud Harradine and Dick Kennedy

HUGH CRUIKSHANK. PHOTO BY BOB YOUNG.

play behind the Victoria Shamrocks, a marked improvement. But the alliance of the teams was awkward and uneasy. In the dressing room, the Salmonbellies changed in one half of the room and the Adanacs stuck to the other half. While they played as a team on the floor, they did not socialize together afterwards, thereby breaking the cardinal rule of winning lacrosse teams—the team that drinks together wins together. At the Russell Hotel after games, the Adanacs would sit on one side of the bar and the Salmonbellies would sit on the other, four tables away. The separation existed even farther afield than the Arena and the Russell. Incredibly, the players were encouraged not to walk on the same sides of New Westminster's streets.

Alfie Wood led the team in scoring with sixty-six goals and eighty points overall, good enough for second in the league. He was followed in team scoring by Jack Northup, Art Pruden, and Hugh Cruikshank.

Pogue played eighteen games to Preston's sixteen. Statistically, there was no difference between the two, Pogue's save average of .688% being all of .001% better than Preston's.

Despite showing well in the playoffs against the Vancouver Combines, the Commandos

The Salmonbellies prior to boarding a Douglas DC-3 at Vancouver International Airport for their opening game of the season against Victoria, May 1950. **Front row l-r:** Hugh Cruikshank ('DC' crest on jacket), John "Hoty" Shaw. **Second row far left to right:** Unidentified, Bob Jones (equip. mngr.), Ian McDonald, Bud Harradine, Bill Jobb, Max Skinner, Harry Preston, Cliff Harrington, Ernie Bradford, George Friend (trainer), Bert Houston, Dick Kennedy. **Third row:** Jake Trotzuk, Bob Raffle, Barry Wood (Jack's son). **Fourth row:** Alf Wood, Jack Wood, Sid Martin. **Missing from photo:** Bill Jiry, Jack Handley, King Crick.

tied the Combines at 15 in overtime in game 1, narrowly lost game 2 (15–12) and game 3 (13–8), and lost game 4 in overtime (14–13). Vancouver went on to play a hard-fought and close-scoring series against the Peterborough Timbermen in the Mann Cup. The Timbermen, led by forward Ross Powless and goalie Moon Wotton, edged Vancouver 13–7 in the seventh game to win the cup.

In 1952, the Commandos were rechristened the Salmonacs in a desperate, half-baked attempt at reconciliation. Art Pruden, who'd joined the Salmonbellies in 1948, replaced Douglas as playing coach. It was an impossible situation for the Salmonacs and unfair to Pruden, who could not really be expected any more than Douglas to command a divided team of which he was still an active player and strongly associated with just one half. Pruden resigned in late February and Blackie Black stepped into the coach's role, hoping to end the dissension between the two factions.

Gord Pogue retired, leaving Preston alone to guard the net, and Northup departed for Victoria, leaving the goal scoring to Alf Wood. The Salmonacs finished second in the league with a 19–13 record to the Victoria Shamrocks' 22–10. Vancouver, now sponsored by beer company Carling and renamed the Pilseners after one of the company's brands, finished third followed by the Pacific National Exhibition (PNE) Indians and the Nanaimo Native Sons.

The Salmonacs lost to the Pilseners 3–1 in the playoffs, and Vancouver was again defeated in the Mann Cup by the Peterborough Timbermen.

In 1953, the year the Korean War ended, the Salmonacs were defeated, managing just six wins in thirty-two games. Had it not been for goaltender Harry Preston, the team might have lost even more games. With Alf Wood not playing, the only Salmonac to crack the top ten in scoring was Bob Raffle at number six. Sports fans were unimpressed; only about 200 people bothered to come out to the Arena on game nights. Attendance stayed that low for the next four years.

Clarence "Spunk" Oddy, grandson of 1890s Salmonbellie Thack Oddy, who joined the Salmonacs that season, was one of the bright spots on the team, scoring thirty-one goals and sixteen assists to win the league's rookie of the year. Preston won the Leo Nicholson trophy for the league's most outstanding goaltender, with a .727% save average.

For a change, the Victoria Shamrocks and not Vancouver met the Peterborough Timbermen (who became the Peterborough Trailermen in 1954) in the Mann Cup. But the western representative hardly mattered to the Timbermen, who once again prevailed, this time 4–1.

The Salmonbellies-turned-Commandos-turned-Salmonacs became the Royals for 1954. Ralph Douglas, playing coach of the 1950 squad, took over the reins in a strictly coaching capacity. Seven members of the 1953 Minto Cup champion junior Salmonacs team moved up to senior, including Doug McRory, Cliff Sepka, Don Sepka, Ivan Stewart, and Jack Barclay.

The Sepka brothers, Stewart, and Barclay—like Preston and Trotzuk—grew up playing lacrosse together in Newton. The Sepka brothers delivered papers together, running them over the long distances between houses because they did not have a bicycle. Later, their father built one from spare parts salvaged from a scrap heap. He also helped the boys clear some bush and level the ground for Newton's first lacrosse box, where the Sepkas, Stewart, Barclay, and others would practice and play.

Balls would frequently fly off into the surrounding bush. When they'd lost most of the balls, they would let their dog smell one. Then Cliff or Don would hide it behind his back, and, substituting a rock for the ball, throw it into the bush. The dog kept on retrieving until it had found every lost ball. The boys also hung an old tire from a rope tied to a tree branch. They'd set it swinging from side to side and take turns throwing balls through the middle.

The Adanacs' contingent had dwindled to just three players: John Douglas, Ted Mosdell, and Harrison Smith. The league's best goalie, Harry Preston, sat out the year. Bill Scuby's understudy, Bill Sampson, took Preston's place for twenty-two of the thirty-two league games.

The Royals, fired by the winning spirit of their rookies, believed they were destined to capture the Mann Cup, just as they'd captured the Minto the previous year. But they soon learned that the difference between junior and senior lacrosse is pronounced. A pattern emerged. The Royals would be in contention for three periods until the opposition's veterans took control, sending them to defeat by two or three goals. The team suffered twenty-seven losses in thirty-two games to finish in the basement.

Only Landess, with fifty-three points, cracked the top-ten scoring list. Right behind him, however, with fifty-two points, was rookie Cliff Sepka, and not far behind him were line mates Stewart and Barclay and Don Sepka. Far down on the scoring list, but high on the hitting list, was rookie Doug McRory. The six-foot-two, 195-pound defenceman was built like Superman and hit like a wrecking ball. Remarkably, he had never touched a lacrosse stick until joining the Salmonacs two years earlier, at the age of nineteen.

Once again, the Shamrocks were the best in BC in 1954. They had five players among the top ten scorers in league play, including Jack Northup in second place. But the big news was a player from Huntsville, Ontario, by the name of Jack Bionda.

The 1953 junior Salmonacs won the first two games of a best-of-five series against the Long Branch Monarchs, went to hospital with food poisoning and lost games three and four, and won game five to become the first New Westminster junior team to win the Minto Cup. **Front row l-r:** Terry Douglas, #7 Murray Duncan, #12 Harry Kelleher, #6 Harry Stewart, #9 Alfie Angell, Jack Faulke. **Second row:** Paddy O'Hunter (trainer), Ivan Stewart, Ken "Truck" McDonald (stand-in coach), Cliff Sepka (holding cup), # 21 Ron Delmonico, Wally Davis. **Third row:** Al Browning (manager), Stan Cowie, Jack Barclay, Don Martin, Barry Pfaff, Noble Collins, Doug McRory. **Back row:** Max Skinner, Don Sepka, Don Frey. **Missing:** coach Ralph Douglas, Floyd Christiiansen (asst. trainer).

BILL ARMSTRONG & STAN COWIE.

The six-foot, 180-pound Bionda was every inch the stereotypical, 1950s all-Canadian boy—blond, with a crewcut and winning smile, he was wholesome to the core. He grew up playing hockey in the winter, but it was summer's lacrosse that he looked forward to. "I didn't play lacrosse to get better," he said, "I played because I loved it."[191] The love was reciprocal. "That Bionda boy—even people who don't like him, love him," observed Huntsville policeman Si Payne.[192] At eighteen, Bionda led the junior Brampton Excelsiors to Minto Cup victory in 1952. He joined Hamilton's senior team in 1953, then the Shamrocks in 1954, capturing the league scoring title with forty-six goals and thirty-three assists. Victoria then defeated the PNE Indians in the league finals before going down 4–1 to perennial champions, the renamed Peterborough Trailermen, in the Mann Cup.

This box hung on a wall at Queen's Park Arena for many years.

*"I hope New Westminster can put lacrosse back on
its feet, like it was at the start of the century, when
the town closed down for games at the old oval."*

Chief Mathias Joe, *Columbian*, August 7, 1959

CHAPTER NINE

FULTON, McKNIGHT, & BIONDA: 1955-1964

In 1955, New Westminster got back their Salmonbellies name and identity, if not their championship-calibre team. The Salmonbellies, coached again by Jack Wood, finished last, with just six wins in thirty-two games. The Nanaimo Timbermen won the 1955 league, with twenty-five wins, followed by the Shamrocks.

Bionda played only seventeen regular-season games for the Shamrocks, but still led the team in goals with thirty-nine, tying Bill Bamford with forty-nine points overall. Bionda, however, was even better in the playoffs, leading the Shamrocks over Nanaimo to advance to the Mann Cup. Professional hockey commitments kept Bionda from the series against Peterborough, but Victoria, led by Archie Browning, Whitey Severson, and Jack Northup, overcame the Trailermen 4–1 to capture their first Mann Cup.

The rudderless Salmonbellies had reached the lowest point in their history. Without a Charlie Welsh and a Herb Ryall, without a Fred Hume and a Grumpy Spring, the team was on the verge of folding—permanently.

In 1956, firefighter Jack Fulton volunteered to help out the Salmonbellies. Fulton was born in 1926 and raised in New Westminster's West End, just two doors down from Grumpy. Fulton was a basketball player, not a lacrosse player, but he'd always taken a keen interest in the Salmonbellies. When he was with the Merchant Navy during World War II, his sister Edith cut out newspaper articles on the team and mailed them to him, a reminder of home. Fulton came out of the Merchant Navy in 1949 with his tugboat master's ticket, and the New Westminster Fire Department hired him the next year to run their boat on the Fraser River. When Fulton volunteered with the Salmonbellies, Wilf Hill was the team's general manager; Fulton became equipment manager.

The Salmonbellies won a couple of early-season games in 1956, but it was obvious they were not going to be championship contenders. Hill and Wood, unable to field a competitive team, were out of ideas and did not want to consider new realities. While other teams spent money to hire players, they would not, holding true to the old amateur ideals stretching back to the 1890s.

Fulton was much younger and more pragmatic. He cared about the future—the "ballyhoo" kind envisioned by Blackie Black—not the past. Taking over as team manager, Fulton asked

Bill Tyler to coach. Tyler didn't want the job—no one did—but reluctantly took it on.

Fulton enjoyed managing, but needed someone at his side to help promote. He thought of his friend and colleague in the fire department, Harry McKnight. A softball player, McKnight coached both a men's and women's team to Canadian championships. He was competitive, social, talkative, and a great promoter. McKnight agreed to pair with Fulton.

The Salmonbellies lost two more games in 1956 than they did in 1955. They also lost one of their great stars. Dad Turnbull died on August 27 at eighty-four.

Wherever Jack Bionda went, Mann Cups followed.

BC SPORTS HALL OF FAME.
PHOTOGRAPH BY JOHN ASKEW.

Despite the team's lackluster performance, McKnight had no doubt where the Salmonbellies were headed. He told Fulton they would win the Mann Cup in 1958. In Vancouver, junior coach Jack McKinnon had the same goal. In 1956, his junior team had won their second Minto Cup title in three years. In the meantime, they all watched as the Nanaimo Timbermen, led by former Peterborough stars Don Ashbee, Don "Nip" O'Hearn, and Bob Allan defeated the Peterborough Trailermen for the 1956 Mann Cup.

When the PNE Indians folded themselves into the Vancouver Pilseners prior to the 1957 season, Fulton recognized the opportunity to pick up some talented players and maybe a coach to replace the reluctant Tyler. He hired Jake Proctor, from St. Boniface, Manitoba. Proctor had fourteen senior seasons under his belt, beginning with the 1941 Adanacs. After four years in the Navy, he returned to New Westminster and played a few games with the Salmonbellies before rejoining the Adanacs in 1946, helping them to a Mann Cup the following year. Known for his lacrosse savvy, Proctor was coaxed out of retirement and into a player-coach role in 1954 by the PNE Indians. He led the Indians into the finals that year and the next and was recruited to coach Vancouver in 1956.

Proctor had a good relationship with his players and in 1957, Fulton was able, with Proctor's help, to recruit four Vancouver veterans (defenceman Jack Byford, Mario and Larry Crema, goaltender Stan Joseph) for $250–500 each and a split of the gate receipts.

Joseph's father, Stan Joseph Sr., had played for the Salmonbellies and the Indians in the 1930s and Stan Jr. grew up surrounded by lacrosse men. There was nothing orthodox about Joseph. He played his own game. He held the shaft of his stick in both hands, with the leather at waist height. During games "he just stood there," recalled Cliff Sepka, "hardly moving."[193] But he had extremely quick reflexes, so quick, in fact, that he was nicknamed "Bunny."

Like all great goaltenders, Joseph was a character. He moaned to Fulton about not having a job. Fulton replied that they got him one as a longshoreman. "Yeah," said Joseph, "but it sounds like a lot of work."[194] He was notorious for losing things, and not caring about it very much. One teammate recalled his dragging his equipment bag onto the ferry after a game on Vancouver Island. A variety of sweaty items spilled from a hole in the bag, leaving a long trail behind. Joseph kept walking. In bars after games, he would serenade his teammates with his impersonation of vocalist Bill Kenny's wistful "Whispering Grass (Don't Tell The Trees)", the Ink Spots' 1940 hit.

With Proctor at the helm and Vancouver veterans on board, the 1957 Salmonbellies won half of their league games. Stan Joseph played all 30 games, with a save percentage of .721%

for the season. Byford had forty-nine assists along with eleven goals to lead the team in points. Sepka led in scoring, with forty-one, followed by Vern Wilkie and Bill Jobb.

"Jobb had a hard shot," recalled Sepka, "I wouldn't even play catch with him—he'd wreck your pocket he threw so hard."[195] Jobb's go-to shot was an underhand sub shot, released with a ferocious whip-like action, often from long range.

The 1957 Salmonbellies made the league semi-finals for the first time in five years. They managed one win against Nanaimo, but the Timbermen took the series and faced the Victoria Shamrocks in the finals.

In twenty-six regular-season games, Victoria's star attraction, Bionda, had scored 102 points, 68 of them goals. He was by now an unmistakable figure in senior Canadian lacrosse circles. Bionda had long arms (a thirty-six-inch sleeve) and bowed legs, and loped rather than ran. He shot from his left side, preferring the side-arm shot to the overhand. When carrying the ball in the heat of battle—looking for an opening, cutting in—his tongue bulged out his cheek. He had a trade-mark "trick" shot. After convincingly faking a shot, he'd coil the stick behind his back and, dipping, release the ball from the side of his heel. "Your stick," he often said, "has to be a natural extension of your arm."[196]

Bionda was deadly. Opposing teams had little choice but to deploy two players to check him. Even then, he was unstoppable. He took a long time to beat his man, but he always did. The way to deal with Bionda was not to check him too hard. If he got angry, he was liable to go on a scoring spree. He was fundamentally lazy, the thinking went, so leave him alone as much as possible and whatever you do, do not rile him.

As great as Bionda was, Victoria was none too happy when, in the third game against Nanaimo, he "assaulted" the referee. The incident earned him a suspension, which is just what Bionda wanted. He had to report to the Boston Bruins' training camp, and a suspension was the only way he was going to get there.[197] Victoria, minus Bionda, defeated Nanaimo in the seventh game and represented the west against the Peterborough Trailermen. Because of a disagreement with the CLA, however, the Long Branch Pontiacs represented the east instead of the Trailermen.[198] Victoria won the Mann Cup 4–0.

While Bionda toiled for Boston and Springfield, Fulton and McKnight wondered if he might be available to the Salmonbellies for the 1958 season. Bionda was known to be unhappy in Victoria. Would he be interested in joining a young and resurgent New Westminster team? Fulton asked him in a letter. Yes, Bionda responded, he was inter-ested. For $3,500. (At that time, the average Canadian took home about $4,000 a year.)

Fulton and McKnight did not have $3,500. Their biggest fundraiser was an annual dinner. It was, however, their chance to get Bionda. They went to their players and asked if they wanted Bionda on the team. Affirmative. Did they understand he would be paid a salary while most of them, other than the former Vancouver players, would not be? No problem, just get him. Fulton and McKnight thought it over and decided that unsalaried players would share gate receipts in lieu of salary and salaried players would be paid through raised money.

As the annual ticket sales drive got underway in April, McKnight appealed to the team's fans for support, reminding them that the Salmonbellies were the only unsponsored club in the

There was no stopping Jack Bionda, who won Mann Cups with Victoria and Nanaimo. But it's his Mann Cups with New Westminster in 1958, '59, '62 and '65 that made him legendary. Jack Barclay takes the hit.

VANCOUVER PROVINCE. PHOTOGRAPH BY JOHN ASKEW.

league."[199] They hoped to double the sales of prepaid books of tickets.

Despite the fact that he got himself suspended to make Boston's training camp, Victoria hated to give up Bionda. Not only had he helped them get to the 1957 Mann Cup, he'd also accounted for 40% of their gate receipts. In April the lacrosse commission approved Bionda's transfer. He was officially a Salmonbellie.

When Fulton and McKnight picked up Bionda at Vancouver's airport, Bionda informed them that he had not played the last two hockey games because he'd hurt his knee. As they drove along, he kept rubbing it. Fulton and McKnight exchanged worried looks. "Holy mackerel," thought Fulton. "We've got all this dough tied up in this guy and he's got a bum knee."[200] Would he be ready to play? Bionda assured them that he would. They reminded him that he was a big investment. As much as they needed him to score goals, they also needed him to put on a show to fill seats.

Bill Jobb joined the Salmonbellies in 1949, persevered through the losing years, and won three Mann Cups before retiring after the 1963 season. Seen here in 1958. Here Nanaimo Timbermen's Irwin "Spud" Morelli tries to check Jobb in 1958.

NEW WESTMINSTER MUSEUM AND ARCHIVES.

Bionda said he'd look after it. And he did. "He had everyone on the team eating out of his hand," recalled Fulton. "He fitted in so well and he was comical. Everybody idolized him because he was that good and a nice guy to boot. Not a drinker, he might have one beer, but he liked the girls. They all chased him and he liked that all right."[201]

After defeating the Shamrocks in Victoria to start the season, the Salmonbellies faced Victoria again in the first game at Queen's Park. Unrecognized among the big turnout that Friday night was a 71-year-old gentleman, who showed up to see Bionda play. He was Édouard "Newsy" Lalonde. Before the game got underway a man who would have surely recognized Lalonde, Willis Patchell, welcomed Bionda on behalf of New Westminster's minor lacrosse association. That evening, the Salmonbellies handed the defending Mann Cup champion Shamrocks their second defeat, 19–5, with Bionda both scoring and assisting three times. He'd been booed in Victoria but was cheered in New Westminster. Bionda raised his teammates' games and made everyone a better player, just as Newsy had done more than forty years earlier.

The Salmonbellies rolled along, seemingly winning at will, and were getting under their rivals' skin. Shamrocks' coach Whitey Severson called them gutless. Vancouver's coach, Jack McKinnon, claimed, "If you start swinging your stick at them, you won't have any trouble with them all night."[202] But by July 2, Bionda, swinging his stick toward the goal, had netted fifty-three, twice as many as any other player in the league. And then, a day later, hard-shooting Bill Jobb scored seven in a Salmonbellies' victory over Nanaimo. Four days after that the "gutless" Salmonbellies proved they could win without Bionda, once again taking down the Timbermen 11–8 in Nanaimo.

Bionda and Sepka played with custom-made elbow, kidney, and shoulder pads. Preston and Trotzuk had been making their own pads for years and happily made sets for their teammates. They purchased fibreboard in eight-foot by four-foot sheets and cut them with a jigsaw according to the patterns they'd made. Soaking the fibreboard pieces in water made them pliable, allowing them to be shaped to fit a player's contours. Thick felt padding was then glued with contact cement to the undersides of the pieces. The pads offered good protection, but also soaked up sweat, growing heavier as the game went. The kidney pads also tended to sag, so Preston and Trotzuk solved the problem with hockey suspenders.

The Salmonbellies won the regular season on seventeen wins and two ties out of thirty games. Bionda's sixty-eight goals and thirty-six assists in twenty-five games earned him his second straight scoring title and his third since coming west in 1954.

Nanaimo disposed of Vancouver in the league semifinals, setting up a showdown with the Salmonbellies. Nanaimo won the sixth game at home to tie the series. On the ferry back to the mainland, Joseph, who had played unevenly, tried to open a beer bottle and cut his hand badly enough to require twenty stitches. He was convinced that he couldn't play the seventh and deciding game. McKnight found him sitting on a stump in front of his home on the North Shore reserve and told him how much they needed him. Joseph held up his wounded paw and shook his head. McKnight told him the team doctor would give him a shot to freeze his hand so he wouldn't feel a thing while he played. Joseph duly received the shot and took to the floor at the Arena.

By the end of the first quarter, Joseph reported that his hand felt much better. He was brilliant in goal all game long, blanking "Skip" MacKay while Bionda scored four times, all on the odd-man play. The Salmonbellies defeated the Timbermen 11–5 to win the league championship for the first time since 1946. McKnight was a happy man. He was also smiling inwardly. His instructions to the doctor prior to the game were to prick Joseph's hand with an empty syringe.

The Ali Baba-coached Welland-Crowland Switsons (formerly the St. Catharines Athletics) won the 1958 Ontario title, with seven players making the top-twelve scoring list. They were a small, fast team, with enough big veteran players such as Don "Nip" O'Hearn to keep their opponents honest. Their style of play was similar to the Salmonbellies'—fast and wide open.

They eliminated the Brampton Excelsiors in the playoffs in four straight games. But the Switsons' success owed a lot to the suspensions handed out to the Peterborough Trailermen players a year earlier for refusing to play in the Mann Cup without Bob Allan. The Peterborough team was the real powerhouse of Ontario. With their veterans suspended, Peterborough had been forced to field a senior team of juniors.

The Switsons, sponsored by vacuum manufacturer Switson Industries, had a turbulent airplane ride to the coast. The turbulence got even worse when they met the Salmonbellies in game 1. The team had trouble hanging onto the ball and appeared disorganized. Coach Teal, substituting for Madsen, admitted they were nervous. In addition, they were used to playing on concrete, they claimed, and couldn't adapt to the Arena's wood floor. The game, played in front of 3,800 fans, was a 20–7 win for the Salmonbellies.

Skip McKay, picked up from Nanaimo, replaced injured players Murray Duncan and Jack Byford. MacKay and Bionda combined on the night for sixteen points against Switsons' goalie Justin Howe.

Directly behind the Salmonbellies' bench, Fred Hume, now the famous "$1 a year in salary" mayor of Vancouver watched the game and liked what he saw: visions of 1937 and 1943.

The Switsons cracked down on Bionda and MacKay in game 2, holding MacKay to one assist and Bionda pointless. Their goaltender, Geordie Johnston, on loan from the Victoria Shamrocks and Howe's replacement, stopped thirty-three shots, but that wasn't enough. The

Quirky, irrepressible goalkeeper Stan "Bunny" Joseph hung with the Salmonbellies for three seasons (1957–59), winning two Mann Cups. In a career spanning three decades and five teams, Joseph played 522 games. He stopped 13,040 of 18,456 shots, a save percentage of a fraction over 70%.

BC SPORTS HALL OF FAME.

Salmonbellies took the game, scoring three unanswered goals in the fourth quarter to win 7–4.

While 2,800 fans saw game 2, 400 fewer showed up for game 3. The Switsons tried Jack Timlock in nets, but he fared no better than Howe and Johnston, and the Salmonbellies won 17–6. Ken Oddy, playing centre on Bionda's line, had five goals, Jack Barclay had three, and Bionda contributed two goals and four assists.

Just 2,000 people showed up for game 4. Was the game's outcome a foregone conclusion or was ABC TV's *Adventures of Ozzie and Harriet*—Wednesday nights at 8:30—simply too irresistible? Whatever the reason for the small crowd, the Salmonbellies won the game 14–6 and with it the Mann Cup. Oddy led all goal scorers with eleven goals and Cliff Sepka had sixteen points, but MacKay's twenty-two points was top overall, earning him the MVP trophy. McKnight's prediction had come true.

In 1959, Fulton and McKnight arranged for a press conference at the King Neptune restaurant on the Fraser River to announce a sponsorship deal with O'Keefes Brewery. The press, especially the *Columbian*, was highly critical. The city and its citizens had supported the team for seventy years. But now, on the heels of the Commandos/Salmonacs misfire, they were taking on the support and the name of a brewery? Now the team known far and wide as the Salmonbellies would be known as the O'Keefes?

City council was none too impressed either. Mayor Beth Wood, wife of Jack Wood, was incensed. Alderman and Parks Commissioner Ken Wright saw no reason, in light of the sponsorship, to continue the city's long-standing practice of discounting the team's rent at Queen's Park Arena. Why, in effect, should the city subsidize a brewery?

The city's merchants were also ticked off, feeling they had been misled when they had been canvassed for money earlier in the spring. As for the fans, they did not think it right that the name Salmonbellies should "drown in a beer bottle."[203]

The furor caught Fulton and McKnight off guard. The Salmonbellies were on the verge of collapse. Where were the fans? Not at the Arena on game nights. Other than turning back a few thousand dollars, where was the city's financial support? Did anyone seriously believe that a modern lacrosse team could be run on the proceeds of a $50-a-plate dinner?

"Let's face it," said McKnight, "It's a great name, but it doesn't put any money into the club. We have been forced to find an alternative."[204] McKnight mentioned the increased cost of such things as sticks and balls, but he did not mention Bionda's salary. "We did," said McKnight, "what was right for the players."[205]

The last thing O'Keefes wanted was to be seen as a villain. They graciously told Fulton to keep the brewery's $4,000 (earmarked to pay Bionda's salary) and stick with the Salmonbellies name. Fulton would not hear of it. They were in for the long haul; they would ride out the controversy. They renegotiated the arena lease with former Salmonbellie and Adanac Stu Gifford, now an alderman.

They ordered new jerseys, white with yellow and blue trim. The O'Keefes name and logo, a German-style tankard, replaced the W and the salmon. The uniforms were different, but underneath, they were still the Salmonbellies. They were not alone when it came to accepting sponsorships and name changes. Nanaimo, funded by another beer company, became the Labatts. In Vancouver, the Pilseners became the Carlings, adopting the corporate name of their sponsor.

"I'm a clumsy skater," said Bionda before the season opener. "As far as that goes, I can't run either."[206] He was telling the truth. He took his time getting up the floor from his own end and even more time to beat his man and get off a shot or a pass. But despite his "handicap," he scored four goals in a 22–8 win over Nanaimo.

It was a false start, however. The team lost the next five games. Were the ghosts of past Salmonbellie teams punishing the O'Keefes? Whatever ailed the players, trainer Paddy O'Hunter nursed them back to health with his prescribed treatment, electricity. "He used suction cups and two live electrical wires," recalled Cliff Sepka. "You never went back."[207]

Nanaimo was in fine health, helped along by their passionate, and inebriated, fans. A beer parlour, the Newcastle, located just across the street from their arena, ensured well-lubricated crowds. The league, however, had a problem on its hands. Referees in Nanaimo were reluctant to make calls against the home team, fearing a deluge of whisky and beer bottles, two-by-fours, rubber hoses, and whatever else was not nailed down. Referee Gordie Folka, a former Salmonbellie, admitted he used "discretion" whenever he was in Nanaimo, which was as infrequently as possible. "It's an explosive situation," he remarked. "You can't call them too close or the crowd could get hot and I'd have a riot on my hands."[208]

In late May, Les Norman, just back from his honeymoon, was in the net for the O'Keefes for the first time. While he split net-minding duties over the season with Joseph, he was clearly being groomed to become the starter. The O'Keefes defeated the Labatts 12–5 for their first win in six outings. Whether or not it was Norman's post-honeymoon debut that kick-started the team, the O'Keefes ran off five straight wins.

On June 18 at Queen's Park Bionda scored three goals with nine assists against Nanaimo, one point short of Salmonbellie Pete Meehan's 1941 record. On June 21, the O'Keefes made it eight wins in a row, defeating Nanaimo at home 14–11.

Referee Ernie Smith, his nerves frayed, was hit in the head by a hard object thrown from the stands. He jumped the boards and went after the guy who had thrown it. Nanaimo's Don Ashbee, a former Peterborough player and the team's playing coach, threatened to pull his team off the floor. It was the same Ashbee who, angered by a referee's call, once grabbed the microphone on his way to the penalty box and announced, "Two minutes to Ashbee—for nothing!"[209] Not that the O'Keefes were behaving like angels. In fact, they were the most penalized team in the league.

They won their tenth straight on June 26. Cliff Sepka—with that slight hesitation in his shot that caused goalies to move, exposing an opening—scored five goals, while Bionda contributed three goals and five assists. On July 16 Bionda scored seven points to close in on Bob Allan's 1956 record of 127 regular-season points. He was, however, still twenty short of Salmonbellie Bill Wilson's 1937 all-time high of 135.

Sepka was hot too, scoring five goals in a 10–4 win over Victoria. Bionda passed Allan's mark on July 30, with a seven-goal, two-assist evening to reach 128. On the same night, Sepka got four goals. Bionda equalled Wilson's mark on August 3 with a goal and six assists in a 15–11 victory over Nanaimo.

Fulton was behind the bench for the game, the increasingly erratic Proctor having been suspended by the league. From time to time Proctor would be absent, due not to suspension but to the "flu." Proctor liked to enjoy a few beers at New Westminster's Dunsmuir Hotel, known as "the Dunny," while perusing the racing form and laying bets. Wilson's record was safe for one more game, Bionda being forced, due to a badly cut face, to sit out a 9–5 loss to the Vancouver Carlings. He was ready for the next game, but before the start was made an honorary chieftain of the Squamish Indian tribe. Chief Mathias Joe, a lacrosse player himself in the early 1900s, anointed Bionda "Cahalla"—top man—in a ceremony at the Arena.

Bionda was presented with an eighteen-inch totem pole and joined in with the Chief and his grandchildren as they danced together at centre floor. "I hope New Westminster can put lacrosse back on its feet," said the Chief. "Like it was at the start of the century, when the town closed down for games at the old oval."[210] Only 1,800 people were in attendance, nowhere near the huge crowds the Salmonbellies had enjoyed "when the town closed down for games."

The O'Keefes' opponent, the Carlings, won the game, but with less than three minutes remaining in the third period, Cahalla took a pass from McRory and, with John Cervi draped all over him, slipped the ball in the right side of the net as he crashed to the floor. He did it: point number 136, breaking Wilson's mark. It was Bionda's only goal and point of the game.

The O'Keefes defeated the Shamrocks four games to one in the playoffs to advance to the Mann Cup finals, where they faced the quietly reinstated Peterborough team, now known as the Mercuries, sponsored by the Ford Motor Company. The Mercuries were a formidable foe led by Bob Allan, who'd helped Nanaimo win the Mann Cup in 1956. Moon Wotton, now a "living legend," a term of respect that also meant "over the hill," played in goal.

Salmonbellies' defenceman Doug McRory played every season 1954 through 1964, won three Mann Cups, retired, and then came back to play thirty games in 1968.

BC SPORTS HALL OF FAME.

The Mercuries, however, had more than enough young players to complement the veterans. One of the youngest was Paul Parnell, who would one day be a legend himself—as a Salmonbellie.

New Westminster won the opener 12–5 on the strength of Bionda's seven points. "They won't take us four straight," declared Wotton after the game. "But we've got to stop Bionda or we're dead."[211]

The O'Keefes won the second game 18–11. Their power play was perfect, producing seven goals on seven penalties. Bionda scored four times and added four assists. One of his shots was so hard it left an inch-deep indentation in Wotton's leather and fibre shin guard. Barclay, a four-time Golden Gloves Champion, punched in six goals and an assist. According to future Salmonbellies GM, Bill Armstrong, "You could tell what kind of a game Barclay was going to have by his yawn during the national anthem."[212] The bigger the yawn, the better Barclay's game.

Game 3 ended in a 14–9 New Westminster victory, with Bionda scoring three times. For Peterborough, Paul Parnell scored twice with one assist, but it was Bob Allan who shocked the Salmonbellies' Rudy Riesinger, stunned Stan Joseph, and dazzled the crowd with a spectacular goal. Running at full speed along the boards with Riesinger checking him closely, Allan reached the blue line and, without breaking stride, unleashed a left-handed backhand shot that found the top left corner of Joseph's net—about 90 feet away. "He was a skinny little guy," recalled fourth-year-man Riesinger, "but his stick was so quick—I'd never seen anything like it."[213]

Barclay must have yawned wide before game 4. He notched four goals—all backhanders—in the O'Keefes' 13–4 win. The O'Keefes swept the series just as they had a year before and earned their fourteenth Mann Cup.

Wotton praised New Westminster's young goaltender, Les Norman, and passed him the torch: "He's now got the name I used to have."[214] By "name" he meant reputation as the best. A lot of credit went to defenceman Jack Byford, who had shackled Bob Allan. McRory had played the four games with his left hand in a cast. Bionda, with twenty-three points in the final series, was named MVP. Over the nine games of the playoffs, he tallied forty-one points, making it 185 points in both league play and playoffs combined. Without question, he delivered in 1959 what he had promised all along: goals, wins, big time showmanship, and fans in seats. "He had incredible anticipation," noted Fulton. "He would pick off a goaltender's pass and pop it right back in the net."[215] He also had a child-like quality. Once, having lost his stick before a game, he asked Fulton if he could borrow his. Using a stick he had never touched before, he tallied three goals and four assists.

Red McMillan, Nanaimo's new coach, knew Bionda from coaching him in Victoria. If Bionda would play for him, Red would give him a 10% interest in a hotel he owned. Fulton, however, already had Bionda's signature on a player's certificate. He was New Westminster property. Fulton had worked out a nice deal. Bionda would be paid $5,000 for the season, and the O'Keefes would pick up $2,000 of it. In return, Bionda would be a company representative.

But Bionda met Fulton at the firehall and told him about McMillan's offer. "I'm committed to you guys," he said, "but I have to go tell Red."[216] When he walked out the door, Fulton knew Bionda was gone. Sure enough, Bionda signed with Nanaimo.

Despite missing Bionda, the O'Keefes were much the same team. Proctor returned as coach. Norman started in goal, Joseph having returned to Vancouver, where he alternated with Don Hamilton, a four-year veteran newly acquired from Victoria. Young netminding prospect Merv Schweitzer, spelling Norman, played seven games for the Salmonbellies.

The O'Keefes led the league by seven points at the halfway mark, but fell into a losing slump. They needed a win on a Saturday night in July in Nanaimo to tighten their hold on second place. However, courtesy of a cross-check by Don Ashbee, they lost Jack Barclay to a broken jaw—no more yawning for a while. What's more, the helmeted Sepka got knocked cold by Tom McVie. As Sepka fell, McVie crashed a knee into his face. The O'Keefes scored twice while McVie served his penalty, and their 10–9 victory snapped a three-game losing streak.

As brutal as games in Nanaimo were, the trip home was almost worse. The Salmonbellies would be showered and out of the arena by 10:30 p.m., but the next Black Ball line ferry wasn't until 6:00 a.m. Most of the players headed over to the beer parlour. The Sepkas, being non-drinkers, watched over the team's equipment bags, sipping on milkshakes.

Inseparable: Jack Barclay, Cliff Sepka, Ivan Stewart. They grew up together, won the Minto Cup in '53 together, and they played twelve seasons together (1954-64), accounting for 2,225 points-together. 1958.

VANCOUVER PROVINCE. PHOTOGRAPH BY LARRY DEAN.

Things were getting increasingly wild on Vancouver Island, even by ICLL standards, and it wasn't just players. Victoria coach Norm Baker attacked referee Earl MacDonald during a game against the O'Keefes and was suspended for the duration of the season.

In August, the association tried to deal with the mayhem in the league. Without naming Nanaimo, they announced fines of up to $500 for rough play, profanity, and arguing with referees. The following night, in New Westminster, Nanaimo racked up fifty-four minutes in penalties in a 13–7 loss. After the contest, McKnight alleged that Nanaimo was trying to injure both Cliff Sepka, their leading scorer, and McRory, their best defenceman. McVie received a one-game suspension, and Ashbee and Proctor were suspended "indefinitely," which turned out to be a few days. It was Ashbee's second suspension. In 1959, he'd been forced to sit out for striking a referee. The association, realizing they had not gone far enough or been specific enough, ordered Nanaimo to post a $500 performance bond.

Through it all, Bionda fulfilled his personal performance "bond," scoring 118 points to win the scoring title for the fourth season in a row.

With Nanaimo up two games to one in the best-of-five playoff series, Bionda delivered the killing blow to New Westminster, scoring with less than forty-five seconds remaining to give Nanaimo a 9–8 victory. After Bionda's goal, an enraged Proctor charged from the bench and headed straight for referee Sid Greenwood. Greenwood's partner, Earl MacDonald, intercepted Proctor and wrestled him to the floor. Once he'd calmed down, Proctor was escorted to the dressing room. Nanaimo then defeated favoured Vancouver in the finals to advance to the Mann Cup against the Port Credit Sailors. The 1960 Mann Cup, one of the great upsets in Mann Cup history, would be the Sailors' one and only cup victory.

From 1953 to 1968 Peterborough's Bobby Allan could almost always find a corner of the net. A great nemesis of the Salmonbellies, in eight trips to the Mann Cup, Allan won four.

PETERBOROUGH & DISTRICT SPORTS HALL OF FAME.

Jack Byford was behind the O'Keefes' bench for the 1961 season. After fourteen seasons (four with New Westminster), stretching back to 1944, 342 games, and 567 points, the rugged defenceman was sticking strictly to coaching. The colourful Proctor, after running the New Westminster show for four years and two Mann Cups, took on an unlikely new role, becoming—of all things—a referee.

The team's most significant acquisition, however, was Paul Parnell, who had met the woman he would marry in New Westminster in 1959, when he was playing for the Mercuries in the Mann Cup. In 1960, he joined Victoria but was unhappy there and requested a transfer.

At first Fulton didn't think he could use Parnell. Thirteen eligible juniors were trying out for the team. But Fulton's opinion changed once he saw him "knocking guys around" during the pre-season practices.[217] He knocked plenty of guys around during the actual season too, and scored a lot of goals. Parnell's dedication to the team was total. He never missed a practice or a game, unless he was seriously injured. Other players might take a short summer vacation, but not Parnell. His will to win was evident when, in the locker room, without fail, he threw up before every game. "The more Paul got up, the better he played," recalled Bill Armstrong, who became the O'Keefes' team manager in 1965. "If he puked between periods, you knew he was on a roll."[218]

There was no puking with Les Norman. He insisted on a pork-chop dinner before every game. With well-fed Norman in goal and empty-gutted Parnell grabbing loose balls "as if he had glue in his stick" and scoring goals, the O'Keefes started the season with eleven straight wins.[219]

In early June, the team arrived in Portland, Oregon, for a four-game exhibition series against Nanaimo, part of the city's annual Rose Festival. Bionda had already established a reputation in the city, for the winter of 1960 was his inaugural season of hockey for the Western Hockey Association's Portland Buckeroos.

Almost 7,000 people came to the first lacrosse game of the series. Bionda putting on his usual display, was checked closely by McRory. The former teammates fought twice. The O'Keefes won the game.

In the second game, Bionda ran into the O'Keefes' Ron Loftus. He pulled ligaments in his right arm, causing him to be out for the remainder of the season. Nanaimo wasn't happy to see their star performer out of action. New Westminster won the second, third, and fourth games in front of large, enthusiastic crowds.

The O'Keefes continued to win after the Portland series. When the season ended, they were 25–4–1. But it was a different story in the playoffs. Vancouver, under player-turned-coach Bob Marsh, won the first two games. Norman was not stopping them as he had been, and his average slipped to less than 70 percent. He was singled out for blame.

Norman improved and the O'Keefes won the third game, but the Carlings won the next

Jack Barclay, master of the around-and-over-the-shoulder goal, Golden Glover, and one third of the deadly Sepka-Stewart-Barclay line. Barclay scored 342 goals in twelve seasons with the Salmonbellies, and won three Mann Cups. Lunging is Vancouver's Bill Chisholm. Unidentified goalkeeper. Undated photo, around 1958.

COLUMBIAN. PHOTOGRAPH BY G. YOUNG.

When a dejected Jack Barclay arrived home after a night of carousing, his wife asked the hard-hitting boxer what was wrong. "I knocked out a guy in a fight at the bar," he said, glumly. "That's not unusual for you," said his wife. "Yeah," said the dispirited pugilist, "but it took me two punches." Here he tussles with Frank Farley (left) of the Peterborough Mercuries in the 1959 Mann Cup.

COLUMBIAN. PHOTOGRAPH BY SEAMUS SMITH.

two to take the title. In Ontario, the Brampton Ramblers defeated the defending Mann Cup champion Port Credit Sailors for the Ontario title—Brampton's first since 1931, the year they beat the Salmonbellies in the last Mann Cup played on grass.

Brampton was not so fortunate against Vancouver. Backed by goalie Don Hamilton, who recorded the only shutout (13–0) in playoff and Mann Cup history in game 3—the Carlings swept the Excelsiors in four straight games to capture the cup.

Harry McKnight and Jack Fulton assembled the 1958 Salmonbellies, bet heavily on Bionda, and won the Mann Cup for the first time since 1943. **Front row:** Rudy Reisinger, Stan Joseph, Harry Preston, John Coleman. **Second row:** Ab Brown, Harry McKnight, Jack Fulton, Jake Proctor, Stan Mahony, Dr. Hugh Radford. **Third row:** Jack Cowie, Stan Radonich, Murray Duncan, Cliff Sepka, Jack Barclay, Ivan Stewart, Bill Jobb, Stan Cowie, Joe Durante, Harvey Russell. **Back row:** Walter Harris, Mario Crema, Ken Oddy, Doug McRory, Don Sepka, Jack Byford, Jack Bionda.

CANADIAN LACROSSE HALL OF FAME. PHOTOGRAPH BY DON LEBLANC.

In 1962, New Westminster drew first blood, defeating Vancouver in the season opener and tying them in the second game to win the two-game, total-points Shrine Cup for the third time in four years. Vancouver suffered a blow when they lost their great goaltender, Don Hamilton, to a company transfer. Coincidentally, a week after Hamilton's transfer, Les Norman stopped twenty-seven shots and recorded the first shutout in ICLL history on May 3, a 23–0 O'Keefes' victory over the Victoria Shamrocks at Queen's Park.

The venerable Stan Joseph and young Merv Schweitzer, who'd spent 1961 with Nanaimo, replaced Hamilton, and Vancouver ran off six straight wins before facing league-leading New Westminster on May 24, Victoria Day, a day that traditionally featured battle royals between New Westminster and Vancouver, going all the way back to the 1890s.

In the "wild and wooley"[220] contest, four players, New Westminster's Jack Barclay and Wayne Shuttleworth and Vancouver's Fred Usselman and Peter Black, received ten-minute game misconducts. A total of ninety-eight minutes in penalties was handed out, the majority to Vancouver. New Westminster prevailed 12–8 on league-leading scorers Sepka and Parnell's four assists and three goals, respectively.

On June 7, Vancouver, in a hard-fought but cleanly played game, took over first place with a 9–8 victory over New Westminster. The teams split their next two encounters. Then, on June 22, Cliff Sepka, in his ninth season, scored twice and added an assist in a game against the Burnaby Norburns to reach 400 career goals and 300 career assists.

Meanwhile, Bionda was idle in Portland. With ten games left in the lacrosse season, he told Fulton he'd play for the Salmonbellies for $1,000. Bionda was in an O'Keefes' jersey against his former Nanaimo teammates on June 28. Playing defence, he made eight interceptions on the way to three goals, an assist, and three stitches to his head.

New Westminster and Vancouver split two games in July. The O'Keefes had been playing the season without McRory, who'd retired at 29 in 1961, convinced he couldn't help the team. But McKnight convinced him otherwise, and McRory was on the floor as if he'd never left, in a crucial showdown with Victoria.

The Shamrocks, having acquired Don Sepka, were trying to overtake the O'Keefes for second place and were up 10–9 when Barclay out-hustled three opponents in the corner for the ball. His pass found Mike Gates, in his second full season with the team, in front of Victoria's net. Gates scored with twenty seconds remaining to send the game into overtime. A few minutes later, Bionda scored the winner, his third goal of the night.

The O'Keefes closed out the season with a win over the Norburns. Sepka scored four times to win the league scoring race with one hundred points on forty-six goals and fifty-four assists. Parnell was right behind him with ninety-six points, fifty-six of them goals, the best in the league.

Vancouver's Sid Warwick chases Paul Parnell chasing the ball in an Inter-city league game in 1962.

CANADIAN WEEKLY.
PHOTOGRAPH BY HAROLD BARKLEY.

A good number of their goals were attributable to Bionda. "Jack would cut through the middle and he'd take two guys with him," recalled Parnell, "and then he'd just flick the ball to you and you'd have an open shot. He'd do that time and time again. He was great to play with. If you needed a goal, he'd get the goal for you. He just had that knack about him. He'd have the stick in his hand all day long."[221] As for Bionda, that night against the Norburns, he got eight points, running his total over the previous four games to twenty-five. But Vancouver, not New Westminster, finished first, and the O'Keefes faced Victoria in the semifinals.

After disposing of the Shamrocks four games to one, New Westminster took on Vancouver in the finals. In the third period of game 1, Sepka scored his third goal of the game, injuring a neck vertebra in the process. New Westminster lost the game 9–6. Sepka, however, was not about to let a neck injury sideline him. He scored five goals in the next game, supported by McRory's hustle and Barclay's fists, in an 11–9 O'Keefes' victory.

New Westminster took the third game 11–5, but Vancouver evened the series with a 13–8

Les Norman stopped twenty-seven Victoria shots on May 3, 1962 to record the first and only shutout in ICLL and WLA regular season play. He sits on the shoulders of Ron Loftus and Gordie Stidolph while Paul Parnell beams.

COLUMBIAN.

After two years with Nanaimo, Jack Bionda played his first game back with New Westminster on June 28, 1962–against Nanaimo. He intercepted eight passes, scored three goals, provided an assist, and received a cut on his head requiring three stitches. O'Keefes won, 12-6.

COLUMBIAN.

victory. On September 11, Vancouver took a one-game lead in the series with an 8–6 overtime win. After the game, New Westminster's fans were critical of Bionda. He'd dropped balls and generally been lacklustre.

McKnight pointed out that Bionda had tallied twenty-three points in the Vancouver series and had been the leading scorer in the semifinals. How much more could one player do? But Bionda was even harder on himself than the fans were. After the game he went outside to practise on his own. In the next game, the sixth, he led all scorers with four goals and three assists in a 12–8 O'Keefes' win, silencing his critics.

Referee Proctor's critics, however, were vocal. At the five-minute mark of the final period, with the O'Keefes leading 10–7, Vancouver coach Alex MacKay held up play to allege to commissioner Tom Gordon that Proctor was drunk and favouring New Westminster. Gordon called Proctor aside and, satisfied he was sober, returned him to the game. After the game, MacKay widened his net of criticism to include referees Earl MacDonald and Bill Stuart and issued an ultimatum: "replace the refs or we quit."[222]

Gordon placated MacKay by bringing in two new refs for game 7, but he retained MacDonald. Playing at home in Kerrisdale Arena, Vancouver fought its way back from a three-goal deficit into a tie at the end of regulation time. In the locker room before the start of overtime, "you could hear a pin drop," said Bionda. "Then everyone started blaming himself for kicking away our big lead. Then something happened like I've never seen before in my playing career. Everyone just got off the bench and hollered 'let's get 'em!'"[223] Six minutes into overtime, Barclay picked off a Vancouver pass and flipped a backhand to Bionda, who scored to make it 10–9. Three O'Keefes' goals later, the game was over.

The O'Keefes picked up Vancouver's great two-way player, John Cervi, for the Mann Cup in Brampton, against the Ramblers. In the first game, Jobb and Parnell led the scoring with three each, McRory and Cervi stood out on defence, and Norman stopped twenty-seven shots. But it was Barclay, playing with ribs injured in the Vancouver series, who came out in the final quarter and sparked a six-goal flurry. On a breakaway, he fired a backhander to score, then set up two more goals for an 11–8 New Westminster victory.

Norman stopped thirty-four shots in the second game, and Barclay further distinguished himself with two over-the-shoulder backhanded goals, one from twenty feet out that drew a big round of applause from Brampton's fans. For good measure, he threw in an ordinary goal to lead all scorers in the 10–5 win.

New Westminster jumped out to a 16–7 halftime lead in game 3. Typical of the team's performance was a play that saw four players touch the ball in the space of four seconds before Cervi scored in the fifth second. Following the goal, Brampton gave the O'Keefes a standing ovation. Bill Jobb scored three goals, one of them a blistering submarine shot that went right through Brampton's goaltender's stick mesh, and added two assists to be named the game's outstanding player. Bionda was not exactly idle, scoring three and assisting on three.

On Saturday, September 22, New Westminster won game four 10–6 and became the first western team to sweep a Mann Cup series in the east. Bionda tallied three goals and four assists to finish the series with sixteen points, four ahead of Cervi (who had six goals—three in the final game—and six assists). Bionda was named the MVP, edging out Norman.

The 1962 Mann Cup victory was New Westminster's seventeenth overall (ten in field lacrosse, seven in box). But it was how the Fulton-McKnight team did it—three sweeps in five years—that was most impressive.

By 1963, the O'Keefes' management realized that Bionda was on the downside of his career. Still, Fulton offered him a $2,500 contract for another season, which Bionda signed. What was apparent to management, however, was far from obvious on the floor. At the end of May, in a game against Nanaimo, Bionda scored five goals with three assists to pass the thousand-point mark in his ten-year ICLL career, only the second player to do so (Victoria's Whitey Severson was the first).

A month later, Bionda scored two goals against Vancouver to reach six hundred career goals. On August 23, he tallied five goals and two assists in a semifinal playoff game against the Shamrocks, giving him sole possession of the goal-scoring record with 637, surpassing Jack Northup's 635 and putting him just six points behind Whitey Severson's all-time points total of 1,111 points. But five days, seven goals, and an assist after that, he bettered Severson's total by two. Severson, years later, said of Bionda: "He had respect and humility, everyone knew he was a superstar—except Bionda."[224]

Bionda won the league scoring title with fifty-one goals and fifty-four assists. As for the team, they defeated Victoria to once again meet archrival Vancouver in the finals. Vancouver took the first game, New Westminster the second, Vancouver the third, New Westminster the fourth.

Stan Joseph, in net for the O'Keefes, played his 500th game on September 11, but allowed 12 goals in a 12–4 loss. And in the sixth game, Vancouver dominated from faceoff to the end of the fourth quarter, winning the game (13–7) and the league title and advancing to the Mann Cup against the St. Catharines Athletics. Vancouver prevailed winning four games and losing two. Gord Gimple scored thirteen goals with six assists in the series and was named the MVP.

In May of 1964, Jack Bionda took a hit during a practice, injuring his back. He played the next game, but was slowed by soreness in a 10–9 loss to Vancouver. His doctor ordered rest. Not even the Salmonbellies' trainer, George Friend, who used steaming hot towels to treat injuries, could fix what was ailing Bionda. With Bionda out indefinitely, McRory returned to the lineup. On July 23, Victoria defeated New Westminster at Queen's Park for the first time since 1959. A noticeable lack of commitment, in the form of midseason trips and vacations, was showing in a number of O'Keefes players. The poor attitude showed in a game against Victoria in which Shamrock goaltender Skip Chapman came within one goal of a shutout in a 10–1 victory. The win lifted Victoria into second place and dropped New Westminster to third.

The *Columbian*'s sports editor, Glyn Lewis, criticized Fulton, McKnight, and coach Byford for fielding weak teams. Fans, said Lewis, paid good money and deserved to see what they thought they were paying for. At the same time, he acknowledged that the team had very little hold on "semi-pros."[225] The age-old issue of professionalism versus amateurism, never far from the surface, was again rearing its head.

Bionda returned to the roster in mid-August for a game against Victoria. Clearly not his old self, he managed just two assists in a 12–11 loss. By the end of the regular season, he had played in only eleven of thirty games, scoring twenty-four goals with eighteen assists—meagre by his standards. The pounding he had taken—and dished out—over the course of ten seasons had taken its toll. His double duty as a hockey player, allowing little if any time for his body to recuperate, had contributed to his decline.

Victoria's Jimmy McNeil chases Paul Parnell in the first game of the best-of-seven western semi-finals in 1962. Parnell threw up before every game, broke scoring records, and led the Salmonbellies to 5 Mann Cup victories between 1960 and 1975.

In 1962 the O'Keefes became the first western team to sweep a Mann Cup series in the east, defeating the Brampton Ramblers in four straight games. **Front row l-r:** Dave Tory, Spider Graham, John Cervi, Jack Fulton, Charlie Saunders. **Second row:** Ron Loftus, Jack Cowie (trainer), Harry McKnight, Jack Byford, Cliff Sepka, Ken Oddy, Les Norman (over Oddy's shoulder), Skip Chapman, Barrie Brownlee (over Chapman's shoulder), Paul Parnell. **Third row:** Jack Bionda (face hidden), Mike Gates (behind Cowie). **Back row:** Bob Allan, Doug McRory, Ivan Stewart, Jim Watson. Missing: Bill Jobb, Jack Barclay and Bill Wilkes, Jr.

CANADIAN LACROSSE HALL OF FAME.

Les Norman deflects a Vancouver Carlings' shot on July 16, 1963. **O'Keefes' players l-r:** Bob Parrent, Wayne Shuttleworth, Mike Gates (#14), Ron Loftus, Bill Wilkes, Jr. (#15). **Carlings' players l-r:** Ron Hemmerling, Fred Usselman, unidentified shooter.

VANCOUVER PROVINCE. PHOTOGRAPH BY DAVID PATERSON.

It took them seven games, but team captain Cliff Sepka and the O'Keefes defeated the Brooklin Merchants to capture the Mann Cup at Queen's Park in 1965.

VANCOUVER PROVINCE. PHOTOGRAPH BY DAVID PATERSON.

Vancouver won the 1964 league with twenty-three wins and nine losses while New Westminster and Victoria finished with identical 18–13–1 records. Victoria defeated New Westminster in a tiebreaker only to lose to them in the semifinal playoffs 3–1.

The Carlings and the O'Keefes met in the playoffs, with Vancouver taking the series 4–2, a repeat of 1963's outcome. The Carlings met the Brooklin Merchants in the Mann Cup. (Brooklin is a community in the town of Whitby, Ontario.) Vancouver lost the first two games, but won the third. They also lost the fourth game, but in the fifth contest, Fred Usselman scored six goals and Cervi notched six points in a Vancouver victory. Down three games to two, with their backs still against the wall, the Carlings won one of the greatest games in Mann Cup history, with Gimple beating Pat Baker with twelve seconds remaining to edge Brooklin 13–12. It was all Vancouver in game 7 as they defeated the Merchants to capture their third Mann Cup in four years.

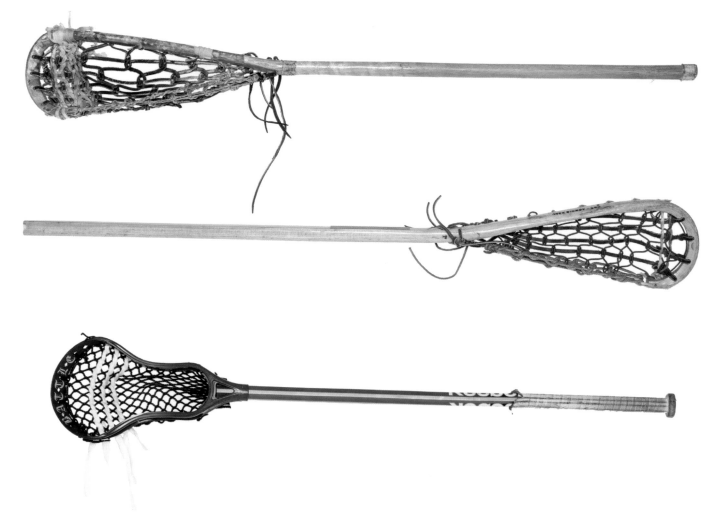

While box lacrosse sticks have evolved since the 1930s, today's sticks look remarkably like the earliest baggataway sticks. The top stick belongs to Al Lewthwaite. The middle stick was used by Jack Bionda.

TOP & MIDDLE STICKS: CANADIAN LACROSSE HALL OF FAME. BOTTOM STICK: PRIVATE COLLECTION. PHOTOGRAPHS BY PHILLIP CHIN.

The sweater worn in the 1970s by Ken Winzoski. Salmonbellies' GM Bill Stevenson designed the iconic emblem.

GAIL WINZOSKI. PHOTOGRAPH BY PHILLIP CHIN.

"They have one helluva lacrosse team."

Peterborough Lakers' coach Bob Allan, 1970

CHAPTER TEN
HARD TO BEAT: 1965-1976

In 1965, Jack Fulton assumed full command of the O'Keefes, McKnight having stepped down at the end of the 1964 season. Fulton brought Bill Armstrong aboard as team manager. Armstrong had helped Jake Trotzuk run the junior Salmonbellies starting in 1958. In 1964, he joined the O'Keefes as secretary-treasurer. Jack Byford resigned as coach, and McRory stepped in.

The Inter-City League lost Nanaimo. The team had asked for $2,000 in travel assistance, but when the league offered just $1,000, the team folded. But Ken Oddy, Lorne Reelie and others organized a new Coquitlam team, the reborn Adanacs. The league recognized that the team needed to be competitive from the start, and so a dispersal draft was held. The Adanacs could choose three players from the existing teams and took Mike Gates, Charlie Saunders, and Jack Barclay from the O'Keefes. In a separate transaction, the Adanacs also acquired Ivan Stewart.

Fulton and Armstrong were down six veterans (Bionda did not return either). But they still had Sepka, Parnell, Wilkes, Shuttleworth, Norman, Reisinger, and more. Reisinger had retired in 1960 after five seasons as a defender with New Westminster, but he was back for another go-around. To their depleted ranks, Fulton and Armstrong added rookies Ron Flaten, Larry Henry, Gord Jakubek, and Mac Tyler, Whoopie's son.

Tyler was another Sapperton product and, like McRory, hadn't started playing lacrosse until junior. Born in 1943, the year his dad played his last game, Tyler was a six-foot-four, 165-pound, gangly "lawn dart."[226] Near-sighted in an era before contact lenses, he wore thick-rimmed, black glasses that became a kind of trademark.

Bill Tyler died in 1962. If he had lived another few years, he could have seen Mac play with the junior Salmonbellies against the Oshawa Green Gaels for the 1964 Minto Cup. Tyler scored the first goal of the series using a move he would employ many times throughout his career. Standing at the crease to one side of an opponent's goal, he would no sooner receive a pass than in one fluid motion, using his extra-long reach, deposit the ball in the far side of the net. Goaltenders absolutely hated it. It was humiliating. And it seemed almost illegal.

The play would reach perfection with the assistance of Paul Parnell. Parnell would fake a shot from the point, drawing out the goaltender, and hit Tyler with a bullet pass. Tyler, looking at an empty net, would whip in the ball. "I used to practise it on my own all the time," he recalled. "I'd stand by the crease at the side of the goal, bounce the ball off the boards, and try to catch it and shoot as fast as I could."[227]

In 1964, Tyler played two games for the senior team and quickly found out about paying your dues in senior lacrosse. "A vet would say to you, 'Get me the ball and get out of the way.'"[228] But, dues paid, he got a permanent spot on the team.

The O'Keefes won the league in 1965 with twenty-one wins against nine losses. Vancouver was just one game off, at twenty and ten. First-year-team Coquitlam, led by ex-Salmonbellies Gates, Oddy, and Barclay, finished at 12–18, while the Shamrocks ended up 7–23. Parnell topped the league's point getters with 109 on 71 goals and 38 assists. Sepka was fourth with eighty points and Shuttleworth came in seventh with sixty-five.

Fulton and the O'Keefes could not believe their good fortune when the Adanacs defeated the Carlings in the semifinals. They might not have been so surprised, not with former O'Keefes Barclay, Stewart, and Oddy in Coquitlam's lineup. In the finals, with New Westminster up three games to one in the fifth game, Sepka tied the score at six, at seven, then at eight in the final quarter to keep the team in the game until rookie Ed McDonald scored the winning goal in a 10–8 victory.

In the first game of the Mann Cup in Queen's Park against the Brooklin Merchants, Sepka led the way with four goals in an 11–5 win in front of 3,500 fans. "The ball bounces too slow for us," said Brooklin coach Bill Vipond after playing on the wood floor. "We prefer a solid, cement floor."[229]

The Merchants discovered that the ball bounced to their liking when they defeated the O'Keefes in the second game 6–5. Brooklin won the third game in overtime, 15–14. Vipond could be forgiven if he was starting to really enjoy Queen's Park's wood floor. Sepka had four goals and Ed McDonald tallied three in the losing cause. Brooklin captured the fourth game 14–9.

In the third quarter of the fifth game, Brooklin goaltender, Don Craggs, was penalized for wrapping his stick around Parnell. An enraged Craggs attacked referee Whitey Severson,

Cliff Sepka drank four times from the Mann Cup.

VANCOUVER SUN.
PHOTOGRAPH BY BOB DIBBLE.

the two spilling to the floor in a wrestling match. Craggs was summarily banished from the game and the remainder of the series. Tempers continued to run high. An irate Brooklin player in the dressing room corridor smashed a press photographer's camera. Parnell, feeling better than he had in weeks, scored two goals, while Ron Flaten and Shuttleworth got three and Tyler got one. The O'Keefes took it 8–7.

Drawn by the O'Keefes' resurgence and Craggs' attack on Severson, 5,500 fans filled the Arena for game 6. With the O'Keefes leading in the first quarter, Brooklin's Bill Castator ran Parnell head first into the boards. Parnell was taken to Royal Columbian Hospital with a concussion.

Backed by Les Norman's exceptional netminding, New Westminster led at the end of every quarter, including the last one: 17–7. Sepka scored four times. Shuttleworth scored one of his three goals off an over-the-shoulder shot while lying prone in front of Brooklin's net. It brought down the house. Brooklin was staying at the Russell Hotel during a beer strike. There was no beer, but there was hard liquor. "I think the whisky was getting to these guys," recalled Fulton.[230]

Before another packed house at the Arena on Saturday, September 25, the O'Keefes faced the Merchants in the seventh and deciding game. Parnell was itching to play, but was forced to watch the game from the sidelines. The score was 2-1 Salmonbellies after the first, 7–2 at the half, 8–2 after the third, and 11–3 at the final whistle. Shuttleworth and McDonald led the winners with two goals apiece. Seven other players scored one each. Les Norman, who'd stopped 90 percent of the shots he faced in the final two games, was named the MVP.

In the spring of 1966, Fulton met with O'Keefe. With all the publicity the team had generated for the brewery by winning the Mann Cup, Fulton felt justified in asking for more money. O'Keefe offered less money and refused to budge.

They finally agreed to pay the team $1,000 to end the relationship. Fulton and Armstrong asked Fred Hume, then 74 and the owner of the Western Hockey League's Vancouver Canucks, for help returning the team to its traditional name. He gave them $500. Fulton then met with Mayor Stu Gifford, told him about the reversion to Salmonbellies, and got a better deal on the Arena rental. The switch to the old name was announced at a press conference at the King Neptune restaurant. Wayne Shuttleworth held up a big spring salmon for photographers. The ghosts of old Salmonbellies were happy once more.

Early season injuries to Sepka, Norman, and Shuttleworth weighed on the Salmonbellies, as did the absence of Bionda. But on June 3 Sepka, in his thirteenth season, was back on the floor and reached 500 career assists, second only to Whitey Severson's 612. After missing another three weeks due to injury, Sepka, in a game against the Adanacs, scored on Merv Schweitzer with minutes left in the game. It was Sepka's third goal to go with two assists. The five points took him to 1,176, surpassing Bionda's all-time league leading mark.

Bionda returned to the Arena on June 29. "Maybe we've seen him in better physical shape," observed Fulton, "but his very presence seemed to inspire a better practice tonight."[231] The following night he scored a goal in an 8–7 win over the Adanacs, but at almost thirty-three, he was not nearly the dominant player he had once been. "How many years does he have left?" wondered the *Columbian*'s Don Cannon. "That nose of his has not got too many more bends left in it."[232]

Junior Salmonbellies Wayne Goss and Ken Winzoski flank equipment manager John "Hoty" Shaw in 1966.

WAYNE GOSS.

On July 2, Bionda scored once and assisted on a goal by Bill Wilkes. Curiously, Wilkes' shot hit both goal posts and the crossbar before going in, almost as if the ball did not want to find the net, as if it wanted to keep going. It was Bionda's 300th—and final—assist as a Salmonbellie. On Thursday, July 7, at Queen's Park Arena, he scored once in a 16–11 loss, his 346th—and final—goal in six seasons as a Salmonbellie. Fittingly, he scored it against the Victoria Shamrocks, the team he'd joined in 1954 and the one he'd left for the Salmonbellies in 1958. Not only was it his last goal for New Westminster, it was his last game for the team. A wrenched knee refused to heal.

The Salmonbellies finished the season in third place with a 13–15–2 record. They lost to Vancouver in the first game of the semifinals. The second game was scheduled for Saturday night, but that afternoon New Westminster's Rayonier-Alaska Pine lumber mill caught fire. Six firefighter Salmonbellies—McRory, Parnell, Shuttleworth, Norman, Bill Cooksley, and Fulton—fought the inferno. On Monday night, the Salmonbellies (minus Norman, who was ill from fighting the fire) lost to Vancouver. Vancouver then took the third game and the series and, after defeating Coquitlam, faced the John Davis-led Peterborough Lakers for the Mann Cup. Vancouver picked up Parnell and Shuttleworth but were still outscored 47–42 and lost four of five close games to the Lakers. Davis led all scorers with ten goals and ten assists and was awarded the MVP trophy.

In 1967, the Salmonbellies lost seven of their first nine games. The biggest issue was a lack of defence, but they also missed Parnell in the first three games and Sepka in the first ten. Mac Tyler, finishing his studies at university, was also late getting started. The team, however, quickly turned things around, winning nine of their next eleven contests. While the Salmonbellies had veteran depth, the new GM, Bill Armstrong, looked increasingly to the juniors to fill the ranks.

The junior Salmonbellies were loaded with locally grown talent. Ed Goss had won the 1966 junior scoring title, with older brother Wayne in third position. In second place was Ken Winzoski, who, despite having one more year of junior eligibility, had already played six senior games. For Winzoski, it was all about winning. "Nobody cares if you finish second," he said.[233] The junior Salmonbellies had won the provincial championship and the right to play the Oshawa Green Gaels for the Minto Cup. It would be the third time in as many years that the teams had battled for the cup, with the Salmonbellies coming out losers twice.

Bill Robinson is a step too late and Paul Parnell's shot appears bound for the net behind Skip Chapman, about 1967.

PAUL PARNELL.

In a July 10 senior Salmonbellies' game against the Adanacs, Lewthwaite scored twice and Winzoski tallied two goals and two assists. On one of his goals Winzoski ran through the entire Coquitlam team to beat Schweitzer with a low shot. The next night, the Salmonbellies defeated Vancouver to move into second place, one point behind Vancouver and Victoria, who were tied for first. Winzoski had three goals in a New Westminster victory, the team's fourth in a row. On July 13, looking for their fifth win, the Salmonbellies lost to Vancouver. In late July, the Salmonbellies defeated the Adanacs 11–10 in overtime on a goal by Parnell, his fifth of the game. The Salmonbellies were now tied for third with the Adanacs, just three points behind Victoria and Vancouver, still tied for first. But they lost the next two games and then a third to Victoria on August 10, and were eliminated from the playoffs.

Vancouver defeated Victoria in the finals and advanced to the Mann Cup, defeating the Brooklin Redmen four games to two to capture their fourth national championship in seven years. On the losing side, John Davis, picked up from Peterborough for the series, won the MVP trophy for the second year in a row.

The 1967 junior Salmonbellies, on the strength of performances like Ed Goss's eleven-goal game, kept on winning all the way to the Minto Cup. Once again, they faced the Green Gaels. Oshawa won the first three games and the Salmonbellies won the next two. But the Green Gaels, powered by some of Gaylord Powless's thirty-three points for the series, took game six 7–4 to capture their fifth straight Minto Cup. For the Salmonbellies, Lewthwaite led with ten goals and six assists, followed by Ray Bennie with fifteen points, Wayne Goss with eleven, and Ed Goss and Winzoski with ten each.

The junior and senior 1967 Salmonbellies became, if not quite one integrated playing unit, at least highly familiar with each other. Their talents, skills, and dedication level ran parallel. And they shared one other important attribute, a commitment to winning. They got their first real chance together in 1968.

Professional lacrosse hadn't been played in eastern Canada since 1931's IPLL and hadn't been seen on the west coast since Vancouver's Con Jones folded his pro team in 1924. The game remained resolutely amateur until demand for a professional league began to heat up in the 1960s.

After the attendance doldrums of the 1950s, the 1960s saw a resurgence in interest in the game. Attendance was strong in the east and in the Lower Mainland because the rivalries were intense and the teams had star players people wanted to see in action. In the west, Victoria, Nanaimo, Vancouver, and New Westminster enjoyed capacity or near-capacity houses. Football, basketball, baseball, and hockey had professionalized many decades earlier, but in the 1960s those sports and others began their expansion into today's celebrity-focused, television-driven business empires.

Morley Kells envisioned professional lacrosse. Kells, born and raised in the lacrosse-playing borough of Etobicoke, Ontario, was a member of the 1955 Minto Cup junior champion team from Etobicoke's Long Branch area. After a senior career, he took up coaching in 1961 and in 1966 he founded and coached the Toronto Maple Leafs of the Ontario Lacrosse Association. A journalist and an ad agency executive, Kells was also the creative director for CBC TV's *Hockey Night in Canada*. He and Jim Bishop had discussed for some time their vision of lacrosse's future.

Kells, ten years Bishop's junior, was on friendly terms with Stafford Smythe and Harold Ballard, co-owners of Maple Leaf Gardens and the Toronto Maple Leafs hockey franchise. Smythe and Ballard liked the way Kells and Bishop's lacrosse teams played. Bruce Norris, owner of the Detroit Red Wings, was looking for a sport he could put into his recently refurbished rink, the Olympia. Smythe told Kells that if he could put together a league he, Ballard, and Norris would enter franchises. Kells lined up Bishop with Norris. Bishop would coach the Detroit team. Canadian TV sports announcer Brian McFarlane would preside over Montreal's entry, the Canadiens. Kells and Bishop then convinced the four western teams to play an interlocking schedule and compete for the national championship.

And so the National Lacrosse League (NLL) was born, consisting of four eastern teams (Montreal Canadiens, Toronto Maple Leafs, Detroit Olympics, and Peterborough Lakers) and four western teams (Victoria Shamrocks, Vancouver Carlings, Portland Adanacs, and New Westminster Salmonbellies).

Salmonbellies' president Dave McDonald estimated the cost of running a NLL franchise at about $40,000 a season, with about half going to player salaries (about $1,000 per player). The best lacrosse talent in Canada abandoned their leagues—the ICLL in the west and the OLA in the east—and turned professional. The ICLL became a senior B league, with teams in Coquitlam, Surrey, Burnaby, and North Vancouver. Brooklin and Brampton remained in the OLA and were joined by teams from Hastings and Mississauga.

Kells and Bishop were determined to move lacrosse from "a slow game featuring brutality to that of a fast-breaking game that focused on conditioning and skills."[234] They introduced the thirty-second rule, whereby a team had thirty seconds after acquiring the ball to either shoot or lose possession, unless they were shorthanded). A shorthanded team had ten seconds to

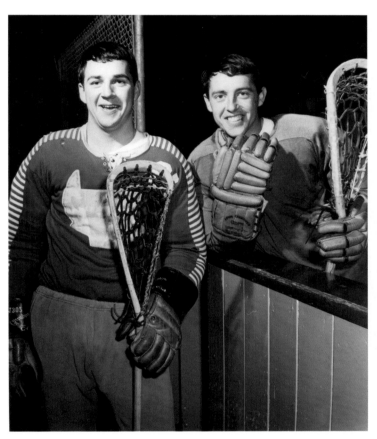

Ed and Wayne, the brothers Goss (rhymes with lacrosse). About 1968.

WAYNE GOSS.
PHOTOGRAPH BY BASIL KING.

get the ball over its offensive "rag" line. And the team that last touched the ball before it went out of bounds lost possession, whereas before the two teams faced off.

In 1968, Winzoski had a lock on one of the two openings for graduating underage juniors. In filling the second spot, Armstrong and Sepka had difficult choices between Ed and Wayne Goss. They were leaning toward Ed, but when they asked for Winzoski's input, he told them that he favoured Wayne, for the two of them had been a potent one-two punch in junior. In the end, they went with Wayne.

Sepka, replacing Wally Henderson, became the Salmonbellies playing-coach in 1968, although he would have preferred to just coach. McRory, who'd sat out 1967, was back for another season. Ken Oddy, who'd played for Coquitlam in 1965 and not at all in 1966 and 1967, returned for another season. Don Wallis, netminder in the Goss-Winzoski junior era, joined the team as Norman's understudy. With Bill Wilkes having retired, Mac Tyler teaching high school in Vernon until the end of the term, and a number of other players injured, the Salmonbellies started the season short of right-handed shooters.

Wayne Goss one-on-one in 1968 with Portland Adanacs goalie Merv Schweitzer. Former Salmonbellie and perennial all-star Mike Gates can only watch.

VANCOUVER SUN. PHOTOGRAPH BY DAN SCOTT.

Parnell, as usual, did most of the team's scoring, followed by Shuttleworth and Goss. Shuttleworth, in his sixth season with the Salmonbellies, switched to offence. He scored four points in a game against Portland on September 7 to reach 101 points, thirty-six more than his previous best. Goss scored as if he were still playing junior, where he averaged six points a game over the 1966 and 1967 seasons. He hit his old stride in a mid-July game against Victoria, tallying four goals and two assists.

When the regular season ended Goss, with ninety-three points, finished third behind Parnell's 130 and Shuttleworth's 101. Winzoski had a good season as well, finishing with sixty-six points. In his fourth full season with the Salmonbellies, Larry Henry had his best season yet, scoring forty-five goals with forty-two assists.

As good as the Salmonbellies' individual stats were, the only stat that really mattered was team wins. In the western division of the NLL the team with the best record was Portland with twenty-four wins in thirty-eight games. Their highest scorer was Mike Gates with 138 points. Vancouver finished second with twenty-two wins, and New Westminster found itself in third place with nineteen wins and nineteen losses.

As the pro teams prepared for the playoffs, the OLA champion Brooklin Redmen defeated the ICLL champion Nanaimo Luckies in four straight games to capture their first Mann Cup. Wayne Shuttleworth continued his hot hand in the first game of the playoffs against Vancouver, scoring five goals on seven shots in an 11–10 Salmonbellies' victory. New Westminster won the second game 7–3, lost the third 11–9, and took the fourth 12–10. Vancouver fought back in the fifth for a 13–5 win and took the sixth game as well. Emotions ran high heading into the seventh game. "At the time some Burrards hated us so much they even refused to drive through New Westminster," remembered Mac Tyler.[235] In the seventh game, Sepka scored three goals and Shuttleworth scored two to pace the Salmonbellies. But with the scored tied 6–6 in the final period, Shuttleworth was sent to the penalty box. Goss, who had not scored a single point all game, rose to the occasion, scoring a shorthanded goal with four minutes remaining to give the Salmonbellies the victory.

The Salmonbellies faced the Portland Adanacs (formerly the Coquitlam Adanacs) in the western division finals. The Adanacs had won eight of ten games against the Salmonbellies in the regular season. In the first game of the finals, after a bench-clearing brawl, the stick of scoring leader Mike Gates somehow ended up in the hands of the Salmonbellies. It was about to be returned to its owner when Parnell asked for it. Bracing it against the floor, he smashed his heel into its pocket a couple of times, stretching it out of shape. "Okay," he said, "you can give it back to him now."[236] A minute later the unsuspecting Gates, attempting to pass, bounced the ball about a foot in front of his feet. Despite his deformed pocket and third year Salmonbellie Ian Bull's tight checking, Gates scored twice with three assists—although not when Bull was on him. (At a post-game celebration, Bull once claimed six glasses of beer as his own by dipping his false teeth in them.) In the midst of all the fighting and foolery, Winzoski shone offensively, scoring three times. But the first star of the game was starting goalkeeper Don Wallis, who'd held the Adanacs scoreless for the first fifteen minutes and allowed only one goal in the second period. New Westminster prevailed 10–7.

The second game of the finals went to the Adanacs 7–6.

Sepka deployed juniors Ed Goss, Ray Bennie, and Dave Matheson for game three. Don Wallis was again in net. Ian Bull was assigned Gates. In the final period, Parnell and Shuttleworth scored a goal apiece to get within one goal of the Adanacs and then Parnell beat Schweitzer to tie it and send it to overtime. In overtime Parnell passed to Goss at the edge of the crease and Goss scored to win the game for the Salmonbellies.

The Salmonbellies took game 4 in Portland 11–6.

New Westminster needed just one more win to advance to the league finals, but the Adanacs scored thirteen times to the Salmonbellies' eleven to take game 5. Wayne Goss led New Westminster with four goals.

In game 6 at Queen's Park, Winzoski scored three times in a 7–3 Salmonbellies' victory to win the series and western laurels. "Winzoski scores his share of goals, is one of the better defensive players, snags enough loose balls for six players, runs all night and, most important, his determination is demoralizing to the opposition."[237] It would take demoralizing determination and then some if the Salmonbellies expected to beat the winners of the eastern division, the Detroit Olympics.

The Bishop-coached Olympics, the professional version of the Green Gaels, had swept their series with the Peterborough Lakers. Eleven of the twenty-four-member team had played for Bishop in Oshawa including Merv Marshall, goaltender on every Green Gaels Minto Cup championship team up to 1968. Of the twenty-two players on the 1968 Salmonbellies team, only eight had not lost at least one Minto Cup to the Green Gaels.

Bishop was a perfectionist who pushed his players to the outer edge of exhaustion in pursuit of winning. In later years he and Winzoski would discuss the philosophical question of whether or not the human body could be worn out. Bishop said it could regenerate itself forever, aging, accidents, and disease aside. Winzoski, who was extremely well conditioned and well read, maintained the exact opposite.

Bishop's Olympics held their training camp in Oakville, Ontario, practising six days a week. On Saturdays, they practised two hours in the morning and two hours in the afternoon. Even during the season, the team practised every night.

Stan Joseph and Les Norman in 1959, the year Norman broke in with the team.

BILL ARMSTRONG.

Playing coach Cliff Sepka is hoisted by his teammates after defeating the Detroit Olympics for the NLL title in 1968. L-r: Dave Tory, Doug McRory, Ed Goss, Mac Tyler, Al Lewthwaite, Cliff Sepka, Ken Oddy, Don Wallis (back of head), Wayne Shuttleworth.

COLUMBIAN. PHOTOGRAPH BY BASIL KING.

For their labour, players were paid $50 a game, $2,000 for a forty-game season. Detroit's wealthy Norris family, who owned the NHL franchise Red Wings, also backed the Olympics. The Olympics lived in and around Oshawa and flew to home games in Detroit on Sundays. Their opponents would be on the same flight there and back. In a baseball-crazed city (the 1968 Tigers won the World Series), the Olympics drew decent crowds, around 3,500 fans for most games.

The Salmonbellies had defeated Detroit in two regular-season games. But the Mann Cup was a best-of-seven series, and the Salmonbellies had come off two long, punishing series with Vancouver and Portland. Having defeated Portland on Friday night, they faced the Olympics Saturday night—the Salmonbellies' fifteenth game in twenty-five nights. Their fatigue showed in the first contest. The two-on-one and three-on-one fast break was a major part of Detroit's game, as it had been for the Green Gaels. The key to it was goaltender Marshall's quick passes to start Detroit's attack in motion. The Salmonbellies could not keep up with it Saturday night and lost 21–12. Powless scored five times for the Olympics, and Sepka, who'd announced that he'd retire at the end of the series, scored three times for the Salmonbellies.

In the second game, Sepka, Parnell, and Shuttleworth combined for sixteen points, including eight goals, in a 16–12 Salmonbellies' victory. Larry Henry scored three goals, and Wayne and Ed Goss (who played in the playoffs as a junior pick-up) had two apiece. Les

Norman stopped thirty-three shots. Detroit's Marshall, used to roaming far from his goal, was checked back into it, putting a damper on his team's fast break. Powless was held to just one goal. Heading to the showers after the game Sepka's legs looked like "rubber bands," wrote the *Columbian*.

Before game 3, Mac Tyler had the fluid drained from his knee (as usual), and lots of tape wrapped around various aching body parts. Norman could still taste his pork chop. Parnell puked. Oddy munched on carrots—a gift from a friend's garden—and went out and scored three goals in the first period. His teammates were impressed by his newfound power and, in the break between periods, munched on carrots as well—and went out and scored eleven goals. Before the night was over, Oddy added two more goals and Sepka four. Parnell tallied two goals and six assists, Shuttleworth notched one goal and six assists, and taped-up Tyler scored once. Even Les Norman got four assists. The veterans accounted for twenty-seven points among them, and the Salmonbellies, having fired seventy-three shots at Marshall, won the game 23–15 to lead two games to one. But it was Cliff Sepka who stood out to the Olympics' coach. "If I was picking a lacrosse team from everywhere in Canada and I could have Sepka," said Bishop after the game, "he'd be my first choice."[238]

Wayne Goss led the way in the fourth game with five goals, followed by Sepka with four and Parnell with two goals and four assists. But the Salmonbellies lost 15–14. Eleven Salmonbellies were in on the scoring in the fifth game, and Norman stopped forty-two shots (twenty-two in the final period). Late in the game Parnell recovered a rebound when everyone had assumed that Detroit would pick up the ball first. He worked his way to the left of Marshall, paid the price of two high checks, and passed to Tyler, who flicked a quick shot into the net to put the Salmonbellies in the lead to stay. At the buzzer, it was 14–12 New Westminster.

Nearly 5,000 fans crammed into the Arena for game 6. Space was so tight that even GM Bill Armstrong couldn't get a seat. He watched the game from a stepladder in the corridor at the Arena's north end. McRory looked after coaching. "McRory was all about common sense. Or uncommon sense, really," recalled Ian Matheson. "He'd allow only the four best shooters to shoot—and the players did as he said. He was a genius coach and the most intelligent businessman I've ever met."[239]

With McRory behind the bench, Sepka was free to concentrate on playing. Trainer George Friend spent two hours before the game working on Sepka's crossed tendons. Armstrong brought in a supply of carrots. Oddy helped himself then hit the floor, promptly scoring five goals, four of them on power plays. When the Salmonbellies scored, the cheering was so loud and prolonged that the players couldn't hear each other, even from just an arm's length away. When Detroit scored, it was as if the Arena were closed for repairs.

The Salmonbellies led 14–12 after two periods. In the final period, the Salmonbellies' defence allowed only nine shots on Norman while the offence exploded in an all out push for victory. In the middle of it, Sepka knocked down a shot, tore down the floor, was checked horizontal in front of the goal, and—sailing through the air—fired a shot past Marshall. It was number 19's nineteenth goal of the series. He received a standing ovation. The Salmonbellies

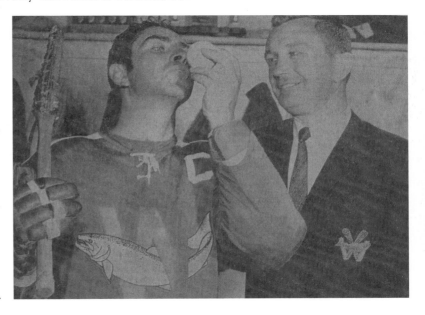

Coach Cliff Sepka watches Paul Parnell celebrate reaching 1,000 points on August 21, 1969. He added five more that night for good measure.

COLUMBIAN.

In 1970 Vancouver Carlings' Don Hamilton kept this one out,
but 921 others from Paul Parnell went in.

BILL ARMSTRONG.

Ken Winzoski eludes Vancouver's Ed "Whitey" Nelson.
Among his many talents, Winzoski was great
at ragging the ball. Before the imposition of the
thirty-second rule, he and Wayne Goss delighted fans
and exasperated opponents by playing catch,
sometimes for the duration of two-minute penalties.

BILL ARMSTRONG.

At 6'3", 225 pounds Al "Lurch" Lewthwaite crunched, punched, squished
and scored with equal skill. His cross-checks lifted opponents off their
feet and threw them miles from where they'd been a second earlier.
His best years were 1968 through 1974. Here he has sent Les Schumaker
(5) sprawling and his stick flying in the course of getting off a shot.
Adanac Dick Crompton (10) checks Ian Bull, and Mike Gates checks
Ray Bennie (7). Merv Schweitzer makes the stop.

COLUMBIAN.

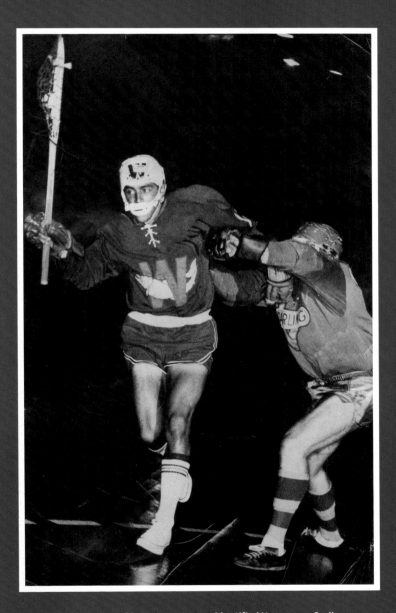

Wayne Goss on his way past an unidentified Vancouver Carling.

WAYNE GOSS.

Dave Tory congratulates Mac Tyler for being named the MVP of the 1970 WLA finals.

MAC TYLER.

fired three more goals to outscore the Olympics eight to two for a 22–14 victory. New Westminster had won the first NLL championship. Bishop also received an ovation. "It was as big a thrill as I've ever had in a loss," said Bishop of the crowd's applause. "If we had to get beat I'd rather lose to them. Once the bitter taste is over you have to say they're worthy champions."[240] Sepka was named MVP and retired after 746 goals and 581 assists in 484 games—an average of 2.74 points per game. But it was the eight juniors and rookies, freeing up the veterans to concentrate on scoring, who deserved a lot of the credit for the championship. Bennie, Matheson, Winzoski, Lynch, the Goss brothers, d'Easum, and Lewthwaite had done the hard checking, dug the balls out of corners, and, when necessary, fought the fights that allowed the veterans to shine. Throughout the lengthy sixty-one game season (including exhibition and playoff games), New Westminster's support of the team and the new professional league had been unstinting. But despite being pros in every sense of the word, not one of the players earned any money.

Mickey Lynch tries to slip a check from Vancouver Carling Brent Ojanen in 1969.

NEW WESTMINSTER MUSEUM AND ARCHIVES.

"I made a $1.69," recalled Tyler. "The girl who babysat our kids earned more than I did," quipped Norman.[241] "We were paid on the basis of wins, losses, and seniority," recalled Lewthwaite. "I made $12 for a win in 1969 and $7 for a loss."[242]

On July 16, 1969, a series of rockets launched Apollo 11 astronauts Neil Armstrong, Michael Collins, and Edwin "Buzz" Aldrin, Jr., toward the moon. Back on Earth, the Adanacs had returned to Coquitlam, the Portland experiment having failed along with the Detroit Olympics: not enough paying customers, not enough revenue. Bishop, however, impressed Norris, who hired him as a vice-president of the Red Wings. The NLL, minus Portland and Detroit, continued to operate.

The Salmonbellies also opted out of the NLL and with Coquitlam, Vancouver and Victoria formed a new entity to replace the ICLL: the Western Lacrosse Association. McRory had taken over from Bill Armstrong, and Sepka was again behind the bench. Veterans Wayne Shuttleworth and Ken Oddy were not yet playing. Winzoski was now playing for the Toronto Maple Leafs. (The NLL team, not the NHL team.)

Wayne Goss was ripping up the Western Lacrosse Association, scoring ten points in a game in June. Goss had been working as a carpenter until Jack Fulton suggested he apply to the fire department. He did and was hired. With so many past and present firefighter Salmonbellies, Goss did not have to explain why he drew the outline of a goal on a wall at the firehall, why he was spending free time shooting at the X marks he had drawn in the goal's four corners, or why he was running around the hall with his stick, bouncing a ball off telephone poles as he ran.

Some abilities Goss was born with: speed, quickness, and anticipation. And some he worked hard to develop: stick skills, endurance, moves. But even so, what accounted for his prowess? At five-foot-eight and 155 pounds, he was on the small side. He scored hundreds of goals, and yet his shot could not, according to at least one observer, "break an egg." Another observer said, "When Goss shot you could read the manufacturer's name—Viceroy—on the ball, it was that slow."[243] He didn't look intimidating, nor did he play with the wild abandon of a Johnny Vernon or a "Blackie" Black. So how did he set all the records he set?

Goss prided himself on working the hardest off the floor to be the best-conditioned player on the floor. His fitness enabled him to keep going when his opponents were exhausted.

He scored most of his goals near the end of a shift. He studied goaltenders for their weaknesses. He made eye contact with the goaltender and shot opposite to where he was looking. His speed and quick moves allowed him to beat opponents one-on-one.

His teammates, knowing his ability, would spread out, giving him the room he needed to beat his man. His back to his check, he would push in relentlessly toward the goal. At the right moment he'd fake to his forehand, tuck his stick into his chest, and then, when he felt his check leaning into him, reverse direction and go under his opponent, emerging free and clear on the other side, ready to shoot. His greatness was not in one or two overpowering strengths. It was in the mobilization of increments. He made the most of the small advantages he created for himself. When opponents tired, he kept going. When goalies looked high, he shot low. When a checker leaned one way, he went the other.

Goss aside, graduating juniors Dave Matheson (nephew of 1930s Adanacs' star Ken Matheson), Mickey Lynch, Steve d'Easum, Ed Goss, Jim Giles, and Al Lewthwaite were also playing well. Giles was a natural athlete, the team's primary prankster, and a quick wit. During one game he tried to score off a backhanded shot. "What the fuck are you doing?" yelled Parnell. A few minutes later Parnell tried his own backhander. Giles stood up on the bench. "What the fuck are you doing?" he yelled, half in jest.[244]

Steve d'Easum, a formidable checker and wily playmaker, was the grandson of Reverend Canon G.C. d'Easum, of New Westminster's Holy Trinity Cathedral. (Reverend d'Easum had presided at Salmonbellies' trainer Tim Mahony's funeral in 1930, when, at the gravesite, the lacrosse stick Mahony had strung for "Buck" Marshall was lowered atop the coffin into Mahony's grave.) At five-foot-six and 180 pounds, d'Easum, known as "Stumpy," was in his first full season of senior lacrosse.

Lewthwaite, who started playing lacrosse in 1957, at the age of seven, in the outdoor box at Hume Park, had a memorable first full season of senior lacrosse. Lewthwaite and his Sapperton gang would play lacrosse from nine o'clock in the morning to dusk. On game nights they'd walk to the Arena, paying ten cents to get in. On one occasion, he hit Vancouver's Bill Chisholm with a bunched up popcorn bag. Chisholm gave him the evil eye and Lewthwaite ran all the way to the cemetery at Cumberland and Richmond Streets, about a mile away.

Vancouver's Gord Frederickson scored 1,069 points 1963-76, and won three Mann Cups. Teammate Don Hamilton backstopped the Burrards to Mann Cups in 1961 and 1975. Salmonbellie Larry Henry (8) watches Hamilton smother one in 1969.

DON HAMILTON.

Lewthwaite and Ray Bennie would hitchhike into Vancouver to see the Salmonbellies' away games. "It was our whole life," recalled Lewthwaite.[245] His sports heroes were slap-shooting leftwinger Bobby Hull of the Chicago Blackhawks, switch-hitting centre fielder Mickey Mantle of the New York Yankees, and hard-hitting defenceman Doug McRory of the New Westminster Salmonbellies. "They were all the same in my mind."[246] He also admired Vancouver's John Cervi, whose play at point he aspired to.

Lewthwaite was three-and-a-half years younger than Winzoski and Wayne Goss, and he looked up to them. But not literally, for he was one of the biggest players around, at almost six-foot-three and 225 pounds. He wore homemade pads, and his back pads were fabricated from the front cover of a Webster's dictionary. His elbow pads were made from soccer shin guards and a layer of blue felt.

Lewthwaite went to the Minto Cup finals twice, losing each time to the Oshawa Green Gaels. But if he had to lose, at least it was to Oshawa. "The Green Gaels were the only team I never hated. They were gentleman. All Jim Bishop's teams were classy."[247]

Lewthwaite prepared for games by visualizing them. He made sure his stick was just as ready as he was. His favourite was the Logan Special, strung with Martin leather. His sticks tended to warp or break from his "exuberant" checking, so 1920s-era field player Ab Brown showed him how to pick out the right grain in a sledgehammer handle, splice and glue it into the neck of the stick, and apply reinforcing fibreglass. "I was quite attached to my lacrosse stick," recalled Lewthwaite. "I looked after it, put Neatsfoot oil on it, you know. I even slept with it," he said.[248] "Ab Brown sat behind the bench," remembered Parnell, "and after the game he'd come down to the dressing room and get all the sticks that needed repair. The next morning we'd go there and they'd be fixed. If he had to he'd do them that night. If a stick was broken he'd fibreglass it for you."[249]

On July 20, Neil Armstrong and Buzz Aldrin landed on the moon's Sea of Tranquility. McRory's goal was to land the Salmonbellies safely in the NLL finals in September. Dissatisfied with the play of goalies Norman, Wallis, and Skip Jolly, McRory asked all-star goalie Joe Comeau, placed on waivers by Coquitlam, to play for the Salmonbellies. Comeau had one condition, that he be given a minimum of ten games to prove himself. Two nights later, he stopped thirty-five of forty-six Vancouver shots in a 12–11 Salmonbellies' victory. "Comeau has himself a regular job," said McRory.[250] Norman called it quits after ten seasons, three Mann Cups, and one NLL championship.

Parnell got his 100th point of the season, 1,000th career point, and five more on August 21 in a game against Vancouver, a 21–13 Salmonbellies' win. New Westminster finished in second place to Coquitlam and faced Vancouver in the semifinals. Vancouver won the first game 14–12. The Salmonbellies took the second game 20–10, the third game 16–11, and the fourth game 14–8.

The main line for Coquitlam was their GAP line of Kerry Gallagher, John Allen, and Kevin Parsons. The Salmonbellies would have to be on them to win the series. In the first game (which the Salmonbellies won 9–8), the Adanacs' Harry Woolley jumped the much smaller Salmonbellies' rookie Walt Weaver (five-foot-nine) and Steve d'Easum (five-foot-six). Lewthwaite, nicknamed "Lurch" after a character in *The Addams Family*, who had been out for three weeks, warned the "Woolley Jumper" to watch his step.

Before the start of the second game, Woolley said to Lewthwaite, "If we're going to fight, let's get it over with."[251] Lewthwaite was not buying it and told him to fuck off. In the last few minutes of the second game the Adanacs' 145-pound Keith Scott, a Golden Gloves boxer, dropped his lacrosse gloves in an attempt to get Lewthwaite to fight and maybe get ejected from the game. Lewthwaite tried to ignore him, but Scott's teammate Alex Carrey came in from behind Lewthwaite's back and started harassing him. Finding himself in a two-on-one fight, Lewthwaite sent Scott flying with a left hook. The Woolley Jumper then tried to jump Lewthwaite. Lurch punched him hard in the head, buckling Woolley's knees. But Woolley came at Lewthwaite again. This time Lewthwaite cracked him in the jaw. But Woolley wanted more. "Woolley, dazed and bewildered, his legs looking like a string of four sausages fluttering in a windstorm, ran at Big Al and grabbed him. Lewthwaite then landed a right upper cut and by then the 'Woolley Jumper' wasn't jumping anymore."[252]

"I don't know why he grabbed me," said Lewthwaite, "he's so weak."[253] Woolley was handed a suspension for the duration of the series, and the Salmonbellies won the game 16–6. Winzoski set a WLA playoff record of seven assists that game.

In the third game, the Salmonbellies scored whenever they were shorthanded. D'Easum ran end to end to score, Winzoski scored three goals, and Tyler scored two. At one point, Lewthwaite and Kevin Parsons squared off. Separated and penalized, they continued, from their respective penalty boxes, to holler at one another over the timekeeper and the PA announcer. Bored with Parsons' jabbering, Lewthwaite pulled out the chunk of lemon he carried in his cheek to keep his mouth lubricated, and hurled it at Parsons. The slimy yellow rind hit Parsons in the mouth. Enraged, he flew out of the box, tripped, stumbled, and fell. Lewthwaite hammered Parsons a few times. It was strictly business, nothing personal. "Unlike some of this teammates, Parsons was a gentleman," said Lewthwaite.[254] The Salmonbellies won 12–7.

In the fourth game, Lewthwaite scored twice from forty-five feet out, proving, although he didn't need to, that he could shoot as well as he boxed. The Salmonbellies won 12–9, sweeping the series. Wayne Goss received the MVP award, while Coach Sepka singled out Winzoski for his playmaking and inspirational defence.

The Salmonbellies travelled to Parnell's hometown, Peterborough, Ontario, for the NLL championship. It was his first time facing his old team in a championship series. But there was more to it than that. His brother-in-law, Cy Coombes, was an outstanding player for the Peterborough Lakers. The team, coached by long-time Salmonbellies' nemesis Bobby Allan, had swept the Toronto Maple Leafs in the eastern finals and had won the league with twenty-seven wins against nine losses, scoring almost 600 goals while allowing slightly more than 400. Seven of their players were in the top ten in scoring. Their lowest top-ten scorer was Larry Ferguson with ninety-two points. The fifth-, sixth-, and seventh-ranked Peterborough scorers each had well over 100 points. Their second-best point getter, Coombes, had racked up 160 points.

Mac Tyler missed wide here, but he put three shots behind Peterborough goalie Pat Baker in the first game of the 1970 Mann Cup.

COLUMBIAN. PHOTOGRAPH BY JOHN SYMONDS.

Coombes had broken into his first full season of senior play with Peterborough in 1958, the same year as Parnell. In 1961, with Peterborough's senior team folding, he played the first of three seasons with Brooklin before rejoining Peterborough in 1964 and helping them win the 1966 Mann Cup.

His 1969 tally included 113 goals—a senior record. Coombes scored most of his goals on breakaways and while working the crease on power plays. But Coombes—like everyone else—was an also-ran in the scoring department compared to John Davis, in his fourth season with Peterborough. Davis piled up 226 regular-season points in 1969 with 103 goals and 123 assists, the all-time record in senior lacrosse. Davis, like Goss, was exceptionally quick and adept at beating his checks one-on-one. He didn't have a great shot, but somehow the ball always seemed to find a way in. A lot of his 123 assists were from passes to Coombes on the crease during power plays.

Davis was well-known to the Salmonbellies, especially the recent juniors, having starred on the Minto Cup winning 1963–65 Oshawa Green Gaels. More recently, he'd been named the Mann Cup MVP in Peterborough's 1966 and 1967 Mann Cup victories.

Pat Baker tended goal for the Lakers. He'd been in net for the Brampton Excelsiors in the Salmonbellies' 1962 Mann Cup win and in goal for Peterborough's 1966 Mann Cup victory over Vancouver.

In game 1, the Salmonbellies checked the Lakers into submission by fighting through their vaunted pick-and-roll plays and shutting down their extremely fast break. Parnell showed no mercy and risked the ire of his sister by forcibly dumping brother-in-law Coombes. The *Columbian* quipped that the only checking they did in the east was at banks—amusing, but not true.

The Lakers' scoring star, John Davis, who averaged four goals and four assists a game during the regular season, had only one assist in the game. But the Lakers' Joe Todd found the net four times with a blistering sub shot. Todd, who seemed to have Comeau's number, caused the Salmonbellies all sorts of trouble throughout the series. For the Salmonbellies, Larry Henry had three goals and Parnell had two in an 11—9 Salmonbellies win.

The Salmonbellies, cooped up in the Empress Hotel, were bored to death, their only diversion being finding new places to eat. "The boys sit around between games playing cards, listening to Mac Tyler's bird imitations and imitations of the big clock across the street from the hotel," said McRory prior to the second game.[255] The Empress was in downtown Peterborough, at the corner of Water and Charlotte Streets. Directly across from it was the old Market Hall, a circa-1900 red brick building with a clock tower. The clock chimed the hours all day and all night long—getting on the players' nerves. It wasn't long before the Salmonbellies devised a plan to make time stand still. Accessing the tower, they attached fishing line to the clock's hands. Then they dropped the line to the pavement, where it would be picked up, carried across the street, hoisted up into one of their rooms, pulled taut, and secured. Viola! No more noisy chiming. At least, that was the plan. In reality, it didn't work, and time went on as inexorably as ever. But at least the operation had killed a few hours of boredom.

The Salmonbellies played disciplined, defensive lacrosse in the second game and got great goaltending from Comeau. Mickey Lynch's play exemplified the team's determination. After Lakers' goalie Baker had come running out of his goal to successfully check Ed Goss in the midst of receiving a long pass, Lynch was in the same position. But Lynch, wiser for having witnessed Baker's check on Goss, held onto the ball, took Baker's hit, and fired into the empty net. Tyler also netted three goals, all on the odd-man play, Shuttleworth counted two goals, and Winzoski tallied two goals and an assist in a 9–6 Salmonbellies' win.

The Salmonbellies entered the third game with a nine-game winning streak. But they had trouble getting the ball up the floor and there were far fewer assists on the goals they scored. In addition, head referee, Bill Hicks, called back three Salmonbellies' goals for crease violations, even though the other referee had signaled a goal each time. Hicks waived each one off, even though he'd been standing at centre for a number of them. The Lakers played without Davis, out after the first game with an injured foot, and Baker excelled in goal. Shuttleworth scored three goals and an assist in an 11–9 Salmonbellies' loss.

In the fourth game, the Lakers scored five goals in the third period to overcome the Salmonbellies' 13–10 second-period lead, winning 15–14. The Salmonbellies scored three goals in the last six minutes of the fifth game to win 8–6. Lewthwaite and 18-year-old rookie Walt Weaver—a standout for the junior Salmonbellies—starred for the senior Salmonbellies, with Lewthwaite scoring the winner. Shuttleworth, Goss, and Tyler each contributed a goal. John Davis returned to the Lakers' lineup for game 6. The Salmonbellies were down 5–4 after the first period and 7–6 after the second. In the third period, they had yet another goal called back, and the Lakers eked out a 9–8 win.

The night before the seventh and deciding game, the Salmonbellies were in a bar enjoying their two-beer-per-player limit. As they were leaving the premises, Lewthwaite was hassled by one of the bar's patrons. After trying to avoid an altercation, Lewthwaite was struck and hit back, sending the guy flying through the plate-glass window of a barbershop. The guy picked himself out of the rubble and, sensibly, began to run. Lewthwaite gave chase, tackled him, and laid on a few more punches. Two cops showed up. Both Lewthwaite and his attacker went to jail. Upon booking Lewthwaite, the cops asked for his shoelaces. "What for?" he asked. So he couldn't hang himself. "Look," said Lewthwaite, "if we lose tomorrow night, I might hang myself, but not now."[256]

Peterborough's Larry Ferguson, Joey Todd, Billy Armour and #10 Carm Collins watch as #7 Paul Parnell zeros in on Pat Baker in the 1970 Mann Cup. #21 Jim Giles is ready for a rebound while #3 Mickey Lynch (background, second from left) patrols the perimeter.
COLUMBIAN. PHOTOGRAPH BY BRIAN KENT.

Meanwhile, McRory had been having drinks with a prominent Peterborough lawyer. The next morning, the lawyer apprised the judge hearing Lewthwaite's case of the situation. McRory briefed Lewthwaite on what to say. "Why did you hit him?" asked the judge. Lewthwaite was supposed to answer that he had tried to stop the other guy from damaging more property, but the honest and outspoken Lewthwaite replied, "Because he hit me!"[257] Regardless, the judge fined the attacker, not Lewthwaite, and, justice having being served, both were released. The incident got around Peterborough, but in the story, it was Shuttleworth who had the fight, not Lewthwaite. Shuttleworth couldn't figure how why,

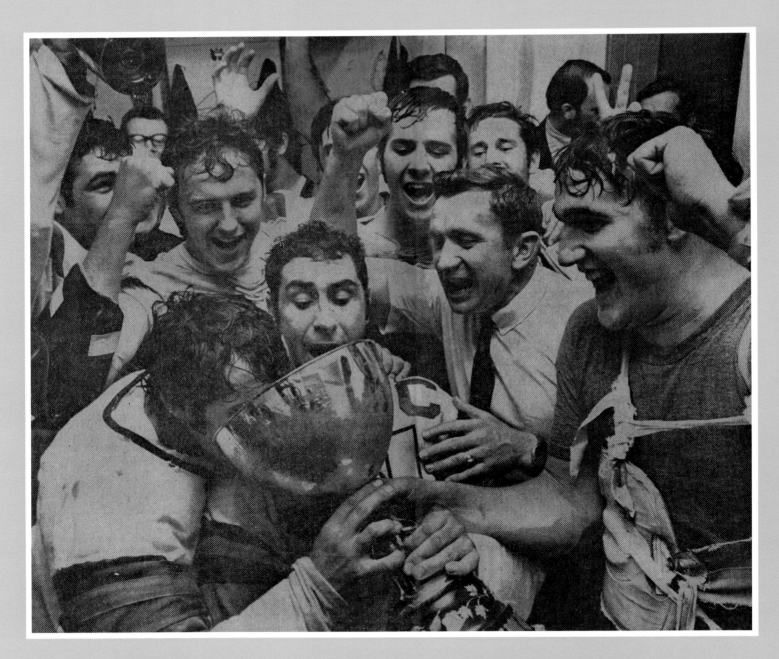

Celebrating their 1970 Mann Cup sweep of the Peterborough Lakers. **First row:** Wayne Goss (drinking from cup), Paul Parnell, Cliff Sepka, Al Lewthwaite. **Second row:** Mickey Lynch, Ed Goss. **Third row:** Ian Bull (face partially blocked by Lynch's fist), Dave Matheson (blocked by Sepka's arm), Larry Henry. **Back left:** coach Keith Jackson (wearing glasses). **Back right:** Ian Matheson.

MAC TYLER. PHOTOGRAPH BY RALPH BOWER.

every time he hit the floor in the seventh game, he was booed and yelled at: "Shuttleworth, you jailbird!"[258]

With the Lakers holding a one-goal lead early in the third period, Wayne Goss took a high hit behind the left ear and was knocked unconscious by Peterborough veteran Ken Henderson. As Goss lay face down on the floor, Henderson grabbed the hair on the back of Goss's head and smashed his face into the floor. The Salmonbellies' bench emptied, but they couldn't get at Henderson. The game was delayed ten minutes while Goss was revived. He was carried from the floor on a stretcher and taken to the hospital with a concussion.

Goss, who had one goal going into the third period and had, to that point, two three-goal games in the finals, wasn't going to score any more from a hospital bed. With the clock ticking down and the score 9–8 for the Lakers, Lewthwaite scooped up the ball in the Salmonbellies' end and ran through the Peterborough team on his way to the net. Baker made a sensational save, and the Lakers were the NLL champions for 1969.

The 1970 Salmonbellies won twenty-two of thirty games, eight more wins than second-place Vancouver, once again playing as the Burrards. But third-place Coquitlam had defeated the Salmonbellies in three of their last four games. The Salmonbellies once again faced the Adanacs in the best-of-seven finals. New Westminster won the first game 13–5 and the second game 9–4 on the strength of hard checking, Comeau's stopping of forty-one of forty-five shots, and Tyler's three second-period goals—the only ones of that period. They won the third game 13–9, with Lewthwaite scoring four goals in total—three on the power play. The Adanacs took the fourth game 11–10, despite Lewthwaite and Tyler each scoring three goals. In the fifth game, a zealous Salmonbellie fan jumped out of the stands and onto Adanacs' coach, Bobby Marsh. The ensuing fracas seemed to fire up Coquitlam, who were down by six, and they went on to a 22–21 overtime win.

With the Peterborough Lakers due to arrive the day after the sixth game, CLA president Jack Fulton was a little anxious about the effect a seventh game would have on the fans' wallets. Would they shell out $3 for each and every game? His worries were over when Wayne Goss scored the Salmonbellies' ninth goal in the third period, putting the game out of the Adanacs' reach. But with the ball in the net, Goss, who had been punched in the head by Adanacs' netminder, Schweitzer, circled behind the goal showering Schweitzer with sarcasm. Irate, Schweitzer went after the trash-talking Goss. The teams emptied their benches, and the referees called off the game with about a minute remaining.

While Wayne had netted the ninth, it was brother Ed who'd led the team that night, with four goals. For the series, Wayne had thirteen goals and eleven assists, but Mac Tyler, with twelve goals in the final four games earned the MVP distinction.

The Salmonbellies faced the Lakers the night after their WLA title victory. The Lakers were much the same team as they were in 1969. The key to defeating them remained the same: shut down their fast break and contain Davis.

The first game saw McRory substituting for Coach Sepka, ill with the flu. Parnell briefed Lewthwaite and Winzoski on how to check Davis. McRory sometimes played five defencemen instead of the usual third line, the better to contain the Lakers' offence. Lewthwaite

Mac Tyler wards off former teammate Wayne Shuttleworth of the Adanacs in game three of the 1971 western semi-finals.

MAC TYLER. PHOTOGRAPH BY RAY ALLAN.

kept Davis close and checked him hard. Davis still managed to score four goals, but not with Lewthwaite on him. Parnell matched Davis with four goals on just five shots and added three assists, Wayne Goss and Mac Tyler scored three each, and the Salmonbellies defeated the Lakers 16–12.

In game 2, Tory broke a bone in his hand, d'Easum broke a bone below his eye, and Lynch broke some of his teeth, but Parnell scored once and assisted on five others while taking his turns checking Davis. Tyler scored twice, Wayne and Ed Goss netted two goals each, and Lewthwaite chalked up three goals and three assists along with one KO—the unfortunate Billy Armour going down—as the Salmonbellies won the game 16–8.

Before the start of the third game, two distinguished-looking men in their late fifties came onto the floor of the Arena for a ceremonial faceoff. In 1934 and 1935, they'd played

They called him "Stumpy" for good reason.
Adanac Keith Scott (18) won't catch Steve d'Easum.
Al Lewthwaite looms at centre. ca. 1972

PHOTOGRAPH BY BASIL KING.

Playing in the one-game Mann Cup championship against the Windsor Warlocks in 1974, Paul Parnell broke Bob Allan's record for most Mann Cup points with 97, and the Salmonbellies won 18-5.

PAUL PARNELL.

together for the Mann Cup-winning Orillia Terriers; in 1936, they were the one-two scoring punch for the Salmonbellies; and in 1937 they and their teammates brought the Mann Cup back to New Westminster after a ten-year absence. Bill Wilkes and Bill Wilson had not seen each other in over twenty-five years. Whether or not Parnell knew the history and the accomplishments of the two gentlemen, he turned in a stellar performance, scoring three goals and two assists in a 14–10 Salmonbellies' victory. In net, Joe Comeau was simply better than Baker that time around.

And Comeau was even better in game 4. Parnell also outdid himself, scoring five goals with two assists while checking Davis who, after three goals in the first period of game one, was held to four goals in the next three games, all on power plays. When Parnell was not on top of Davis, Lewthwaite was. Lurch also dealt decisively with a challenge from the Lakers' big

In 1972 the Salmonbellies were beset by a string of crippling injuries, fought a fire, set scoring records, grabbed a bull by the horns, got star performances from steady regulars, and played over fifty games on their way to their fifteenth Mann Cup. On the bench September 21, 1972 during the second game of the Mann Cup: Dave Matheson, Steve d'Easum (5), Mickey Lynch (3), Fred Greenwood, Mac Tyler (11). Trainer George Friend behind. Top Centre: Morley Kells.

MAC TYLER. PHOTOGRAPH BY BASIL KING.

man, Ron Liscombe. Liscombe, attempting to take the heat off Davis, initiated a fight with Lewthwaite, but like so many before him, he couldn't finish what he started. As Lewthwaite landed blows to Liscombe's head, Wayne Goss tangled with Tim O'Grady and d'Easum battled Ken Henderson, who'd knocked Goss cold in the final Mann Cup game in 1969.

The adrenaline was tapering off when Ed Goss, taking exception to O'Grady's treatment of his brother, thrashed the Laker. The younger Goss finished the night as the Salmonbellies' second leading scorer, with twenty-one points in the Peterborough series and forty-six points over the combined ten-game playoffs, his 4.6-point average putting him in the company of Davy, Wilkes, Wilson, Bionda, and Sepka.

When the dust settled, the Salmonbellies had defeated the Lakers 14–8 in game 4, winning their fourteenth Mann Cup in four games straight. Parnell, the ex-Peterborough

The 1972 New Westminster Salmonbellies. **Front row l-r:** George Friend (trainer), Bob Holmes, Jim Giles, Joe Comeau, Pat Thorp, Kerry Gallagher, Steve d'Easum, Don Sepka (Assistant Trainer). **Middle row:** Bill Workman, Bill Stevenson (General Manager), Larry Henry, Tracy Wright, Ed Goss, Dave Matheson, Wayne Goss, Ian Matheson (President), Jim Glanville (Secreatry Treasurer) **Back row:** Ken Winzoski, Paul Parnell, Fred Greenwood, Al Lewthwaite, Mac Tyler, Mickey Lynch, Ray Bennie.

CANADIAN LACROSSE HALL OF FAME.

boy, had racked up thirteen goals and twelve assists against his old friends and took home the MVP award. Sepka, another Mann Cup victory in his pocket, announced his retirement from the game.

Two months later, on November 21, a man inextricably linked with the history of the Salmonbellies, Vancouver Lacrosse Club star Édouard Newsy Lalonde, died in Montreal at the age of 83. He may have been, in the words of Frank Selke, Jr., "as mean a player as ever played," but he brought an excitement to the game like few others.[259]

Parnell replaced Sepka as coach for the 1971 season, and Tyler became captain. Joe Comeau was back in net, backed up by a renewed and un-retired Les Norman, who hadn't played in 1970. The Salmonbellies finished in first place with twenty-two wins in thirty-one games. At the opposite end of the scale, Victoria finished last with twenty-two losses.

In the league semifinals, Coquitlam defeated Victoria, and New Westminster defeated Vancouver, setting up another Salmonbellies-Adanacs final series. Former Salmonbellies' star Wayne Shuttleworth led Coquitlam in scoring. Shuttleworth, like Norman, hadn't played in 1970, but was back with a vengeance in 1971, racking up 143 points to win the individual scoring honour by two points over Wayne Goss.

The Salmonbellies jumped to a 5–0 lead in the first game and went on to win 12–7, but lost the second game 15–9. In game 3, Ed Goss tallied three goals and two assists, and the Salmonbellies won 14–11. With Les Norman in goal, New Westminster took the fourth game 15–12 in front of a capacity crowd of 2,500 at Coquitlam's arena. Ed Goss was outstanding once again, scoring five times, while Giles hit the back of the net four times. The only bad news concerned Lewthwaite's chronic problem knee, which he re-injured during the game. It was so swollen he could barely walk.

A rare colour slide of the Salmonbellies and the Adanacs at the Arena in June 1973, an off year for the reigning Mann Cup champions. Sandy Lynch is about to shoot while Keith Scott (18) and Jim Aitchison (3) give chase. Fred Greenwood (10) looks left.
PAUL PARNELL.

Merv Schweitzer is ready for an Adanacs' shot. Schweitzer was with the Adanacs for seven years, but he started his career in 1960 with the Salmonbellies. He would play thirteen games for them in 1973, including this one in June, before retiring. **L-r:** Paul Parnell, Wayne Goss.
PAUL PARNELL.

Lewthwaite's absence was a critical factor in game 5. Playing without the fear of being crunched by the big man, the Adanacs posted a 10–7 victory. With the Salmonbellies leading the series 3–2 the Adanacs mounted an all-out charge in game 6, but New Westminster prevailed 12–11 in overtime. Ed Goss, with two goals in the game and twenty-two points in the series, was named MVP. "It was as if everything slowed down for me in the Adanacs series," said Goss. "The ball was huge and I could see where it had to go. I guess I was in some kind of zone."[260]

Earlier in the season, the Salmonbellies had defeated the Brantford Warriors in the Arena. But if they wanted to repeat as Mann Cup champions, they'd have to beat the Warriors at home in Brantford, Ontario. Brantford was home to the Six Nations Mohawk tribes and was where Alexander Graham Bell lived when he invented the telephone in 1874.

It was still 1874 in Brantford, as far as Parnell was concerned. The playing coach showed some wit in assessing the team's shabby old accommodations at the Graham Bell Hotel.

"You don't move too quickly in the rooms—or you'll bruise your elbows. In case of fire we won't be using the fire escape—the players don't want to get rope burns."[261] He wasn't kidding about the rope fire escapes, which were attached to old cast-iron radiators.

Lewthwaite was with the team, but was limping and it was doubtful he would play. Larry Henry, who, along with Goss and Giles, had been instrumental in winning the Coquitlam series, couldn't make the trip due to work commitments and an expecting wife. Brantford capitalized on their zone defence, fast-break offence, and offensively minded goalkeeper Bob McCready in the first game, winning 15–4. Paul Suggate scored four goals for Brantford. Lewthwaite watched helplessly on the sidelines as big Rick Dudley intimidated the smaller Salmonbellies. Wayne Goss received a cut above his left eye that required fourteen stitches.

No trip to Brantford was complete without paying one's respects to the game's greatest living stick maker, Joe Logan of the Six Nations Indian reserve in the village of Ohsweken. In the eyes of many players, including the Salmonbellies, Logan's sticks were beautiful works of

1973 was a frustrating year for Ed Goss and his teammates, losing all ten games against the Burrards. Here, Doug Hayes blocks Ed's shot, sparing Don Hamilton the trouble. Ward Sanderson behind Goss.

COLUMBIAN. PHOTOGRAPH BY PETER BATTISTONI.

art. A visit to his workshop was like dropping in on Cézanne at his studio. Logan made his sticks in a shed behind his house—a small space, with wooden pop cases and empty cream-soda bottles scattered around. "He made his sticks out of hickory that he cut, shaped, bent, and hung to cure," said Jim Giles. "Other makers didn't cure their sticks, and they'd bend when you checked—but Logan's didn't."[262]

In game 2, with Norman in goal, Ed Goss scored three goals to Parnell's two and Tyler's one, but the Warriors matched the Salmonbellies and added four more to take the game 10–6. In game 3, the Salmonbellies outshot Brantford, but scored only ten times to the Warrior's twelve—of which Powless generated four. Kells' Warriors won the fourth game 17–13 for their first Mann Cup. Powless and Ron MacNeil led with fifteen points each. Goalkeeper McCready's ten assists proved his importance to the Warriors' offence.

The 1971 season was done, and so was Les Norman. In his twelve-year, 368-game career with the Salmonbellies, he stopped 9,960 of 13,143 shots for a save percentage of .758. He was a league all-star seven times, top goalie three times, league MVP in 1961, playoff MVP in 1962 and Mann Cup MVP in 1965.

Dave Tory also packed it in. He'd played ten full seasons with the Salmonbellies between 1961 and 1971, missing only 1963. In 352 combined regular-season and playoff games, he scored 233 goals and 219 assists for 452 points, an average of forty-five points a season. He also had three Mann Cup championships to his credit.

On May 1, 1972, Canadian heavyweight boxing champion George Chuvalo went twelve rounds in Vancouver with the greatest heavyweight boxer in history. While Chuvalo did not win the fight, Muhammad Ali did not knock him down. The reigning heavyweight champion in Canadian lacrosse, Al Lewthwaite, was not looking for a fight two nights after the Ali-Chuvalo bout, but Vancouver's Stan "Butch" Skyrzyk insisted on one. Skyrzyk sucker-punched Lewthwaite. Lewthwaite's retaliation brought Ward Sanderson off the bench, which brought everyone else into the melee. The referees restored order and sent the teams to their respective dressing rooms to cool down for twenty minutes. Skyrzyk was handed three major penalties, a ten-minute misconduct, and a game misconduct. Lewthwaite received the same treatment, minus one major penalty.

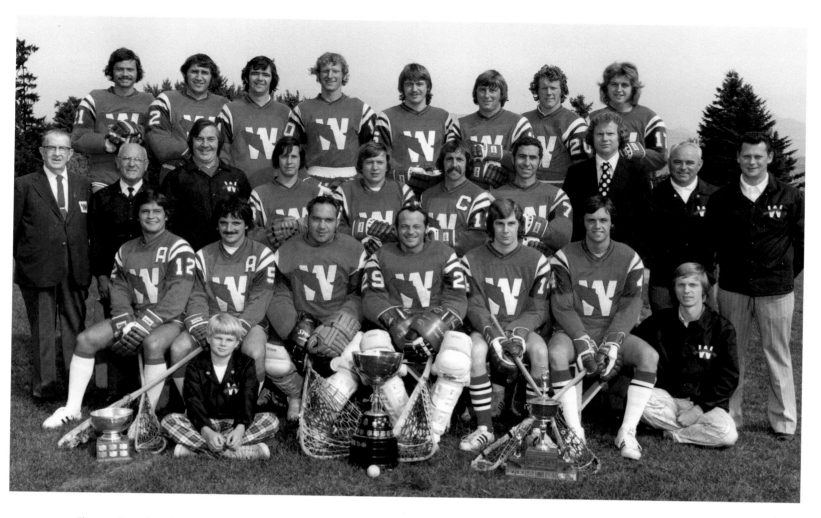

The 1974 Mann Cup champions. **Front row:** Ken Winzoski, Steve d'Easum, Joe Comeau, Skip Jolly, John Hannah, Dave Matheson, Dr. D. Metzak.
Middle row: Bill Workman (supporter), George Friend (trainer), Ron Hemmerling (coach), Larry Henry, Ian Kennedy, Wayne Goss, Paul Parnell, Dave Lumb (equipment), Creighton O'Malley, Max Skinner. **Back row:** Jim Giles, Bill Robinson, Jim Grady, Fred Greenwood, Walt Weaver, Gary Stevens, Bill Mosdell, Harvey Olson. The boy is Creighton O'Malley's son. **Missing:** Al Lewthwaite, Bob Tasker.
CANADIAN LACROSSE HALL OF FAME.

Every team the Salmonbellies faced seemed to have a designated Lewthwaite-baiter and would-be brawler. In Vancouver, it was traditionally Sanderson. In Coquitlam, it was Woolley and Parsons. In Peterborough, it was Billy Armour and Ron Liscombe—not to mention the assailant he sent through the barbershop window. Wherever Lewthwaite played, he was a marked man. But he took no penalties in his next game and scored the tying goal in the third period, one of two he scored that night. Following each counter, he showboated a little, going into what he called "Lurcher's Shuffle." "You'll see a lot of it this year," he predicted, "about 50 times, more or less."[263]

On the night of the Lewthwaite-Skyrzyk bout, Paul Parnell, in his thirteenth WLA season, picked up two assists to overtake Cliff Sepka as the WLA's all-time scoring leader, with 1,328 points. Two games later, he added four assists to reach 616, five more than previous assist leader Whitey Severson.

Parnell's resolute determination and Lewthwaite's cockiness exemplified the spirit of the Salmonbellies as they embarked on the team's eighty-first season. The Salmonbellies added three players to their roster: Tracey Wright, who'd scored seventy-seven goals one season as a junior Salmonbellie; Fred Greenwood, a former Oshawa Green Gael and a member of the 1968 Detroit Olympics; and all-star Kerry Gallagher, who'd been scoring goals for Coquitlam since 1965. The Salmonbellies could have added high-scoring Huntsville brothers Brian and Ivan Thompson to their roster, but McRory, knowing the team would have been too strong with them, offered them to Victoria, who signed them up.

From midnight to 9:00 a.m. on July 27, 1972, the New Westminster Fire Department was busy fighting a fire. That night, on only a couple of hours of sleep, Parnell took a pass from fellow firefighter Wayne Goss to score goal number 747, one more than what had been

Paul Parnell gave nothing less than all out efforts, and expected the same from his teammates. From 1961 when he broke in with the Salmonbellies until his retirement in 1975, the team won five Mann Cups and one NLL title.

BC SPORTS HALL OF FAME.

Cliff Sepka's WLA record. Steve d'Easum, in a knee brace, returned to the lineup after seven weeks of recovery. Before the torn knee d'Easum, in three seasons, had scored 274 points, but the injury forced him to concentrate less on goals and more on playmaking and defence.

The Salmonbellies wrapped up the league title in August, defeating the Lakers 10–6 in an interlocking game at the Arena. The team then travelled to Ontario for a series of games. Henry, Wright, Lynch, and Ed Goss had also sustained injuries over the course of the regular season. But the eastern tour, comprising five games in ten nights, exacted an even worse toll. Giles pulled a hamstring, Winzoski sprained an ankle, Ed Goss dislocated his shoulder and twisted his knee, and Parnell tore knee ligaments. Lewthwaite sustained a serious injury as well, but it was between games. In Toronto to play the Shooting Stars, Lewthwaite, Bennie, and Dave Thwaites dropped into an arcade to pass the time. They found themselves in front of a Bull Strength Tester and had to try it. Grabbing a bullhorn in either hand, Bennie tried to push them together. He did well, but Thwaites did even better. There was no way Lewthwaite was going to lose. He took the horns and squeezed with everything he had, snapping his pectoralis major muscle in the process.

Parnell, speaking for the team, blasted the CLA for insisting on the series, coming as it did at the end of the regular season, just before the playoffs. "It's time they stopped using the players as the only means of promoting the game," he said.[264] But even with seven men out of the lineup, including Parnell, his leg in a cast, the Salmonbellies defeated the Burrards 9–7 on August 17.

The injuries, however, continued. Wayne Goss was the next to go down with a bad charley horse. The Salmonbellies not only lost the first game of the semifinals to the Shamrocks, they also lost the services of Ed Goss, who'd returned too soon and twisted his right knee. He was now out for the duration. Tyler pulled a hamstring and Lewthwaite re-injured his chest muscle. Somehow, Parnell played, his ankle heavily taped. Battered and bruised, braced and taped, the Salmonbellies took to the floor for game 2 on August 30. At one point, Wayne Goss got into position to take a faceoff. Victoria's Dave Thomson, a 200-pounder in his first senior season, attempting to intimidate Goss, tried to slam his knee into Goss's face. The blow was only glancing, but Mac Tyler took exception to Thomson's intention.

There was no stopping the ferocity Tyler had inherited from his no-holds-barred Salmonbellie father, Whoopie. Off came the gloves and down from Tyler's six-foot-four, 230-pound frame came a bone-crushing right hand to Thomson's face. As Thomson tumbled, Tyler kept pummelling.

Victoria's players, attempting to go to Thomson's aid, were blocked by Salmonbellie Dave Thwaites, who hovered protectively over Tyler as he administered a whooping. Thomson, assessed a major penalty and a game misconduct, was carried off the floor. The Salmonbellies won the game to go up two games to one. The following night, they handed Victoria their third and final loss.

The Salmonbellies and the Burrards met in the finals for the first time on September 8, with New Westminster winning 12–11. The archrivals then alternated wins over the next five games. After six games, very little separated them, Vancouver having scored sixty goals to win three and New Westminster having scored sixty-two to win three. Fred Greenwood shone for the Salmonbellies.

New Westminster went into the seventh game minus Tyler, who was out with an injury. Lewthwaite, who wanted to play, was rigged with a special brace pinning his right arm to his side, but he was judged not quite ready. Without several key players and with others in dubious states of health, the Salmonbellies found themselves down a goal in the third period. Dave Matheson, who'd stepped up his game in response to his team's injuries, ventured a shot from twenty-five feet out, beating Dave Evans to tie the game at nine. Seconds later Matheson, who'd scored just eighteen goals in the regular season, found the back of the net on another twenty-five footer. Goss then flipped a Barclay-like over-the-shoulder pass to Parnell, who scored the insurance. Parnell, who only weeks earlier had been in a cast, had three goals and three assists in the deciding game. For his fifteen goals and nine assists in the series, he was awarded the MVP trophy.

There was no time for the Salmonbellies to celebrate their victory and recuperate. The very next night, September 17, they were back on the floor at Queen's Park to battle the defending champion Brantford Warriors for the Mann Cup. Allowed to pick up a player, the Salmonbellies turned to Vancouver's Bob Salt, who was in his eighth season. Built like a Pontiac GTO, Salt was a big reason for Vancouver's success that year, scoring forty-three goals and thirty-five assists during the regular season and performing even better in the playoffs. Salt, they hoped, would fill Ed Goss' shoes.

In game 1, Salt was what the Salmonbellies needed (and more), tallying three goals and four assists in a 13–8 victory. Parnell scored the first goal, the last goal, and two in between. Comeau stopped thirty-five shots. Lewthwaite, his right arm braced to his side, played his first full game in five weeks.

In game 2, Wayne Goss won most of the faceoffs, the team incurred just two minor penalties, Gallagher scored three goals with three assists, and Ray Bennie, in his best season ever, banged in three goals as the Salmonbellies won 13–11. "The guys are tired," said Parnell after the game, understating things, "we've played 50 games this year."[265]

Tired or not, Parnell scored two key goals at the start of the second period of game 3 to give the team a three-goal edge. He scored a third to pass another of Sepka's WLA records, 113 hat tricks. In the third period Larry Henry went on a scoring binge, netting four. Comeau yet again made saves when the team needed them. Lewthwaite, playing with one good arm and one he couldn't raise above shoulder height, checked as if nothing were wrong. The Salmonbellies won the game 20–9.

A couple of nights later, Parnell scored three goals with four assists in game 4 as New Westminster prevailed 18–16 and drank from their 15th Mann Cup. His hat trick tied Bionda for most three-point games in Mann Cup history. With fifty-four playoff points, Parnell won MVP, while Wayne Goss topped all scorers with fifty-seven. Joe Comeau stopped more than three out

Salmonbellies' button designed by Paul Parnell's wife Joan.
CANADIAN LACROSSE HALL OF FAME.

of four shots. As for big Al Lewthwaite, who'd performed the Lurcher Shuffle thirty-one times during the regular season and garnered eighty-six points, he somehow managed to score four goals with eight assists in six playoff games—with his arm braced to his side. "For my money," said Salmonbellies GM Bill Stevenson, "the 1972 team was the strongest ever."[266]

The 1973 Salmonbellies, under coach Keith Jackson, were collectively tired and worn out. Mac Tyler had to have most of the moving parts of the left side of his body—elbow, hip and knee—drained of fluid before each and every game. But it was a stiff check that ultimately did him in. He went into the boards near the Salmonbellies' bench in a twisted position, injuring his lower back. In extreme pain, he should have been carried off the floor, but in a time-honoured tradition he didn't want anyone to see that he was hurt, so he crawled to the bench. With a bad back, a shot knee, and—later—a split lip, he decided it was time. He played twenty games in his tenth—and final—season, retiring with three Mann Cup championships and an NLL championship to his credit. In all, he'd played 305 games, scored 307 goals, and assisted on 262 goals. His best season was 1970 with sixty-nine combined regular- and post-season goals and fifty assists. "What makes a championship team is the dressing room. If everyone respects each other and is committed to winning, you can win—but put an asshole in a dressing room and you have a problem."[267] Asked why he kept playing even though he had to have his knee, elbow, and wrist drained, not to mention other possible reasons (such as no summer vacations, fresh injuries, no pay for playing), he said, "Pride and work ethic to some degree," but that in the end, he "just didn't want to let anyone down."[268]

"I guess we don't want to win badly enough," said Parnell in July with the Salmonbellies floundering.[269] His will to win was certainly undiminished, scoring thirty-two goals with sixty-four assists over the twenty-five game schedule—second only to Coquitlam's Parsons. Lewthwaite was healthy for all but four games and ended the season with sixty-six points. But the Salmonbellies finished dead last with just seven wins. Worse still, they lost all ten games against the Burrards, who met the Peterborough Lakers in a televised single-game Mann Cup final, and lost 9–5.

Ron Hemmerling coached the Salmonbellies in 1974. Hemmerling had played nine seasons for the Vancouver Burrards/Carlings between 1957 and 1968, including on their 1961, 1963, and 1964 Mann Cup teams. His non-stop witticisms, jokes, and quips made him popular with the players. "It was like having Rodney Dangerfield as your coach," recalled Lewthwaite. "He even looked like Dangerfield. Before the national anthem, we'd all be out on the floor laughing. Our opponents couldn't figure out what was going on. Well, it was Hemmerling. He really kept us loose and relaxed."[270]

On June 5, Parnell—thirty-six years old and in his fifteenth WLA season—scored three goals with five assists as the Salmonbellies defeated Victoria, making him the WLA's all-time leading scorer at just two points shy of 1,600. The Salmonbellies won their first nine games before finally losing to Victoria.

Later, in a victory over the Adanacs, Wayne Goss had four assists and three goals—two of them shorthanded in the third period—to reach 900 career points, the eighth player in WLA history to reach that mark. At 11:01 of the first period, Parnell notched 1,600 points and Lewthwaite scored two with four assists to reach 500 points.

The Salmonbellies continued to win through July and August. When the regular season ended after twenty-four games, New Westminster had twenty wins—more than enough for first place. In the WLA finals, the Salmonbellies swept the Burrards in three games, earning the right to face the Windsor Warlocks at the Arena. The odds favoured the Salmonbellies, for the east's best players were playing pro in the NLL. The format was the same as 1973—a one-game final to be broadcast by the CBC. The Warlocks were young and inexperienced, but their run-and-gun offensive style had won them fourteen of twenty regular-season games. Their best point getter was John McDonald, followed by brothers Norm and Bill Hope. In goal was rookie Grant Bryck.

In reality, the Warlocks were closer to the level of a senior B team, and the game was a mismatch reminiscent of the 1958 Welland-Crowland Switson series. In front of 4,127 fans and a national TV audience, Parnell broke Bob Allan's record for most Mann Cup points with ninety-seven while Winzoski tallied four goals (two shorthanded) and two assists in an easy 18–5 Salmonbellies' victory. Comeau was once again virtually unbeatable, and Winzoski's efforts earned him the MVP award.

After the game Ab Brown, whose first Mann Cup appearance was in 1918, did what he always did, checking the Salmonbellies' sticks for damage. His inspection completed, he slipped away quietly into the night.

In 1975, Hemmerling returned to coach the Salmonbellies. Six players—including Lewthwaite, Winzoski, Bennie, and Ed Goss—opted to play for pro teams in the NLL. Giles sat out the WLA season with a separated shoulder. Comeau skipped the season, so Skip Jolly went into net. Despite the loss of veterans, the Salmonbellies finished the regular season in first place, with seventeen wins and seven losses. Wayne Goss topped the scoring chart with fifty-two goals and ninety-four assists.

The Salmonbellies faced third-place Vancouver in the best-of-five semifinals. In game 1, Bill Mosdell scored six goals, and Wayne Goss got five goals and two assists in a 15–14 Salmonbellies' win. In game 2, Goss was slashed and broke a finger, while Mosdell suffered a separated shoulder. The loss hit the team severely. They were short two more players for game 3 (Walt Weaver had the flu and Gary Stevens was working) and went down 12–9. On August 20, goalie Bill Scriver scored New Westminster's final goal in the fourth game—the first WLA goalie to ever score in a regular-season game—but the Salmonbellies lost to Vancouver in the playoffs for the first time since 1966.

Wayne Goss welcomes to his right Jan Magee and to his left Jim Johnston. Magee and Johnston hailed from Peterborough, but played the 1976 season with New Westminster. Johnston had 151 points in 38 combined regular season and playoff games, while Magee contributed 83 points in 29 combined games.

BILL ARMSTRONG.

Parnell had four assists and reached 1,801 career points (all but thirty-one of them with New Westminster). The game was his 587th and final game. In sixteen seasons, he played on five Mann Cup teams and one NLL championship team, scoring 921 goals and 880 assists, an average of 112 combined regular-season and playoff points a season—over three points a game. His best year was 1965, when he scored seventy-one in the regular season and thirteen in the playoffs on the way to a Mann Cup victory, but 1968 was close with eighty-two combined goals and a Mann Cup. During his six years of playing in championships, only once did he average fewer than three points a game—2.72 in 1962. And in his best year, 1974, he averaged 4.28 points a game. "Parnell shone in the really tough ones," said Jack Fulton. "He would get beat up something awful. He was the heart and soul of the team. He played the same way he worked as a fireman—he gave it everything he had."[271]

The Vancouver Burrards, led in scoring by Bob Salt, Bill Rawson, and WLA rookie of the year, Ron Pinder, advanced to the 1975 Mann Cup against the Brampton Excelsiors. Gord Frederickson's power-play goal in overtime of game 1 gave Vancouver an 11–10 victory. Game 2 was an easy 16–8 Vancouver win and another Mann Cup. Pinder was MVP.

Joe Comeau looks to see where the ball has gone as the Adanac is about to collide.
Steve d'Easum and Brent Ojanen look on.

COLUMBIAN. PHOTOGRAPH BY JOHN SYMONS.

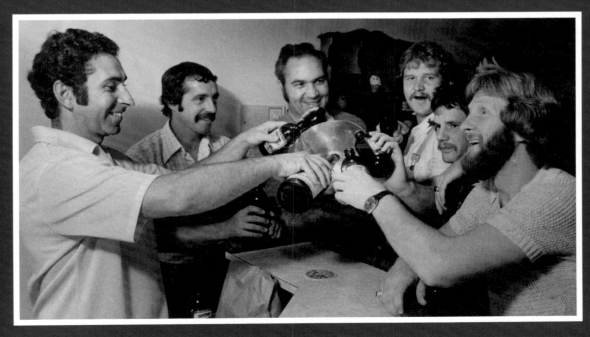

Back in New Westminster, the 1976 Mann Cup champions celebrated at Paul Parnell's house.
From left: Paul Parnell, Wayne Goss, Joe Comeau, Don Brown, Bill Mercer and Dave Wilfong.

DON BROWN.

Bill Stevenson returned as the Salmonbellies' president for 1976, and Barry Erlandson took on the general manager's role. Wayne Goss began the season as the team's playing-coach, but discovered it was too early; he still had lots to offer strictly as a player. Seven games into the season, retired Vancouver player Bob Babcock took over coaching duties. Expensive air travel and low attendance, with the exception of Montreal and Philadelphia, sealed the fate of the NLL. The 1976 Summer Olympics had taken over the Montreal Forum and without Montreal's participation, Quebec opted out of the league.

The NLL's demise brought Lewthwaite, Winzoski, Bennie, Ed Goss, and Tasker back into the Salmonbellies' fold. At Lewthwaite's urging, four of his Tomahawks teammates—Chuck Medhurst and former Peterborough juniors Dave Wilfong, Jan Magee, and Jim Johnston—signed on with the Salmonbellies.

The *Columbian* wrote that Johnston was "the most talented and colourful lacrosse player since Jack Bionda." In his first season out of the Peterborough juniors, he nearly won the NLL scoring title. Along with Lewthwaite's picks from the Tomahawks, the 1976 Salmonbellies were a mix of eastern players, other NLL returnees such as Bob and Brian Tasker, junior drafts and trades, and premature retirement returnees Ray Bennie and Wayne Spooner. Bennie had last played for the team in 1973 and Spooner in 1972.

After a season of pro lacrosse, Ed Goss thought he still wanted to play, but realized he no longer had the heart for it, so retired. Lewthwaite re-injured his knee early on and played only two regular-season games. In the first, he came up with seven assists.

On June 21, the Salmonbellies lost to Nanaimo, their sixth defeat in a row and fourth under Babcock. They sat dead last in the standings. With the team at three wins and eight losses, Comeau came back. When he spoke a hush fell over the dressing room; he recommended better checking.

On June 24 Vancouver's Sanderson jumped Dave Wilfong. Goss, tired of Sanderson and tired of losing, retaliated with a cross-check, followed by well-aimed punches that closed both of Sanderson's eyes. "We have mixed feelings about Sanderson," said Babcock, "on the one hand he's a menace, but on the other hand we score a lot of goals when he's on the floor."[272]

As for Goss, his pre-game routine was to eat a spaghetti dinner at 4:30 in the afternoon, sleep for an hour, listen to the three-part harmony of the band America and head to the Arena. Asked on July 26 what he'd do if he won a million dollars in a lottery, he replied, with characteristic wit, "just keep playing lacrosse until the money ran out."[273]

With Comeau in net, Goss blackening eyes, and the team checking, the Salmonbellies started to win again. Lewthwaite returned to the lineup for a game against Nanaimo on July 10. He was unsteady on his sore knee, but handed out three punishing checks that inspired his teammates to another convincing victory of 19–10. They won their next twelve games and finished in second place. In the semifinals, New Westminster defeated the Adanacs four games to one. Nine days later they met the Burrards in the finals.

The time off was no help to the Salmonbellies, and they lost game one 9–8. They won game two 13–9 and game three 13–12. (A pattern was developing. Whenever the team scored Goss's number, thirteen, they won.) They lost game four 14–11, but won game five when they once again tallied thirteen goals to Vancouver's nine.

Legendary Six Nations stick maker Joe Logan poses in front of his workshop with Salmonbellies John Hannah, Don Brown, and Bob Geddes in 1976.

DON BROWN.

In game six, Vancouver hit seven goalposts, but that wasn't bad luck according to Comeau. "The pipes are part of my equipment," he noted matter-of-factly.[274] The Salmonbellies scored Goss's number, plus one extra, defeating Vancouver 14–7.

For the Mann Cup, the Salmonbellies picked up the third Tasker brother, Dave, of the Burrards, junior Mario Govorchin, and the WLA's third-leading scorer, Dave "the Dude" Durante of the Adanacs. The nickname was bestowed on Durante by his Adanacs teammate, goalie Dave Wedlock. When the coifed, cologned and stylishly dressed Durante joined his teammates for an après game drink, Wedlock exclaimed, "Look! It's the Dude!" The Dude's original ambition was to play in the NHL, but when his hope of a university scholarship fell through, he turned to lacrosse. He knew where he wanted to play, his dad Joe had won a Mann Cup with the 1958 Salmonbellies, but the Dude signed with the Adanacs in 1973. He

In seven seasons with the Salmonbellies, netminder Joe Comeau won four Leo Nicholson trophies and four Mann Cups. Only Les Norman and Rod Banister have played more box lacrosse games in goal for the Salmonbellies.

BILL ARMSTRONG

won the WLA scoring title the next year using a stick rejected by the man that finished second: Paul Parnell. The irony was not lost on Durante.

The Salmonbellies were 3–0 in previous Mann Cup encounters with Brampton, losing in 1930, '31, and '42. The 1976 Salmonbellies were counting on their ball control style of play to carry them to victory.

In the first game, Salmonbellie Chuck Medhurst scored six goals, but injuries to Brian Tasker and Jim Johnston left the team one line short for the second and third periods. Three goals by Ted Greves and two goals and three assists by Mike French led the Excelsiors to a 14–10 victory.

A number of Salmonbellies, led by team prankster Jim Johnston, called Ward Sanderson and asked, tongue-in-cheek, about his availability. Winzoski, Mosdell, Bennie, and Brown checked the way Comeau demanded his defenceman to check, and he stopped all but four Brampton shots in game 2, including eighteen in the third period. At the other end of the floor, Durante scored three goals with five assists and Dave Tasker tallied three goals in a 10–4 Salmonbellies' win. The cost of victory, however, was a hard slash to Wayne Goss's knee, causing him to wear a brace for the remainder of the series.

The Salmonbellies were up 9–3 going into the third period of game 3, but they collapsed and Brampton scored nine to win 12–11. With all three Tasker brothers playing on the same line, the Salmonbellies—on the strength of Comeau's play and Brian Tasker's four goals and three assists—won game four 10–6. "They didn't play that well," said Brampton coach John McCauley. "It's just that we played worse."[275]

Babcock noticed a certain "uptight" quality to his players in the dressing room that didn't bode well for game 5.[276] In the second period, McCauley replaced Gary Powless in net with Larry Smeltzer of the Fergus Thistles. Once again, the Salmonbellies collapsed in the third period and were outscored 6–1. Greves scored two in the third and four overall. Tom Patrick scored Brampton's final goal for an 11–10 victory. In game 6, Dave Wilfong scored three times, the Salmonbellies forechecked, and the team outscored Brampton 5–2 in the third period to prevail 15–12.

The seventh game was set for Friday night, but Brian Tasker had a fire department qualifying exam to write in Vancouver that day. He flew out Thursday, wrote the exam, and returned to Brampton a few hours before game time. The Salmonbellies led 6–1 at the end of the first period, but were tied at eight late in the third. When Brampton failed to advance the ball out of their end within ten seconds, Jim Johnston, not pranking this time, scooped it up and passed to Bob Tasker who was all alone in front of goalie Larry Smeltzer. Tasker's shot found the net with 7:34 left in the game, and the Salmonbellies held on for a 9–8 victory and their fourth Mann Cup in six years.

After three previous Mann Cup losses the Salmonbellies had finally defeated Brampton. Comeau chalked up seven points on seven assists—his last ever. The Tasker brothers accounted for seventeen goals and twenty-two assists. Eight goals and seventeen assists by Coquitlam pickup Dave Durante earned him the MVP award.

The last of the Salmonbellies' old guard—a member of the 1908 Minto Cup heroes—died in New Westminster on November 8, 1976, at the age of ninety. Jimmy Gifford had outlived his four brothers and teammates, Will, Tom, Hugh, and Jack. The generous, boisterous, sentimental Scot retained his vitality, often not knowing his own strength. Greeting the women of the family in bear hugs you could hear vertebrae cracking; men massaged their hands after one of his vice grip handshakes. Jimmy's loathing of Newsy Lalonde, whom he outlived by six years, continued until the end. He even refused to attend the opening ceremony of the Canadian Lacrosse Hall of Fame in 1966 because Lalonde was also going to be a charter inductee.

Newsy didn't care for Jimmy.
VANCOUVER ARCHIVES. PHOTOGRAPH BY W.J. CAIRNS.

Jimmy didn't care for Newsy.
NEW WESTMINSTER MUSEUM AND ARCHIVES.

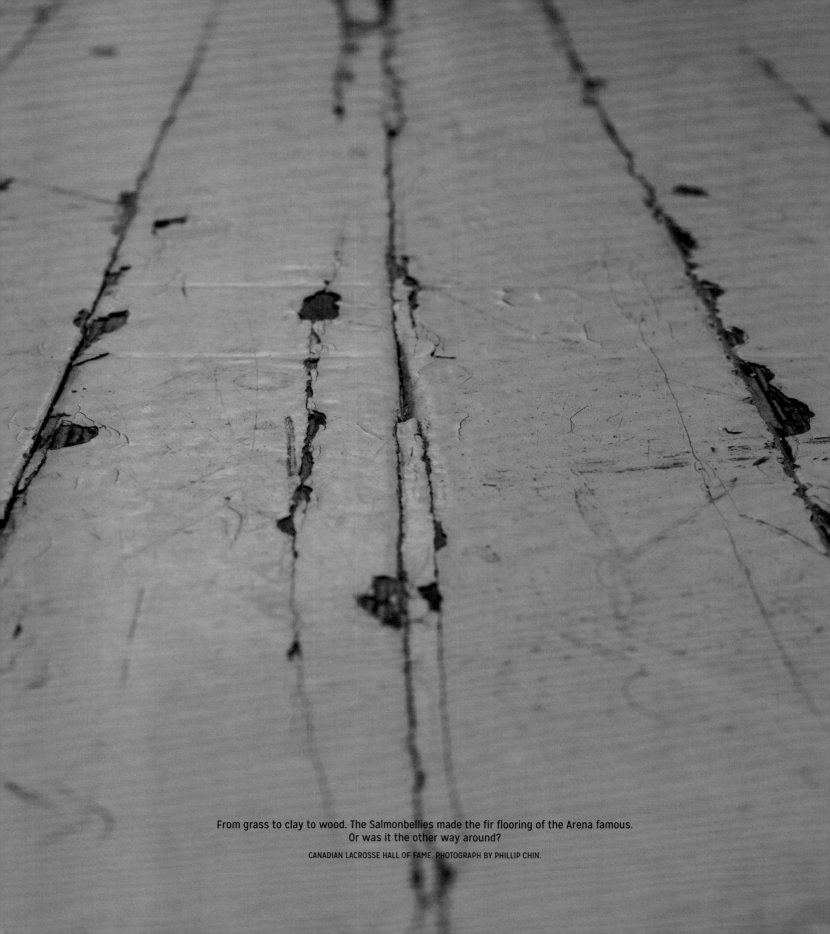

From grass to clay to wood. The Salmonbellies made the fir flooring of the Arena famous.
Or was it the other way around?

"You'd have seen 23 Salmonbellies dead on the floor from exhaustion before you'd have seen us lose another [Mann Cup] at home."

Geordie Dean, 1989

CHAPTER ELEVEN
CHAMPAGNE AND GLORY: 1977-1991

At the start of the 1977 season, Ed Goss had not been in a Salmonbellies' uniform in three years, but he played nine games, scoring nine goals and two assists, his last points in a career that saw him win two Mann Cups and score 437 points on 192 goals and 245 assists in 163 games, an average of over 2.5 points a game. Winzoski retired as well, having won four Mann Cups and scoring 573 WLA points on 205 goals and 368 assists in 270 games as a senior and thirteen games as a junior pickup—an average of two points a game. With Ted Gernaey in net, the Salmonbellies finished third in the 1977 standings (12–12) and were defeated in the semi-finals by the Burrards. Vancouver, led by Doug Hayes, won four straight against the Brampton Excelsiors to win the Mann Cup four games to two. Hayes and Mike Smith shared the Mike Kelly trophy. It was Vancouver's fourteenth and last Mann Cup.

Lloyd Solomon became the Salmonbellies' GM in 1977, at the age of twenty-six—the youngest ever to hold the position. He put an organized system in place, attending junior and senior B games and compiling comprehensive scouting reports on prospects. In 1978, he acquired Ivan Tuura and Eric Cowieson.

The 1978 Salmonbellies went 12–11–1 before losing to the Adanacs in the first round of the finals. The Peterborough Red Oaks, led by MVP Tim Barrie, defeated high scoring Ron McNeil and the Victoria Shamrocks in the 1978 Mann Cup. In 1979, Solomon took over as Salmonbellies' president, Al Lewthwaite took on the coaching duties, and Casey Cook became general manager. Cook, who was born in Holland but grew up in Burnaby, played junior lacrosse in Coquitlam, played up for the senior Adanacs in 1966 and 1967, and played fourteen games of senior in Coquitlam. In 1969, he played for both the New Westminster Blues of the ICLL amateur league and the Salmonbellies. That same year he joined the staff of the Vancouver Parks Board. Before joining the Salmonbellies, he was with the Burnaby Cablevision team.

Defenseman Dan Richardson also joined the team that year. Richardson was born in 1957 in Powell River, BC, and moved to New Westminster with his family in 1966. A couple of years later, his dad took him to a lacrosse game at the Arena—a 1968 championship game against the Detroit Olympics—and the next day bought him and his brother lacrosse sticks at Peterson's sporting goods store in New Westminster.

Richardson played three years for the junior Salmonbellies. By the time he was drafted by the Nanaimo Timbermen in 1979, he was six-foot-four and weighed 220 pounds. His banking career precluded him moving to Nanaimo, so he was traded to the Salmonbellies. A defenceman, he scored only a handful of goals, but he kept things light-hearted in the dressing room, nailing teammates' flip-flops to the floor and freezing players' boxer shorts.

Things got more serious when the Salmonbellies, 17–12–1 for the 1979 regular season, met the Victoria Shamrocks in the semifinals. Defenceman Jim Lynch was Victoria's leading regular-season scorer, followed by Bob Cool, defenceman Chris Hall, and Kevin Alexander. Alexander, however, had only played twelve regular-season games, compared to the other three with twenty-nine games each. The Salmonbellies also had to contend with Ivan Thompson, Ranjit Dillon, Larry Bell, Dan Green, and Larry Smeltzer, winner of the Leo Nicholson Trophy as the league's most outstanding goaltender. Victoria was simply too strong, and defeated the Salmonbellies four games to one. They were even better in the Mann Cup, sweeping the Peterborough Red Oaks in four games. Wayne Goss, picked up by Victoria for the series, scored twelve points in three games.

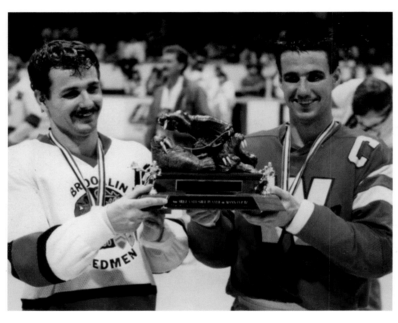

Eric Cowieson (right) played eighteen seasons with the Salmonbellies, fourteen of them as captain, but at the start of every year he was never sure he was good enough. When the team retired his number, he admitted being "a little uncomfortable" seeing his name hanging from the rafters at the Arena with the team's five other all-time greats. In 1987 he shared the Mann Cup MVP award with Jim Meredith.

MARK TUURA.

Solomon and Lewthwaite saw to it that New Westminster native Steve Manning—who refused to play for any team but New Westminster—joined the Salmonbellies for the 1980 season. The rugged defenceman hit hard and often, in the tradition of Patchell, McRory, and Lewthwaite. Mark Tuura and goaltender Rod Banister were signed. The Salmonbellies also engineered a deal that saw the team trade Govorchin for WLA all-star Dave Durante and his brother Ray, a skillful centreman. The Dude, who'd scored 477 points in six seasons with the Adanacs, fit in perfectly with New Westminster's plans. While the Dude was strong physically, his competitive edge was cerebral. He kept a mental playbook on his opponents and he used his vocal chords to skewer opponents and inhabit their heads. Furthermore, he didn't care about statistics, personal records or even, when it came right down to it, the regular season. The Dude only cared about winning Mann Cups.

Entering the 1980 season, Wayne Goss led the WLA with thirty-six first goals of the game and thirty-six game-winning goals. He also led the league in shorthanded goals, with 118, fifty-eight more than second-place Ranjit Dillon. Goss's value as a penalty killer kept him out of power plays until halfway through his career, but he was still fourth in the league with 116. Goss was setting the pace ten games into the season with thirty-five points when a ruptured disc in his back knocked him out of further play. Cowieson was appointed interim captain. The team finished 11–13 during the regular season, but defeated Coquitlam in the semifinals and Victoria in the finals.

The Salmonbellies faced the Excelsiors in the Mann Cup in Brampton. Their hosts had arranged for them to stay at a hotel featuring mud-wrestling contests and door-knocking hookers who roamed the hallways all night long. They stayed only a couple of nights at their fleabag accommodations before booking into something reasonable near the airport. They didn't have the same choice when it came to dressing rooms. Brampton's ramshackle arena was so small it couldn't accommodate all the players, forcing many to change in the hallway. Those who did squeeze into the room inhaled turpentine fumes, the result of a suspiciously recent coat of oil-based paint.

The heat and humidity were oppressive. The Excelsiors' dressing room was air-conditioned; the Salmonbellies' was not. Wherever they went for beer, locals tried to goad them into fighting. But the lowest blow was Brampton's claim that they'd lost their red game jerseys. Brampton's spies had reported correctly that the Salmonbellies' red game jerseys were older models, not made of the new lightweight mesh material. By claiming that they only had white uniforms in which to play, the Excelsiors hoped to force New Westminster—also equipped with new, lightweight, *white* mesh jerseys—into playing exclusively in their heavier reds. Given the heat and humidity, that would have been another distinct advantage for Brampton. So coach Lewthwaite saw to it that the Salmonbellies "lost" their red jerseys, too.

Led by Barry Maruk, Bram Wilfong, and high-scoring brothers Bob and Jim Wasson (picked up for the series from the Peterborough Lakers), the Excelsiors won the first two contests. The Salmonbellies were without Brian Tasker, stranded in Calgary because of an air traffic controllers' strike in Toronto. His brother Bob scored nine points in game 3, and the Salmonbellies notched nine power-play goals to win 17–10. Brian Tasker joined the team for game 4, but Brampton outshot the Salmonbellies and won 9–8. The fifth game and the Mann Cup went to the Excelsiors—their first cup in forty-nine years.

The absence of a number of players, including Brian Tasker, altered the Salmonbellies' chemistry at the start of the 1981 campaign and reduced their goal-scoring ability. But a strong nucleus of veterans and the addition of big defenceman Lyle Robinson augured well. The Salmonbellies, however, sat at the bottom of the league in July. They couldn't score. They couldn't win at home. With the team at six wins and nine losses, Cook did what GMs sometimes must do, and fired Lewthwaite. A few days later, Lewthwaite was rehired, only to resign. Cook added coach to his GM duties. New Westminster finished fourth at 10–13–1, seven wins behind first-place Coquitlam and two wins ahead of last-place Nanaimo. But in the first game of the semifinals against Vancouver, Mark Tuura's game-winning goal led to three more wins in a four-game series sweep.

The Adanacs took the first game of the finals 10–7. Their goaltender, Greg Thomas, who'd played fifteen games with the Salmonbellies in 1973, knew better than to rule out his opponents after just one game. "Even though New Westminster doesn't have the gunners," he told the *Columbian,* "they have the guts."[277] Ivan Tuura, inactive for most of the season with an injury, returned to the lineup for game 2, along with Brian Tasker. Tasker scored three goals and two assists to lead the Salmonbellies to a 13–9 win. Tasker was not in the lineup for game 3, but the Salmonbellies still won 16–14. Tasker scored four times in game 4, and with the score tied at fifteen, Goss bounced in the winner, his third of the match to go with four assists. The Salmonbellies won the deciding game 13–10, earning the right to again face the Excelsiors in the Mann Cup, this time at Queen's Park.

Montreal Canadiens legend and lacrosse player John Ferguson watches the junior Salmonbellies with lacrosse greats Tommy McVie, Jack Bionda, and Paul Parnell in 1978.

COLUMBIAN. PHOTOGRAPH BY BASIL KING.

Future Salmonbellies President and GM Dan Richardson battles Vancouver's Eric Otterstrom for a loose ball in 1980. Bob Tasker is partially hidden by Otterstrom's stick. Doug Hayes is behind Tasker.

COLUMBIAN. PHOTOGRAPH BY PETER BATTISTONI.

Geordie Dean, Jack Bionda and Dave Durante in 1982, Dean's rookie year.

COLUMBIAN. PHOTOGRAPH BY TOM BRAID.

The first game, an 11–8 New Westminster victory, was relatively uneventful, but early in the second period of the second game, with the Salmonbellies leading 7–5, referee Reg Higgins disallowed a goal by Brampton's Gord Keates. Keates responded with a two-handed slash to Higgins's wrist. Keates was ejected and Higgins went to Royal Columbian Hospital. The Salmonbellies scored five power-play goals and four shorthanded goals on their way to a 14–5 win. Goss, playing in what he'd announced would be his last Mann Cup series, had two goals and four assists, while the Dude had two goals and three assists.

Goss went into game 3 with eight Mann Cup assists so far in the series and fifty-four over his career, tying him with John Cervi. Goss had scored the first goals in games 1 and 2, and the first two in game 3. Attempting another goal, he was hit hard and knocked cold. Not even knowing if he'd gotten the shot away, he was led off the floor, groggy but otherwise in one piece. Durante contributed three goals and the Salmonbellies won 12–10.

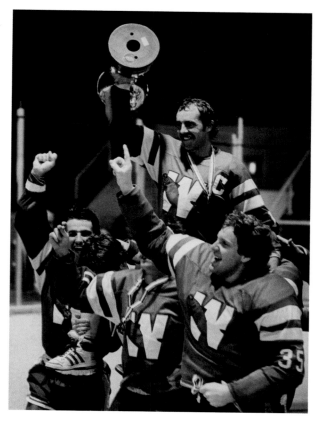

Goss took to the floor in game 4 needing six points to tie Paul Parnell's Mann Cup scoring record of ninety-seven points. He matched Parnell with five minutes and twenty-two seconds remaining in the third period. And then, with time running out, he grabbed a loose ball and shovelled it to New Westminster junior pickup Terry Oiom. Oiom, a big, strong player with a hard overhand shot, bulged Brampton's net with six seconds to spare. It was Oiom's third goal of the series and Goss's fifth assist and seventh point of the night. The Salmonbellies won the game 24–10 and swept the series, erasing all thoughts of fleabag hotels, hookers, turpentine, and humidity.

The respectful Excelsiors stayed on the floor to congratulate Goss. "What a way to go out of the game," Goss said.[278] He'd come into the senior game fourteen seasons earlier in 1968, the year the Salmonbellies surprised everyone in defeating Bishop's Olympics. He sold peanuts right there in the Arena. He learned lacrosse at Fred Hume's park in Sapperton. He studied Jack Barclay's faceoff technique. He chose number 13 to be linked with Ken Winzoski. He played side-by-side with his brothers Bob and Ed. He'd been cut, slashed, hacked, and knocked out. Now, there he was, in his last year as a player, clutching the Mike Kelly MVP silverware.

"Wayne had a drive and determination that was unmatched," said Casey Cook. "As a coach, you tell the guys what needed to be done, and Wayne would have this look that you were talking directly to him. He'd go out and do it, and that set an example for everybody."[279] Goss played 475 games and scored 1,852 points,[280] setting forty-one WLA and Mann Cup records. He helped the Salmonbellies win an NLL title and five Mann Cups, setting the record for most assists and points in the national championship.[281]

Now he was out of the game, but he'd written himself into it forever. "He was a premiere centre-man. He was a penalty killer. Only about one-third into his career did he start playing on the power play because he did so many other things," wrote lacrosse historian Stan Shillington.[282] Goss, in Shillington's opinion, "is the greatest all-round player in box lacrosse history."[283]

With the 1982 season just weeks away, Goss, now coaching the Salmonbellies, was helping a friend build a cabin at Pitt Lake. He was working on the roof when a loose board tripped him up, sending him tumbling ten metres onto the rocks below. He was airlifted to hospital where he lay unconscious for two weeks. He'd suffered a severe brain-stem injury that affected his balance, co-ordination, and speech. Doctors doubted that he would walk or talk again.

Wayne Goss clutches his fifth and final Mann Cup in 1981. Eric Cowieson (left) and goalie Rod Banister (right) raise their arms in triumph.

COLUMBIAN.
PHOTOGRAPH BY PETER BATTISTONI.

He spent the next five years, not behind the bench, but in rehabilitation. With the resolve he'd demonstrated as a player, Goss progressed slowly but steadily from a wheelchair to a walker to canes to just his feet. Taking up horseback riding as a form of therapy led to his winning medals at the BC Equestrian Disabled Games. He worked just as hard on his speech, recovering a lot of it.

The 1982 Salmonbellies acquired Geordie Dean, a standout junior in Coquitlam who'd won rookie of the year and league MVP. The four-time junior all-star scored 378 points in 100 games and played senior games for Vancouver, Coquitlam, and New Westminster, racking up fifty points in forty games. He was a tough, physical player who bowled opponents over on his way to the net. Dean played up for the Salmonbellies in the 1980 Mann Cup and was drafted by New Westminster in the first round in 1982. The Salmonbellies, captained by Cowieson, won

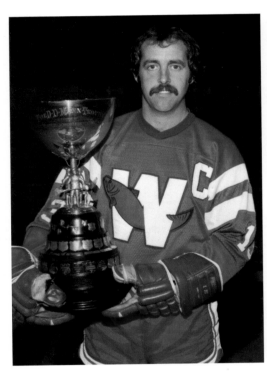

Wayne Goss scored 1,840 points in 462 games in a Salmonbellies uniform, an average per game of 3.98, the most so far. He's fourth behind Paul Parnell, John Davis and John Tavares on the all-time career points list, with 1,852 combined regular season, playoff and Mann Cup points.

WAYNE GOSS.

the 1982 WLA title. With Banister and rookie Doug Zack splitting goaltending duties, the Salmonbellies defeated the Adanacs in the finals, but couldn't successfully defend the Mann Cup, losing in Peterborough to the Lakers, four games to two.

The 1983 Salmonbellies, 13–11 for the season, lost to Vancouver and Victoria in the round-robin semifinals. Led by Kevin Alexander, John Crowther, and Bob Cool, Victoria defeated Peterborough 4–2 in the Mann Cup.

The 1984 Salmonbellies topped the league, but lost in the WLA finals to defending Mann Cup champion Victoria Payless. Victoria, led by high scoring Kevin Alexander, was defeated 4-1 in the Mann Cup by the John Grant led Peterborough Lakers. That same year, after sixteen seasons, 512 games, 164 goals, 689 assists, a pro league championship, and five Mann Cups, Steve "Stumpy" d'Easum retired.

The Salmonbellies finished third in 1985 and defeated Victoria four games to three in the finals. For the Mann Cup, they took on the Brooklin Redmen, who were making their first Mann Cup appearance in sixteen years after defeating the Peterborough Lakers 4–1 in the OLA finals. The Redmen had played together a long time. They were well coached, skilled, and had great goaltending. And they had the requisite nasty side. "In every important respect," noted the Dude, "they mirrored us."

The Salmonbellies, playing at home, won the first three games. No team had ever been up three and lost a Mann Cup championship. The worst collapses had been twenty years earlier when Brooklin, up 3–1 over Vancouver in 1964 and 3–1 over New Westminster in 1965, wound up losing both. But 1985's first three Mann Cup games were close and could have gone either way. "We were maybe a bit lucky and were surprised to be up three," recalled Cowieson.[284] After the Redmen won the next two games, "a little panic" set in.[285] They lost game 6 too.

In game 7, with the teams tied at five and only a few minutes left, Brooklin's left-handed shooter Ken Colley cut across the top of the crease toward his wrong shooting side. Salmonbellie goalie Rod Banister tracked him, guessing he would shoot low to the short side. But Colley fired a backhand shot. Banister, moving right as the shot went left, dropped to his knees and blocked the shot with his left thigh, but as he went to trap the ball Cowieson tried to scoop it up. "I am not sure if I distracted him when I tried to trap it," said Banister later, "but unfortunately the ball somehow flipped off of his stick and went right into the net.[286] The Salmonbellies lost the game 6–5 and with it, the Mann Cup, setting a record with four Mann Cup game losses in a row. "It was the lowest point of my career," said Cowieson.[287] He and the Salmonbellies vowed it would not happen again.

In 1986, the Salmonbellies signed several new players to the team, including Holland-born Ben Hieltjes, who came to Canada with his family at the age of six and took up lacrosse in New

Westminster "just for something to do in the summer."[288] The commitment that his first two coaches, Dave Wilfong and Bob Salt, had for the game rubbed off on Hieltjes, but after his team won the BC intermediate championship, he almost dropped out of lacrosse. Intermediate felt "a little rag-tag" to him, but the sharper pace of junior revived his interest.[289] Hieltjes played to win; lacrosse was not for summer fun. His goal was to be the best player on the floor, every time out.

Quinlan and Zack shared the goaltending, Banister being sidelined for the season. Brian Baker led the team in scoring with sixty-five points, followed by Dean with fifty-eight. The Salmonbellies much preferred to play in the Arena, winning ten of eleven games at home. The league's best penalty killers, they tied Victoria with fourteen wins and ten losses at the top of the standings in regular season play.

The Salmonbellies fell behind the Burrards in the semifinals three games to two, but won the next two. Victoria won the first game of the finals, and the Salmonbellies the next, with Dean scoring the first goal for his 500th career point. In the same game, Bob Johnston notched four assists and his 300th career point. Other players also racked up the points, but the key man was goalie Shawn Quinlan, MVP.

The Salmonbellies advanced to the Mann Cup finals in Whitby against Brooklin, determined not to repeat 1985's embarrassing collapse. If they were going to win, however, it would be on the strength of their defence. Only two Salmonbellies averaged more than a goal a game, and the team itself averaged less than ten a game.

Game 1 saw Hieltjes score five goals and Vilneff score two shorthanded in a 14–10 Salmonbellies' victory. In game 2, Brooklin led 8–3 in the second period. Doug Zack replaced Quinlan in net, but the Redmen still won 11–6. Todd Lorenz broke an 11–11 tie with three seconds left on the clock and the Salmonbellies won game four.

The Salmonbellies had to beat the weather along with the Redmen. "Our guys were losing 10 to 12 pounds a game, the place was so humid," recalled Casey Cook. "Our guys were getting stomach cramps, and we had to make sure everybody was always hydrated."[290]

In game 4, eight game misconducts were handed out at the end of the first period after the Salmonbellies got the better of Brooklin in a 15-minute bench-clearing brawl. Although the Redmen won the game 6–5 it was the turning point in the series. "Once they knew they couldn't intimidate us," recalled the Dude, "we knew we were going to win the cup." In game 5, Brooklin outshot the Salmonbellies, but New Westminster scored three shorthanded goals and won 10–8.

In game 6, Brooklin's netminder, Wayne Colley, stopped everything the Salmonbellies threw at him for the first thirty-six minutes. "I couldn't believe how long it took us to get one lousy goal," said d'Easum, "I was starting to think about a seventh game."[291] At the other end of the floor, Quinlan made great saves, including three on Kevin Van Sickle breakaways. John Gilchrist finally scored New Westminster's first goal to make it 4–1 and Steve Voelpel scored the second right after.

Regardless of the score, the Salmonbellies had been dominating the third period of every game. The third period of game 6 was no different and the Salmonbellies posted an 8–6 win, redeeming themselves for 1985, becoming the first team to win in the east in ten years,

In his sixteen seasons with New Westminster, number 5 Geordie Dean broke records that still stand in 2013.

GEORDIE DEAN.

and (most importantly) holding aloft their twenty-second Mann Cup.

Jubilation filled the dressing room. Todd Lorenz had led the team in goal scoring with seven, but MVP Dean led overall with nineteen points, followed by Baker with seventeen, Hieltjes with eleven, and Shaughnessy and Cowieson with ten each. Quinlan was outstanding in goal. Coach d'Easum, drenched in champagne and glory, couldn't stop smiling all the way back to New Westminster.

In 1987, Ben Hieltjes was the league's top goal scorer, with forty-six goals and best overall point-getter with eighty-three. He was followed by other Salmonbellies: third-place Johnston with seventy-four, fourth-place Dean with sixty-four, sixth-place Lorenz with sixty-three, and ninth-place Scott Patterson with fifty-eight. For the first time in decades, the Salmonbellies had five players in the league's top ten scorers. The team scored 306 points and allowed just 209 (the best for-and-against record in the league) and posted twenty wins in twenty-four games to easily claim the league title.

Adanacs' Mario Govorchin checks Dave Durante in 1982. The two men switched teams in a 1980 trade.

DAVE DURANTE.

The Salmonbellies defeated the Richmond Outlaws in the semifinal and the Adanacs in the finals to advance to the Mann Cup for the third time in three years. Once again they encountered the Brooklin Redmen. Despite playing at home in Queen's Park Arena, Cowieson's thirteen goals, Dean's twelve assists, and a twenty-point effort by six-year veteran Paul Dal Monte, the Salmonbellies couldn't beat the Redmen, who won four of seven games to reclaim the cup.

The loss crushed the entire team, but Dave Thornhill, who hadn't played in 1986, was especially dejected. When he was ten years old, Wayne Goss gave him five of his old helmets, early-model three-piece SK-100s, with number 13 and bloodstains emblazoned on each one. Whenever Thornhill looked at them, he wondered if one day he might be good enough to play for the Salmonbellies. He played for the 1980 junior Salmonbellies and was drafted into the senior ranks in 1981, but didn't play that year. He left the Arena as quickly as he could, not bothering to collect his finalist medal. He brooded for days. "There was such a high level of expectation being a Salmonbellie. Not a pressure to win, but an expectation. It was an intoxicating environment. It was all about the Mann Cup. The fun was the winning."[292] Thornhill never played again.

Terry Blair took over Cook's GM duties in 1988. Blair had refereed in the WLA from 1982 through 1987 and served as the head referee for Canadian field lacrosse from 1983 to 1988. He first watched the Salmonbellies in the late 1960s, but his initial exposure to the team was as an eight-year-old in East Vancouver in 1948. "One night I was listening to radio station CKNW. The sports announcer said that the Vancouver Burrards had lost eight to four to the New Westminster Salmonbellies. I had never heard of the Salmonbellies—we were from Alberta—and I thought it was the funniest name ever for a team. I went downstairs and told my parents about this team with the hilarious name. They laughed just as hard as me."[293]

With Blair at the helm, the Salmonbellies took league honours again in 1988, winning sixteen of twenty-four games. Coquitlam's Jim Veltman led the scoring race, followed by Hieltjes, and it was the Adanacs who defeated the Salmonbellies four games to three in the league finals to face the Redmen (undefeated in twenty-eight league and playoff games) in the Mann Cup. The Redmen won four games to two, capturing their third Mann Cup in four years.

The 1989 Salmonbellies, co-coached by Casey Cook and John Hannah, won twenty-one of twenty-four games to finish eighteen points ahead of second-place Coquitlam. Dean topped all scorers in the league with 101 points, 75 of them assists. But it was defence, anchored by goalies Banister and Quinlan, that made the biggest difference. The duo led the WLA, allowing fewer than eight goals a game on average. The Salmonbellies defeated Vancouver in the semifinal and faced the Adanacs in the finals. "This whole thing's going to be won by execution, not elocution," said Cook, "so let's go to it."[294] They went to it, executing a four-game series sweep, setting up yet another showdown with Brooklin.

The Redmen were even stronger than they'd been in 1988, thanks largely to Gary Gait, whose fifty-eight goals helped them remain undefeated in regular-season play. In fact, they hadn't been beaten since 1986. The Redmen went undefeated in the round-robin semifinals, but Peterborough beat them in the eastern finals, ending Brooklin's unprecedented winning streak at eighty-four games. Peterborough took the series to seven games, but the Redmen pulled out the victory, aided by a thirty-three-goal performance by Gait and twenty-one goals by Derek Keenan.

As the Redmen flew west, the largest sockeye run in seventy-five years was heading east up the Fraser River. Fifteen hundred gillnetters cast their nets, each trying for their share of the estimated ninety million fish. The sheer volume of fishing boats made navigation difficult for other industries using the waterway. Tempers flared as tugboats towing barges and log booms tangled with nets.

When the last run of that size occurred, the world was at war, Con Jones offered to buy the Salmonbellies lock, stock, and barrel, and Newsy Lalonde enjoyed a sixty-six-goal lacrosse season for the Montreal Nationals. The Redmen were flying into the land of the sockeye.

One of the Salmonbellies' greatest fans, seventy-year-old Pat Power, could hardly wait for the Mann Cup series to start. He remembered Winston Churchill in Queen's Park in 1929, the first box game at the Arena in 1932, the Hamilton Tigers' Mann Cup win in 1933, American singer Bing Crosby at a game, and the "great thrill" he felt when Fred Hume announced the signing of Wilson, Wilkes, Downey, and Anthony for the 1936 season.[295]

Steve Manning (left) and Lyle Robinson flank Eric Cowieson lofting the Mann Cup after their 1986 victory over the Brooklin Redmen.

STEVE MANNING.

The championship got underway on September 6. The Salmonbellies' defenders—Manning, Cowieson, Ogilvie, and Robinson—built a fortress around Banister and prevented Brooklin's top guns from cutting through, finding an opening, and getting off an inside shot. Instead, the Redmen were left with long shots from the outside—the Salmonbellies' "thin red line" all over again.

Banister, a big man, had all the corners covered. The teams battled to a 3–3 tie at the end of the second period. The Salmonbellies' Don McNeill, in his second season with the team, scored two goals in rapid succession (at ten and twenty-three seconds of the third period) and New Westminster went on to win 9–3. Hieltjes scored three goals, two on the power play and one shorthanded.

In the second period of the second game Brooklin outran and outscored the Salmonbellies 8–1 on their way to a 12–8 win. The Redmen's Brian Nikula (born and raised in New Westminster) and Eric Perroni each scored three goals.

Seventeen minutes into the second period of the third game, with the Salmonbellies up 6–3, the Dude stole the ball from the Redmen's Barry Brear and faked out Wayne Colley to score. The Salmonbellies won 10–5, with Hieltjes scoring the winning goal plus two more.

Ivan Tuura, John Gilchrist and Geordie Dean (the trio were New Westminster firemen) celebrate their 1986 victory.

IVAN TUURA.

In the third period of the fourth game, with Brooklin leading 7–6, Hieltjes scored his second of the game to tie it. Durante, Ogilvie, and Deschner followed with goals of their own, but Gait scored his third of the game to close the gap. As determined as Gait was, the Salmonbellies' defence was that much more determined. At one point, Gait was hit by all five Salmonbellies. The fifth hit, a hip check, sent him to the floor just before he could get his shot away. Nikula scored his second of the game to get the Redmen within one, but Salmonbellies' rookie Mike Kettles scored to make it 11–9, and Paul Jones scored into an empty net to secure the victory.

Dean hadn't scored a single goal in four games, but in the fifth match he broke out of his slump, netting four. Brooklin, however, won 12–8.

In the sixth game, Hieltjes got two goals and two assists and Paul Jones got three goals. The Salmonbellies' defence held firm, allowing the Redmen just four goals to the Salmonbellies' ten. Looking down from the stands, Pat Power was overjoyed. The Salmonbellies had won the cup for the twenty-third time, denying the Redmen a third straight championship. "You'd have seen 23 Salmonbellies dead on the floor from exhaustion before you'd have seen us lose another one at home," said Dean, who'd scored twice in the final game to finish the series with six goals and fourteen assists.[296] Hieltjes, with ten goals and nine assists, was named the MVP. The classy Hieltjes deflected the credit to his teammates.

Durante, then thirty-seven years old, had played his forty-seventh Mann Cup game, beating the previous record by three games. His three goals and four assists in the series brought his totals to thirty-five Mann Cup goals and sixty-five assists, moving him ahead of Wayne Goss, Paul Parnell, and Bob Allan on the all-time Mann Cup scoring list. He'd announced he'd be retiring from lacrosse after the series, but driving home following the fourth game, reflecting on the goal he had scored to put the team in the lead 8–7, he questioned whether or not he was ready to bow out. "You can always quit," he said, "but you can never come back."[297]

On December 17, Flickie Doyle died at the age of 85, leaving Ab Brown and Jack Wood as the only remaining players from the 1928 Olympic Salmonbellies. According to the pact they'd agreed to sixty-two years earlier, they were to retrieve the stored bottles of rum and toast their teammates. But Brown was ninety-five and on medication that prevented him from consuming alcohol. Wood was eighty-eight, but his drinking days were over, too. Besides, most of the rum,

Ivan Tuura makes a spectacular catch with Vancouver's Don MacDonald in pursuit. ca. 1987.

IVAN TUURA.

Salmonbellies' number 25 Mark "Rubber Band Man" Tuura looks for an opening as Adanac Jeff Eder closes in during the sixth game of the 1987 WLA playoffs.

THE PROVINCE. PHOTOGRAPH BY TIM PELLING.

stored since the 1960s at the Hall of Fame, had mysteriously "evaporated" over the years. So the two remembered their teammates soberly.

The Salmonbellies won seventeen of twenty-four games in 1990 and finished first in the WLA, but the fourth-place Burnaby Lakers defeated them in the semifinals 4–3. In the finals, the Burrards beat the Lakers, then lost four straight to the Paul Gait-led Brooklin Redmen in the Mann Cup, their third cup in four years.

Jack Fulton's son Jack took over as the Salmonbellies' co-coach, along with Steve Manning, for the 1991 campaign. After an outstanding junior Salmonbellies career, Fulton had played one full season, 1979, with the senior Salmonbellies, scoring seventy-three points. Manning had retired after the team's 1986 Mann Cup victory, having played 193 games and scoring 177 points as a defensive specialist.

The Salmonbellies facing off with the Brooklin Redmen in a 1987 Mann Cup game.

MARK TUURA.

Number 11 Ben Hieltjes defending against the Brooklin Redmen in a 1987 Mann Cup game.

MARK TUURA.

Geordie Dean vs. Vancouver's Terry Oiom in 1988.

GEORDIE DEAN.

In thirteen seasons with the Salmonbellies (1982-1995) Todd Lorenz scored on 380 shots, contributed 477 assists, and helped the team win three Mann Cups.
MARK TUURA.

Exhaustion and disappointment register on the faces of Paul Dal Monte, Geordie Dean, Mark Tuura, Rod Banister, Steve Voepel, Kevin Shires, and Ben Hieltjes after their overtime loss to the Brooklin Redmen in game seven of the 1987 Mann Cup. Manager Greg Crawford and coach Steve d'Easum stand behind Shires and Hieltjes.
PHOTOGRAPH BY DAVE LORD.

The Redmen appear to have Mark Tuura surrounded in the '87 Mann Cup.
MARK TUURA.

In Hieltjes, now in his sixth season, Fulton and Manning had a player at the peak of his powers. Hieltjes had missed eight of twenty-four games in 1990 due to field lacrosse commitments but was ready in 1991 to add another Mann Cup to the two he already had. On June 1, he notched his 500th career point. His teammate, the Dude, had been out of the lineup with a pulled hamstring until June 23, but in his first appearance scored his 700th career goal. The Salmonbellies, with Rick Mang in net, won fifteen of twenty-four regular-season games, and defeated Victoria 4–1 in the semifinals and Coquitlam 4–3 in the finals.

Mang had been sensational in net all season long, being named to the first all-star team and winning the Leo Nicholson trophy. Backed by Mang, the Salmonbellies faced their old adversaries, the Redmen, in the Mann Cup.

Dave "The Dude" Durante helped the Salmonbellies win four Mann Cups in a twenty-year WLA career (1971–1991). In total he played 552 games, scored 609 goals, and made 900 assists for 1,509 points. He is seventh on the list of all-time Salmonbellies scorers with 893 points in 380 games.

DAVE DURANTE.

The Redmen were without coach Vipond and players Gait, Nikula, and Keenan. New Westminster won the first game 17–3 and the second 13–5. Brooklin led 8–6 after two periods of the third game, but the Salmonbellies scored six last-period goals to win 12–9. Dean's assist on a Scott Patterson goal made him the leading scorer in Mann Cup history with 108 points, one more than Peterborough's Jim Johnston. Seconds later, Dean fired a goal past the Redmen's Brian Arnold. The Salmonbellies won the fourth game 8–5 for their twenty-fourth Mann Cup. Seven Salmonbellies tallied more points in the series than Brooklin's best, Peter Parke, who had three goals and three assists—very un-Brooklin-like stats. Hieltjes was top scorer in the series with seven goals and sixteen assists, and Dean, with four goals and sixteen assists, set Mann Cup records for most assists and most points and was named the MVP.

In the fourth game of the series, the Dude had stick-checked a player, stolen the ball, and scored on Colley, but he knew his eighteen-year career was over. Although he was nearing 40 years old he believed he could still play effectively, but the game had lost its appeal to him. Off the floor players were becoming increasingly transient, going wherever the most money was offered. Transience, so far as the Dude was concerned, killed socializing, taking the fun out of the sport. On the floor referees were ignoring the rules governing checking; the long standing tradition of two hands fifteen inches apart on the stick was abandoned for one hand on the stick and the other hand holding an opponent. The emerging offence/defence system didn't appeal to Durante either. He retired having scored 609 goals and 900 assists for 1,509 points in 552 games, an average of 2.73 a game. A lot of credit for the Salmonbellies' three Mann Cup wins in the 1980s must go to Durante, according to author Cleve Dheensaw, for "he was the catalyst, the engine that made the machine run."[298]

In the dressing room after the 1991 Mann Cup, the Salmonbellies sprayed champagne as the Rolling Stones blasted from the stereo system. Rookie Colin Sinclair, who'd had a great series and led all goal scorers with ten, told a reporter, "We dominated in the '60s and '70s, and I think we're going to do it in the '90s."[299] Sinclair wasn't alone in assuming great things for the team. Reporter Dan Hilborn, in an editorial the day after the victory, lamented the state of lacrosse in Ontario. With the best eastern players bailing for BC, "we can look forward to a bunch of Mann Cup parades around the Lower Mainland."[300] Indeed, after an easy sweep of Ontario's best, it looked as if nothing could stop the Salmonbellies. Sinclair, however, played another eight seasons with New Westminster and never won a second Mann Cup.

Another man who'd sipped from Sir Donald's cup, in 1927, never to sip again, Ab Brown, died on December 7, 1991, at the age of ninety-six. He'd been around forever, expertly repairing sticks, free of charge. By the time he died, there were no more wooden sticks to repair anyway.

As of 2013, the 1991 Salmonbellies are New Westminster's last Mann Cup champions. **Back row (l-r):** Rusty Wills (trainer), Rob Dick, Scott Patterson, Gord Frederickson, Jamie Malanfant, Todd Lorenz, Ben Hoskin (trainer). **Middle row:** Terry Blair (GM), Rick Wills (team mangr.), Doug Taylor, Colin Sinclair, Brad Dickson, Darrell Digby, Mike Kettles, Paul Jones, Paul Dal Monte, Don McNeill, K.C. Cook (Pres.) **Front row:** Dave Durante, Andy Ogilvie, Steve Manning (coach), Rick Mang, Eric Cowieson, Rod Banister, Jackie Fulton (coach), Ben Hieltjes, Geordie Dean, Travis Taylor (ball boy), Kenny Downie (ball boy). **Missing from photo:** Greg Crawford (asst. coach), Eric Perkins (equip. mngr.), Jody Twa.

CANADIAN LACROSSE HALL OF FAME.

For most of his long life lacrosse players in New Westminster knew Ab Brown as an expert stick repairer who wouldn't take a nickel for his work. Few knew that in his twenty-two years with the Salmonbellies he won ten BC championships, three Mann Cups, and was a member of the Salmonbellies team that represented Canada at the 1928 Olympic games. In 1977 an outdoor lacrosse box in New Westminster was named in his honour. Brown died on December 7, 1991, at ninety-six.

COLUMBIAN. PHOTOGRAPH BY CRAIG HODGE.

The gloves and the game may have changed since the Salmonbellies first competed
for the Mann Cup, but the goal is the same: winning.

"It is harder to be a good winner than a good loser."

Morley Kells

CHAPTER TWELVE
THE ELUSIVE MANN: 1992-2013

The Salmonbellies topped the WLA in 1992, defeated Victoria Payless in six games in the semifinals and the Burnaby Lakers in five games to advance to the Mann Cup championship with the Brampton Excelsiors. In the last two minutes of game 2, Hieltjes was cross-checked in the throat and was done for the series. His vocal chords were so damaged he couldn't talk for six weeks. The Excelsiors took the series four games to one.

The 1993 Salmonbellies, minus a retired Hieltjes, were defeated in the league semifinals by the Burnaby Lakers. Brampton repeated as Mann Cup champions.

In 1994, the Vancouver Burrards moved to Surrey and the old North Shore Indians team was revived. The Salmonbellies won the league, and defeated Surrey in the semifinals and the Adanacs in the finals. In the series, Cowieson sustained a punctured lung. Every breath was painful, but he donned a flack jacket to play the Six Nations Chiefs for the Mann Cup. He played all six games, but the Salmonbellies lost 4–2.

In 1995, New Westminster won twenty-one of twenty-five WLA games. Hieltjes, two years into retirement, watched from the stands and wondered if he had one more Mann Cup in him. He played a few regular-season games and qualified for the playoffs. After defeating Burnaby in the semifinals and Victoria in the finals, the Salmonbellies again faced the Les Wakeling-coached Chiefs. Wakeling had coached the Excelsiors to Mann Cups in 1992 and '93. John Tavares, Paul Gait, and brothers Rich, Darris, and Travis Kilgour led the team on the floor.

In game 1, Hieltjes, marked by the Chiefs for special treatment, was cross-checked from behind by Miles General. Falling heavily and unconscious into the endboards, Hieltjes received several hard right hands from General before the attack was halted. Hieltjes suffered a concussion and whiplash and never returned to the floor. General was suspended and charged with common assault.

Over the course of the series, Dean set Mann Cup records for most goals (sixty-seven) most assists (ninety-four) and most points (161). The Salmonbellies, however, lost the series 4–2. The Chiefs' Paul Gait received the MVP award. The Chiefs piled up 150 minutes more in penalties than New Westminster, but Wakeling insisted that the Salmonbellies were the more aggressive team. "We knew they were going to try anything they could to win it this year."[301]

As for General's suspension, Wakeling said it was "just ridiculous," adding, "I've seen a lot worse hits during the time I've been coaching."[302]

General was convicted of assault and served jail time. "I felt bad for lacrosse," said Hieltjes, "that people might judge the game by that incident."[303] After three Mann Cups, 762 total points in 249 games (an average of three a game), Ben Hieltjes retired for good.

Another veteran, who, at the start of every season, was never sure he was good enough to play and who needed a first goal "to take the pressure off,"[304] called it a career too. Eric Cowieson, who'd played 161 consecutive games between May 17, 1984 and May 12, 1988, second only to Parnell's 195 consecutive games, retired after eighteen years with the team (fourteen as captain) and four Mann Cups.

When the Salmonbellies retired his number six, the ever-humble Cowieson admitted being "a little uncomfortable" seeing it hanging in the Arena's rafters with the team's other greats.[305]

Canadian box lacrosse was undergoing fundamental change yet again in the early 1990s. American college field lacrosse, the popularity of the professional box lacrosse league (NLL), and the introduction of aluminum shafted, plastic headed sticks altered the way the game was played. Wood lacrosse stick manufacturers couldn't match the market's demand, so an alternative was sought. The new sticks were lighter, easier to wield, and were less of a weapon to be feared. Checks didn't hurt as much. Deeper pockets allowed for one-handed operation and "shovel" passes became more common. The ancient First Nations belief that the stick joined man spiritually to earth was being severed—A.J. Smith of the Coquitlam Adanacs was the last WLA player allowed to use a wooden stick (2003–2004). Field lacrosse's offence/defence system greatly influenced the box game, virtually eliminating the transitional, fast break offence. A new kind of player began to emerge, one that played either offence or defence. The era of the two-way player was coming to an end.

In a tight race in 1996, the North Shore Indians finished first in league play then knocked out the Salmonbellies in the semifinals. But the Chiefs, led by John Tavares, won their third straight Mann Cup, defeating the Victoria Shamrocks in four straight.

The Salmonbellies finished in fifth place in 1997 and didn't make it to the semifinals. The Shamrocks, led by Gary Gait, went to the Mann Cup and defeated the Niagara Falls Gamblers.

Goalie Matt Disher played 203 games in net for the Salmonbellies, 1998 through 2007. He faced 8,993 shots and stopped 7,050 of them for a save percentage of 78.4, fifth all-time behind Rick Mang, Rod Banister, Shawn Quinlan and Doug Zack.

PHOTOGRAPH BY PAUL HORN.

Geordie Dean called it a career. In 506 games from 1982 to 1997, he'd accumulated 1,412 points on 569 goals and 843 assists, an average of 2.8 points a game. His points include 53 hat tricks, 109 power play goals, 53 shorthanded goals, and 39 game winners. He played in fifty-three Mann Cup games in nine series, winning three. While his Mann Cup goal and point marks have since been surpassed, his Mann Cup assists record still stands.

In his day, Jack Wood had seen a few lean lacrosse seasons not unlike the Salmonbellies' 1997 campaign. The talented player, dedicated coach, and last of the 1927 Mann Cup champions and 1928 Olympic team, died in New Westminster on September 10, 1997, at the age of ninety-four.

In 1998, Green Gaels' founder, Jim Bishop, driving home from his office in Bowmanville, Ontario, fell asleep at the wheel and crashed. The man who had helped out former players fallen on hard times and who never forgot a birthday was gone. "Jim taught me that it is harder to be a good winner than a good loser," said Morley Kells in his eulogy.[306]

The 1998 Salmonbellies had to contend with being good losers, having failed to reach the semifinals. The Brampton Excelsiors, led by Jim Veltman and MVP-winning goaltender Paddy O'Toole, defeated the Coquitlam Adanacs for the Mann Cup. The Salmonbellies, however, added goaltender Matt Disher to the lineup. Disher would be a stellar performer over the next ten seasons, with a save percentage of .788% in 184 league games, and .765% over thirty-seven playoff games.

Randy Radonich, a former BCLA president and WLA commissioner, became the Salmonbellies GM in 1999. That year, the Salmonbellies were knocked out in the first round of the playoffs. The Shamrocks, led by reunited twins Paul and Gary Gait, defeated Brampton to win the Mann Cup.

The Salmonbellies failed to get past the first round of playoffs through to 2002. Dan Richardson, former player and a team director since 1994, became assistant GM prior to the 2003 season. That year, the Salmonbellies failed to make the playoffs, and Casey Cook retired as president. Corinne Perriman took his place, the first woman to hold the position. Bob Salt replaced Frank Neilson as coach, his second stint.

In 2004, the Salmonbellies again didn't make the playoffs, and in 2005, they lost in the semifinals. For years the Arena's famous tongue-and-groove fir floor had shown its age. Splinters were a constant danger, and the floor could no longer be held together with plywood patches. The 67-year-old floor was retired. Sections were sold off and a large piece of the faceoff circle was mounted on the Arena's south wall.

Richardson took full charge of the team in 2006. Like Hume and Fulton before him, he started rebuilding by trading veterans, stockpiling draft picks, and generally mending fences with everyone, including the minor league system.

With a new hard maple floor underfoot, the 2006 Salmonbellies returned to the league finals for the first time in eleven seasons, but were defeated by Victoria, who in turn lost to Peterborough in the Mann Cup. In 2007, the Adanacs beat out the Salmonbellies in the WLA finals, then lost to Peterborough in the Mann Cup.

In 2008, New Westminster won the WLA with seventeen wins and only one loss and returned to the Mann Cup for the first time since 1995. They were defeated in four games by the Brampton Excelsiors.

The 2009 Salmonbellies finished second behind the Victoria Shamrocks in league play and won eight straight games against the Langley Thunder and Coquitlam Adanacs in the playoffs. Again, they faced the Brampton Excelsiors for the Mann Cup, this time at the Arena.

Down on the Fraser River, the predicted massive sockeye run collapsed, only two million of the estimated thirteen million fish returning. The Salmonbellies' more superstitious fans didn't think it boded well. The Salmonbellies won three games in regulation play and lost three games in overtime.

The score in the closing seconds of the third period of game seven stood at 7–6 in the Salmonbellies' favour when, during a stoppage in play due to a Brampton penalty, the Salmonbellies, for some reason, called a time out. Brampton pulled their goaltender, and the teams reconvened on the floor. The referee awarded the ball to the WLA's 2009 MVP, the Salmonbellies' Ilija Gajic, in his third season.

Salmonbellies stalwart Craig Stevenson played fourteen continuous seasons with the team (1993-2006). "Howie" played 352 games in total, scoring 391 goals with 642 assists for 1,033 points. He's the sixth highest scoring Salmonbellie in the team's history.

PHOTOGRAPH BY PAUL HORN.

Pat Maddalena gets airborne against the Maple Ridge Burrards. Maddalena played two seasons for New Westminster, 2000-2001.

PHOTOGRAPH BY PAUL HORN.

Gajic turned and sprinted for his own end, pursued on his left by Brampton's Mike Carnegie and on his right by Brodie Merrill. With his teammates spread out as directed in Brampton's end, Gajic was alone behind goalie Tyler Richards. With no one to pass to and with no time outs remaining, Gajic's only options were to lob the ball far down into Brampton's end or to run it out.

He chose to run. He dashed to his right, trying to elude Carnegie. Carnegie, however, managed to slow him down a step or two, allowing Merrill to hit and squeeze Gajic farther along the boards. As Gajic went down, the ball popped out.

Brampton's Bill Greer recovered it. Greer passed to Carnegie, a right-handed shooter who was about twenty feet out, directly in front of the Salmonbellies' goal. Carnegie was a checker, not a goal scorer. In four seasons with Brampton, he'd tallied a grand total of two goals. Carnegie had teammates to his left and to his right. All that stood in his way were Salmonbellies' defenders Jordan Hall and Peter McFetridge and goalie Tyler Richards. Carnegie, with just sixteen seconds remaining, took his chance and drilled a shot. Richards dipped slightly down

Tyler Richards adjusts the net in a 2011 game.

PHOTOGRAPH BY DAVID ZUSKIND.

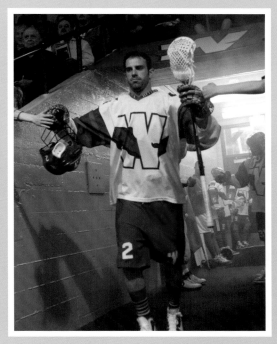

Wade DeWolff lays some glove on two young fans on his way to the floor in 2011.

PHOTOGRAPH BY DAVID ZUSKIND.

A very displeased Kyle Ross receives an escort to the penalty box in 2011.

PHOTOGRAPH BY DAVID ZUSKIND.

and to his left as Carnegie's shot sped in the exact opposite direction. Carnegie, a player who seldom found top corners, found one against a goalie who seldom gave them away.

Suddenly the game was tied at seven. The Salmonbellies were as demoralized as the Excelsiors were ecstatic. Regulation time ended. Fifty-five seconds into overtime, Colin Doyle, an accomplished Mann Cup scorer, took a pass from NLL MVP Dan Dawson, and put Brampton in front 8–7. Brampton then added another goal to capture the cup for the second straight year, the MVP award going to Shawn Williams.

Feisty, crafty, hustling and combative, Salmonbellies' number 9 Ilya Gaijc had an immediate impact on the team when he scored 64 points in his first twenty games with the Salmonbellies in 2007. (Seen here in 2012.)

PHOTOGRAPH BY DAN BRODIE.

Ian Hawksbee, a 2005 addition to the team, lets it go in game one of the Salmonbellies' 2011 playoff series against the Langley Thunder.

PHOTOGRAPH BY DAVID ZUSKIND.

In 2010, New Westminster defeated the Maple Ridge Burrards 4–1 in the semifinals and the Shamrocks 4–0 in the finals, but lost 4–2 to the Peterborough Lakers in the Mann Cup. It was Peterborough's 13th Mann Cup victory and the Salmonbellies' third Mann Cup defeat in three years.

In 2011, the Salmonbellies lost to the Langley Thunder in the WLA finals. The Thunder were defeated by Brampton in the Mann Cup, and Brampton goalie Anthony Cosmo earned his third Mann Cup MVP.

In 2012, the Salmonbellies struggled offensively and, although they won most of their home games, they lost most of their away games and failed to make the WLA playoffs. In 2013, they again failed to make the WLA playoffs.

The New Westminster Salmonbellies were Canada's winningest team during field lacrosse's pro era, capturing twelve Minto Cup championships between 1908 and 1924. The Salmonbellies' "farm team", the New Westminster Royals, were Canada's greatest amateur field team, winning six Mann Cups between 1915 and 1924. When the two teams merged as the Salmonbellies, the team won Mann Cups in 1925 and 1927 and represented Canada at the 1928 Olympic games. In 1937, the Salmonbellies captured their first box lacrosse Mann Cup championship and have won thirteen since. Including the two Mann Cups won by the New Westminster Adanacs in 1939 and 1947, the city's senior teams have won a combined twenty-four Mann Cups. Including the Salmonbellies' 1968 NLL pro championship, New Westminster has won thirty-five field and box lacrosse championships—more than any other Canadian senior men's lacrosse team.

But as of July 2013, twenty-two years have passed since the Salmonbellies last won the Mann Cup, by far their longest winless streak, eight years longer than the 1944–1957 dry spell.

In 2013/14, the Salmonbellies celebrate their 125th anniversary, the longest-running lacrosse team in Canadian history. When will they win a twenty-fifth Mann Cup? Some observers are keeping a close watch on the Fraser River's sockeye run, the strength of which—if history is any indication—may have some bearing on the fortunes of the New Westminster Salmonbellies.

Minto and Mann. The ultimate symbols of skill, stamina, strength, smarts, speed and—most of all—of the will to win.

CANADIAN LACROSSE HALL OF FAME. PHOTOGRAPH BY PHILLIP CHIN.

Thing of blood, sweat and tears: the sweater worn by Ed Downey in the 1940s.

ACKNOWLEDGEMENTS

Heartfelt thanks to this book's first enthusiasts

Ian "Stick" Matheson, for getting the ball rolling.
David McDonald and the McDonald family, for extraordinary encouragement and selfless support.
Jim Glanville, for bringing it all together and making everything work.
Jack Fulton, for 1956 to 2013 and beyond.
Paul Parnell, for inspirational leadership and knowing the value of history.
Dave "Slack" Matheson, for a sharp memory and sharper insights.

And thank you to

The City of New Westminster,
The Citizens of New Westminster,
Mayor Wayne Wright and City Council,
and City Manager Paul Daminato, for your enthusiastic support and your generous contribution to the creation of this book.
(And thank you Amy Chan!)
The New Westminster Museum and Archives
and The New Westminster Public Library, for your tips, leads, photos, microfiche and all-round support.
The Canadian Lacrosse Hall of Fame, for generously opening your doors, cabinets and treasure boxes and allowing it all to be photographed, and for lending your time and full support.
Bill Armstrong, for your collection of photos and your unstinting assistance.
Stan Stewardson, for collecting history and sharing it with the world.
Darren Flintoff, for giving the book its second wind.

Al "Lurch" Lewthwaite, for great stories, humour, and bone crunching honesty.
Wayne Goss and Carol Goss, for graciousness, class, and wit.
Bill Scuby, for your support, friendship and garlic.
Dan Richardson, for somehow always finding the time to lend a hand.
Bert Houston,
Hugh Cruikshank,
Jake Trotzuk,
Stan Cowie,
and Ralph Burton, for keeping the flames burning.
Larry "Wamper" Powers, for your invaluable wampsbibleoflacrosse.
The *Columbian*, for your writers and photographers through the ages.
Salmonbellies players,
Coaches,
GMs,
Wives, sons, daughters and grandchildren of all the above,
the Salmonbellies Alumni Association
and Salmonbellies fans, for sharing your stories, donating your money, and lending your photos.

This book is further indebted to

Coriana Constanda,
Erika Zell,
and Alyssa McLeod, for your enthusiasm, research skills, and organizational abilities.
Jennifer Adrian, for hours and hours of interview transcriptions.
Golya Mirderikvand, for meticulous (and miraculous) object and photographic conservation/
preparation work.
Donald MacDonald, for getting this book across the finish line. (Thanks, bro.)
Barbara Adamski, for asking great questions and keeping the narrative on track.
Phillip Chin, for bringing photographic brilliance, expertise and consummate professionalism
to this project.
Vici Johnstone, for believing in this story and publishing it.

An extra-special thank you to

Stan Shillington, for keeping score. (No Shillington, no stats, no stories–no book!)
Basil King, for having the inner eye and shutter finger to capture lacrosse stories on film like
no one else before or since.

Last and most, thank you to

David Hayes, for your unwavering support, planning, patience, attention to detail, and sublime
visual talent in making this book the thing of beauty that it is.

Without the generous support of the following individuals and organizations this book would not have been possible. Thank you.

Bill Armstrong
Alan Benson
Julian Brambleby
Richard Bryson
Jack Butterworth
Derek Carey
John Cervi
Stan Cowie
Susan Flatters
Darren Flintoff
Jack Fulton, Sr.
Jack Fulton, Jr.
Martin Gifford
Jim Giles
Larry Gill
Jim Glanville
Steve Goodwin
John Goodwin
Pete Goodwin
Paul Goodwin
Wayne Goss
Ed Goss
Diane Gray
John Gregg
John Hannah
Patrick Julian
Harry Keen
Sid and Cindy Landolt
Peter Legge
Bill Lewis
Al Lewthwaite
Jim Lightbody

Donald MacDonald
Malcolm Family
Manning Family
David Matheson
Ian Matheson
Mollie McDonald
David McDonald
Steve McDonald
Bruce McDonald
Gary McLaughlin
Craig Moulton
Mike O'Keefe
Erik and Linda Otterstrom
Paul Parnell
Dan Perreault
Bill Popowich
Bruce Richardson
Shawn and Corrine Rouse
Stan Stewardson
Merv Schweitzer
Bill Scuby
Jake Trotzuk
Mark Tuura
Mac Tyler
Ken Wallin
Walt Weaver Family
Dave Wilfong
Jason Winslade

City of New Westminster
Salmonbellies Alumni Association
Finally Holdings Ltd.
SierraSil Health Inc.

SOURCES

BOOKS

Beers, William George. *Lacrosse: The National Game of Canada.* Montreal: Dawson Brothers, 1869.

Bishop, Charles Wallace. *The Canadian YMCA in the Great War.* Toronto: National Council of Young Men's Christian Associations of Canada, 1924.

Christopherson, Stanley, Eric Green, E.T. Sachs & F. Sachs. *Hockey and Lacrosse.* London: George Routledge & Sons, 1909.

Dheensaw, Cleve. *Lacrosse 100: One Hundred Years of Lacrosse in B.C.* Victoria: Orca Book Publishers, 1990.

Fisher, Donald M. *Lacrosse: A History of the Game.* The Johns Hopkins University Press, 2002.

Kerr, J. B. *Biographical dictionary of well-known British Columbians; with a historical sketch.* Vancouver: Kerr & Begg, 1890.

Matthews, Major James Skitt. *Early Vancouver.* Vancouver: City of Vancouver, 2011.

Mitchell, Michael Kanentakeron. *Teiontsikwaeks: Lacrosse—The Creator's Game.* Ronathahon:ni Cultural Centre, 2010.

Savelieff, David S., Jr. *Canada's National Game: A History of the Sport of Lacrosse in B.C..* Vancouver: n.d.

Vennum, Thomas, Jr. *American Indian Lacrosse: Little Brother of War.* Smithsonian Institution Press, 1994.

Weyand, Alexander M., & Milton R. Roberts. *The Lacrosse Story.* Baltimore: H. & A. Herman, 1965.

PUBLISHED ARTICLES

Adamski, Barbara K. "An Upstream Battle." *Walrus*, May 2007.

Best, William Gage. "Canada's Apostle of Lacrosse." *Star Weekly*, 1944.

Bouchier, Nancy B. "Idealized Middle-class Sport for a Young Nation: Lacrosse in Nineteenth Century Ontario Towns 1871–1891." *Journal of Canadian Studies*, 1998.

Edwards, Brendan F.R. "Andrew Paull and the Value of Literacy in English." *BC Studies*, no. 164 (winter 2009–10).

Greene, Ronald. "Con Jones & the Don't Argue Tokens of Vancouver, B.C." *British Columbia History 39*, no. 4 (2006).

Mason, Daniel. "Professional Sports Facilities and Developing Urban Communities: Vancouver's Recreation Park, 1905–1912." *Free Online Library*, 1997.

Schrodt, Barbara. "Lacrosse in British Columbia Prior to World War I: A Case Study of Sport in an Emerging Urban Setting." *NASSH Proceedings*, 1990.

RULEBOOKS AND PAMPHLETS

Constitution and Rules British Columbia Amateur Lacrosse Association. Vancouver: Evans & Hastings, 1899.

Myron. *An Outline of Lacrosse History.* Shell Oil Company of British Columbia, 1935.

Wells Gray. "Lacrosse in British Columbia." Spalding's Athletic Library. Vol. 1, No. 4, *Official Canadian Lacrosse Guide 1910.* Montreal: Canadian Sports Publishing Co., 1910.

Wildlife Review Magazine. Fish & Game Branch, Department of Recreation & Conservation, 1960.

UNPUBLISHED MATERIAL

Leaf, George Herbert. "Memories." Manuscript, New Westminster Archives, ca. 1951.

Mahony, Tim. "History of the New Westminster Lacrosse Club." Manuscript, New Westminster Public Library, ca. 1910.

Tracy, Michael. "The Start of Field Lacrosse in New Westminster." Memo, New Westminster Public Library, 1984.

STATISTICS

Powers, Larry. "Wamps Bible of Lacrosse." http://www.wampsbibleoflacrosse.com.

Shillington, Stan. "Who's Who in Lacrosse 1933–2007: 75 years of Major Senior 'A' Box Lacrosse History."

WEBSITES

Canada Sports Hall of Fame. Retrieved from http://www.sportshall.ca.

Dundas, G. "Thistles Lacrosse History—The Canadian Story." Retrieved from http://www.geocities.com/thistlesforever/index2.html (now defunct).

"History of the A's—The St. Catharines Senior Athletics Lacrosse Club." Retrieved from http://www.athleticslacrosse.com/new_page_3.htm.

"Major Matthews' Early Vancouver." Retrieved from http://former.vancouver.ca/ctyclerk/archives/digitized/EarlyVan/index.htm.

Moore, Dustin. "The Evolution of Box Lacrosse in Ontario." Retrieved from http://www.olhof.ca/pages/history.html.

Peterborough Lakers. Retrieved from http://www.peterboroughlakers.ca.

Powers, Larry. "A history of lacrosse in Durham Region." Retrieved from http://wampsbibleoflacrosse.com/newstats/book.html.

Shillington, Stan. "Down Memory Lane". Articles retrieved from http://bclaregistration.com/general/memory-lane/index.cfm.

Stewart-Candy, David. "Brief History of Senior & Professional Lacrosse in British Columbia, Canadian Lacrosse Almanac 1886–2012." Retrieved from www.pdfcast.org/pdf/canadian-lacrosse-almanac-2012.

Stewart, Miller. Over The Hill, CBC Radio, June 26, 1964. Retrieved from http://archives.cbc.ca/sports/lacrosse/topics/824/ (now defunct).

ARCHIVES

BC Archives
City of New Westminster Archives
City of New Westminster Public Library
Canadian Lacrosse Hall of Fame

B.C. Sports Hall of Fame
City of Vancouver Archives
City of Toronto Archives
Old Hastings Mill Store Museum

NEWSPAPERS

The Daily Columbian
The Weekly Columbian
The British Columbian
The Columbian
The Royal City Record
The Royal City Record Now
The Burnaby and New Westminster News

The Vancouver Daily Province
The Vancouver Sun
The Winnipeg Free Press
The Toronto Telegraph
The Montreal Gazette
The Ottawa Citizen

Basil King, *Columbian* photographer supreme and member of
the Canadian Lacrosse Hall of Fame. Cheers!

PHOTOGRAPHS—PUBLIC COLLECTIONS

City of New Westminster Public Library
City of New Westminster Archives
Canadian Lacrosse Hall of Fame
Vancouver Public Library

City of Toronto Archives
B.C. Sports Hall of Fame
Canada's Sports Hall of Fame
Canadian Museum of Civilization

PHOTOGRAPHS—PRIVATE COLLECTIONS

Bill Armstrong
Lauren Bomhof (Barclay)
Dan Brodie
Don Brown
Ralph Burton
Stan Cowie
Hugh Cruikshank
Geordie Dean
Pat Downey
Ted Downey
Dave Durante
Tracy Fulton (Black)
Jim Giles
Wayne Goss

Don Hamilton
Paul Horn
Al Lewthwaite
Steve Manning
Don Oxenbury
Paul Parnell
Bill Scuby
Stan Stewardson
Jake Trotzuk
Mark Tuura
Ivan Tuura
Mac Tyler
David Zuskind

AUTHOR'S INTERVIEWS

Cliff Adams
Bill Armstrong
Lauren Bomhof (Barclay)
Terry Blair
Don Brown
Ralph Burton
Eric Cowieson
Hugh Cruikshank
Steve d'Easum
Pat Downey
Ken Downey
Dave Durante
Jack Fulton, Sr.
Tracy Fulton (Black)
Martin Gifford
Jim Gifford
Jim Giles
Jim Glanville
Wayne Goss
Carol Goss
Ed Goss
Fred Greenwood
Ben Hieltjes
Paul Horn
Bert Houston
Steve Laleune

Al Lewthwaite
Jim Lightbody
Donald MacDonald
Steve Manning
Ian Matheson
Dave Matheson
David McDonald
Ken Oddy
Paul Parnell
Rudy Reisinger
Dan Richardson
Rollie Rose
Cliff Sepka
Bill Scuby
Lloyd Solomon
Rob Steele
Bill Stevenson
Dave Thornhill
Jake Trotzuk
Mark Tuura
Ivan Tuura
Mac Tyler
Elaine Tyler (Wintemute)
Walt Tyler
Gail Winzoski

ENDNOTES

CHAPTER ONE

1 *Daily Columbian*, June 8, 1937.

2 In historical documents, "Mowat" also appears as "Mowatt."

3 Major James Skitt Matthews, *Early Vancouver*, Vol. 2 (Vancouver: City of Vancouver, 2011), 33.

4 Stanley Christopherson, Eric Greer, E.T. Sachs and F. Sachs, *Hockey and Lacrosse*, 1909.

5 Matthews, *Early Vancouver*, Vol. 2, 33.

6 Vancouver's team: Captain W.S. Taylor, Alfred Ernest "Bony" Suckling, J.B. Simpson, James Smith, David Smith, Edward Albert "Chub" Quigley, Joe Bigham, Ed Murphy, H.E. Rankin, and four other players whose given names are unknown: McDougall, Boultbee, Thompson, and Page.

7 *Daily Columbian*, July 13, 1891.

8 Matthews, *Early Vancouver*, Vol. 3, 33.

9 *Daily Columbian*, October 6, 1891.

10 Ibid.

11 *Columbian*, July 14, 1893.

12 *Daily Columbian*, August 1, 1893.

13 Ibid.

14 Tim Mahony, "History of the NWLC" (unpublished manuscript, City of New Westminster Archives, ca. 1910).

15 *Daily Columbian*, July 16, 1894.

16 In the spring of 1895 the Moonlighters and the West Enders merged into the Maple Leafs. The two Vancouver teams became the Vancouver Juniors and, with the Victoria Juniors and the Nanaimos, the Intermediate League was born. The Victoria Juniors became the first Intermediate League champions in 1895.

17 *Daily Columbian*, August 9, 1897. "The crowd from Vancouver which, on former occasions, had 'beefed' a good deal about 'salmon bellies' &c., realized on Saturday the full force of a genuine salmon 'run,' which ignored the insignificant opposition of 12 Vancouver nets."

18 George Herbert Leaf, "Memories" (unpublished manuscript, City of New Westminster Archives, ca. 1951).

19 Matthews, *Early Vancouver*, Vol. 5, 33.

20 Ibid.

21 Ibid.

22 Rob Steele (Jimmy Gifford's grandson), interviewed by the author, 2011.

23 Ibid.

24 Leaf, "Memories."

25 Matthews, *Early Vancouver*, Vol. 7, 63.

26 Mahony, "The History of the NWLC."

27 A.P. Garvey, "Thirty-four years in lacrosse and still playing is record of Alex 'Dad' Turnbull," *Winnipeg Free Press*, August 10, 1918.

28 *Daily Columbian*, June 5, 1899.

29 *British Colonist,* October 4, 1899.

30 "Hip! Hip! Hip! Hurray!" repeated 3 times. A fourth and final round is the "tiger."

31 *Daily Columbian,* October 9, 1899.

CHAPTER TWO

32 *Daily Columbian,* June 25, 1900.

33 "No one seems to remember just who was responsible as author of the ditty..." Stan Moncrief, "Stan's Slants," *Columbian,* January 18, 1951.

34 George Herbert Leaf, "Memories" (unpublished manuscript, City of New Westminster Archives, ca. 1951).

35 *Daily Columbian,* August 21, 1900.

36 *Daily Columbian,* August 15, 1900.

37 *Daily Columbian,* August 21, 1900.

38 *Daily Columbian,* August 29, 1900.

39 *Daily Columbian,* August 28, 1900.

40 *Weekly Columbian,* August 30, 1900.

41 Ibid.

42 John Bower "Bouse" Hutton (1877–1962). Goalie for the Ottawa Capitals, winners of the first Minto Cup in 1901 and another in 1904. In 1902 he was the fullback for the Ottawa Rough Riders, Canadian football champions. He won two Stanley Cups as the goalie for the Ottawa Silver Seven, in 1903 and 1904.

43 Ottawa newspaper clipping (paper not known), in files of Archie MacNaughton, Canadian Lacrosse Hall of Fame.

44 *Daily Columbian,* September 9, 1900.

45 *Daily Columbian,* September 8, 1900.

46 *Daily Columbian,* September 10, 1900, citing the *Ottawa Citizen.*

47 *Daily Columbian,* September 8, 1900, citing the *Montreal Gazette.*

48 *Daily Columbian,* September 10, 1900.

49 *Daily Columbian,* September 4, 1900, citing the *Montreal Gazette.*

50 *Daily Columbian,* September 26, 1900.

51 Ibid.

CHAPTER THREE

52 According to Vancouver player George Matheson (1899-1918), the Salmonbellies "[a]t first wore red sweaters and navy blue short trousers, not maroon sweaters, but a sort of dark red; barn red. Then, after a year or two, they had a salmon across the chest, but it was only for one year; then they took it off." Major James Skitt Matthews, *Early Vancouver,* Vol. 4 (Vancouver: City of Vancouver, 2011), 33.

53 George Herbert Leaf, "Memories" (unpublished manuscript, City of New Westminster Archives, ca. 1951).

54 Ibid.

55 *Daily Columbian,* October 12, 1901.

56 *Daily Columbian,* June 30, 1902.

57 Ibid.

58 *Daily Columbian,* July 22, 1903.

59 *Daily Columbian,* September 16, 1903.

60 "Are Champions Indeed," *Daily Columbian,* September 21, 1903. Urban released thirty-five Living Canada films in 1903–1904, plus Canada's first filmed drama, the fifteen-minute-long *Hiawatha, the Messiah of the Ojibway.* In 1906 several of the films were re-edited, condensed, and re-released under the title *Wonders of Canada.* Unfortunately, none of the thirty-five films is known to have survived.

61 A.P. Garvey, "Thirty-four years in lacrosse and still playing is record of Alex 'Dad' Turnbull," *Winnipeg Free Press,* August 10, 1918.

62 Ibid.

63 *Daily Columbian,* October 3, 1905.

64 *Daily Columbian,* October 9, 1905.

65 *Columbian,* October 23, 1906.

66 Ibid.

67 *Daily Columbian,* September 12, 1907.

68 *Daily Columbian,* September 28, 1907.

69 *Ottawa Citizen,* May 9, 1917.

70 Though Bill and Len Turnbull were brothers, they were not related to Dad Turnbull.

71 *Daily Columbian,* October 14, 1907.

72 *Daily Columbian,* October 12, 1907.

73 Eugene Field (1850–1895), *The Little Book of Western Verse* (Charles Scribner's Sons, 1889).

74 *Columbian,* July 13, 1908.

75 *Daily Columbian,* July 12, 1908.

76 Murton, *Toronto Telegram,* July 22, 1908, reprinted in the *Daily Columbian,* July 27, 1908.

77 Ibid.

78 Ibid.

79 Ibid.

80 Ibid.

81 *Daily Columbian,* July 30, 1908.

82 Ibid.

83 Laura Mary Sinclair (Rutledge), letter to Archie Miller, New Westminster archivist, October 9, 1985, in files of Canadian Lacrosse Hall of Fame.

84 *Daily Columbian,* July 29, 1908.

85 *Daily Columbian,* September 26, 1908.

CHAPTER FOUR

86 *Vancouver Sun,* May 10, 1910.

87 *Daily Columbian,* September 19, 1910.

88 *Daily Columbian,* September 10, 1910.

89 Ted Reeve, *Toronto Telegram,* July 26, 1961. Reeve, 1902–83, won Mann Cups with the Oshawa Generals in 1929 and the Brampton Excelsiors in 1930. He wrote a weekly lacrosse column for the *Toronto Telegram* from 1923 to 1927.

90 *Toronto Mail and Empire,* May 1926. Retrieved from http://www.athleticslacrosse.com/new_page_3.htm.

91 George Herbert Leaf, "Memories" (unpublished manuscript, City of New Westminster Archives, ca. 1951).

92 *Daily Province,* May 23, 1911.

93 Laura Mary Sinclair (Rutledge), letter to Archie Miller, New Westminster archivist, October 9, 1985, in files of Canadian Lacrosse Hall of Fame.

94 *Daily Province,* May 25, 1911.

95 Rob Steele (Jimmy Gifford's grandson), interviewed by the author, 2011.

96 *Daily Province,* June 26, 1911.

97 *Daily Province,* June 27, 1911.

98 *British Columbian,* August 17, 1911.

99 *Daily Province,* August 16, 1911.

100 Clipping from unknown newspaper, September 1, 1911.

101 *Toronto Star Weekly,* August 5, 1944.

102 *Daily Province,* September 5, 1911.

103 *Hedley Gazette,* September 21, 1911.

104 Macbeth, Act 3, scene 1.

105 Frank J. Selke (1893–1985) interview, 1973, National Archives of Canada.

106 *British Columbian,* July 2, 1912.

107 Ibid.

108 *British Columbian,* July 13, 1912.

109 *British Columbian,* July 20, 1913.

110 Ibid.

111 *British Columbian,* July 8, 1914.

112 Retrieved from http://bcla.centraldesktop.com/spirit2 doc/2362421/w-WillisPatchellMemoryLane.

113 Private Robert Percival Dauphinee, 6th Canadian Railway Transport Corps, letter, *Columbian,* August 16, 1917.

114 *BC Veterans Weekly,* October 7, 1922.

115 *British Columbian,* July 2, 1920.

116 *British Columbian,* April 18, 1922.

117 *British Columbian,* June 19, 1922.

118 *Vancouver Sun,* June 24, 1922.

119 Joe Lally credited Brennan with first introducing box lacrosse in 1922. Lally cited the Montreal Forum as the location, not Mount Royal Arena, but the Forum was not built until 1924, so Lally must be confusing the two. The Mount Royal Arena, converted into an auditorium after 1926 and later into a commercial building, burned down in 2000. A Provigo supermarket now stands on the site.

120 *British Columbian,* September 17, 1923.

121 *British Columbian,* May 22, 1924.

122 Ibid.

123 *British Columbian,* June 2, 1924.

CHAPTER FIVE

124 Louis S. Nixdorff, 1928 Olympic Games Collection, 1926–1978, #443, National Museum of American History, http://amhistory.si.edu/archives/ d9443f.htm.

125 Ibid.

126 Ibid.

127 Ibid.

128 Ibid.

129 *New York Times,* 1928.

130 Nixdorff, 1928 Olympic Games Collection.

131 Ibid.

132 Ibid.

133 A monument and drinking fountain erected in Mahony's honour stands on the west side of New Westminster's city hall, the former site of Duke of Connaught High School.

134 Tim Mahony, "History of the NWLC" (unpublished manuscript), ca. 1910, City of New Westminster Archives. (Mahony referred to himself in the third person.)

135 Frank Selke Sr., interview, 1973. Retrieved from http://wampsbibleoflacrosse.com/newstats/Frank-Selke-Sr-Interview-1973.pdf.

136 *British Columbian,* September 2, 1930.

137 Basil O'Meara, *Montreal Star,* retrieved from http://wampsbibleoflacrosse.com/newstats/Chapter-4.pdf.

138 Frank J. Selke, interview, National Archives of Canada, 1973.

139 Cliff Adams, interviewed by the author, 2011.

CHAPTER SIX

140 In 1930, CLA president Joe Lally donated a cup in his name, open to competition among teams from Canada, the US, England, and Australia.

141 *British Columbian,* April 28, 1933.

142 *British Columbian,* June 15, 1933.

143 *British Columbian,* November 8, 1939.

144 *British Columbian,* October 10, 1933.

145 David S. Savelieff, Jr., *Canada's National Game: A History of the Sport of Lacrosse in B.C.* (Vancouver, n.d.).

146 *British Columbian,* August 25, 1934.

147 *British Columbian,* October 9, 1934.

148 *British Columbian,* October 15, 1934.

149 Michael Kanentakeron Mitchell, *Teiontsikwaeks: Lacrosse—The Creator's Game* (Ronathahonni Cultural Centre, 2010). Quoting Stan Shillington.

150 *British Columbian,* May 10, 1954.

151 *Vancouver Sun,* October 13, 1937.

152 *Vancouver Sun,* October 13, 1935.

153 Ralph Burton, interviewed by the author, 2013.

154 Denny Boyd, *Vancouver Sun,* 1966.

155 *Vancouver Sun,* October 10, 1937. "Drop the handkerchief" was a game played by elementary school girls.

156 Ibid.

157 Ibid.

158 *British Columbian,* October 14, 1937.

159 Ibid.

160 Ibid.

CHAPTER SEVEN

161 Bill Scuby, interviewed by the author, 2012.

162 Ibid.

163 Ibid.

164 *British Columbian,* September 1, 1939.

165 *British Columbian,* September 5, 1939.

166 Ralph Burton, interviewed by the author, February 2013.

167 *British Columbian,* September 29, 1939.

168 *British Columbian,* October 5, 1939.

169 Ibid.

170 *British Columbian,* October 6, 1939.

171 *British Columbian,* October 12, 1939.

172 *British Columbian,* October 27, 1939.

173 Jake Trotzuk, interviewed by the author, 2011.

174 Stu Keate, *Vancouver Province,* 1942.

175 *British Columbian,* August 20, 1942.

176 Jack Patterson, *Vancouver Sun,* September 12, 1942.

177 *St. Catharines Standard,* June 22, 1961.

178 Paul Whiteside, "Thistles History," retrieved from http://wampsbibleoflacrosse.com/newstats/ ThistlesHistory.pdf

179 Scuby, 2011.

180 *Columbian,* July 12, 1943.

181 Bert Houston, interviewed by the author, 2012.

182 *British Columbian,* October 6, 1943.

183 *British Columbian,* October 14, 1943.

184 Whiteside, "Thistles History."

185 *Columbian,* October 16, 1944.

CHAPTER EIGHT

186 *British Columbian,* May 27, 1947.

187 Ken Croft, interview, retrieved from http://www.athleticslacrosse.com/weiner_croft.htm

188 *British Columbian,* September 22, 1949.

189 *Vancouver Province,* February 24, 1950.

190 Stan Moncrief, "Stan's Slants," *The British Columbian,* January 18, 1951.

191 *Royal City Record,* 1990.

192 Roy McGregor, *National Post,* November 9, 1999.

CHAPTER NINE

193 Cliff Sepka, interviewed by the author, 2011.

194 Jack Fulton, interviewed by the author, 2011

195 Sepka, 2011.

196 *Royal City Record,* 1990.

197 Bionda played four seasons in the NHL.

198 The Trailermen's star, Bob Allan, had reneged at the beginning of the season on his agreement to play for Nanaimo. The CLA warned the Trailermen that Allan, being Nanaimo's property, couldn't play in the Mann Cup. But the Trailermen, including Allan, went to Victoria for the Mann Cup anyway. The situation came to a head not long before the start of game 1. The Trailermen refused to play without Allan. The CLA warned the team that failure to play, minus Allan, would cost the whole team five-year suspensions from all amateur sports. Incensed, the Trailermen refused to step onto the floor. The CLA responded by having the Trailermen evicted from their Victoria hotel, confiscating their return plane tickets, and imposing the playing ban on all the players but one. The Pontiacs were no match for the Shamrocks and were outscored 51–23. The playing ban was rescinded after a year.

199 *British Columbian,* April 11, 1958.

200 Fulton, 2011.

201 Ibid.

202 *British Columbian,* July 1, 1958.

203 *British Columbian,* May 23, 1959.

204 *British Columbian,* May 14, 1959.

205 Ibid.

206 *British Columbian,* May 5, 1959.

207 Sepka, 2011.

208 *British Columbian,* May 13, 1959.

209 Sepka, 2011.

210 *British Columbian,* August 7, 1959.

211 *British Columbian,* September 16, 1959.

212 Bill Armstrong, interviewed by the author, 2011.

213 Rudy Reisinger, interviewed by the author, 2012.

214 *British Columbian,* September 22, 1959.

215 Ibid.

216 Fulton, 2011.

217 Ibid.

218 Armstrong, 2011.

219 Dave Matheson (Salmonbellies player), interviewed by the author, 2012.

220 *British Columbian,* May 25, 1962.

221 Paul Parnell (Salmonbellies player), interviewed by the author, 2011.

222 *British Columbian,* September 13, 1962.

223 *British Columbian,* September 15, 1962.

224 Whitey Severson, Salmonbellies newsletter.

225 *Columbian,* July 26, 1964.

CHAPTER TEN

226 Mac Tyler, interviewed by the author, 2012.

227 Ibid.

228 Ibid.

229 *Columbian,* September 14, 1965.

230 Jack Fulton, interviewed by the author, 2011.

231 *Columbian,* June 29, 1966.

232 *Columbian,* July 2, 1966.

233 Gail Winzoski, interviewed by the author, 2012.

234 Michael Kanentakeron Mitchell, *Teiontsikwaeks: Lacrosse—The Creator's Game* (Ronathahon:ni Cultural Centre, 2010).

235 Tyler, 2012.

236 Jim Giles, interviewed by the author, 2012.

237 Don Cannon, *Columbian,* October 5, 1968.

238 Don Cannon, *Columbian,* October 9, 1968.

239 Ian Matheson, interviewed by the author, 2012.

240 *Vancouver Sun,* October 15, 1968.

241 Bill Armstrong, interviewed by the author, 2011.

242 Al Lewthwaite, interviewed by the author, 2012.

243 Matheson, 2012. Matheson was quoting an unnamed source.

244 Giles, 2012.

245 Lewthwaite, 2012.

246 Ibid.

247 Ibid.

248 Ibid.

249 Paul Parnell, interviewed by the author, 2011.

250 Don Cannon, *Columbian,* July 30, 1969.

251 Lewthwaite, 2012.

252 *Columbian,* September 12, 1969.

253 Ibid.

254 Lewthwaite, 2012.

255 *Columbian,* September 24, 1969.

256 Lewthwaite, 2012.

257 Ibid.

258 Ibid.

259 Frank Selke, Sr., 1973, National Archives of Canada.

260 Ed Goss, interviewed by the author, 2012.

261 *Columbian,* September 15, 1971.

262 Giles, 2012.

263 *Columbian,* May 7, 1972.

264 *Vancouver Sun,* August 15, 1972.

265 *Columbian,* September 21, 1972.

266 Bill Stevenson, interviewed by the author, 2012.

267 Tyler, 2012.

268 Ibid.

269 *Columbian,* July 15, 1973.

270 Lewthwaite, 2012.

271 Fulton, 2011.

272 *Columbian,* June 25, 1976.

273 *Columbian,* July 27, 1976.

274 *Columbian,* September 3, 1976.

275 *Columbian,* September 13, 1976.

276 *Columbian,* September 15, 1976.

CHAPTER ELEVEN

277 *Columbian,* August 17, 1981.

278 *Columbian,* September 11, 1981.

279 Casey Cook, *New Westminster Record,* March 19, 2012.

280 An average of 3.98 points a game. The figure is that much more extraordinary when his not playing on power plays is taken into account. Seven times Goss scored over 100 points in regular season play, his best year coming in 1975 with 146 points on 52 goals and 94 assists.

281 Goss earned a sixth Mann Cup after being picked up by the Victoria Shamrocks for the 1979 finals.

282 John Wawrow, "Wayne Goss: The Boss of Lacrosse," *Royal City Record.*

283 Stan Shillington, "Down Memory Lane." Retreived from http://bclaregistration.com/general/memory-lane/goss-wayne.cfm.

284 Eric Cowieson, interviewed by the author, 2012.

285 Ibid.

286 Rod Banister, interview, February 21, 2008, retrieved from www.lacrosseinsidethegame.com/2008/02/21/647/.

287 Cowieson, 2012.

288 Ben Hieltjes, interviewed by the author, 2012.

289 Ibid.

290 Casey Cook, Salmonbellies newsletter.

291 *Royal City Record,* September 13, 1986.

292 Dave Thornhill, interviewed by the author, 2012.

293 Dr. Terry Blair, interviewed by the author, 2012.

294 *Royal City Record,* August 19, 1989.

295 *Royal City Record,* September 7, 1989.

296 *Royal City Record Now,* September 16, 1989.

297 Ibid.

298 Cleve Dheensaw, *Lacrosse 100: One Hundred Years of Lacrosse in B.C.* (Victoria: Orca Book Publishers, 1990).

299 *Royal City Record Now,* September 15, 1991.

300 Dan Hilborn, *Royal City Record Now,* September 15, 1991.

CHAPTER TWELVE

301 *Windspeaker* 13, no. 6 (1995).

302 Ibid.

303 Ben Hieltjes, interviewed by the author, 2012.

304 Eric Cowieson, interviewed by the author, 2012.

305 Dean #5, Cowieson #6, Parnell #7, Bionda #12, Goss #13, Sepka #19.

306 Morley Kells, "Eulogy of Jim Bishop 'The Coach' 1929–1998," *Teiontsikwaeks—Lacrosse: The Creator's Game,* ed. Michael Kanentakeron Mitchell (Ronathahonni Cultural Centre, 2010).

INDEX